AF758674

International Arbitration and Forum Selection Agreements

International Arbitration and Forum Selection Agreements

Drafting and Enforcing

Seventh Edition

by

Gary B. Born

Wolters Kluwer

Published by:
Kluwer Law International B.V.
PO Box 316
2400 AH Alphen aan den Rijn
The Netherlands
E-mail: lrs-sales@wolterskluwer.com
Website: www.wolterskluwer.com/en/solutions/kluwerlawinternational

Sold and distributed by:
Wolters Kluwer Legal & Regulatory U.S.
920 Links Avenue
Landisville, PA 17538
United States of America
E-mail: customer.service@wolterskluwer.com

ISBN 978-94-035-3299-8

e-Book: ISBN 978-94-035-3309-4
web-PDF: ISBN 978-94-035-3319-3

© 2025 Kluwer Law International BV, The Netherlands, and/or subsidiaries, its licensors, and contributors. All rights are reserved, including those for text and data mining, AI training, and similar technologies.

No part of this publication may be reproduced, stored in a retrieval system, or transmitted in any form or by any means, electronic, mechanical, photocopying, recording, or otherwise, without written permission from the publisher.

Permission to use this content must be obtained from the copyright owner. More information can be found at: https://www.wolterskluwer.com/en/solutions/kluwerlawinternational/rights-and-permissions

Table of Contents

Preface and Acknowledgements to the First Edition

Disputes have a critical impact on international commercial dealings. Properly handled, contractual disagreements need not jeopardize, and can enhance, a company's bottom line. Handled ineffectively, disputes can produce unjust or disproportionate liability, extravagant legal costs, adverse publicity, and worse. These risks are especially great in international commercial transactions, where parties' expectations and national legal systems differ widely.

This book examines the principal means for reducing the risks inherent in international commercial disputes. Specifically, it examines international forum selection clauses and international arbitration agreements, as tools for choosing tribunals to resolve parties' international commercial disputes. The book seeks to explain, in concise and accessible language, the advantages and disadvantages of different types of dispute resolution provisions. It then details the various options which are available in drafting these provisions, providing representative text for each. The emphasis throughout is on simple, practical, and durable solutions.

This book would not have been possible without the assistance of countless colleagues, students, clients, and competitors, rendered over the course of decades. Any list of acknowledgements would fail properly to attribute the enormous credit due to those who have assisted. In particular, I wish to acknowledge the care and ingenuity of Elke Jenner and the research of Joe Profaizer, Kevin Pettican, and Susie Williams. As always, John Berger provided invaluable editorial advice.

Gary B. Born
March 1999

Preface and Acknowledgements to the Seventh Edition

This is the seventh edition of a guide to drafting international arbitration and forum selection agreements. First published in 1999, the guide discusses one of the principal means for reducing the risks inherent in international commercial disputes—namely, international forum selection and arbitration agreements. The guide focuses on practical observations and model clauses, with both hopefully drafted in concise and accessible language.

This edition of the guide is updated to August 2025, and seeks to take into account developments since the previous editions were published (in 1999, 2005, 2010, 2013, 2016, and 2021). Nonetheless, one striking aspect of the dispute resolution provisions discussed in this edition is how little they have changed in the past 20 years. Now, as then, simple forum selection clauses and arbitration agreements provide the most practical and durable mechanisms for reducing the risks and costs of transnational disputes.

This expanded seventh edition of the guide also introduces a number of additional model provisions which can be used either to supplement agreements to arbitrate (and forum selection clauses) or to replace them (as with expert determination provisions). This edition also introduces, for the first time, more specific assessments of both selected national legal systems (providing observations as to their suitability for foreign parties) and international arbitral institutions.

As with prior versions, the guide is not a substitute for consideration of the circumstances and needs of particular transactions, or specialized advice about dispute resolution mechanisms for those transactions. Rather, it provides language and identifies issues in order that such consideration and advice can be more focused and efficient.

As with its predecessors, this seventh edition is only possible because of the invaluable assistance of my colleagues, students, clients, and competitors. In particular, Katrin Frach provided exceptionally diligent and careful assistance, as did Shadia Ajam, Erica Li, Gilliam Collinsworth-Hamilton and Laurie Labbaye. My publishers at Kluwer Law International, particularly Gwen de Vries, have also provided characteristically invaluable editorial advice and assistance.

Any comments, criticisms and queries are welcome by email to gary.born@wilmerhale.com.

Gary B. Born
August 2025

Chapter 1

Planning for International Dispute Resolution

A. IMPORTANCE OF CONTRACTUAL FORUM SELECTION IN INTERNATIONAL DISPUTES

Recent decades saw an unparalleled expansion of global trade and investment. That expansion weathered political, financial and other crises, and, notwithstanding recurrent crises, appeared for many years more likely than not to endure.

Recent events have raised questions regarding the future development of cross-border trade and investment. Protectionist measures in many nations, as well as concerns regarding international supply chains, have threatened to suspend or reverse the historic expansion of global trade and investment. The consequences of these developments for the future remain uncertain.

Together with prosperity, increased international trade and investment brought about an increased number of international commercial and investment disputes. At the same time, recent protectionist measures and other developments have also increased the risk of cross-border disputes. Consequently, business enterprises of every description can find themselves entangled in legal proceedings with foreign companies or governments, sometimes before distant, unsympathetic, or corrupt tribunals. The costs of these proceedings, and the consequences of losing, are often substantial.

Almost every international commercial controversy poses a critical preliminary question: "Where, and by whom, will this dispute be decided?" The answer to this question often decisively affects a dispute's eventual outcome. It can mean the difference between winning and losing, between *de minimis* damages and a multimillion-dollar, euro, pound, yen, rupee, or renminbi award.

There are many reasons why the same dispute can have materially different outcomes in different fora. Procedural, choice-of-law, substantive, and other legal rules differ from one jurisdiction to another. The character, competence, and integrity of tribunals also vary substantially among different states. Other considerations, such as inconvenience, local bias, and language, may make a particular forum much more favorable for one party than another. These differences are almost always more pronounced across international borders than within purely domestic political systems, and they have become more, not less, significant in recent years.

Because of the importance of forum selection, parties to international transactions often include contractual dispute resolution provisions in their agreements. As detailed below, these provisions significantly reduce the uncertainties inherent in international commercial disputes, and can sometimes offer a substantial measure of legitimate partisan advantage. As a consequence, it is almost always advisable to include a contractual dispute resolution provision in any international contract. These provisions typically take the form of: (1) forum selection clauses, or (2) arbitration agreements. Either form of agreement can be and frequently is combined with a choice-of-law clause, selecting the substantive law applicable to the parties' relationship.

B. FORUM SELECTION AGREEMENTS

A forum selection clause is an agreement which either permits or requires its parties to pursue their claims against one another in a designated national court. Forum selection agreements can be either "exclusive" (i.e., requiring that all litigation between the parties be pursued solely in their contractual forum, and nowhere else) or "non-exclusive" (i.e., permitting litigation between the parties in their contractual forum, but not prohibiting claims from being brought in other courts which possess jurisdiction). Forum selection agreements are also sometimes referred to as "jurisdiction clauses," "choice of forum agreements," or "forum clauses."

C. INTERNATIONAL ARBITRATION AGREEMENTS

An arbitration agreement is similar in some respects to a forum selection clause, but it also has vitally different features. Briefly stated, international arbitration is a means for finally resolving a dispute, pursuant to the parties' voluntary agreement, through the decision of a non-governmental decision-maker, selected by or for the parties (an "arbitrator"), who applies adjudicative procedures affording the parties an opportunity to be heard, prior to making a binding and enforceable award. As this definition indicates, international arbitration has several distinctive characteristics.

First, international arbitration is ordinarily *consensual*—the parties must agree to arbitrate their differences. Second, arbitrations are decided by *non-governmental decision-makers*—arbitrators are not, and do not act as, government representatives, but are private persons selected by the parties (or on their behalf, typically by an arbitral institution or other appointing authority). Third, arbitration produces a *final and binding award*—rather than a merely precatory recommendation—which is generally capable of enforcement against the award-debtor or its assets through national courts. Fourth, arbitration permits substantial procedural *flexibility*—the parties are free to select arbitrators, or to adopt specialized procedures, appropriate for their particular transaction, industry, and other needs. At the same time, these procedures are typically *adjudicative*, permitting each party the opportunity to present its evidence and to be heard according to quasi-judicial procedures. Finally, international arbitration is intended to be *neutral*, in that it usually seeks to provide a dispute resolution mechanism that takes place outside either party's home jurisdiction and judicial system, and that adopts no single nation's litigation procedures.

Almost all international commercial arbitrations occur pursuant to arbitration clauses contained within underlying business agreements. These clauses typically provide for the arbitration of future disputes relating to the contract pursuant to a specified set of procedural rules (often promulgated by an established arbitral institution). Some investment arbitrations also occur pursuant to arbitration agreements contained in investment or other contracts, although many such arbitrations arise from the arbitration provisions in bilateral investment treaties ("BITs").

Finally, unlike most forum selection agreements, international arbitration clauses are generally subject to a specialized international legal regime. This regime includes a number of multilateral (or bilateral) treaties providing for the validity and enforceability of international arbitration agreements and awards. It also includes arbitration legislation in most developed and many other nations, which is supportive of the international arbitral process. These instruments contribute significantly to the efficacy of arbitration as a means of resolving international disputes, ordinarily in a manner which is more expert, efficient, expeditious, even-handed, and enforceable than national court proceedings.

D. FUNCTIONS SERVED BY FORUM SELECTION AND ARBITRATION AGREEMENTS

Both forum selection and arbitration agreements serve vital functions in international transactions. First, such provisions may offer one party a favorable forum for resolution of future disputes. For example, financial institutions may require borrowers to accept resolution of disputes before a court in London or New York, thereby ensuring a convenient, competent, and presumptively sympathetic decision-maker. Conversely, a Korean company might urge its European counterparty to accept dispute resolution in Korean courts, for understandable reasons.

Second, even if a party cannot obtain agreement on its preferred forum, it can at least preclude litigation in highly undesirable fora. For example, parties from Japan and the United States might agree upon dispute resolution exclusively in a neutral third state (such as England, Singapore, or Switzerland). Dispute resolution could take the form of either proceedings before a neutral national court or an international arbitral tribunal in a disinterested jurisdiction. Either course would reduce the risk that one party would be required to litigate in the other party's home-courts (or some other undesirable forum).

Third, an exclusive forum selection or arbitration agreement can preclude parallel or multiplicitous litigation of the same dispute in two or more fora at the same time. Absent agreement on a contractual forum, each party may pursue litigation in the forum that it perceives to be most favorable to it. Given the likelihood of overlapping jurisdiction in different national courts in many international disputes, this can lead to protracted jurisdictional litigation, inconsistent (and perhaps unenforceable) judgments, and multiple sets of lawyers and legal fees. An exclusive forum selection or arbitration agreement can confine litigation of the parties' dispute to a single forum, thereby reducing the expense and uncertainty resulting from parallel proceedings.

Fourth, a forum selection or arbitration agreement makes the parties' contractual relationship more predictable. Parties are better able to assess their rights and duties when there is relative certainty as to the tribunal that may finally resolve their disputes. This is particularly true when a forum selection or arbitration agreement is combined with a choice-of-law provision.

Fifth, in appropriate cases, a contractual dispute resolution mechanism can be tailored to the parties' specific needs. A forum selection clause can select a court with significant commercial (or other) expertise relevant to the parties' transaction; an arbitration agreement can provide for the appointment of arbitrators with particular qualifications, or parties can make such appointments themselves. Dispute resolution provisions may also address issues such as disclosure or discovery, procedural timetables, availability of appeals, remedial authority, and allocation of legal costs. All of these factors can enhance the predictability and commercial appeal of dispute resolution procedures.

Sixth, a contractual dispute resolution provision can seek to reduce the difficulties that are often encountered in enforcing national court judgments abroad. Thus, the parties' contractual commitment to a specified judicial forum reduces the risk of successful jurisdictional challenges during an enforcement action. As discussed below (See p. 168 below), arbitration agreements provide particular advantages in this respect because of the favorable international legal framework for enforcing arbitral awards.

For all of these reasons, it is almost always advisable to include either a forum selection or arbitration agreement in any significant international contract or set of contracts. Likewise, it is virtually always wise to agree upon a choice-of-law clause in international commercial agreements. These provisions materially reduce the uncertainties that accompany international dispute resolution and, if drafted with care, may provide a measure of legitimate partisan advantage. Conversely, there is seldom any justification for not including a dispute resolution provision in a commercial contract. The only real issue is whether this dispute resolution provision should be an arbitration clause or a forum selection clause.

E. CHOOSING BETWEEN FORUM SELECTION CLAUSES AND ARBITRATION AGREEMENTS

Deciding whether to adopt a forum selection clause, on the one hand, or an arbitration agreement, on the other, in a particular international transaction is sometimes not a straightforward decision. As detailed below, numerous considerations affect this choice, including the identities and interests of the parties, the types of disputes likely to arise under the parties' commercial agreements, the need for enforcement of the parties' dispute resolution agreement and any resulting judgments or awards outside the contractually specified forum, the importance of confidentiality and procedural flexibility, the importance of multi-party solutions, and the benefits (or costs) of appellate review. Of course, all of these considerations must be viewed from the perspective of what terms a party can realistically achieve in particular contractual negotiations with its counterparty.

It would be imprudent to prescribe a single dispute resolution mechanism for all transactions or parties. There are too many variables, which inevitably counsel in different directions in different transactions for different parties. Nonetheless, it is both possible and useful to identify various considerations affecting the choice between a forum selection clause and an arbitration agreement. Evaluating these considerations in the context of a particular transaction and counterparty, or particular category of transactions, will often indicate what form of contractual dispute resolution mechanism is most desirable for a party. It is also possible (See pp. 14-15 below) to formulate a number of general guidelines to assist parties in choosing between international forum selection and arbitration agreements in particular cases.

1. Favorable Forum

Commentary on dispute resolution often extols the virtues of "truly international" or "neutral, competent" tribunals. That is commendable. The primary objective of any commercial party, however, must be an agreement to future dispute resolution in the forum where it will have the best chance of definitively prevailing in future disputes. Other considerations—including particularly the enforceability of a dispute resolution agreement and any resulting judgment or award—may influence or override this objective in particular cases. Nonetheless, ensuring that disputes are resolved in the most favorable forum for a particular party is the starting point, and often the ending point, for any analysis.

In many cases, choosing the most favorable forum for a party means choosing the local courts in that party's principal place of business. In an international transaction, these courts will be convenient and familiar to the hometown party, and to its regular outside counsel; these courts will also probably be somewhat inconvenient and unfamiliar to the counterparty. This is especially true where differences in language, culture, and legal traditions exist. Where local courts are subject to political, media, popular, or other pressures, the attractions of a home-court judicial forum are further sharpened. The same is true if a company is a substantial local employer, a "national champion," or otherwise potentially favored in local courts. Recent trends towards protectionism make these considerations particularly important.

Despite the foregoing advantages, a company is not always best served by litigation in its home-courts. Corporate restructurings, widespread employee layoffs, local animosities or competition, and other factors may bias hometown courts against a local company. In some cases, various procedural aspects of litigation can make a counterparty's home-courts a more favorable venue than the party's own courts: these include the availability (or unavailability) of discovery, the applicable rules of law, the rules for allocation of the parties' costs for legal representation, the length of time required for a decision, or trial by a lay jury or judge. More generally, a party that obtains a favorable decision in its own domicile may be required to enforce the judgment in its counterparty's home forum, with the attendant uncertainties, costs, and delays. It is therefore prudent to examine critically reflexive assumptions about the desirability of litigating at home in all cases. Nonetheless, in practice, this assumption will often either prove correct or be difficult to rebut satisfactorily.

Conversely, characteristics that make one party's local courts attractive to it will often make them unacceptable to counterparties. If nothing else, a healthy concern regarding the potential for home-court bias usually prompts parties to refuse to agree to litigate in their counterparty's local courts; again, protectionist and other trends in recent years underscore this point. The costs of overcoming this mistrust during contractual negotiations, with any degree of confidence, are usually uneconomical. As a consequence, outside of lending and similar transactions, it is often difficult for a party to obtain its counterparty's agreement to resolve future disputes in its own local courts.

Even so, the primary objective of any party will remain negotiating for a forum that will resolve future disputes in its favor. Identifying this forum requires determining the kinds of disputes that are likely to arise under the parties' agreement and considering how they might be resolved in different possible contractual fora. Among other things, this analysis is influenced by the characteristics of different tribunals (e.g., judge versus lay jury), procedural and choice-of-law rules, language, rules for allocating litigation costs, and likely approaches to damages.

2. Appellate Review

Another important factor to consider in deciding whether to choose an arbitration clause or forum selection clause concerns appellate review. A salient feature of international commercial and investment arbitration is the absence, in most cases, of appellate review of arbitral awards. Judicial review of awards in most developed countries is narrowly confined to issues of procedural fairness, jurisdiction, and public policy. If any scrutiny of the arbitrators' substantive decisions is permitted, it is ordinarily highly deferential. (See pp. 130-131 below.) This contrasts markedly with the availability of appellate review of first instance judgments under national court systems, which may allow either de novo relitigation or fairly searching reconsideration of both factual and legal matters.

There are both advantages and disadvantages to appellate review mechanisms. Dispensing with appellate review reduces both litigation costs and delays, which often may result in an appellate decision that is no more satisfactory than the first instance decision. On the other hand, it also means that an eccentric, or simply wrong, arbitral decision cannot be corrected. (It is partially for this reason that many arbitration agreements provide for three-person arbitral tribunals in cases of any significant magnitude, thereby reducing the risk of erroneous decisions.) Deciding which of these tradeoffs to accept in a particular case often requires consideration of the types of disputes that a contract might produce. It also requires considering the possibility of drafting an arbitration clause to provide for some measure of appellate review. (See pp. 130-131 below.)

3. Efficiency and Expedition

It has long been said that arbitration offers a cheaper, quicker means of dispute resolution than national court proceedings. It is also fashionable, at least in some circles, to describe arbitration as a slower, costlier option. In reality, both international arbitration and international litigation can involve significant expense and delay, and it is difficult to generalize about which mechanism is necessarily quicker or cheaper in every case. Nonetheless, some general conclusions can be drawn.

International arbitration is sometimes not cheap, particularly in substantial cases. The parties are required (generally subject to later allocation of arbitration costs by the tribunal) to pay the fees of the arbitrator(s) and, usually, an arbitral institution. The parties will also have to pay the logistical expenses of renting hearing rooms, travelling to the arbitral seat, lodging, and the like. This entails expenses that generally do not exist in national court litigation.

Nonetheless, the additional expenses of arbitration will usually pale in comparison with the costs of legal representation if there are parallel or multiplicitous proceedings in national courts (followed by appellate proceedings). This can be the case where the parties have been unable to agree upon an exclusive forum selection clause, or where their clause is held unenforceable. Parallel judicial proceedings can be particularly costly where one party is obliged to commence multiple actions in different nations (e.g., to deal with unauthorized use of intellectual property in several jurisdictions). Likewise, the expenses of arbitration will typically not approach those that are incurred if there is relitigation of factual issues in national trial and appellate courts. Arbitration also usually does not have the potential for costly, scorched-earth discovery and other procedural steps which exist in some common law jurisdictions.

International arbitration is also not always speedy. Under leading institutional arbitration rules, smaller arbitrations (involving amounts in dispute of less than USD 5 million) can frequently be completed in six months or less. Outside of some specialized contexts, however, substantial disputes often require between 12 and 36 months to reach a final award, albeit with possibilities for earlier summary dispositions. Procedural mishaps, challenges to arbitrators, and litigation over jurisdictional issues in national courts can also delay these timetables, as can crowded schedules of busy arbitrators and counsel. It is possible to achieve greater expedition, through either drafting a "fast-track" arbitration clause or adroit procedural tactics, but there are limits to how quickly a major commercial arbitration can realistically and reliably be resolved.

Nonetheless, in many jurisdictions, national court proceedings are subject to even more significant delays. In some states, even relatively small civil actions can easily take at least a decade to resolve. The possibility of de novo or otherwise rigorous appellate review, and new trial proceedings, adds a significant risk of additional lengthy delays to those in first instance courts. As discussed above (See pp. 6-7), arbitration typically does not involve appellate review, thereby avoiding the delay inherent in appellate proceedings and reducing the risk that new trial proceedings will be required (in the event of appellate reversal of an initial trial court decision).

On balance, therefore, international arbitration does not necessarily have dramatic speed and cost advantages as compared to national court proceedings. Broadly speaking, however, the absence of appellate review and the advantages of procedural flexibility mean that arbitration is usually materially less slow than litigation in most states, although there will inevitably be exceptions to this generalization. Conversely, arbitration will virtually never face the types of lengthy delays that are common in some court systems, where overcrowded dockets produce 10 or 20-year-long litigations.

4. Expertise and Even-Handedness

Many national courts are distressingly inappropriate choices for resolving international commercial disputes. In some states, local courts have little experience with international transactions or disputes; in others, basic standards of judicial integrity and/or competence are lacking. These observations have become more, not less, accurate in recent years.

More generally, national courts inevitably apply local procedural rules to international disputes, which may be ill-suited for parties from different legal traditions and regions of the globe. The need to translate evidentiary materials or legal authorities into the language of the forum may create practical problems and jeopardize a judge's comprehension of the case.

On the other hand, some national judiciaries include very talented judges with considerable experience in resolving international disputes. The courts of England, Switzerland, New York, Singapore, and a few other jurisdictions are able to resolve complex transnational disputes with a fairly high degree of reliability. Additionally, with English increasingly serving as the language of international commerce, translations may not be necessary in courts in non-English-speaking jurisdictions.

Proponents of international arbitration routinely hold out the promise of neutral, highly competent decision-makers. In this view, parties can select arbitrators with substantial experience in resolving international commercial disputes. They can also choose arbitrators whose nationality is different from that of the companies involved (thus reducing the risks of partiality or parochial prejudice). More broadly, a three-person tribunal, composed of arbitrators drawn from different legal traditions, will often adopt a truly neutral procedural regime, while giving all parties confidence in the arbitration's procedural fairness.

Nonetheless, selecting arbitrators can be a challenging enterprise, particularly in some contexts (such as investment arbitration). The parties will sometimes be unable to agree directly upon the choice of a sole or presiding arbitrator, thereby requiring appointment by an arbitral institution. Only a limited number of arbitral institutions have proven track records in international disputes, and inexperienced arbitral institutions can make unfortunate appointments, while even experienced arbitral institutions sometimes make mistakes in their appointments. The absence of appellate review of arbitral awards makes inappropriate appointments especially damaging.

On balance, arbitrators selected by one of the leading international arbitral institutions (as discussed below, being the International Chamber of Commerce, the London Court of International Arbitration, the Singapore International Arbitration Centre, the American Arbitration Association, and the International Centre for Settlement of Investment Disputes) are likely to have somewhat greater competence and neutrality than most national courts. (See pp. 47-49 below.) A few national judiciaries (or specialized courts within such judiciaries) may offer nearly comparable competence, and may provide comparable procedural neutrality in particular cases. Even here, however, hardly any national courts can offer the breadth of resources and experience possessed by a tribunal of three experienced international arbitrators chosen by the parties after a dispute has arisen. And, just as poor or unsuitable arbitrators can be chosen, even the best national judicial systems have trial judges or lay juries that international businesses would understandably prefer to avoid.

5. Enforceability of Dispute Resolution Agreements

As discussed below (See pp.168-169), in most national courts, international arbitration agreements are more readily enforced and more broadly interpreted than forum selection clauses. This is largely because of a network of international arbitration treaties and "pro-arbitration" legislation in a substantial number of states. The 1958 United Nations Convention on the Recognition and Enforcement of Foreign Arbitral Awards ("New York Convention"), to which some 172 nations are currently party, is particularly important in facilitating the enforceability of international arbitration agreements. (See pp. 163-164 below.)

In contrast, there are only a few regional arrangements which seek to establish effective international enforcement regimes for forum selection clauses. The most notable is the Brussels I Regulation in the European Union (Regulation 44/2001/EC and its recast version 1215/2012/EU), which replaced the 1968 Convention on Jurisdiction and the Enforcement of Judgments in Civil and Commercial Matters ("Brussels Convention"). (See pp. 157-158 below.) There are also a few industry-specific arrangements providing enforcement mechanisms for international forum selection clauses (such as treaties governing the carriage of goods by sea). In general, however, international forum selection agreements do not presently benefit from anything comparable to the New York Convention.

Additionally, some states impose limitations on the enforceability of forum clauses, such as requiring a "reasonable relationship" between the parties' contract and the forum or considering *forum non conveniens* objections to the parties' contractual forum. Similarly, "public policy" or "mandatory law" limitations are usually less significant in arbitral than in judicial proceedings. For these reasons, it is often easier to obtain effective enforcement of an international arbitration agreement than of a forum selection clause.

As discussed below (See p. 23), the Hague Conference on Private International Law's 2005 Convention on Choice of Court Agreements ("the 2005 Convention"), which entered into force in Mexico and EU countries (except Denmark) in October 2015, and subsequently in Singapore (in 2016), Montenegro and Denmark (in 2018), Ukraine (in 2023), Albania and Moldova (in 2024), and North Macedonia and Switzerland (in 2025), provides more uniform international standards governing the enforcement of forum selection agreements than historically existed. Other states have, however, declined to accede to the 2005 Convention, correctly doubting its utility and wisdom. Even if a significant number of other states ratified the 2005 Convention, its limitations and exceptions would leave the enforceability of forum selection clauses subject to significant uncertainties. At least for the foreseeable future, international arbitration agreements will therefore enjoy a substantial "enforceability premium" as compared to forum selection clauses.

6. Enforceability of Awards or Judgments

Like international arbitration agreements, international arbitral awards enjoy the protection of the New York Convention, as well as favorable national arbitration legislation in many countries. These instruments provide a "pro-enforcement" regime, with only limited grounds for denying recognition to an arbitral award. Particularly in major trading states, there is substantial, successful experience with the enforcement of international arbitral awards. (See pp. 175-176 below.)

In contrast, there are only a few regional arrangements for the mutual enforcement of foreign judgments (in particular, the Brussels I Regulation (recast) in the EU), and there is no global counterpart to the New York Convention for foreign judgments. Many major trading states, including the United States, are not party to bilateral or multilateral agreements on the enforceability of foreign judgments. In the absence of international treaties, the recognition of foreign judgments in many nations is subject to local law, which often makes it difficult or impossible to obtain effective enforcement. As a consequence, there is generally a greater likelihood that an international arbitral award will actually put the parties' dispute to rest than will a national court judgment. Of course, where a regional or other treaty for the mutual recognition of foreign court judgments is applicable, the advantages of arbitral awards may be less significant.

As noted above, the 2005 Convention prescribes broad international standards applicable to the recognition and enforcement of judgments based on forum selection agreements. Although it has been ratified by a dozen or so nations, the 2005 Convention is subject to important exceptions, limitations, and defects, which will likely detract materially from its efficacy. At least for the foreseeable future, like international arbitration agreements, arbitral awards will therefore enjoy a substantial "enforceability premium" as compared to national court judgments.

7. Confidentiality of Dispute Resolution Proceedings

A potentially important consideration in designing dispute resolution provisions is the extent to which proceedings will be confidential. Broadly speaking, international arbitration is more likely than national court litigation to produce a private, confidential dispute resolution process, but there are seldom any guarantees of absolute confidentiality.

Most national court proceedings offer little by way of confidentiality to the parties. Hearings and court dockets are open to the public and the press in many countries, and parties are often free to disclose the contents of proceedings and submissions to third parties. Competitors, regulatory authorities, and press representatives are sometimes able to scrutinize the parties' submissions and evidence. Of course, this may affect what disputes are litigated and how the litigation occurs. Moreover, public disclosure may impede negotiated compromises by hardening positions or fueling emotions, and may become an independent instrument in the parties' hostilities.

In contrast, international arbitration is usually more confidential than national court proceedings. Arbitral hearings are virtually always closed to the press and public, and in practice, both submissions and awards often remain confidential. The contrast with open public dockets and court proceedings is significant.

Nonetheless, many national laws impose no clear duty of confidentiality on parties to international arbitrations, and arbitral awards are sometimes made public, either in enforcement actions or otherwise. It is possible to reduce these risks of disclosure by a counterparty through appropriately drafted confidentiality provisions. (See pp. 142-144 below.) Even if this is done, it remains the case that both arbitral awards and submissions in arbitral proceedings will, in principle, be subject to demands for disclosure by governmental regulators and that disputes with foreign states in investment arbitrations and otherwise will frequently entail public disclosures.

Although international enterprises often wisely prefer confidential dispute resolution mechanisms, parties sometimes affirmatively desire that certain disputes and their outcomes be made public. Where a company has a standard form contract, used with numerous counterparties, it may want interpretations of the contract to become publicly known and binding through precedent as widely as possible. Thus, financial institutions, intellectual property licensors, and franchisors may see litigation as a way to generate awareness or case law that has an impact beyond the parties to a litigation. Arbitration does not generally offer the same possibilities.

8. Multi-Party and Multi-Contract Issues

Arbitration agreements in multi-party or multi-contract transactions are seldom straightforward. (See pp. 125-127 below.) Drafting an arbitration agreement that binds all relevant parties in a complex (or not-so-complex) transaction can require considerable foresight and drafting skills. In some cases, parties to related transactions will refuse to agree to multi-party arbitration. In other cases, institutional arbitration rules will be ill-suited to resolve a complex dispute.

Despite these obstacles, it is generally possible, with a measure of effort, to draft arbitration agreements even for complex multi-party, multi-contract transactions. Moreover, recent versions of many institutional arbitration rules provide for multi-party and multi-contract arbitrations (including provisions for consolidation, intervention, and joinder of parties). Nonetheless, it is sometimes more prudent to rely on the jurisdictional authority of national courts. In many states, national law readily permits the exercise of jurisdiction over all related parties in a complex transaction. A forum selection clause may possess some advantages in these circumstances over an ad hoc arbitration agreement.

9. Solomonic Arbitral Compromises Versus Crisp Judicial Decisions

It is sometimes said that arbitrators are prone to issue Solomonic or "baby-splitting" awards, which compromise the parties' positions with little regard for applicable law. This may well be true in some domestic arbitration contexts (where compromises are sometimes what the parties expect and desire in agreeing to arbitrate). The image of compromise verdicts is much less true, but not entirely wrong, in international arbitration.

Most international arbitrations involve the application of law to fact, much like a national court proceeding. It is true that some international arbitrators are reluctant to grant summary dispositions, dismissing a party's claims prior to a full evidentiary hearing (other than on jurisdictional grounds). Even so, most international arbitrations are more principled and predictable in the application of law to fact than trials before most national court judges or lay juries. A significant, but relatively uncommon, exception to this are the relatively rare cases where the arbitrators are expressly authorized to decide *ex aequo et bono* or as *amiable compositeur*. (See pp. 124-125 below.)

Three-person arbitral tribunals frequently seek to produce unanimous awards, which can result in a degree of compromise or horse-trading. In some cases, this can produce outcomes that may be somewhat less crisp and principled than those of a rigorous national court judge—but no more so than many other available national litigation processes (e.g., many national court judges or juries). On the other hand, a three-person tribunal will often arrive at a more principled and rigorous factual and legal analysis than that of most national trial courts (where a single judge with limited experience hears the dispute).

International arbitrators can also encounter pressures arising from the consensual nature of the arbitral process. In order to ensure a measure of procedural civility and because they lack most types of coercive governmental authority, some arbitrators can be reluctant to make procedural or interim decisions that one party will regard as draconian.

10. Facilitating Amicable Settlement

It is sometimes said that arbitration is more likely than litigation to permit parties to amicably settle their differences. This hypothesis is attributed to the fact that arbitration is consensual from the outset by virtue of the parties' arbitration agreement. Similarly, arbitral proceedings generally involve some measure of procedural cooperation between the parties—for example, in choosing arbitrators and agreeing to a procedural timetable. Some arbitral institutions also have "arb-med" mechanisms that encourage the parties to mediate their disputes, including in the course of an arbitration.

It is far from clear, however, that international arbitration is systemically more likely than litigation to produce negotiated settlements. There is no reliable empirical data on the subject, and anecdotal experiences vary. Nonetheless, the arbitral process does present parties with opportunities for both procedural cooperation and more general settlement discussions. Approached constructively, these opportunities can be used to pursue a negotiated resolution, at least where parties are so inclined.

F. PLANNING FOR DISPUTE RESOLUTION IN INTERNATIONAL CONTRACTS

As discussed above (See p. 1), it is almost always advisable to include a dispute resolution provision in international commercial contracts. That conclusion has become particularly true in recent years, as a consequence of increased volatility and uncertainty in international trade and investment relations.

The dispute resolution mechanism that a party can realistically obtain in a particular transaction often depends upon its own negotiating strength and its counterparty's interests and leverage. Like other contractual terms, the dispute resolution clause is a product of bargaining, compromise, and drafting ability.

Putting aside the question of what can actually be achieved in a particular set of negotiations, it is wrong to adopt an unqualified preference for either international forum selection clauses or international arbitration agreements. Both mechanisms have strengths and weaknesses, some of which are more significant in given circumstances than others. Deciding which mechanism is appropriate in a specific case, and for a particular party, usually requires careful consideration of the parties' proposed agreement, their likely future disputes, and their respective interests.

That said, the following general guidelines for drafting international dispute resolution provisions can be offered.

First, if it is not expected that an agreement or award will need to be enforced abroad, then a forum selection clause selecting a party's home-courts may be the simplest, most desirable option. Enforcement abroad will typically not be necessary where both parties have assets within the contractual forum, and particularly where the local party does not have assets elsewhere. In these circumstances, the convenience, familiarity, and presumptive sympathy of a party's home-courts will usually outweigh other considerations. The same conclusion generally applies if a bilateral or other treaty provides for the effective enforcement of a party's home-court judgments in its counterparty's place of business. This general conclusion will not apply, however, where proceedings in a party's courts are subject to excessive delays or to a lack of basic judicial competence or integrity, as is true in an unfortunate number of jurisdictions.

Second, even if enforcement abroad is a likely necessity, the advantages of a truly favorable home-court forum may outweigh difficulties in enforcement. This requires a party to assess on a case-by-case basis how great the benefits of the local forum are, how important enforcement abroad may be, and how significant any enforceability issues will likely be. It will also require a case-by-case assessment of issues of cost and speed, expertise, integrity, and similar factors in the various potentially available fora.

Third, if enforcement abroad is sufficiently important *or* if a favorable local forum cannot be obtained in negotiations, then international arbitration in a favorable or neutral forum is generally the most desirable alternative. In almost all cases, a well-drafted international arbitration agreement will ensure a dispute resolution mechanism that is sufficiently competent, predictable, and neutral to warrant acceptance. Thus, parties should ordinarily have no reason to reject an otherwise attractive deal merely because of the need to agree to international arbitration. Indeed, arbitration is generally materially more attractive than a forum selection clause selecting a neutral judicial forum. This is because of the greater likelihood of successfully enforcing arbitration agreements and awards, the relative advantages of the arbitral process as compared to national court procedures, and the parties' ability to select expert, experienced decision-makers for particular disputes.

Fourth, the courts of a few developed nations can be selected as neutral fora, subject to confirming the willingness and suitability of such courts to resolve particular disputes. These courts include those of England, New York, Switzerland, Singapore, and a limited number of other nations. There may be instances where the procedural and other characteristics of particular national courts (e.g., discovery or jury trial) make them more attractive to a party than other fora, even if the courts are in a neutral third state.

Fifth, litigation in the courts of a counterparty *or* in most national courts (e.g., those lacking proven experience in international commercial disputes) is generally not an attractive outcome. If such a choice is considered, it should be preceded by careful review of the consequences. There will be cases where the inability to obtain a satisfactory dispute resolution provision is a good reason for walking away from an otherwise acceptable commercial transaction. The risks that arise from litigation in an inappropriate national court, or arbitral seat, have increased in recent years, making it particularly important to avoid proceedings in such fora.

The following chapters discuss the implementation of these observations. Chapters 2 and 3 address the drafting of forum selection clauses and international arbitration agreements. Chapters 4, 5, 6, and 7 then provide an overview of the issues that arise in enforcing both dispute resolution agreements and resulting judgments or arbitral awards. Finally, Chapter 8 considers the drafting and enforcement of choice-of-law clauses.

A number of model or representative international forum selection clauses and arbitration agreements are set out in the chapters that follow. In addition, Appendix I contains a collection of model arbitration clauses recommended by leading international arbitral institutions. Appendix J sets forth a collection of all the representative arbitration and forum selection clauses that are contained in the text of this book.

Before continuing, a word about routinized, smaller-scale transactions is appropriate. Contracts for smaller sales and other transactions are seldom extensively negotiated, and the costs of legal review of dispute resolution provisions for such transactions are virtually never justified. In these cases, the most sensible course is inclusion of a standard form institutional arbitration clause or a simple forum selection clause in contractual documentation. Each of these options is considered below in Chapters 2 and 3.

Chapter 2

Drafting International Forum Selection Clauses

As we have seen, a forum selection clause is a contractual term providing for litigation of the parties' disputes in a specified national court. Forum selection clauses are often used in connection with other provisions related to dispute resolution, such as choice-of-law clauses, service of process provisions, and waivers of foreign sovereign (or state) immunity. (See pp. 30-34 below.)

Like other contractual arrangements, forum selection clauses are largely a product of the contracting parties' interests, negotiations, and drafting abilities. This chapter discusses issues that commonly arise in drafting international forum selection agreements.

Preliminarily, the interpretation and enforcement of international forum selection agreements often raise choice-of-law questions. In general, the law applicable to a forum selection clause is either that of the parties' chosen contractual forum or the parties' underlying agreement. (See p. 161 below.)

A. EXCLUSIVE VERSUS NON-EXCLUSIVE FORUM SELECTION CLAUSES

There is a vital difference between "exclusive" and "non-exclusive" forum selection clauses. There are also important variations in the ways that different national courts approach the interpretation of such provisions.

1. Exclusive Forum Selection Clauses

An exclusive (or "mandatory") forum selection clause *requires* that disputes covered by the clause be resolved solely in the specified forum, and nowhere else. The following language is a representative example of an exclusive forum clause:

> The parties agree that any dispute relating to this Agreement shall be resolved exclusively by the courts of _________, and no others.

Other formulations of exclusive forum selection clauses are discussed below. (See pp. 21-22.) Exclusive forum selection clauses are also sometimes referred to as "derogation" clauses because they preclude litigation in courts which would otherwise possess jurisdiction, as well as specify the court where litigation may occur.

2. Non-Exclusive Forum Selection Clauses

A non-exclusive (or "permissive") forum clause *permits* parties to litigate their disputes in the contractual forum, but *does not require* that disputes be resolved there. Thus, litigation can also be pursued in other fora that may have jurisdiction under applicable law(s) over the parties and the dispute. The following provision is a representative example of a non-exclusive forum clause:

> The parties submit to the non-exclusive jurisdiction of the courts of _________ for any disputes relating to this Agreement.

Other formulations of non-exclusive forum selection clauses are discussed below. (See p. 22.)

Non-exclusive forum selection clauses are also sometimes referred to as "prorogation" clauses or "submissions to jurisdiction." Particularly to common law audiences, these labels reflect the clauses' function of conferring personal jurisdiction (*rationae personae*) over the parties on the courts of the contractual forum, without necessarily purporting contractually to divest other courts of the jurisdiction they might possess over the parties. In some civil law states, the term "prorogation clause" can refer more broadly to both exclusive and non-exclusive forum selection clauses.

3. Choosing Between Exclusive and Non-Exclusive Forum Selection Clauses

A variety of considerations affect a party's decision whether to use an exclusive or a non-exclusive forum selection clause. First, an exclusive forum clause is more likely to prevent parallel or multiplicitous litigations in different national courts. In contrast, a non-exclusive forum clause generally leaves both parties largely free to commence litigation in other fora of their choice. Where litigation tactics make this attractive, a party will do so, with the attendant expense and possibility of inconsistent results in different proceedings.

Second, and conversely, an exclusive forum clause may, in some jurisdictions, preclude a party from seeking relief in fora outside the contractual forum, even when there are strong practical reasons for doing so. For example, a licensor of intellectual property could be prevented by some exclusive forum selection clauses from seeking injunctive relief outside the contractual forum to halt unauthorized uses of the licensed property. Alternatively, a creditor might be precluded from freezing or otherwise proceeding against funds located outside the contractual forum.

These consequences of an exclusive forum clause are by no means inevitable. There are persuasive arguments under the laws of many jurisdictions (including the EU, the United States, England, and Singapore) that exclusive forum selection clauses should not be interpreted as extending to questions of provisional measures and similar ancillary litigation. In addition, as discussed below (See pp. 34-35), there are ways of drafting forum clauses that address these concerns. Nonetheless, there is inevitably some risk that an exclusive forum selection clause will prevent or impede a party from pursuing avenues of judicial relief which would otherwise be available.

Third, exclusive forum selection clauses are more likely in some jurisdictions than non-exclusive ones to raise questions of validity or enforceability. As discussed below, exclusive forum agreements are presumptively enforceable in most major trading nations. (See pp.157-159.) Nonetheless, there are numerous exceptions to this rule that can have important practical consequences. These issues exist with respect to the enforceability of the forum clause itself and with respect to judgments eventually rendered in the contractual forum. In contrast, enforceability objections to non-exclusive forum clauses are much less likely to be significant.

On balance, parties to international transactions are often better served by an exclusive forum selection agreement than by a non-exclusive one. The former reduces the risk of litigation in undesirable or unanticipated fora, which can be of substantial importance in international disputes. Where there is a need to preserve particular avenues for judicial relief outside the contractual forum, clauses can be drafted to provide expressly for this. (See pp. 22-23 below.) Although there are enforceability questions about exclusive forum clauses, failing to prevail on such issues generally has little consequence beyond converting an exclusive forum selection clause into a non-exclusive forum selection clause.

B. DRAFTING EXCLUSIVE AND NON-EXCLUSIVE FORUM SELECTION CLAUSES

One might think that determining whether an international forum selection clause is exclusive or permissive would be only a straightforward question of interpreting the text of the contract. In fact, as outlined below (See p. 24), different national courts adopt significantly differing approaches to the interpretation and enforcement of forum clauses.

It is important to understand these different approaches in drafting international forum selection clauses. Depending upon the law that is applied and the courts where litigation occurs, the same forum selection language can often be construed in different courts as either exclusive or non-exclusive. As a consequence, it is advisable to draft forum selection clauses to expressly address the question of exclusivity. This reduces the potential effect of differing approaches to construction.

1. Common Law Approach to Exclusivity of Forum Selection Clauses

Courts in some common law jurisdictions generally will not interpret forum selection clauses as exclusive, absent some affirmative showing that the parties so agreed. U.S. courts are particularly reluctant to hold that a forum selection agreement is exclusive. The underlying rationale of most U.S. decisions is that parties should not be lightly presumed to have contractually waived otherwise existing access to judicial remedies. In cases of ambiguity, therefore, a forum selection clause will be interpreted by U.S. courts as permissive or non-exclusive, rather than exclusive. Thus, a forum selection clause must ordinarily provide that disputes shall "only" or "exclusively" be resolved in the contractual forum in order to be deemed exclusive by U.S. courts. English courts take a broadly similar approach to interpreting forum selection clauses in most circumstances, but without adopting an express presumption of non-exclusivity. Under English law, a forum selection clause will be interpreted objectively to determine the parties' intentions, with some evidence of an affirmative exclusion of alternative fora being required in order to sustain an interpretation of exclusivity.

2. Civil Law Approach to Exclusivity of Forum Selection Clauses

In contrast to the common law approach, some legal systems resist the notion that parties may confer jurisdiction on the courts of one country, while simultaneously reserving the right to proceed in other fora. Under this view, jurisdiction ought, as a matter of principle, to be fixed in a single judicial forum. This position is followed in both the EU and a number of civil law states.

Forum selection clauses in EU Member States are often governed by the Regulation on Jurisdiction and the Recognition and Enforcement of Judgments in Civil and Commercial Matters. The Regulation, which was first adopted in 2000 as Council Regulation (EC) No. 44/2001 and is known as the "Brussels I Regulation," was revised in late 2012. The "recast" Brussels I Regulation, Regulation (EU) No. 1215/2012 applies to proceedings commenced on or after January 10, 2015. The Brussels I Regulation is applicable broadly to civil and commercial matters, with exceptions for revenue, customs, administrative matters, status or legal capacity of natural persons, matrimonial matters, inheritance, bankruptcy, social security, and arbitration. Courts in nations outside the EU, including the United States, Japan, China, and other non-European states, are not bound by the Brussels I Regulation (or by its predecessor, the Brussels Convention), but in EU courts, the recast Brussels I Regulation applies to non-EU, as well as EU, parties.

Under the Brussels I Regulation, a court of an EU Member State, which is designated by a forum selection clause, possesses exclusive jurisdiction over disputes covered by the clause. In contrast to the U.S. approach, the European regulation treats forum selection agreements as presumptively exclusive (i.e., exclusive unless the parties have agreed otherwise), requiring the parties to pursue litigation solely in their contractual forum.

While the rules relating to forum selection clauses under the older version of the Brussels I Regulation (Article 23 of EC Regulation 44/2001) apply whenever a dispute involving a forum selection clause is brought before a court in an EU Member State (other than Denmark), and at least one party is domiciled in such a state, the rules under the recast version (Article 25 of EU Regulation 1215/2012) apply regardless of the domicile of the parties. (As discussed below, these rules are subject to exceptions for certain claims by insureds, consumers, and employees, as well as to some claims regarding real property, internal corporate affairs, and arbitration. (See pp.160-161)) Both versions expressly permit parties to agree upon non-exclusive forum selection clauses, but any such agreement must overcome a presumption of exclusivity.

In addition, the Brussels I Regulation apparently preserves the approach under the former Brussels Convention, which recognized the validity of forum selection agreements that are binding on only one party (or "asymmetrical clauses"). Such a clause permits the party for whose benefit the forum clause was concluded to sue *either* in the chosen court *or* in the courts of any other EU Member State which would have jurisdiction over the disputes. (See pp. 28-30 below.) In effect, the clause is exclusive for one party and non-exclusive for the other.

A number of European states outside the EU (including Switzerland, Norway, and Iceland) are subject to substantially similar rules to the Brussels I Regulation by virtue of the Convention on Jurisdiction and the Recognition and Enforcement of Judgments in Civil and Commercial Matters 1988 ("Lugano Convention"). Article 17 of the 1988 Lugano Convention (Article 23 of the revised 2007 Lugano Convention) is similar to Article 23 of EC Regulation 44/2001 and Article 25 of EU Regulation 1215/2012, and the same issues and conclusions that apply under the Brussels I Regulation also arise under the Lugano Convention. Beyond the Brussels I Regulation, national law in a number of civil law states interprets forum selection clauses as exclusive in cases of doubt. For example, Article 5 of the Swiss Law on Private International Law, which was inspired by the Brussels Convention, adopts a presumption that forum selection clauses are exclusive. In the words of Article 5, "[u]nless otherwise agreed, a choice of forum is exclusive." Thus, Switzerland has, as is the case under the Brussels I Regulation, adopted the reverse presumption from that applied in U.S. courts: in order for a forum selection clause to be deemed non-exclusive, it must contain language expressly providing for such a result. Other civil law jurisdictions follow similar approaches, as does the 2005 Convention. (See p. 23 above.)

3. Drafting Exclusive Forum Selection Clauses

Whichever type of forum clause is desired, parties should expressly address the question of exclusivity. This is advisable in order to avoid uncertainties resulting from different rules of construction in different jurisdictions.

Where an exclusive forum selection clause is desired, language that specifically excludes litigation in other courts should be included. This is advisable in order to overcome the presumption adopted by U.S. and some other common law courts against exclusive forum selection agreements.

The following clause is a suitable model:

> The courts of _________ shall have exclusive jurisdiction over all disputes relating to this Agreement.

Or:

> All disputes relating to this Agreement shall be resolved exclusively by the courts of _________, and no others. [Each of the parties irrevocably submits to the jurisdiction of the courts of _________ for the purpose of resolving such disputes.]

Alternatively:

> In relation to any legal action or proceedings arising out of or in connection with this Agreement ("Proceedings"), each of the parties irrevocably submits to the exclusive jurisdiction of the _________ courts with regard to such Proceedings and waives any objections to Proceedings on the grounds of venue or on the grounds that proceedings have been brought in an inappropriate forum.

It is wiser to avoid ambiguous formulations such as "This Agreement is governed by _________ courts" or "Disputes shall be determined by the courts of _________."

4. Drafting Non-Exclusive Forum Selection Clauses

Conversely, if a non-exclusive forum selection clause is desired, that also should be clearly stated. This is advisable in order to maximize the chances of overcoming EU, Swiss, and similar presumptions favoring exclusive forum agreements. The following is a suitable model:

> The parties irrevocably submit to the non-exclusive jurisdiction of the courts of _________ for any disputes relating to this Agreement.

Or:

> The courts of _________ shall have non-exclusive jurisdiction to decide actions relating to this Agreement, without prejudice to the right of either party to commence such actions in any other court of competent jurisdiction.

Alternatively:

> All disputes relating to this Agreement may be submitted by either party to the non-exclusive jurisdiction of the courts of ________. [The parties irrevocably submit to the non-exclusive jurisdiction of the courts of ________ for the purpose of resolving such disputes.] Nothing contained herein shall affect the rights of either party to submit any such dispute to any other courts of competent jurisdiction.

Alternatively:

> In relation to any legal action or proceedings arising out of or in connection with this Agreement ("Proceedings"), each of the parties irrevocably submits to the non-exclusive jurisdiction of the courts of ________ save that this submission shall not affect the right of any party to take Proceedings in any other court or courts having jurisdiction, to the extent permitted by law.

Of course, all of these formulations may be affected in particular cases by applicable law, which can require amendments or alternative approaches.

Finally, as discussed above, forum selection clauses can be non-exclusive for one party and exclusive for the other. Such clauses were expressly permitted by Article 17 of the Brussels Convention and are also generally enforceable in other leading jurisdictions. The drafting of such "asymmetrical" forum clauses is addressed below. (See pp. 28-29.)

C. HAGUE CONVENTION ON CHOICE OF COURT AGREEMENTS

The Member States of the Hague Conference on Private International Law finalized the text of a proposed Convention on Choice of Court Agreements in 2005. In 2007, Mexico became the first state to ratify the 2005 Convention, followed by the European Union with the exception of Denmark (in 2015), Singapore (in 2016), Montenegro and Denmark (in 2018), the United Kingdom (in 2020), Ukraine (in 2023), and Moldova, Albania, Switzerland and North Macedonia (in 2024). The United States and China have signed the 2005 Convention (in 2009 and 2017, respectively), but have not ratified it. The 2005 Convention, which is reproduced in Appendix B, requires Contracting States to recognize and enforce exclusive forum selection clauses by accepting jurisdiction (when the parties have so agreed) and by declining jurisdiction (when the parties have agreed upon exclusive jurisdiction in another forum). The 2005 Convention also requires recognition and enforcement of foreign judgments obtained in proceedings based on a valid exclusive forum agreement.

Significantly, under the 2005 Convention (in Article 3(b)), a choice of court agreement shall be deemed to be exclusive unless the parties have expressly provided otherwise. The 2005 Convention gives Contracting States the option to agree that they will recognize and enforce judgments obtained in proceedings based upon non-exclusive forum selection agreements. However, a state is only bound in respect of non-exclusive jurisdiction agreements if it has issued a separate, optional declaration to that effect.

In all cases, the 2005 Convention's provisions are subject to significant exceptions, including for "null and void" agreements and for "manifest injustice," public policy, or other "exceptional reasons." The 2005 Convention is also inapplicable to a number of categories of agreements and disputes, including matters involving consumers, employment, intellectual property (except copyright), insolvency, and antitrust/competition law. Commentators have cited significant shortcomings in the 2005 Convention, which counsel strongly against its ratification. There has been no practical experience to date with the 2005 Convention, and its application between jurisdictions in which the 2005 Convention has entered into force will present challenges.

If the 2005 Convention were to come into force among more states, it could enhance the enforceability of forum selection agreements. As noted above, however, this appears unlikely, and the 2005 Convention's exceptions would likely materially detract from its practical utility, even if it were ratified by additional states. Absent further developments, the 2005 Convention is likely to have only limited effect on parties' selection and drafting of international dispute resolution provisions.

D. SCOPE OF FORUM SELECTION CLAUSES

A critical issue in drafting forum selection agreements is the question of "scope"—what categories of claims or disputes are subject to a forum clause? Particularly common are questions whether a forum selection agreement applies to statutory claims or claims in tort or delicts (such as allegations of fraudulent inducement of a contract, defamation, unfair competition, breach of fiduciary duty, etc.). Similar issues arise with respect to claims based on related contracts or transactions, amendments, guarantees, and the like.

1. Scope of Forum Selection Clause Generally Determined by Parties' Agreement

The categories of disputes which are subject to a forum selection clause are largely a matter of the parties' intentions and drafting. Most developed legal systems allow forum selection clauses to encompass virtually all contractual disputes and at least some non-contractual disputes (such as tort or statutory claims). U.S., English, and other common law courts have frequently held so, even without statutory authorization. Likewise, in most civil law jurisdictions, forum clauses may extend to a broad array of contract, tort, and statutory claims. In Switzerland, for example, Article 5 of the Swiss Law on Private International Law provides that a forum selection clause may apply to any matter of "financial interest."

2. Formulae for Scope of Forum Selection Clauses

Several formulations are commonly used to define the breadth of forum selection clauses: (i) "all disputes *arising under* this Agreement"; (ii) "all disputes *arising out of* this Agreement"; (iii) "all disputes *relating to* this Agreement"; and (iv) "all disputes *arising in connection with* this Agreement." Alternative formulations are also encountered, including: (v) "all disputes relating to this Agreement, *including any question regarding its existence, validity, breach, or termination*"; and (vi) "all disputes relating to this Agreement *or the subject matter hereof*." National courts do not generally apply presumptions favoring either an expansive or a narrow reading of the scope of a forum selection clause. As discussed below, this contrasts with the approach of many courts to arbitration clauses, where a strong presumption that the parties intended to arbitrate disputes often applies to questions of scope. (See p.169.) Instead, courts typically apply general principles of contract interpretation, without pro-coverage presumptions, to resolve disputes about the scope of forum clauses. Some national courts have drawn fine distinctions between different formulae contained in forum selection clauses. Several such decisions have concluded that the phrase "*arising under* this Agreement" is less expansive than the phrase "*relating to* this Agreement"; they have reasoned that the former formula includes only contractual claims based on the terms of the parties' agreement, while the latter extends to quasi-contract and non-contractual claims. Most other courts, including a number of common law courts, have rejected such distinctions.

3. Advantages of Forum Selection Clauses with Broad Scope

In general, it is prudent to draft forum clauses with an expansive scope. This reduces the risk of time-consuming preliminary litigation over questions of jurisdiction. It also makes it more likely that all of the parties' disputes can be settled in a single, consolidated proceeding in the contractual forum, thus avoiding the possibility of inconsistent results and legal expenses from multiple proceedings. Of course, a party may have reasons for preferring multiple proceedings in a particular transaction, with different dispute resolution mechanisms for different categories of disputes, in which case an alternative approach may be appropriate.

4. Drafting Forum Selection Clauses with Broad Scope

Drafting a broad forum selection clause involves several elements. First, the drafter should ordinarily begin with a preamble providing that "*all disputes, claims, controversies, and disagreements*" are subject to litigation in the contractual forum. This formula is generally preferable to shorter references to "disputes" or "any disputes" because it reduces the risk of debates over what constitutes a "dispute."

Second, the drafter's chosen preamble should usually be combined with two or more broad connecting formulae, such as disputes "*relating to*" or "*arising in connection with*" the parties' agreement. It is better to use several expansive connectors, rather than just a reference to disputes "arising under" or "arising from" the parties' agreement. This is because the former formulae increase the likelihood that a clause will reach non-contractual or quasi-contractual claims, as well as disputes concerning the existence or validity of the parties' underlying contract. As noted above (See p. 25), some jurisdictions adopt narrow interpretations of the phrase "arising under," underscoring the advisability of broader formulations.

Finally, it is often desirable to include a reference which is broader than disputes relating to the parties' "Agreement" or "Contract." For example, forum selection clauses often extend more broadly to disputes relating to "this Agreement, or the subject matter of this Agreement." Such a provision reduces the risk that conduct by the parties, or other occurrences, relating to their contract, but arguably not necessarily entailed in its performance, will fall outside the scope of the forum selection clause.

Taken together, these guidelines produce a "broad" forum selection clause along the following lines:

> All disputes, claims, controversies, and disagreements relating to or arising out of this Agreement, or the subject matter of this Agreement, shall be subject to the exclusive [or non-exclusive] jurisdiction of the courts of ________, and no others.

A somewhat shorter version, more familiar to drafters outside the common law world, would provide:

> All disputes relating to this Agreement shall be subject to the exclusive [or non-exclusive] jurisdiction of the courts of ________.

Of course, the interpretation and enforcement of particular forum selection clauses must be considered under their applicable law(s), which may, in particular cases, require changes to the above clauses.

5. Exclusions from Scope of Forum Selection Clauses

A forum selection clause can exclude certain categories of disputes from its coverage. For example, particular contractual provisions can be carved out from the scope of otherwise applicable forum clauses, either because the parties wish to be free of any restrictions with respect to the litigation of excluded disputes or to provide an alternative form of dispute resolution for such disputes. An example of a provision excluding particular disputes from a forum selection clause is as follows:

> All disputes relating to this Agreement, with the exception of claims arising under Article III [or: claims for payment under Article IV], shall be resolved exclusively in the courts of ________.

An exclusion of this sort would ordinarily be accompanied by provisions setting forth a separate dispute resolution mechanism for disagreements falling within the exclusion. This could take the form of either a forum clause selecting an alternative judicial forum, an arbitration clause, or a clause referring certain disputes to a technical expert (e.g., an accounting firm or engineer). For example, an accounting firm might be designated to resolve disputes concerning price adjustments, or a technical expert might be designated to resolve disputes concerning the quality of certain goods or the adequacy of particular types of contract performance.

Contractual exclusions of this sort may have some appeal by channeling highly technical disputes to appropriately qualified experts. Nonetheless, these sorts of provisions frequently give rise to jurisdictional disputes as to whether or not a dispute falls within an exclusion and may also raise significant questions as to the scope of judicial review. As a consequence, save in special circumstances and where great care is taken in drafting, such exclusions are usually ill-advised.

Finally, mandatory national law or public policy may render exclusive forum selection clauses unenforceable as applied to particular non-contractual claims. This is especially likely with respect to statutory protections enacted for the benefit of specific classes of litigants that are perceived to require legislative protection, such as consumers, securities investors, employees, insureds, distributors, or franchisees. Examples of such protections are detailed below. (See pp. 160-161.) The circumstances in which mandatory law will render forum selection agreements unenforceable are almost always a question of national law, which varies significantly between jurisdictions. The effects of mandatory law on the enforceability of a forum clause are also generally a question which cannot be affected by a choice-of-law clause selecting the applicable substantive law.

E. SELECTING THE CONTRACTUAL FORUM

A forum selection clause must designate the parties' chosen court. First, this requires deciding what court a party wishes to select, and then negotiating that preference with the counterparty. The considerations relevant to this choice are discussed above. (See pp. 4-13.) As also noted above, recent protectionist and other trends have made it particularly important to select an appropriate forum for dispute resolutions with care; the risks of bias, lack of independence, inexperience and the like in national court proceedings in many jurisdictions have materially increased over the past decade.

Second, a forum selection clause must accurately and effectively specify the court upon which the parties have agreed. At a minimum, this requires correctly identifying the relevant court and geographic location. In addition, it may also require choosing among several courts in a particular location. For example, selecting a court in a particular U.S. locale may permit choosing between federal and state courts, while in England and France, parties can choose between different types of local courts. Likewise, a few jurisdictions have established so-called "international" courts, with different attributes than local courts (e.g., the Abu Dhabi Global Market Courts or the Singapore International Commercial Court), as discussed below

(See pp. 35-37); if parties wish to provide for dispute resolution in such courts, they generally must be specifically identified.

Conversely, parties should be careful not to select a court which, under local law, cannot exercise jurisdiction over their dispute. Local counsel should be consulted in such cases regarding the availability of different options and which court should be selected.

Finally, selecting a forum also requires selecting a particular geographic locale. Although this can be straightforward, some care is appropriate. In particular, the precise location should be clearly stated (e.g., not merely "New York," which could include the entire state). In some countries, a general reference to national courts (e.g., Swiss courts), without specifying a particular geographical location (e.g., a canton), may not be valid under local law. Again, advice from local counsel in the contractual forum should ordinarily be sought.

F. ASYMMETRICAL (OR "ONE-SIDED") FORUM SELECTION CLAUSES

As noted above (See pp. 20-21), forum clauses may be exclusive as to one party, while leaving the other party free to initiate litigation in courts other than the contractual forum. These types of clauses are often used in financial transactions, where lenders reserve the right to commence actions against the borrower in any forum, or in any of several specified fora. The following is a representative example of an asymmetrical forum clause:

> The parties agree that all disputes relating to this Agreement shall be resolved exclusively in the courts of ________, provided however that [Party A] shall be also free to pursue claims in any court of competent jurisdiction, including, without limitation, the courts of ________ and ________.

An alternative formulation is:

> The parties agree that all disputes relating to this Agreement shall be resolved exclusively in the courts of ________, unless [Party A] chooses to bring action in ________.

An English formulation provides:

> This Agreement shall be governed by and construed in accordance with English Law and the parties irrevocably agree for the exclusive benefit of the Lenders that the courts of England are to have jurisdiction to settle any disputes which may arise out of or in connection with this Agreement and that accordingly any suit, action, or proceeding arising out of or in connection with this Agreement (in this Article [X] referred to as "Proceedings") may be brought in such courts and the Company hereby irrevocably submit to the jurisdiction of such courts.

> Nothing contained in this Article [X] shall limit the right of the Lender to take Proceedings against the Company in any other court of competent jurisdiction, nor shall the taking of proceedings in one or more jurisdictions preclude the taking of Proceedings in any other jurisdiction, whether concurrently or not.

Another version of an asymmetrical forum clause, permitting one party to elect to arbitrate (rather than litigate) future disputes, provides:

> The parties irrevocably submit to the non-exclusive jurisdiction of the courts of ________ for resolution of any disputes, claims or controversies relating to this Agreement. Notwithstanding the foregoing sentence, and at the sole option of [Party A], any disputes, claims or controversies relating to this Agreement shall be finally resolved by arbitration. ... If a court action has been initiated by [Party B] prior to or at the time that [Party A] elects to submit the dispute(s) to arbitration, then [Party B] shall forthwith take all necessary steps to discontinue and dismiss such court action.

As with other examples of asymmetrical forum selection clauses, this provision raises enforceability issues. Although they are generally enforceable in most developed states, asymmetrical clauses raise issues of enforceability in some jurisdictions on the grounds that they lack mutuality or are unconscionably one-sided. In particular, caution is appropriate in cases involving a disparity in bargaining power or sophistication.

Courts in many states, including the United States and EU Member States, will likely require that asymmetrical forum clauses be expressed with particular clarity. The following text is representative of a clause drafted to satisfy this condition:

> All disputes relating to this Agreement shall be submitted to the courts of ________. This provision is for the sole benefit of ________, which shall retain the option of submitting any such disputes to any other courts of competent jurisdiction.

Whatever formulation is adopted, a party desiring an asymmetrical forum clause should ensure that this intention is expressed with sufficient clarity.

G. FORUM SELECTION CLAUSES: SELECTING THE DEFENDANT'S PLACE OF BUSINESS

Some forum selection clauses do not choose a single court or fixed geographic location. Instead, these clauses provide that future disputes will be resolved in the place where the respondent in a given action (whichever contracting party that may prove to be) has its principal place of business. This clause requires that a party wishing to initiate litigation do so only in the courts of its adversary.

Such provisions are designed to discourage over-hasty resort to litigation by requiring a claimant to pursue its action in its counterparty's home-courts. They also reflect the notion that a party should be permitted to defend itself against legal claims on its own "home ground."

A significant disadvantage of such arrangements is that they do little or nothing to bring predictability to the parties' relations, since the contractual forum is not known until litigation actually begins. Such provisions can also encourage undesirable pre-litigation procedural maneuvering and self-help measures. This may reward, or at least not appropriately discourage, breaches of contractual commitments by making it more difficult to obtain judicial relief. This sort of provision should be used only in rare circumstances and with caution.

A representative example of a clause specifying the defendant's domicile as the contractual forum is as follows:

> Any suit relating to this Agreement brought by Buyer shall be brought in ________ [or: the place where Seller's principal place of business is located]; any suit relating to this Agreement brought by Seller shall be brought in ________ [or: the place where Buyer's principal place of business is located].

Although there is relatively limited precedent, national courts that have considered the issue have in principle upheld the validity and enforceability of such clauses.

H. PROVISIONS COMMONLY ACCOMPANYING FORUM SELECTION CLAUSES

There are various ancillary contractual provisions which are frequently used in conjunction with forum selection clauses. In some cases, these provisions are either necessary or highly desirable.

1. Consent to Service of Process

Forum selection clauses can be accompanied by contractual provisions regarding service of process, typically on a local agent within the contractual forum. A representative example of such a clause for use in the United States is as follows:

> ________ irrevocably designates, appoints, and empowers ________, with offices on the date hereof at ________, as its agent with respect to any action or proceeding in ________ to receive, on its behalf, and in respect of its property, service of any and all legal process, summons, notices, and documents which may be served in any such action or proceeding and agrees that the failure of the agent to notify ________ of any such service of process will not impair or affect the validity of service. ________ further irrevocably consents to the service of process out of any of the courts listed in Article [X] by the mailing of copies by registered or certified mail, postage prepaid, to ________ at its address set forth in Article [X], such service to become effective 30 days after such mailing. If for any reason ________ shall cease to be available to act as agent, ________ agrees to designate a new agent in ________ on the same terms and for the same purposes.

A similar clause, drafted along English lines, is:

> ________ hereby irrevocably appoints ________ of ________ as his agent for the service of process in England in connection with this Agreement. Service of process on ________ at the above address shall be deemed, for all purposes, to be due and effective service, and service shall be deemed completed whether or not forwarded to or received by ________.

The purpose of such provisions is to simplify the practical task of completing service of process in a valid manner. The existence of a local agent, within the territory of the contractual forum, generally means that service of process need not be effected on the defendant in its home country under otherwise applicable rules governing the service of process abroad. This can be of significant practical importance because the service of process abroad can be cumbersome under either international agreements (such as the 1965 Hague Convention on Service Abroad of Judicial and Extrajudicial Documents in Civil or Commercial Matters) or domestic law (which may require specific judicial leave).

2. Allocating Legal Costs

A forum selection agreement can be accompanied by provisions regarding the allocation of the costs of legal representation. For example, parties can agree that the prevailing party may recover the fees and other costs of legal counsel from the unsuccessful party. Alternatively, an agreement may provide that each party will bear its own legal expenses, regardless of whether it prevails on its claims.

Outside the United States, many jurisdictions apply some sort of rules allocating liability for the prevailing party's costs of legal representation to the unsuccessful party (also termed "fee-shifting"). In many countries, these rules are based on local statutory provisions.

If parties wish to avoid fee-shifting, they will generally need to provide so expressly, in order to avoid otherwise applicable local rules in most countries. Sample clauses addressing this issue are set forth below. (See pp. 109-112.) Because such provisions implicate matters of public policy and judicial administration, their validity and enforceability in particular national courts must be confirmed.

3. Waiver of Foreign Sovereign or State Immunity

International trade frequently involves dealings with foreign states or foreign state-related entities. This can present special litigation problems because these entities may enjoy varying degrees of foreign sovereign or state immunity under applicable national law.

In many cases, a foreign state that engages in "commercial activity" will not enjoy immunity from claims relating to that activity. Nonetheless, parties are usually well-advised to include express waivers of sovereign immunity in commercial agreements with foreign states or state-related entities. Such waivers can help avoid disputes about what constitutes "commercial" activity, and can also extend to the enforceability and execution of judgments (and provisional measures) against the foreign state's assets.

The precise terms of a waiver of foreign sovereign immunity should be considered in the light of applicable law(s) in the parties' contractual forum(s). Such a provision could be formulated as follows:

> The parties agree that the matters that are subject to this choice of court agreement are commercial transactions and agree not to claim and to waive any immunity from suit, execution, pre-judgment, or post-judgment attachment, or other legal process in any jurisdiction in connection with any litigation between the parties pursuant to this choice of court agreement or otherwise.

The following formulation is used in U.S. practice:

> The Borrower is subject to civil and commercial law with respect to its obligations under this Agreement. The execution, delivery, and performance by the Borrower of this Agreement constitute private and commercial acts rather than public or governmental acts. Neither the Borrower, nor any of its Properties or revenues, is entitled to or will claim any right of immunity in any jurisdiction from suit, jurisdiction, judgment, attachment (whether before or after judgment), set-off, or execution of a judgment or from any other legal process or remedy relating to the obligations of the Borrower under this Agreement.

A standard waiver of state immunity under English law provides:

> To the extent that the Borrower may in any jurisdiction claim for itself or its assets immunity from suit, execution, attachment (whether in aid of execution, before judgment or otherwise), or other legal process and to the extent that in any such jurisdiction there may be attributed to itself or its assets any such immunity (whether or not claimed), the Borrower hereby irrevocably agrees not to claim and hereby irrevocably waives such immunity to the full extent permitted by the laws of such jurisdiction.

Note that these model clauses expressly address the question of enforcement of judgments against (and attachments of) foreign state assets, as well as the question of immunity from claims. This express waiver is, in many instances, required under applicable national legislation on the subject of state immunity from execution and attachment.

4. Choice-of-Law Clauses

Forum selection agreements are frequently accompanied by choice-of-law clauses. These are discussed below in Chapter 8.

5. Waiver of *Forum Non Conveniens*

Even if a national court can exercise personal jurisdiction over a foreign defendant, the *forum non conveniens* doctrine and related theories may permit dismissal of the action in some common law countries. Under the *forum non conveniens* doctrine, trial courts have broad, and often fairly discretionary, authority to dismiss claims on grounds of inconvenience.

Forum selection clauses can address the *forum non conveniens* doctrine and related rules, requiring each party to waive any right to assert the doctrine in the contractual forum. The following formulation is a representative approach:

> The Parties irrevocably waive any objection to venue in those Courts and any objection based on the doctrine of *forum non conveniens* or similar grounds that those Courts are inconvenient for determination of a dispute.

Waivers of *forum non conveniens* defenses are most frequently encountered in loan agreements and similar financial transactions.

An exclusive forum clause should be interpreted as a waiver of *forum non conveniens* arguments by committing both parties to litigate solely in the contractual forum. Nonetheless, where a higher degree of certainty is desired, the issue can be directly addressed.

6. Waiver of Jury Trial

A forum selection clause can also be accompanied by a term waiving rights to a jury trial. Jury trials are virtually unknown outside the United States, where they are both a constitutional requirement and a source of substantial concern to many defendants. Contractual waivers of jury trials are appropriate for transactions relating in some fashion to the United States, and are common in U.S. commercial and banking transactions. The following formulation is a representative example of a jury trial waiver:

> [Borrower] expressly waives any right to a trial by jury with respect to disputes relating to this Agreement and agrees not to seek or claim any such right.

An alternative formulation provides:

> Each party to this Agreement waives its prospective right to a jury trial of any claim or cause of action arising out of this Agreement, or any dealings between any of the parties hereto relating to the subject matter of this Agreement. The scope of this waiver is intended to be all-encompassing of any and all disputes that may be filed in any court and that relate to the subject matter of this Agreement or the loan documents, including, without limitation, contract claims, tort claims, and all other common law and statutory claims. This waiver is irrevocable, meaning that it may

> not be modified either orally or in writing, and this waiver shall apply to any subsequent amendments, supplements or modifications to this Agreement, or to any other document or agreement relating to the transactions. The parties acknowledge that they have consulted with legal counsel regarding this provision and that they have freely and voluntarily entered into it.

Waivers of jury trial rights raise questions of enforceability under U.S. law, particularly in the consumer context. In general, however, U.S. courts have enforced such waivers, subject to a variety of exceptions similar to those for forum selection agreements. (See pp. 159-161 below.)

I. APPLICATION OF FORUM SELECTION CLAUSES TO ACTIONS SEEKING PROVISIONAL OR INTERIM RELIEF

An important practical issue is whether a forum selection clause applies to proceedings seeking provisional or interim relief in aid of litigations which have been (or will be) commenced in the contractual forum on the merits of the parties' dispute. For example, a party may seek to freeze its counterparty's assets, to halt unauthorized use of intellectual property, or to obtain otherwise unavailable evidence—all in places outside the contractual forum. In many developed civil law legal systems, a standard worded forum selection clause will generally not be interpreted as extending to these sorts of ancillary actions. The Brussels I Regulation (in Article 31 of EC Regulation 44/2001 and Article 35 of EU Regulation 1215/2012) and the Lugano Convention (in Article 24) contain provisions expressly permitting such actions. In common law jurisdictions, such as the United States and England, authorities are less clear, but should produce the same result.

To reduce uncertainties, parties can agree upon a forum selection clause that expressly excludes actions for provisional or similar relief, as the following clause illustrates:

> Nothing in this Agreement shall prevent either party from applying to a court that would otherwise have jurisdiction for provisional or interim measures, including, but not limited to, any claim for preliminary injunctive relief.

Licensors of intellectual property, including trademarks, patents, and trade secrets, often insist upon provisions for obtaining relief outside the contractual forum when their licensee makes unlicensed use of their property. The following is a model:

> All disputes relating to this Agreement shall be resolved exclusively in the courts of _________, provided that claims alleging unlicensed or otherwise unauthorized use of the [Trademarks] may be asserted in any court of competent jurisdiction.

Alternatively:

> All disputes relating to this Agreement (with the exception of claims arising under Article [X]) shall be resolved exclusively in the courts of ________.

As noted above (See pp. 18-19), many national courts will interpret even a broadly worded exclusive forum selection clause as permitting ancillary litigation outside the contractual forum. Nonetheless, where applicable law is unclear or where it is important to preserve such options, an express reservation should generally be made.

J. FORUM SELECTION CLAUSES IN ROUTINE TRANSACTIONS

Much international business takes the form of smaller, routine transactions. Contractual documentation for these transactions is virtually never individually tailored. In these circumstances, a standard form contract should typically contain a simple forum selection clause which will not provoke objections from counterparties and which will not raise unnecessary issues of enforceability or interpretation.

In many cases, the most sensible course is an exclusive forum selection clause specifying one party's domicile, combined with an equally simple choice-of-law clause:

> All disputes relating to this Agreement shall be subject to the exclusive jurisdiction of the courts of ________, and shall be decided in accordance with the laws of ________.

Alternatively, a non-exclusive forum selection clause, again typically selecting the drafting party's home-courts, can be used. Additionally, as discussed below, a simple arbitration clause providing for arbitration under a set of leading institutional arbitration rules in a recognized jurisdiction can offer an effective solution. (See p. 156 below.)

K. FORUM SELECTION CLAUSES SELECTING INTERNATIONAL COMMERCIAL COURTS

Over the last 20 years, a number of nations have established so-called international commercial courts with specialized procedures, designed to hear cross-border commercial disputes. Forerunners of contemporary international commercial courts include the Commercial Court in London (established in 1895) and the Commercial Division of the New York Supreme Court (established in 1995), both of which have specialized panels of judges and are intended to hear complex commercial disputes, both international and domestic. More recently, jurisdictions in the Middle East, Asia, Europe and elsewhere have established courts with specialized procedures for international commercial disputes. Although termed "international" commercial courts, these courts are not genuinely international, but are instead domestic institutions that combine elements of both international arbitration (e.g., foreign nationals participating as judges, freedom from local procedural rules, proceedings in English) and litigation (e.g., standing panels of judges, an appeal mechanism, and mandatory jurisdiction).

The first contemporary international commercial court was established in the Dubai International Financial Center ("DIFC"), a unique legal regime within Dubai, United Arab Emirates. The DIFC is an "offshore" jurisdiction, designed to attract foreign trade and investment to Dubai, in which local Sharia and other law does not apply. One element of the DIFC is the DIFC court system ("DIFC Courts"), established in 2006, in which panels of both local and foreign judges preside over cases, applying common and civil law principles. The DIFC Courts' jurisdiction extends to commercial cases where the parties' contract includes a forum selection clause specifying the DIFC, as well as commercial disputes arising in the DIFC. The DIFC Courts have heard nearly 1,000 cases annually in recent years (with a total value of claims of approximately USD 2 billion).

Other states in the Middle East, including Abu Dhabi, Qatar and Kazakhstan, have also recently created "international" courts to provide investment-friendly legal environments within their respective financial centers. These include the Abu Dhabi Global Market Courts in Abu Dhabi ("ADGM Courts"), the Qatar International Court and Dispute Resolution Centre, also known as the Qatar International Court, in Doha, Qatar, and the Astana International Financial Center in Kazakhstan. All of these courts offer panels that include both local and foreign judges (typically retired judges from common law jurisdictions); have procedural and substantive rules other than local law; and have proceedings which are often conducted in English. Like the DIFC Courts, these courts' jurisdiction typically extends to cases where the parties' contract includes an appropriate forum selection provision. Both the ADGM Courts and DIFC Courts are frequently selected by the parties in regional and local transactions.

More recently, several Asian and European jurisdictions also established "international" courts to resolve international commercial disputes. In 2015, Singapore created the Singapore International Commercial Court ("SICC"), staffed by members of the Singapore judiciary as well as practitioners or retired judges from other jurisdictions. Similarly, the Chinese International Commercial Court was established in China to hear international commercial disputes related to China or its Belt and Road Initiative. A number of European countries (including the Netherlands, Germany and France) have also established international commercial courts within their domestic court systems, typically staffed only with local judges, although often applying flexible procedures and hearing cases in English.

Experienced practitioners are generally skeptical of "international" commercial courts in most circumstances. Although international commercial courts are modelled in part on international arbitration, they generally combine the least desirable, rather than the most desirable, attributes of arbitration and litigation: litigants lose the ability to select arbitrators, to enforce arbitration agreements and awards under the New York Convention, to benefit from the extensive procedural experience and practice in international arbitration, and to obtain an expeditious final decision, which arbitration provides, while also losing the procedural certainty of national court litigation. Most parties are also skeptical about the suitability of both local and retired foreign judges for international disputes, as well as uncertain about the long-term independence of so-called international courts (which are ultimately part of local judicial systems).

As a consequence, prudence generally counsels decisively against specifying any such courts in contractual dispute resolution provisions. That is particularly true for foreign or international parties in transactions with local counterparties. If parties nonetheless wish to submit disputes to international commercial courts, the language used in each such court's model clause should ordinarily be used.

The following is the model clause recommended by the ADGM Courts:

> Any dispute arising out of or in connection with this contract, including any question regarding its existence, validity or termination, shall be subject to the exclusive jurisdiction of the Abu Dhabi Global Market Courts.

The SICC recommends the following for submission to its exclusive jurisdiction before a dispute arises:

> Each party irrevocably submits to the exclusive jurisdiction of the Singapore International Commercial Court all disputes arising out of or in connection with the present contract, including any question relating to its existence, validity or termination.

The DIFC recommends that the following language be used:

> Any dispute, difference, controversy or claim arising out of or in connection with this contract, including (but not limited to) any question regarding its existence, validity, interpretation, performance, discharge and applicable remedies, shall be subject to the exclusive jurisdiction of the Courts of the Dubai International Financial Centre ("the DIFC Courts").

Other international courts have also published model forum selection clauses, which are typically available on either the courts' websites or promotional materials (and which are often periodically updated).

Chapter 3

Drafting International Arbitration Agreements

Almost all international arbitrations occur pursuant to arbitration clauses contained in commercial contracts concluded well before any dispute arises. It is, of course, possible for parties to agree to submit an existing dispute to arbitration, and this sometimes happens. (The resulting agreement is called a "submission agreement" or "*compromis*"; a model of such an agreement is set forth in Appendix H.) Typically, however, it is difficult to negotiate a submission agreement once a concrete dispute has arisen and litigation tactics have been explored by the parties. As a consequence, relatively few disputes are arbitrated pursuant to submission agreements.

Instead, most arbitration agreements provide for the submission of future disputes to arbitration. A selection of model institutional arbitration clauses for use in commercial contracts, including provisions for use in contracts with states and state-related entities, is contained in Appendix I. Nonetheless, parties are in principle free to draft their international arbitration agreement in whatever terms they wish and in practice, this freedom is liberally exercised. Like forum selection clauses, arbitration agreements are largely a product of the parties' interests, negotiations, and drafting skills.

International arbitration agreements can be very short, very long, or somewhere in between. Although such provisions should virtually always be avoided, national courts have upheld arbitration clauses that are as brief as "English law—arbitration, if any, London according ICC Rules," or "arbitration—Hamburg, Germany." At the other extreme, arbitration agreements in large, multi-party transactions sometimes take the form of separately executed documents running to dozens of pages and (purportedly) addressing almost every conceivable procedural eventuality. A selection of commonly used international arbitration clauses is contained in Appendix J.

In many commercial circumstances, the most sensible drafting approach is a relatively short arbitration clause identical to or based closely on one of the model clauses recommended by a leading arbitral institution. These model clauses provide a tested form of wording that avoids ambiguities, internal inconsistencies, gaps, and other defects that can arise as by-products of hasty drafting or negotiation; they also incorporate institutional arbitration rules, which typically contain provisions addressing a wide range of issues that are difficult to satisfactorily or efficiently deal with in an ad hoc arbitration clause. For these reasons, absent unusual circumstances and specialized advice, it is almost always wise to avoid lengthy arbitration agreements, drafted in an effort to suit a specific transaction, and instead rely entirely or largely on short model clauses.

Alterations or additions to a model institutional arbitration clause should be made with care and with the advice of expert counsel to avoid unforeseen inconsistencies, conflicts, or similar problems. There is also some risk that departures from the model wording of a particular institutional arbitration clause may lead to procedural uncertainties (i.e., challenges to the arbitral tribunal's jurisdiction) based on speculation about the parties' reasons for making such changes. For this reason, it is usually advisable to adopt the wording recommended by a particular institution except where specialized advice counsels otherwise.

Whatever basic approach is adopted, however, a number of issues should be considered in drafting an international arbitration agreement. These issues are outlined below. The discussion first addresses a handful of critical elements that must be included in virtually every international arbitration clause. It then considers a number of additional elements which may be either desirable or necessary in particular cases.

A. CRITICAL ELEMENTS OF INTERNATIONAL ARBITRATION AGREEMENTS

There are several critical elements that must be addressed in almost every international arbitration clause. These are:

- Agreement to binding arbitration.
- Scope of the arbitration agreement.
- Selection of an arbitral seat (or place of the arbitration).
- Use of an arbitral institution and its rules.
- Appointment, number, and qualifications of the arbitrators.
- Language of the arbitration.
- Formalities, capacity, and validity.
- Choice-of-law clause.

In particular cases, other provisions may be either vital to an effective international arbitration agreement or advantageous to one party. These provisions are also detailed below. (See pp. 109-149)

1. Agreement to Binding Arbitration

It is elementary that any arbitration clause must clearly set forth the parties' *agreement to arbitrate*. This means that their agreement should expressly refer to "arbitration" (rather than to mediation, settlement, "ADR," accounting, or some other form of non-judicial resolution). These other forms of alternative dispute resolution are not categorized as "arbitration" under many international treaties and national arbitration statutes, and will often not qualify for the "pro-enforcement" safeguards provided by these instruments. Care should also be taken to avoid unfamiliar labels or qualifications, such as "*arbitrato irrituale*" in Italy, which can refer to forms of dispute resolution other than arbitration.

The requirement that the parties agree to arbitrate also means that a defined category of disputes should be referred to arbitration for a *binding* or *final* disposition (See below on the "scope" of arbitration clauses). The clause ought not treat arbitration as a possible future option, applicable only if the parties so agree after a dispute arises, nor ought it suggest that arbitration will produce merely a recommended or optional result, as opposed to a binding, enforceable award.

In essence, an appropriately drafted arbitration clause should provide: "All disputes *shall be finally resolved* by arbitration ... ." All the model clauses set forth below, and almost any usable arbitration agreement, include some variation of this formula.

Some arbitration clauses contain language providing that "all disputes may be resolved by arbitration" or "all disputes may be submitted to arbitration ... ." These types of formulations should generally be avoided because some courts interpret their use of the word "may" as providing only for an "optional" or "non-mandatory" possibility of arbitration, without mandatorily binding either party to submit future disputes to arbitration. These interpretations are erroneous (and isolated), but it is prudent to avoid such formulations and instead use unequivocally mandatory language.

2. Scope of Arbitration Agreement

Critical to any arbitration clause is its "scope"—that is, the categories of disputes or claims that will be subject to the agreement to arbitrate. For example, are all disputes between the parties bearing any conceivable connection to their contractual relations subject to arbitration? Or will only contract claims that clearly arise under the express terms of the parties' agreement, and not non-contractual claims, be arbitrated? Alternatively, should particular types of claims be carved out or excluded from an otherwise broad arbitration agreement?

The contractual scope of an arbitration clause must be distinguished from the question of whether particular issues or disputes are legally capable of being arbitrated. The latter issue, often referred to as whether a dispute is "arbitrable" or "objectively arbitrable," is discussed below. (See p. 170 .)

a. Formulae for Scope of Arbitration Agreements

As with forum selection agreements, there are a handful of formulae that are frequently used to define the scope of international arbitration clauses. These formulae include: (i) "all disputes *arising under* this Agreement"; (ii) "all disputes *arising out of* this Agreement"; (iii) "all disputes *in connection with* this Agreement";

and (iv) "all disputes *relating to* this Agreement." Alternative formulations include: (v) "all disputes relating to this Agreement, *including any question regarding its existence, validity, breach, or termination*"; and (vi) "all disputes relating to this Agreement *or the subject matter hereof.*"

As already discussed, some national courts have drawn surprisingly technical distinctions between these different formulae. For example, disputes often arise over the question of whether an arbitration clause extends to tort (delict) or other non-contractual claims. A few national courts have reasoned that a dispute only "arises under" a contract if a party's claims are contractual ones, seeking to enforce the terms of its contract; under this rationale, some courts have concluded that tort, quasi-contract, statutory, or other non-contractual claims do *not* "arise under" the parties' agreement. In contrast, more expansive phrases such as "relating to" and "in connection with" are generally held to extend broadly to contractual and non-contractual claims having some reasonable relation to the parties' contract.

Many other courts have refused to consider fine distinctions between the foregoing formulae, instead interpreting arbitration agreements expansively (and sometimes holding that this is properly a decision for the arbitral tribunal). Nonetheless, the possibility of such restrictive interpretations should be recalled when drafting arbitration agreements.

b. Advantages of Arbitration Agreements with Broad Scope

As a general rule, it is wise to draft international arbitration clauses as broadly as possible to encompass all disputes having any connection with the parties' dealings. It is usually better to avoid—except in fairly unusual and compelling circumstances—efforts to exclude particular types of disputes from arbitration. This is particularly true given developments over the past decade, which have increased the risks of biased, non-independent or otherwise unsatisfactory results in many national courts.

Faced with a live dispute, and the temptations of forum shopping or perceived attractions of delay, few parties will lack the ingenuity to cast their claims or defenses in terms that purport to fall outside a narrow, or exception-filled, agreement to arbitrate. In turn, this will almost inevitably lead to parallel proceedings in both the arbitral forum and national courts, and to jurisdictional disputes over the application of a clause to particular claims. None of these fosters rational, efficient resolution of the parties' underlying dispute.

c. Drafting Arbitration Agreements with Broad Scope

Drafting a broad arbitration clause, like drafting an expansive forum selection clause, requires addressing several components.

First, it is generally desirable to begin with a descriptive preamble broadly submitting "*all disputes, claims, controversies, and disagreements*" to arbitration, rather than a simple reference to "any disputes" or "all claims." This reduces the risk of litigation or arbitral proceedings over whether a "dispute" is involved (as distinguished, in some litigants' submissions, from a mere "claim" or "disagreement").

Second, this preambular formula should ordinarily be used together with one or more broad connecting phrases, such as disputes "*relating to*" or "*arising in connection with*" the parties' agreement. It is usually desirable to avoid confining an arbitration clause merely to disputes "arising under" or "arising from" an agreement because of the risk that these formulae will exclude non-contractual claims. (See pp. 24-27 above.)

In addition, disputes sometimes arise over the question of whether an arbitration clause extends to disputes regarding the formation of a contract (e.g., claims of fraudulent inducement or invalidity) or the termination of a contract. Some arbitral institutions' model clauses (such as that of the London Court of International Arbitration ("LCIA")) address this possibility by expressly providing that disputes, including "any question regarding [the contract's] existence, validity or termination," will be arbitrated.

In general, courts in developed states have concluded that commonly used arbitration clauses extend to disputes about the validity, enforceability, and legality of the parties' underlying agreement. (See p. 169 below.) Nonetheless, where the issue is considered important, an arbitration clause can be drafted to apply expressly to disputes relating to the validity of the parties' underlying contract, "*including its existence, formation, validity, enforceability, performance, or termination.*" Where an arbitral institution's model clause contains such a reference, agreements to arbitrate in accordance with the institution's rules should virtually always preserve the reference.

Finally, references to the "subject matter of the Agreement" are also often appropriately included in arbitration clauses. This widens the scope of the arbitration agreement and will ordinarily extend to disputes regarding the formation and validity of the underlying contract. Taken together, the foregoing guidelines produce a "broad" arbitration clause along the following lines:

> All disputes, claims, controversies, and disagreements relating to or arising out of this Agreement, or the subject matter of this Agreement, shall be finally resolved by arbitration. ...

Or:

> All disputes, claims, controversies, and disagreements relating to or arising out of this Agreement (including the formation, existence, validity, enforceability, performance, or termination of this Agreement), or the subject matter of this Agreement, shall be finally resolved by arbitration. ...

An alternative formulation, drafted as concisely as possible, provides:

> All disputes relating to this Agreement shall be finally resolved by arbitration.

As noted earlier, where a set of institutional arbitration rules is incorporated, care should be taken in considering alterations to the institution's model clause. Although the addition of language in order to broaden the scope of a clause is often appropriate, any changes to a model clause may be subject to special scrutiny in the event of future disputes.

Finally, issues of interpretation and enforceability under the law(s) applicable to particular arbitration clauses must also be considered. The foregoing examples and commentary are useful as a general matter and may be sufficient in particular cases. Nonetheless, they are not a substitute for advice in specific cases.

d. Exclusions from Scope of Arbitration Agreements

Even where the parties have agreed to a broad international arbitration clause, there may be claims or disputes that one party does *not* want submitted to arbitration. Exceptions to the scope of arbitration agreements (such as exceptions to forum selection clauses) should be used cautiously and drafted carefully because they can lead to jurisdictional disputes and other uncertainties. In appropriate contexts, however, carefully drafted exceptions may be useful. A generic provision providing for exclusion of particular matters from the parties' agreement to arbitrate can be drafted along the following lines:

> With the exception of those claims which are specifically excluded (pursuant to [Article X(2)] below) from arbitration under this [Article X(1)], all disputes, claims, controversies, and disagreements relating to or arising out of this Agreement shall be finally resolved by arbitration. ...

Or:

> Claims under the following Articles of this Agreement are specifically excluded from arbitration hereunder: [Articles V, VII, and ...].

Ordinarily, exclusions from the scope of the agreement to arbitrate should be avoided except in unusual circumstances; the examples identified below are some of the instances where exclusions may be appropriate. Where such an exclusion is used, the excluded disputes should almost always be the subject of a specific forum selection (or other dispute resolution) provision.

i. Injunctive Relief for Intellectual Property Rights

Licensors of intellectual property sometimes wish to expressly retain the right to seek immediate remedies against unauthorized uses of their property by licensees.

Among other things, licensors may insist on preserving their ability to obtain immediate provisional relief from national courts in the place where unauthorized use of their property occurs, rather than first proceeding through an arbitration and then, sometime later, enforcing the award locally. As discussed below, many institutional arbitration rules permit parties to seek injunctive relief in aid of arbitration from national courts, notwithstanding their agreement to arbitrate. (See p 134-137) In many cases, this may offer sufficient procedural protection for intellectual property licensors.

However, if further flexibility to seek injunctive relief against unauthorized use of intellectual property is desired, the following language can be used:

> Any violation of Article [X] hereof [relating to trademarks, patents, trade secrets, copyrights] would cause irreparable injury to [Licensor]. [Licensor] may, in addition to any other rights under this Agreement and notwithstanding the arbitration agreement contained in this Article [Y], seek specific performance of Article [X] and any other available provisional relief in any court of competent jurisdiction against any violation of such Article [X].

Such exceptions can also be graduated, depending upon the time at which they are invoked:

> Prior to the appointment of the arbitrator(s), either party may seek provisional or interim measures from any court of competent jurisdiction. After the appointment of the arbitrator(s), the arbitrator(s) shall have exclusive power to consider and grant requests for provisional or interim measures.

Exceptions such as these sometimes create more problems than benefits. They may conflict with the parties' chosen institutional arbitration rules or applicable law, while making parallel proceedings more likely. Nonetheless, some national courts hold that arbitration agreements (particularly agreements providing for institutional arbitration that include the possibility of emergency arbitration (See pp. 136-137 below)) exclude the parties' right to seek court-ordered provisional measures. Where access to court-ordered provisional relief is important, formulations such as those set forth above should be used.

ii. Validity of Intellectual Property Rights

Alternatively, some intellectual property owners wish to preclude any arbitral consideration of disputes concerning the ownership or validity of their intellectual property. This is because of the (typically mistaken) perception that arbitrators may lack the expertise to efficiently resolve complex intellectual property disputes or that the absence of appellate review in such circumstances is inappropriate. Where this view is adopted, the following clause may be used as a model:

> All disputes arising out of or relating to this Agreement, except "Licensed Mark Disputes" (as defined below), shall be finally resolved by arbitration in accordance with [identify institutional rules]. "Licensed Mark Disputes" shall constitute all disputes relating to the Licensor's ownership of, the validity of, or the registration of any Licensed Mark.

If such a provision is adopted, it should be combined with a forum selection clause applicable to the category of intellectual property disputes which is excepted from arbitration. (See pp. 34-35 above.) A representative provision, to be used with the foregoing provision, is as follows:

> All Licensed Mark Disputes shall be subject to the [exclusive] [non-exclusive] jurisdiction of ________.

In some jurisdictions, disputes over the ownership or validity of intellectual property (particularly patents) may raise "non-arbitrable" issues of public policy. (See p. 177 below.) In these instances, a forum selection clause should be used, preferably alone or alternatively in combination with an arbitration clause applicable to arbitrable issues.

iii. Payment Obligations

Parties also sometimes seek—usually unwisely—to exclude payment obligations from the scope of arbitration clauses. The theory underlying this approach is that arbitral proceedings may take several months to get underway and that arbitrators may be more likely than national courts to adopt Solomonic decisions that dilute contractually crisp payment obligations. Financial institutions, in particular, sometimes exclude payment obligations from the parties' arbitration agreement. To implement this objective, one party's payment obligations can be placed in a single article, which can then be excluded from the scope of the arbitration clause:

> With the exception of Buyer's payment obligations under Article [X] hereof, all claims, controversies, disputes, and disagreements arising under or relating to this Agreement shall be finally resolved by arbitration in accordance with ...

In general, however, this approach should be avoided. The jurisdictional and other uncertainties that result from such a bifurcated dispute resolution scheme usually outweigh any potential benefits.

Of course, if payment (or other) obligations *are* excluded from an arbitration agreement, then a separate forum selection agreement for such disputes is usually appropriate. For example:

All disputes [arising under] [in connection with] the Buyer's payment obligations under Article [X] hereof shall be subject to the [exclusive] [non-exclusive] jurisdiction of the courts of ________.

3. Institutional Versus Ad Hoc Arbitration

International (and domestic) arbitration can be either (a) institutional, or (b) ad hoc. Institutional arbitration is conducted pursuant to procedural rules promulgated by a particular arbitral institution, which generally also "administers" the arbitration. The administration of an arbitration typically involves performing administrative or supervisory functions such as selecting and removing arbitrators (whenever the parties default or fail to reach an agreement on these issues), serving requests for arbitration and some other submissions, scrutinizing awards, and dealing with the arbitrators' and arbitral institution's fees.

In contrast, ad hoc arbitration is conducted without an administering authority and, generally, without the aid of institutional procedural rules. It relies instead on the parties' cooperation, backed by potential recourse to national courts for such matters as the appointment of arbitrators in case of defaulting or disagreeing parties. As explained in greater detail below, virtually all experienced international arbitration practitioners prefer institutional arbitration to ad hoc arbitration because of the heightened predictability, stability, and institutional expertise provided by the former, and because institutional arbitration rules often provide useful default mechanisms for enhancing the arbitral process (e.g., replacing arbitrators, corrections to awards). For example, one empirical study found that 79% of the surveyed arbitrations were administered by institutions.

a. Institutional Arbitration

If institutional arbitration is desired, the parties must choose an arbitral institution and refer to it in their arbitration clause. It is almost always wisest to rely on one of a few established international arbitral institutions. This avoids the confusion and uncertainty that comes from inexperienced administrative efforts and ill-considered appointments of arbitrators or challenging decisions. This conclusion is particularly important given developments over the past decade, including some nations' shuttering of arbitral institutions or efforts to assert governmental control over the institutions' functions. As a consequence, a "flight to quality," favoring established institutions with a proven track record and assurances of independence, is both observable in practice and advisable.

A number of organizations provide institutional arbitration services. Some of the best-known of these organizations are discussed below. These institutions typically possess published arbitration rules, a decision-making body that appoints arbitrators and makes certain other decisions, and a professional staff that administers individual arbitrations. Importantly, an arbitral institution does *not* resolve the parties' underlying substantive dispute or otherwise act as an arbitrator; rather, the arbitral institution administers proceedings which are conducted and decided by individual arbitrators.

The precise functions of arbitral institutions vary among different institutions. In general, however, an arbitral institution will receive requests (or notices) for arbitration made pursuant to its rules, transmit such requests (or notices) to the respondent, confirm the parties' nominations of arbitrators, appoint arbitrators when the parties are not able or willing to do so, consider challenges to the independence or qualifications of arbitrators, and decide on requests for extensions of time for the filing of initial submissions. In addition, some institutions also fix the amounts of the arbitrators' fees, collect the parties' advance payments of fees and costs, and (in some instances) scrutinize and comment on arbitrators' draft awards. The rules of each arbitral institution detail how the foregoing functions are performed.

Of course, the services rendered by professional arbitral institutions come at a price, in addition to the fees and expenses of the arbitrators. Every arbitral institution has a fee schedule that specifies what that price is. The amounts charged by institutions for particular matters vary significantly, as does the basis for calculating such fees. For example, some institutions use hourly charges while others charge based on a percentage of the amount in dispute.

b. International Arbitral Institutions

Leading international arbitral institutions include:

- International Chamber of Commerce International Court of Arbitration ("ICC").
- London Court of International Arbitration ("LCIA").
- American Arbitration Association ("AAA") and its international arm, the International Centre for Dispute Resolution ("ICDR").
- Singapore International Arbitration Centre ("SIAC").
- Stockholm Chamber of Commerce Arbitration Institute ("SCC").
- Vienna International Arbitral Centre ("VIAC").
- International Centre for Settlement of Investment Disputes ("ICSID"), insofar as investment disputes are concerned.
- Permanent Court of Arbitration ("PCA").

Other institutions active in specialized or regional settings include:

- Abu Dhabi International Arbitration Centre ("arbitrateAD").
- Asian International Arbitration Centre ("AIAC"), formerly the Kuala Lumpur Regional Centre for Arbitration ("KLRCA").
- Australian Centre for International Commercial Arbitration ("ACICA").

- Cairo Regional Centre for International Commercial Arbitration ("CRCICA").
- China International Economic and Trade Arbitration Commission ("CIETAC").
- Dubai International Arbitration Centre ("DIAC").
- German Institution of Arbitration ("DIS").
- Hong Kong International Arbitration Centre ("HKIAC").
- Indian Council of Arbitration ("ICA").
- Inter-American Commercial Arbitration Commission ("IACAC").
- JAMS International ("JAMS").
- Japan Commercial Arbitration Association ("JCAA").
- Korean Commercial Arbitration Board ("KCAB").
- Netherlands Arbitration Institute ("NAI").
- Swiss Chambers' Arbitration Institution ("SCAI").
- World Intellectual Property Organization ("WIPO").

The contact details of these, as well as selected other national or regional institutions, are contained in Appendix F.

There are also a number of less widely known regional or national arbitral institutions. Many of these institutions were founded, or first promoted for significant international matters, during the 1980s, while others were founded only recently. Accordingly, some of these institutions lack the experience and track records that sophisticated users require.

i. International Chamber of Commerce

The ICC's International Court of Arbitration was established in Paris in 1923. The ICC has historically been regarded as the world's leading international commercial arbitral institution, and has less of a national character than other leading arbitral institutions. Its annual caseload was well above 300 cases per year during much of the 1990s, and, on average, registered nearly 800 new cases filed per year from 2009 to 2015. In 2024, 831 requests for ICC arbitration were filed, involving parties from 136 jurisdictions. Most of these cases were international disputes, with seats of arbitration located in more than 60 countries, and many involving very substantial sums. The ICC's caseload involves parties from around the world, with an increased presence compared to 2023 in North and West Europe, Sub-Saharan Africa, Latin America and the Caribbean, South and East Asia, and the Pacific.

The ICC's model arbitration clause provides:

> All disputes arising out of or in connection with the present contract shall be finally settled under the Rules of Arbitration of the International Chamber of Commerce by one or more arbitrators appointed in accordance with the said Rules.

The ICC administers arbitrations under the ICC Rules of Arbitration, which are periodically revised, most recently in 2021, and which include the Expedited

Procedure and Emergency Arbitrator Rules. The ICC has also issued the ICC Mediation Rules, the ICC Expert Rules (for the Proposal or Appointment of Experts and Neutrals, and for the Administration of Expertise Proceedings), the ICC Dispute Board Rules (including Appendix III on the Challenge of DAAB Member(s) under the 2017 FIDIC Contracts), and the ICC DOCDEX Rules.

Under the ICC Rules, the ICC (through the International Court of Arbitration ("ICC Court")) is extensively involved in the administration of individual arbitrations. Despite its name, the ICC Court is not, in fact, a "court," and does not itself decide disputes or act as an arbitrator. Rather, the ICC Court is an administrative committee that acts in a supervisory and appointing capacity under the ICC Rules. Among other things, the ICC Court and its Secretariat are responsible for service of the initial Request for Arbitration; fixing and receiving payment of advances on costs of the arbitration by the parties; confirming nominations of arbitrators (made by the parties and/or co-arbitrators or by other agreed appointing authorities); appointing arbitrators if a party defaults or if the parties are unable to agree upon a presiding arbitrator or sole arbitrator; considering challenges to the arbitrators, including on the basis of lack of independence or contractually required qualifications; reviewing and approving so-called "Terms of Reference," which define the issues and procedures for the arbitration; reviewing a tribunal's draft award for formal and other defects (including drawing the tribunal's attention to the points of substance); and fixing the arbitrators' compensation and the final administrative expenses.

The ICC Court maintains a sizeable legal and administrative staff of over 100 persons, with more than 30 nationalities, organized as a Secretariat. Specialized teams of counsel, deputy counsel, and administrative staff are assigned to particular geographic, linguistic, or cultural regions.

The ICC Secretariat is substantially involved in the day-to-day administration of arbitrations. The ICC Court's method of appointing arbitrators varies depending on whether a co-arbitrator, on the one hand, or a sole or presiding arbitrator, on the other hand, is involved.

If the ICC Court is appointing a co-arbitrator (where a party has failed to do so), it will often select a national from that party's home country. In contrast, if the ICC Court is appointing a sole arbitrator or a presiding arbitrator at the outset of a case, it will often act upon recommendations made by a third country's "national committee" of the ICC, which is usually an organization representing the international business interests in a specific country. Currently, more than 90 countries and territories have ICC National Committees or Groups. The ICC will not select a presiding or sole arbitrator who is of the same nationality as one of the parties (unless the parties do not object). Although arbitrators from Northern and Western Europe have represented half of those appointed in ICC arbitrations (49.9% in 2024), the diversity of nationalities represented among ICC arbitrators has increased over the last three decades (arbitrators were nationals of 62 different countries in 1995, 68 in 2005, 77 in 2015, and 91 in 2024).

ICC arbitrations can be (and are) seated almost anywhere in the world. In 2024, ICC arbitrations were seated in 107 cities and conducted in 62 countries or independent territories. Over the last 15 years, an increasing number of arbitrations have been seated outside of Western Europe and North America, including in Asia, the Middle East, and Latin America. Nonetheless, the most common places of ICC arbitrations have been in England, France, Switzerland, the United States, as well as Singapore, Brazil, Mexico, and the United Arab Emirates. (See pp. 84-87 below.) The ICC has opened case management offices in Hong Kong, New York, Singapore, São Paulo, and Abu Dhabi. ICC has also established a Hearing Centre in Paris, providing custom-built hearing spaces and designed to facilitate access for guests with reduced mobility.

The ICC's administrative fees are based on the amount in dispute between the parties. With respect to arbitrators' fees, the ICC Rules fix both a minimum and a maximum amount which can be charged based on the amount in dispute. With respect to administrative fees and charges, the ICC Rules provide for a sliding scale of charges that is again based on the amount in dispute between the parties. The ICC Rules require that the parties pay an advance on the anticipated costs of the arbitration calculated by the ICC Court. The advance on costs is equally divided between the Claimant and the Respondent, although one party may pay the full amount in order to enable the arbitration to proceed if the other party defaults.

Amendments to the ICC Rules in 2012, 2017, and 2021 reflected a concerted effort to increase the efficiency and speed of ICC proceedings. Among other things, the ICC Rules require arbitrators to conduct a case management conference and propose a number of case management techniques. The ICC Rules also require arbitrators to provide statements of availability prior to appointment and to inform the parties at the close of the proceedings of the expected timing of the award. While ICC arbitration has occasionally been criticized as costly and complex, recent amendments have been implemented to enhance efficiency. For example, an arbitrator fee reduction mechanism was introduced in the "ICC Note to Parties and Arbitrators" in 2016, to address unjustified delays in the submission of draft awards to the ICC Court. The recent launch of a new version of the "ICC Case Connect" online case management platform also aims at enhancing efficiency through streamlined workflows and secure collaboration.

Despite criticism of its costs and delays, the ICC generally remains the institution of preference for many sophisticated commercial users, particularly in Europe. The ICC's proven track record, worldwide reputation, and comparative predictability will likely help it maintain this position for the foreseeable future, particularly given increased concerns over the past decade regarding the reliability of newer or regional institutions.

ii. London Court of International Arbitration

Founded in 1892, the LCIA is, by many accounts, the second most popular European arbitral institution after the ICC. Its annual caseload, which is generally increasing, has exceeded 300 disputes in recent years (with 362 cases in 2024). One can anticipate that the LCIA will become more popular with commercial users in coming years, given the "flight to quality" that recent global events have produced.

The LCIA has made a determined, and generally successful, effort in recent years to overcome perceptions that it is a predominantly English organization. Among other things, it appointed five successive non-English presidents between 1994 and 2015, as well as a further non-English President in 2025, and its vice-presidents include non-English practitioners. In 2024, 95% of LCIA arbitrations were of an international nature (involving one or more international parties), and 75% of cases involved only international parties without any UK parties.

The LCIA administers arbitrations under a set of arbitration rules, the LCIA Rules, which were revised in 1998, 2014 and 2020. Although identifiably English in drafting style and procedural approach, the LCIA Rules generally provide a sound basis for international dispute resolution, particularly for parties desiring a common law approach. Broadly speaking, LCIA arbitrations are administered in an efficient but less comprehensive fashion than ICC cases. Among other things, the LCIA Rules contain no Terms of Reference procedure and do not provide for institutional review of draft awards. The LCIA's administrative fees are calculated based upon the time spent by LCIA personnel (as of December 2023, GBP 300/hour for the Registrar/Deputy Registrar, GBP 285/hour for Counsel, and GBP 220 or GBP 190/hour for the Secretariat, depending on the activity).

In contrast to most other institutional arbitration rules, the LCIA Rules set out the powers of an LCIA arbitral tribunal in some detail. The powers to order disclosure of documents and security for legal costs (i.e., a deposit or bank guarantee securing the estimated amounts which an unsuccessful claimant would be liable to reimburse to a successful respondent for its costs of legal representation) are prominently included among the arbitrators' powers.

The LCIA's appointments of arbitrators have historically been drawn predominantly from the English bar and retired judiciary. This is in part because many LCIA cases have involved contracts governed by English law and/or foreign parties specifically providing for the appointment of English-qualified arbitrators. When not constrained by such provisions, the LCIA's selections of arbitrators tend to be more diverse. The LCIA fixes the arbitrators' fees according to the time expended by the arbitrators and subject to maximum hourly rates published by the LCIA.

Most LCIA arbitrations are seated in London. Absent contrary agreement by the parties or factors pointing to another more convenient location, London will ordinarily be selected as the arbitral seat by the LCIA.

A particular procedural advantage of the LCIA Rules is their provision for expedited formation of the arbitral tribunal and expedited appointment of replacement arbitrators. The LCIA Rules also permit joinder of third parties in arbitrations, subject to prescribed conditions, and consolidation of arbitrations.

The LCIA has made largely unsuccessful efforts to establish foreign presences. It established a successful partnership in Dubai (the Dubai International Financial Centre-LCIA ("DIFC–LCIA") Arbitration Centre) in 2008, which applied rules closely modelled on the LCIA Rules. The DIFC-LCIA was abolished, however, in 2021 by governmental decree (which also assertedly transferred the DIFC-LCIA's functions to a Dubai arbitral institution, the DIAC). The LCIA also established an arbitration center in Mauritius, the LCIA-Mauritius International Arbitration Centre ("LCIA-MIAC"), which was closed in 2018, and similarly made unsuccessful efforts to establish an "LCIA-India," which was terminated in 2016. Despite these events, the LCIA remains a leading choice of parties in both the Middle East and Africa.

The LCIA model arbitration clause for future disputes provides:

> Any dispute arising out of or in connection with this contract, including any question regarding its existence, validity or termination, shall be referred to and finally resolved by arbitration under the LCIA Rules, which Rules are deemed to be incorporated by reference into this clause.
>
> The number of arbitrators shall be [one/three].
>
> The seat, or legal place, of arbitration shall be [City and/or Country].
>
> The language to be used in the arbitral proceedings shall be [_________].
>
> The governing law of the contract shall be the substantive law of [_________].

iii. American Arbitration Association and International Centre for Dispute Resolution

The AAA was founded in 1926 and is based in New York (with approximately 25 regional offices throughout the United States). The AAA is the leading U.S. arbitral institution, and handles one of the largest numbers of arbitral disputes in the world. The AAA's caseload has increased significantly over the past two decades. In 1997, it reported a total annual caseload of 11,130 arbitrations (under its Commercial Rules), rising to 17,620 cases in 2018. Similar growth is reported in international cases. The AAA reports that its international caseload has increased from 453 cases filed in 1999 to 848 new international filings in 2023 (although the 2023 figure is somewhat lower than that in other recent years).

The primary arbitration rules administered by the AAA are the AAA Commercial Arbitration Rules ("AAA Rules"), most recently revised in September 2022; these rules are used in a large number of domestic U.S. arbitrations.

Non-U.S. parties have sometimes been reluctant to agree to arbitration under AAA Rules, fearing parochial predisposition and unfamiliarity with international practice. In 1996, to enhance its position as an international arbitral institution, the AAA established the International Centre for Dispute Resolution ("ICDR"), which has exclusive responsibility for administering the AAA's international arbitrations. The ICDR International Dispute Resolution Procedures ("ICDR Rules"), most recently revised in 2021, are applied where parties have agreed to them or to AAA arbitration in an "international" dispute, but without specifying a particular set of AAA Rules.

The ICDR Rules are based principally on the UNCITRAL Arbitration Rules (reproduced in Appendix E), and were intended to permit a measured amount of flexibility and a minimum amount of administrative supervision. Under all versions of AAA Rules, the AAA administrative staff plays a less significant supervisory role regarding certain substantive matters than does the ICC Secretariat or SIAC Registrar. Among other things, the AAA does not receive or serve initial notices or requests for arbitration, does not require or review a Terms of Reference, does not scrutinize draft awards (except for non-substantive content and accuracy), and plays a less significant role in setting the arbitrators' fees. The AAA's administrative charges are based on the amount in dispute. With respect to the arbitrators' fees, arbitrators fix their own rates, which are published on their resumes for parties to consider when receiving a list of potential arbitrators. Compensation under the ICDR Rules is based on the "time spent by the arbitrators," taking into account their stated rates and the "size and complexity of the case."

Most ICDR and AAA appointments of arbitrators in international cases are generally based on a list-procedure, with names drawn from over 750 panelists maintained by the ICDR and presented to the parties for expressions of preference. Although the AAA's lists were historically dominated by U.S. practitioners, the ICDR increasingly seeks to appoint arbitrators with international experience in appropriate cases. The ICDR has administrative facilities in New York, Houston, Miami, and Singapore, and access to hearing facilities through its global network of 85 cooperative agreements, enabling it to administer arbitrations in many parts of the world.

A model AAA arbitration clause, selecting the ICDR International Dispute Resolution Procedures, provides:

> Any controversy or claim arising out of or relating to this contract shall be determined by arbitration in accordance with the International Arbitration Rules of the International Centre for Dispute Resolution.

A model AAA arbitration clause, selecting the AAA's Commercial Arbitration Rules, provides:

> Any controversy or claim arising out of or relating to this contract, or the breach thereof, shall be settled by arbitration administered by the American Arbitration Association in accordance with its Commercial [or other] Arbitration Rules, and judgment on the award rendered by the arbitrator(s) may be entered in any court having jurisdiction thereof.

Numerous other sets of AAA arbitration rules also exist, some of which provide for specialized types of disputes (e.g., construction, employment, consumer), and can be selected in the parties' arbitration agreement. The AAA has also recently launched an online "ClauseBuilder" tool to assist users in drafting clear and appropriate arbitration and mediation agreements.

iv. Singapore International Arbitration Centre

The Singapore International Arbitration Centre ("SIAC") was established in 1991, initially for disputes arising out of construction, shipping, banking, and insurance. In recent years, SIAC has broadened its focus to all categories of commercial disputes and has become the leading international arbitral institution in Asia and one of the most successful arbitral institutions in the world. Although its caseload has declined in recent years, SIAC administered 625 new cases in 2024, and 91% of cases filed with the SIAC were international in nature.

SIAC-administered arbitrations are ordinarily governed by the SIAC Rules, which are based on the United Nations Commission on International Trade Law ("UNCITRAL") Arbitration Rules, with significant modifications, and have been periodically revised (most recently in January 2025). The 2025 SIAC Rules are aimed at streamlining the efficiency and speed of proceedings and further enhancing the quality and fairness of SIAC-administered arbitrations, including by the introduction of new procedures (the Streamlined Procedure, Preliminary Determination and Coordinated Proceedings); expansion of the cases eligible for the Expedited Procedure; and enhancements to the Emergency Arbitrator procedure.

Under Article 14 of the SIAC Rules, an Expedited Procedure may be applied in arbitral proceedings. This is a fast-track procedure, requiring an award to be made within six months of the tribunal's constitution and providing that the Registrar may extend the time for making such an award. The procedure is applicable where the parties have agreed to the application of the Expedited Procedure prior to the constitution of the tribunal or if the SIAC Court of Arbitration determines that one of three criteria is satisfied: at the time of the application, the amount in dispute does not exceed SGD 10 million (roughly USD 7.5 million) but exceeds SGD 1 million (roughly USD 750,000); at the time of the application, the amount in dispute does not exceed SGD 1 million and the President has determined under Article 13.1(b) that the Streamlined Procedure shall not apply to the arbitration; or the circumstances of the case warrant the application of the Expedited Procedure.

In cases where emergency interim relief is needed, the SIAC Rules allow a party to make an application for emergency interim relief and provide the President with the power to appoint an emergency arbitrator if the application for emergency relief is accepted. Under Article 12.1 and Schedule 1 of the SIAC Rules, parties may apply for urgent interim relief prior to the constitution of an arbitral tribunal through an emergency arbitrator (and prior to the commencement of a SIAC arbitration). SIAC has considerable experience with emergency arbitrator applications: since 2010, the institution has received 173 applications, with emergency arbitrators appointed in all cases, and interim relief granted in whole or in part in more than half of all proceedings.

SIAC's organizational structure is similar to that of the ICC with respect to case management. It has a Court of Arbitration that comprises leading practitioners from around the world, and an experienced Secretariat with specialized lawyers to manage the administration of cases. SIAC draft awards are scrutinized by the

Registrar for issues of both form and substance, and can only be rendered by the tribunal if approved by the Registrar as to their form. While the Registrar manages the formal review and scrutiny process, the Registrar may, where appropriate, consult the SIAC Court before approving the draft award. Timelines for scrutiny are reportedly shorter than at the ICC: two to three weeks for final awards, and one to two days in the case of emergency arbitrator orders and awards.

SIAC maintains a Panel of Arbitrators, composed of leading international and regional arbitration practitioners who reflect a broad base of expertise, knowledge and experience. In 2015, SIAC released an Arb-Med-Arb clause, in collaboration with the Singapore International Mediation Centre ("SIMC"), which allows for a dispute to be referred to arbitration and then suspended while mediation at SIMC is attempted. If the dispute is settled through mediation, the agreement is recorded as a consent award, which may be enforced under the New York Convention. If the dispute cannot be settled through mediation, the parties may resume the arbitral proceedings.

A model arbitration clause, as recommended by SIAC, provides:

> Any dispute arising out of or in connection with this contract, including any question regarding its existence, validity or termination, shall be referred to and finally resolved by arbitration administered by the Singapore International Arbitration Centre ("SIAC") in accordance with the Arbitration Rules of the Singapore International Arbitration Centre ("SIAC Rules") for the time being in force, which rules are deemed to be incorporated by reference in this clause.
>
> The seat of the arbitration shall be [Singapore].
>
> The Tribunal shall consist of ________________ arbitrator(s).
>
> The language of the arbitration shall be ________________.
>
> The law governing this arbitration agreement shall be _________.
>
> [*Parties may wish to agree to the supervisory jurisdiction of the Singapore International Commercial Court (SICC) for international commercial arbitrations where Singapore is chosen as the seat of arbitration. If so, include:*
>
> In respect of any court proceedings in Singapore commenced under the International Arbitration Act 1994 in relation to the arbitration, the parties agree (a) to commence such proceedings before the Singapore International Commercial Court ("the SICC"); and (b) in any event, that such proceedings shall be heard and adjudicated by the SICC.]

In January 2017, SIAC published a set of rules specifically for investment arbitration. The SIAC Investment Arbitration Rules can be incorporated into investment contracts or referred to in bilateral investment treaties.

v. *Stockholm Chamber of Commerce Arbitration Institute*

Founded in Sweden in 1917, the SCC Arbitration Institute ("SCC") has a long history of providing arbitration services to Swedish and international parties. It operates as a non-profit and independent entity within the Stockholm Chamber of Commerce, which is in turn an independent business organization.

During the Cold War, the SCC developed into a substantial forum for disputes involving parties from the USSR and (subsequently) China. The SCC's status as a forum for dispute resolution originates from the Optional Clause Agreement signed in 1977 between the U.S. (through the AAA) and the USSR (through the USSR Chamber of Commerce and Industry). This agreement enabled the resolution of U.S.-Soviet commercial disputes in Sweden with the assistance of the SCC. In 1984, the SCC and the China Council for Promotion of International Trade ("CCPIT") entered into a cooperation agreement, resulting in China transferring many of its international disputes to the SCC.

Following these developments, the SCC sought to position itself as a forum for investor-State dispute settlement ("ISDS"), having administered its first investment dispute in 1993. Both "Stockholm" and "SCC" are listed as forums for the resolution of disputes between investors and states arising out of 94 bilateral investment treaties ("BITs") and the Energy Charter Treaty ("ECT").

The SCC offers a wide range of dispute resolution services, including arbitration, expedited arbitration, mediation and express dispute assessment proceedings to Swedish and international parties. The SCC Arbitration Rules were most recently revised in 2023 and include an emergency arbitrator mechanism and specific rules of ISDS disputes. Today, the SCC Arbitration Rules are reportedly the third most commonly used set of arbitration rules in investment disputes. The SCC Rules for Expedited Arbitrations, which constitute a separate body of rules to which the parties must opt in, were also revised in 2023. The SCC Rules for Expedited Arbitration achieve time and cost efficiency through a stated "front-loading" of the procedure. The SCC has adopted Procedures for the Administration of Cases under the UNCITRAL Arbitration Rules, which entered into force on January 1, 2015 and were last revised in 2023. Moreover, new SCC Mediation Rules entered into force on January 1, 2025.

In 2024, the SCC administered 204 cases, of which 105 (51%) were international, i.e., at least one of the parties was not Swedish. In international disputes, the SCC frequently appoints non-Swedish arbitrators. SCC arbitrations are usually seated in Stockholm, although parties frequently agree on other seats in Sweden and elsewhere. In the absence of party agreement, the SCC Board decides the seat based on factors including the nationality of the parties, practical considerations, cost-effectiveness, and the parties' expectations.

The SCC recommends that the following clause be used in contracts providing for arbitration under the SCC Arbitration Rules:

> Any dispute, controversy or claim arising out of or in connection with this contract, or the breach, termination, or invalidity thereof, shall be finally settled by arbitration in accordance with the Arbitration Rules of the SCC Arbitration Institute.
>
> *Recommended additions:*
>
> The seat of arbitration shall be [...].
>
> The language to be used in the arbitral proceedings shall be [...].
>
> This contract shall be governed by the substantive law of [...].

vi. Vienna International Arbitral Centre

The VIAC has historically conducted only international commercial arbitrations, reflected in a requirement that at least one of the parties must be of non-Austrian origin or the dispute must be of an international character. From 2018, the VIAC absorbed the jurisdiction of the nine regional chambers of commerce in Austria and now also administers domestic proceedings. In 2016, the VIAC adopted Mediation Rules, and in 2021, the VIAC adopted specialized rules for investment arbitration and mediation.

Since its inception, the VIAC has administered some 2,000 proceedings and is one of the premier international arbitral institutions in Central and Eastern Europe. The VIAC has historically had a caseload of roughly 50 new cases per year. In 2024, VIAC's caseload registered a 35% increase in 2023, with 45 new cases and a total of 71 pending cases. Twenty-two percent of the VIAC's cases involved amounts in dispute in excess of EUR 10 million, and the aggregate amount of all disputes under VIAC administration in 2024 was EUR 2 billion.

The VIAC administers arbitrations submitted to it through its Secretariat. VIAC arbitrations are administered in accordance with the VIAC Rules of Arbitration and Mediation ("VIAC Rules"). The VIAC Rules were revised in 2006 (when new rules were adopted in light of revisions to the Austrian Arbitration Law, which is based on the UNCITRAL Model Law), 2013, 2018 (adding joinder and consolidation provisions), 2021 (expanding VIAC's authority to administer investment and ad hoc proceedings, introducing third-party funding rules for transparency, and adding annexes for ad hoc cases and succession disputes) and 2025 (revising the fee structure for mediation-related disputes and adding supplementary rules for corporate disputes).

Under the VIAC Rules, the VIAC is responsible for, among other things, the confirmation of receipt of the statement of claim; the fixing and reviewing of the advance on costs payable by the parties at the outset of the proceedings; confirming the appointment of arbitrators nominated by the parties; deciding arbitrator challenges for lack of impartiality or independence; and appointing arbitrators in the event that the parties are unable to agree upon a sole or presiding arbitrator. Under the VIAC Rules, both the administrative fees of the VIAC and fees of the arbitrators are fixed on the basis of the amount in dispute, according to a schedule of fees included in Annex 3 of the VIAC Rules.

The VIAC model arbitration clause provides:

> All disputes or claims arising out of or in connection with this contract, including disputes relating to its validity, breach, termination or nullity, shall be finally settled under the Rules of Arbitration of the International Arbitral Centre of the Austrian Federal Economic Chamber in Vienna (Vienna Rules) by one or three arbitrators appointed in accordance with the said Rules.

VIAC was originally designed primarily as a venue for East/West economic disputes. These origins are reflected in the fact that a significant proportion of VIAC's caseload still includes parties from Central and Eastern Europe (although parties from more than 65 states used VIAC services from 2013 to 2024).

vii. International Centre for Settlement of Investment Disputes

The International Centre for Settlement of Investment Disputes ("ICSID") is an international organization established by the Convention on the Settlement of Investment Disputes between States and Nationals of Other States ("ICSID Convention" or "Washington Convention") of 1965. As of August 2025, there were 158 Contracting States and seven Signatory States to the ICSID Convention.

As one of the five institutions of the World Bank Group, ICSID is headquartered in Washington, D.C. While most ICSID arbitrations are governed by the ICSID Convention and the ICSID Additional Facility, ICSID also administers arbitrations under the UNCITRAL Arbitration Rules, as well as other ad hoc arbitrations, conciliations and mediations. The ICSID Convention is discussed below. (See pp. [150–153] below.)

ICSID jurisdiction is generally confined to "investment" disputes, involving claims by foreign investors against host states. Major international infrastructure and natural resource projects often include ICSID arbitration clauses. ICSID arbitration has also frequently been included in the dispute provisions of bilateral investment treaties, which proliferated during the 1990s. ICSID has adopted a set of procedural rules for arbitrations conducted under the ICSID Convention, titled the ICSID Convention Arbitration Rules, as well as a separate, corresponding set of procedural rules for investment arbitrations conducted under the ICSID Additional Facility (available for certain investment disputes that would not fall under the ICSID Convention), titled the ICSID Additional Facility Arbitration Rules. These rules were last revised in 2022 and added new investor-State Mediation Rules.

ICSID's caseload has significantly increased over the past decades, rising from one case filed per year, on average, in the 1970s and two cases filed per year, on average, in the 1980s, to 52 cases in 2015 and 55 cases in 2024. ICSID has administered over 1,000 investor-State disputes, with 341 cases pending in 2024.

viii. Permanent Court of Arbitration

The Permanent Court of Arbitration ("PCA") was established by the 1899 and 1907 Hague Conventions for the Pacific Settlement of International Disputes. The PCA is an intergovernmental organization with 124 Member States, including two countries, Timor-Leste and Vanuatu, which joined in 2024. One of the PCA's most significant functions is under the UNCITRAL Rules; the PCA Secretary-General is designated under the UNCITRAL Rules as responsible for selecting an appointing authority for UNCITRAL arbitrations (where the parties have not otherwise agreed). The 2010 UNCITRAL Rules also permit parties to designate the Secretary-General of the PCA directly as appointing authority.

The PCA enjoyed very modest usage during its first 70 years of existence (only 25 arbitrations were submitted to PCA tribunals during this period). More recently, the PCA's caseload has significantly expanded, now including substantial numbers of investment and contract-based disputes. In 2024, the PCA administered 243 cases: seven were state-to-state disputes, 114 were investor-State disputes under bilateral or multilateral investment treaties and national investment laws, and 114 involved disputes arising under contracts or other agreements to which at least one party was a state, state-controlled entity, or intergovernmental organization.

As originally established, the PCA was a registry for state-to-state arbitration conducted pursuant to the Hague Conventions. The PCA's governing body later recognized that the institution was able to administer a broader range of disputes. During the 1990s, the PCA promulgated four sets of procedural rules, for arbitrations involving particular types of parties, all of which were based on the 1976 UNCITRAL Rules and which have been adopted by parties on various occasions: Optional Rules for Arbitrating Disputes between Two States (1992); Optional Rules for Arbitrating Disputes between Two Parties of Which Only One Is A State (1993); Optional Rules for Arbitration Involving International Organizations and States (1996); and Optional Rules for Arbitration between International Organizations and Private Parties (1996).

In 2012, the PCA published a new set of rules ("PCA Rules"), which effectively consolidated and replaced the PCA's existing four sets of rules (although the older rules were not withdrawn and technically remain in existence). The PCA Rules are similar to the 2010 UNCITRAL Rules, providing greater flexibility to the parties than the PCA's earlier rules, but are also specifically tailored for cases involving states, state-controlled entities, and intergovernmental organizations.

Parties seeking PCA-administered dispute resolution services are free to either adopt the PCA's Rules or agree to PCA administration of cases conducted under other rules, such as the UNCITRAL Rules or ad hoc rules of procedure. The PCA may also assist parties in drafting procedural rules or arbitration clauses for particular disputes or instruments.

The PCA headquarters is located in The Hague, within the premises of the Peace Palace, and it has permanent overseas presences in Singapore and Mauritius.

The PCA's International Bureau provides highly skilled support services for arbitrations conducted under PCA auspices. Additionally, the PCA frequently provides hearing facilities and meeting rooms at the Peace Palace, which are available free of charge for PCA-administered proceedings. The PCA has also entered into "Host Country Agreements" with a number of its Member States, including Argentina, Austria, Brazil, Chile, China (in relation to Hong Kong SAR), Costa Rica, Djibouti, India, Ireland, Malaysia, Mauritius, Paraguay, Portugal, Singapore, South Africa, Uruguay, and Vietnam, which establish a legal framework under which PCA-administered proceedings can be conducted in the territory of the host country on an ad hoc basis, providing for similar privileges and immunities for participants in its proceedings as the PCA enjoys in the Netherlands. Furthermore, pursuant to these agreements and other cooperation agreements that the PCA has concluded with other institutions, the PCA is able to access hearing and meeting facilities in a number of locations free of charge for use in PCA-administered proceedings.

The PCA also operates a "Financial Assistance Fund," established in 1994, to assist developing countries by offsetting costs related to international arbitration or other means of peaceful dispute settlement offered by the PCA. PCA Member States that are listed on the Organization for Economic Co-operation and Development ("OECD") Development Assistance Committee's "List of Aid Recipients" may benefit from access to the Fund. As of September 2020, the PCA had provided grants to 10 states from different regions around the world.

The PCA recommends that the following clause be used in contracts providing for arbitration under the 2012 PCA Rules:

> Any dispute, controversy or claim arising out of or relating to this contract, or the breach, termination or invalidity thereof, shall be settled by arbitration in accordance with the PCA Arbitration Rules 2012.

In addition to the foregoing arbitral institutions, there are a number of regional or otherwise more specialized institutions. In recent years, some of these institutions have become important regional players that competently administer both local and international disputes. Other institutions remain less experienced and/or more specialized, and foreign parties should exercise caution when considering them for transactions, particularly with local counterparties. In addition, there have been instances where purported "arbitral institutions" putatively administered what were fraudulent or otherwise unlawful proceedings, including in the absence of any agreement to arbitrate. Of course, institutions of this nature must be avoided.

ix. Abu Dhabi International Arbitration Centre

The Abu Dhabi International Arbitration Centre ("arbitrateAD") was established in February 2024. It is the result of a reorganization of the previous Abu Dhabi Commercial and Conciliation Centre ("ADCCAC"), which was formed under the auspices of the Abu Dhabi Chamber of Commerce & Industry. On February 1, 2024, the 2024 arbitrateAD Rules replaced the 2013 ADCCAC Rules. While cases registered under the ADCCAC Rules before this date continue to be administered and resolved under the provisions of the ADCCAC Rules, new cases filed from this date onward are administered by arbitrateAD under its Arbitration Rules.

In its first year of operation, arbitrateAD administered more than 30 disputes and is now the principal arbitral institution in Abu Dhabi and, arguably, the United Arab Emirates. It is an important addition to the disputes landscape in the Middle East, serving both local and international parties.

arbitrateAD recommends the following model arbitration clause:

> Any disputes, controversies, or claims of any nature (contractual or non-contractual), arising out of or having a connection with this contract, including, inter alia, the execution, interpretation or termination of the contract, ("Disputes"), shall be referred to and finally resolved by arbitration in accordance with the Rules of Arbitration of the Abu Dhabi International Arbitration Centre ("Rules").
>
> The number of arbitrators shall be [one or three].
>
> The seat of arbitration shall be ______________ [Abu Dhabi Global Market (ADGM), or other City/Country].
>
> The language of the arbitration proceedings shall be ______________.
>
> The law governing Disputes shall be the substantive law of ______________ [Jurisdiction].

x. *Asian International Arbitration Centre*

The Asian International Arbitration Centre ("AIAC"), formerly named the Kuala Lumpur Regional Centre for Arbitration ("KLRCA"), was established in Malaysia in 1978 to promote international commercial arbitration in the Asia/Pacific region. The AIAC administers arbitrations under its rules, which are based on the UNCITRAL Arbitration Rules.

The KLRCA and AIAC have periodically revised their Rules, most recently in 2023 (based on the 2021 UNCITRAL Rules with minor modifications).

The KLRCA and AIAC had limited caseloads for the first few decades of their existence, but have since reportedly increased to 172 new cases in 2021, from only seven filed in 2016. As its name change reflects, the AIAC aspires to provide a viable alternative to SIAC, HKIAC and ACICA in commercial arbitrations involving parties from the Asia/Pacific region.

The AIAC recommends the following model arbitration clause:

> Any dispute, controversy or claim arising out of or relating to this contract, or the breach, termination or invalidity thereof shall be settled by arbitration in accordance with the AIAC Arbitration Rules.

xi. Australian Centre for International Commercial Arbitration

The Australian Centre for International Commercial Arbitration ("ACICA") was established in 1985 on the initiative of the Institute of Arbitrators, Australia. The ACICA promulgated new rules, based on the UNCITRAL Arbitration Rules, in 2005, which were revised in 2011 (incorporating emergency arbitrator provisions), 2016 (adding provisions on consolidation, joinder and expedited procedures), and 2021 (improving online practices).

ACICA enjoys a growing reputation, particularly in arbitrations involving parties from the Asia/Pacific region. In such arbitrations, ACICA promotes itself as providing a credible alternative to either the HKIAC or SIAC. The ACICA will also act as appointing authority under the UNCITRAL Arbitration Rules.

The ACICA recommends the following model arbitration clause:

> Any dispute, controversy or claim arising out of, relating to or in connection with this contract, including any question regarding its existence, validity or termination, shall be resolved by arbitration in accordance with the ACICA Arbitration Rules. The seat of arbitration shall be [Sydney/Melbourne/Perth/Brisbane/Adelaide], Australia [or choose another city]. The language of the arbitration shall be English [or choose another language]. The number of arbitrators shall be one [or three, or delete this sentence and rely on Article 11 of the ACICA Arbitration Rules].

xii. Bahrain Chamber for Dispute Resolution

The Bahrain Chamber for Dispute Resolution ("BCDR") was established in 2009. Although it operated in partnership with the AAA at the outset, in 2022, the BCDR became independent of the AAA.

The BCDR administers arbitrations under the BCDR Arbitration Rules, which were last revised in 2022. According to the BCDR's 2022 annual report, 45 new cases were registered in 2022, with a total value of approximately USD 450 million. Around two-thirds of the 421 cases filed with the BCDR from its inception to 2022 involved at least one non-Bahraini party, although only 5% of these cases involved exclusively international parties, suggesting that the main users of the BCDR were Bahraini. The BCDR issued Sports Arbitration Rules in March 2022, which largely mirrored the BCDR Arbitration Rules.

The BCDR recommends the following model arbitration clause:

> Any dispute arising out of or in connection with this contract, including any question regarding its existence, validity or termination, shall be finally settled by arbitration in accordance with the Rules of Arbitration of the Bahrain Chamber for Dispute Resolution. The arbitral tribunal shall consist of [specify one or three] arbitrator[s]. The place of arbitration shall be [specify town and country]. The language of the arbitration shall be [specify language].

xiii. Cairo Regional Centre for International Commercial Arbitration

Established in 1979, the Cairo Regional Centre for International Commercial Arbitration ("CRCICA") is an independent non-profit international organization under the auspices of the Asian-African Legal Consultative Organization ("AALCO"). Pursuant to an agreement concluded in 1987 between AALCO and the Egyptian government, the CRCICA directs its services primarily towards Middle Eastern and African trade and investment disputes, particularly in the Arab world. The CRCICA has administered over 1,747 cases since its establishment, including 76 new cases in 2024.

The CRCICA arbitration rules, most recently revised in 2024, are based on the UNCITRAL Rules, with modifications relating principally to the CRCICA's role as an arbitral institution and an appointing authority. The CRCICA reportedly maintains a list of more than 500 national and international arbitrators. Both the administrative fee that is charged by the CRCICA and the arbitrators' fees are calculated by reference to the amount in dispute between the parties. Although distinctly regional in character, the CRCICA has not infrequently been considered, both by parties within and outside the region, as an appointing authority in international commercial matters.

xiv. Center for Arbitration and Mediation of the Chamber of Commerce Brazil-Canada

The Center for Arbitration and Mediation of the Chamber of Commerce Brazil-Canada ("CAM-CCBC") was founded in 1979 and is one of the leading arbitral institutions in Latin America, with its headquarters in São Paulo.

Since 1989, the CAM-CCBC has administered more than 1,670 arbitrations, of which around 15% are international. In 2024, CAM-CCBC administered 126 new arbitrations. The CAM-CCBC Rules were extensively revised in 2022 and are now broadly similar to the UNCITRAL Rules. The CAM-CCBC issues Administrative Resolutions dealing with specific procedural aspects of CAM-CCBC arbitrations (such as arbitration with Brazilian state entities and third-party funding).

The model CAM-CCBC arbitration clause provides:

> Any dispute arising out of or in connection with the present contract, including its interpretation or performance, shall be finally settled by arbitration, administered by the Center for Arbitration and Mediation of the Chamber of Commerce Brazil-Canada ("CAM-CCBC"), under its Rules and the Arbitral Tribunal shall consist of [one(1)/three(3)] arbitrators appointed in accordance with the said Rules.

Parties considering use of CAM-CCBC should also consult the discussion below on Brazil as an arbitral seat (See pp. 87-88).

xv. China International Economic and Trade Arbitration Commission

The China International Economic and Trade Arbitration Commission ("CIETAC") was established in 1956. Also known as the Court of Arbitration of China Chamber of International Commerce, CIETAC is headquartered in Beijing, with branches in a number of other Chinese cities, including Hong Kong. CIETAC enjoys a privileged position in Chinese arbitration by virtue of governmental measures; it also has a unique depth of experience in Chinese-related disputes.

In 2024, CIETAC handled 6,013 new cases (of which 758 were foreign-related arbitrations). CIETAC has revised its Arbitration Rules a number of times in the past 65 years, most recently in 2023, which became effective as of January 1, 2024 ("CIETAC Rules"). Successive revisions of the Rules have sought to bring CIETAC's practices further in line with leading international arbitral institutions by affording greater party autonomy, transparency, and efficiency. The CIETAC Rules contain emergency arbitrator procedures. CIETAC is typically more involved in the procedural administration of arbitrations than most other arbitral institutions, including in scrutinizing awards.

Particularly in recent years, non-Chinese parties have frequently questioned the neutrality and transparency of CIETAC's case administration and arbitrator appointments, particularly in cases involving Chinese counterparties. Under current Chinese law and judicial practice, foreign investors and other foreign parties doing business related to China may provide for arbitration with non-Chinese seats or administered by foreign arbitral institutions. Despite apparent efforts to improve the professionalism and neutrality of CIETAC arbitration, foreign users increasingly prefer other arbitral institutions, including for China-related transactions. Developments over the past decade in China and elsewhere suggest that this preference is likely to become more pronounced in the coming years. As a consequence, foreign and international users should virtually never accept CIETAC arbitration, particularly in matters with local counterparties; parties should also consider the discussion below of China as an arbitral seat (See pp. 90-91). Conversely, Chinese and Hong Kong parties may have a different perspective.

When drafting a CIETAC arbitration clause, it is important to select a language for the arbitration (See pp. 102-103 below), provide that the presiding arbitrator be of a neutral nationality (See pp. 98-100 below), and provide that the parties are free to choose arbitrators outside the CIETAC list.

xvi. Dubai International Arbitration Centre

In 2004, Dubai's Commercial Conciliation and Arbitration Centre was reorganized and renamed as the Dubai International Arbitration Centre ("DIAC"). DIAC's caseload has increased from just 34 cases in 2004 to 355 cases in 2023. The DIAC Arbitration Rules (the "DIAC Rules"), which were adopted in 2007, were influenced by the ICC Rules. The DIAC Rules were extensively revised in 2022, and new Mediation Rules were introduced in 2023.

In 2021, the Ruler of Dubai abolished the DIFC-LCIA and Emirates Maritime Arbitration Centre by Decree 34/2021, which purported to merge the operations of these institutions with DIAC. The Decree resulted in disputes regarding the meaning and effect of existing DIFC-LCIA arbitration agreements, at least some of which were referred to DIAC. Since 2021, DIAC has adopted a number of steps to internationalize and strengthen the quality of its Arbitration Court, Registrar and administrative team.

Approximately half of the claimants and arbitrators involved in recent DIAC cases were from outside the Gulf Cooperation Council. Most DIAC arbitrations are conducted in English. DIAC-appointed arbitrators are frequently leading international arbitration practitioners or retired judges.

DIAC recommends the following model arbitration clause:

> Any dispute arising out of or in connection with this contract, including any question regarding its existence, validity or termination, shall be referred to and finally resolved by arbitration under the Arbitration Rules of the Dubai International Arbitration Centre, which Rules are deemed to be incorporated by reference into this clause.
>
> The number of arbitrators shall be [one/three].
>
> The seat of arbitration shall be [City and/or Country].
>
> The language to be used in the arbitration shall be [language].
>
> The governing law of the contract shall be the substantive law of [State or Country].

xvii. German Institution of Arbitration ("DIS")

The German Arbitration Committee was originally founded in 1920 to administer arbitrations in Germany. In 1992, the Committee merged with the German Arbitration Institute to form the German Institution of Arbitration ("Deutsche Institution für Schiedsgerichtsbarkeit e.V." or "DIS") to provide nationwide arbitration services in

Germany for all sectors of the economy. The DIS Arbitration Rules (published in English translation as well as in the authoritative German text) are intended for both national and international arbitrations; the DIS Rules were most recently revised in 2021, specifically regarding the Schedule of Costs at Annex 2.

Despite having a highly competent staff, DIS's caseload has struggled in recent years, declining significantly from earlier figures. In 2023, roughly 60% of the DIS annual caseload of 70 arbitrations involved domestic transactions with German parties.

The DIS recommends the following model arbitration clause:

> All disputes arising out of or in connection with this contract or its validity shall be finally settled in accordance with the Arbitration Rules of the German Institution of Arbitration ("DIS") without recourse to the ordinary courts of law.
>
> The arbitral tribunal shall be comprised of [please enter "a sole arbitrator" or "three members"].
>
> The seat of the arbitration is [please enter city and country].
>
> The language of the arbitration shall be [please enter language of the arbitration].
>
> The rules of law applicable to the merits shall be [please enter law or rules of law].

xviii. Hong Kong International Arbitration Centre

Established in 1985, the Hong Kong International Arbitration Centre ("HKIAC") developed into Asia's leading international arbitral institution prior to the departure of the British administration. In more recent years, HKIAC has faced increasing challenges and has reported decreasing caseloads. In 2024, HKIAC stated that it administered 352 new arbitrations, of which 249 cases were under the 2024 HKIAC Administered Arbitration Rules ("HKIAC Rules") and the UNCITRAL Arbitration Rules.

The HKIAC Rules, which are based on the UNCITRAL Rules, contain a number of innovations, including provisions on diversity, environmental impact and information security; enhanced tribunal powers to determine preliminary issues; and more stringent time limits on tribunals in respect of closing proceedings and rendering of awards. In recent years, HKIAC has established representative offices in Seoul, Beijing and Shanghai, and has introduced a tribunal secretary service allowing the Secretariat members to act as tribunal secretary.

The Hong Kong government has expressed its support for the development of international arbitration in Hong Kong, and has declared that it is in the process of developing a legal hub with state-of-the-art hearing facilities for Hong Kong-based arbitral institutions, including HKIAC. Nonetheless, particularly in recent years, potential users of HKIAC have voiced increasing concerns about the stability and judicial independence of Hong Kong, and many foreign parties are unwilling to designate HKIAC (or a Hong Kong seat), particularly in disputes involving Chinese parties. (See pp. 90-91 below.) Recent developments suggest that these concerns are likely to increase among most foreign and international users, while Hong Kong and Chinese users are likely to have different perspectives.

The HKIAC recommends the following model arbitration clause for arbitrations administered under its rules:

> Any dispute, controversy, difference or claim arising out of or relating to this contract, including the existence, validity, interpretation, performance, breach or termination thereof or any dispute regarding non-contractual obligations arising out of or relating to it shall be referred to and finally resolved by arbitration administered by the Hong Kong International Arbitration Centre ("HKIAC") under the HKIAC Administered Arbitration Rules in force when the Notice of Arbitration is submitted.
>
> The law of this arbitration clause shall be [... (Hong Kong law)].
>
> The seat of arbitration shall be [... (Hong Kong)].
>
> The number of arbitrators shall be [... (one or three)].
>
> The arbitration proceedings shall be conducted in [... (insert language)].

xix. Indian Council of Arbitration

The Indian Council of Arbitration ("ICA") was established in 1965 and, at least until the establishment of the former LCIA-India, was regarded as India's pre-eminent arbitral institution. The ICA Rules are tailored to the provisions of the Indian Arbitration and Conciliation Act 1996, and were most recently revised in 2022. Many users remain cautious about seating arbitrations in India, noting historically interventionist attitudes of Indian courts. The ICA handled eight international arbitrations in 2010, and slightly more in later years.

xx. Inter-American Commercial Arbitration Commission

The Inter-American Commercial Arbitration Commission ("IACAC") was established in 1934 as a product of the Seventh International Conference of American States in Montevideo, Uruguay. IACAC consists of over 20 national sections that provide decentralized administration of commercial arbitrations according to the IACAC Rules of Procedure ("IACAC Rules"). The IACAC Rules resemble the UNCITRAL Rules and were most recently updated in 2002. The IACAC issued Administrative Procedural Guidelines in 2008 (and revised in 2017) for arbitrations conducted under the IACAC Rules.

IACAC Member States include most North and South American nations as well as Spain and Portugal. Article 3 of the Inter-American Convention on International Commercial Arbitration, or "Panama Convention," provides that unless parties have agreed otherwise, the IACAC Rules will govern arbitration proceedings conducted in Convention Member States. In the United States, IACAC arbitrations are administered by the ICDR.

Though its efforts over time have contributed to the greater acceptance of international arbitration throughout Latin America, IACAC itself has not been able to achieve the same level of recognition as many of the major international arbitral institutions. Between 2001 and 2019, IACAC administered relatively few arbitrations.

The ICDR suggests the following model clause for incorporation of the IACAC Rules:

> Any dispute, controversy, or claim arising from or relating to this contract, or the breach, termination, or invalidity thereof, shall be settled by arbitration in accordance with the Rules of Procedure of the Inter-American Commercial Arbitration Commission in effect on the date of this agreement.

xxi. Istanbul Arbitration Centre

The Istanbul Arbitration Centre ("ISTAC") was established in 2015 in Turkey. It administers arbitrations under the ISTAC Arbitration and Mediation Rules, which came into force in October 2015. The ISTAC aims to resolve arbitrations within six months, although it also provides fast-track arbitration and emergency arbitration services and has issued the Fast-Track Arbitration Rules and the Emergency Arbitrator Rules.

In 2024, the ISTAC handled 167 new cases, an increase from 138 in 2023. Of these disputes, 80% were resolved between six months and one year, with the remaining resolved over one year. Domestic disputes made up 87% of these cases; of the remaining 13% of international disputes, parties included companies from China, Russia, Iran, Switzerland, the U.S., and the U.K.

xxii. JAMS International

In 2011, JAMS, a leading domestic mediation and arbitration provider in the United States, combined with the ADR Center in Italy to form JAMS International, headquartered in London. JAMS handles an average of 18,000 arbitration and mediation cases a year throughout the world. JAMS has its most substantial presence in North America, where its panel of "neutrals" is comprised largely of former judges and practicing lawyers. JAMS International is still in the process of compiling its panel of neutrals.

The JAMS International Arbitration Rules, adopted in 2011 and most recently revised in 2021, are similar to most other leading international arbitration rules. They include a liberal consolidation provision and the opportunity for online filing and email communications thereafter. JAMS International's fees are relatively modest when compared with other provider organizations. In 2024, JAMS handled 266 new international cases.

JAMS recommends the following model arbitration clause for international disputes:

> Any dispute, controversy or claim arising out of or relating to this contract, including the formation, interpretation, breach or termination thereof, including whether the claims asserted are arbitrable, will be referred to and finally determined by arbitration in accordance with the JAMS International Arbitration Rules. The tribunal will consist of [three arbitrators][a sole arbitrator]. The seat of the arbitration will be [location]. The language to be used in the arbitral proceedings will be [language]. Judgment upon the award rendered by the arbitrator(s) may be entered by any court having jurisdiction thereof.

A unique feature of JAMS is its "Mediator-in-Reserve Policy for International Arbitrations," which encourages parties to mediate their disputes. JAMS has also adopted "Efficiency Guidelines for the Pre-Hearing Phase of International Arbitrations," which contain guidelines similar to those in the International Bar Association ("IBA") Rules on the Taking of Evidence in International Arbitration, discussed below. (See pp. 116-118.)

xxiii. Japan Commercial Arbitration Association

The Japan Commercial Arbitration Association ("JCAA") and the Japan Shipping Exchange ("JSE") are Japan's only permanent arbitral institutions. The JCAA was founded by the Japan Chamber of Commerce and Industry in 1950, with a particular focus on international commercial disputes.

The JCAA has adopted the JCAA Commercial Arbitration Rules, most recently revised in 2021, which are designed to handle a wide range of international transactions. In 2024, 19 new arbitrations were registered with the JCAA. In general, most of the JCAA's cases have involved at least one non-Japanese party.

The model JCAA arbitration clause provides:

> All disputes, controversies or differences arising out of or in connection with this contract shall be finally settled by arbitration in accordance with the Commercial Arbitration Rules of The Japan Commercial Arbitration Association. The place of the arbitration shall be [city name], [country name].

xxiv. Korean Commercial Arbitration Board

The Korean Commercial Arbitration Board ("KCAB") was founded in 1966 and is authorized to administer arbitrations under the Korean Arbitration Act. The KCAB has two sets of arbitration rules, one for domestic arbitration and the other for international arbitration. The KCAB's International Arbitration Rules were most recently revised in 2016.

Over the past 55 years, the KCAB has administered some 9,000 arbitrations. In 2024, the KCAB administered 352 arbitrations, including 301 domestic arbitrations and 51 international arbitrations.

The model KCAB arbitration clause provides:

> Any disputes out of or in connection with this contract shall be finally settled by arbitration in accordance with the International Arbitration Rules of the Korean Commercial Arbitration Board.
>
> The number of arbitrators shall be [one/three].
>
> The seat, or legal place, of arbitral proceedings shall be [Seoul/Republic of Korea].
>
> The language to be used in the arbitral proceedings shall be [language].

xxv. Mumbai Centre for International Arbitration

The Mumbai Centre for International Arbitration ("MCIA") was established in October 2016 as a joint initiative between the Government of Maharashtra and business and legal communities in India and abroad, with the aim of promoting institutional arbitration in India.

The MCIA focuses on India-related arbitrations and aspires to become India's premier forum for dispute resolution. The MCIA's arbitration rules ("MCIA Rules") came into effect in 2016 and were most recently revised in 2025. The MCIA Rules currently contain features such as an accelerated timeline for low-value or simple disputes; mechanisms catering to multi-party and multi-contract scenarios; and an emergency arbitrator procedure. In 2017, the Supreme Court of India recognized the MCIA as an appointing authority, buttressing the status of the institution. In 2024, the MCIA received 34 new case filings.

xxvi. Netherlands Arbitration Institute

Established in 1949, the Netherlands Arbitration Institute ("NAI") is the leading commercial arbitral institution in the Netherlands. The NAI offers a number of alternative dispute resolution services, including the administration of arbitrations and mediations. The NAI registered 56 new cases in 2024. The total amount in dispute as of December 31, 2024 was EUR 3.4 billion.

The most recent version of the NAI arbitration rules ("NAI Rules") came into effect in December 2024. Noteworthy provisions of the 2024 NAI Rules include (i) the establishment of an NAI Case Management Committee; (ii) additional provisions regarding arbitrators' independence and impartiality; (iii) expedited proceedings for disputes under EUR 1 million; (iv) various amendments to enhance the efficiency of arbitral proceedings, including mandatory midstream conferences; and (v) an NAI Arbitration platform.

The NAI Rules provide for emergency arbitration proceedings, where provisional relief may be granted (with or without a pending arbitration). Under the Netherlands Arbitration Act and the NAI Rules, it is not necessary to commence arbitral proceedings on the merits after initiating emergency arbitration proceedings. Where requests for these proceedings are accepted, the NAI will appoint an arbitrator within one business day, with the median duration of proceedings being 38 days.

If the parties have not agreed on the place of arbitration, the NAI Rules provide that Amsterdam shall be the default place of arbitration.

The NAI recently co-founded sector-specific arbitral institutions for aviation and art disputes (i.e., the Hague Court of Arbitration for Aviation and the Court of Arbitration for Art).

The NAI recommends the following model arbitration clause:

> All disputes arising in connection with the present agreement, or further agreements resulting therefrom, shall be settled in accordance with the Arbitration Rules of the Netherlands Arbitration Institute.

xxvii. Saudi Center for Commercial Arbitration

The Saudi Center for Commercial Arbitration ("SCCA") was established by Saudi Cabinet Decree No. 257 of March 15, 2014 to administer arbitrations, mediations and other alternative dispute resolution proceedings. The SCCA operates in conjunction with the Saudi judicial system and is supported by the Saudi government. Nonetheless, to reflect its independence from the government, the SCCA board is given operational autonomy, and it is composed of non-governmental officers.

The SCCA is the first institutional arbitration center in Saudi Arabia, and it administers cases under the SCCA Arbitration Rules ("SCCA Rules"), which were first published in July 2016 and last revised in May 2023. The SCCA Rules were based on the UNCITRAL Model Rules and were drafted by a working group comprising the SCCA and the International Centre for Dispute Resolution of the American Arbitration Association ("ICDR-AAA").

The revised SCCA Rules provide for the formation of the SCCA Court, which is charged with making key administrative decisions related to SCCA-administered arbitrations. The revisions also expanded the tribunal's powers to determine the most effective format for hearings, reject changes in party representation as a procedural safeguard, encourage parties to resort to mediation where appropriate and limit the length of written statements or requests. Since 2016, the SCCA has reportedly administered a significant number of cases.

The SCCA recommends the following model arbitration clause:

> Any dispute, controversy or claim arising out of or relating to this contract, or the breach, termination or invalidity thereof, shall be settled by arbitration administered by the Saudi Center for Commercial Arbitration (SCCA) in accordance with its Arbitration Rules.

xxviii. Swiss Arbitration Centre ("Swiss Centre")

Switzerland's major cities have historically maintained local Chambers of Commerce and Industry, each of which administered institutional arbitrations, including international arbitrations. In 2004, these Chambers adopted a unified set of arbitration rules, the Swiss Rules of International Arbitration ("Swiss Rules"), and designated an Arbitration Committee to oversee arbitrations conducted under the Swiss Rules by each of the Chambers. A 2012 revision of the Swiss Rules consolidated the administrative structure by replacing the Arbitration Committee oversight with the Swiss Chambers' Arbitration Institution ("SCAI"), an independent association that, like the ICC and SIAC, consists of an Arbitration Court and the Secretariat. In 2021, SCAI was renamed Swiss Arbitration Centre, with the Swiss Arbitration Association ("ASA") being the majority shareholder. This restructuring also included a light touch revision of the Swiss Rules in the same year.

Arbitrations under the Swiss Rules generally benefit from the pro-arbitration Swiss Private International Law Act ("PILA") and from the availability of substantial numbers of practitioners and potential arbitrators with impressive arbitration experience in Switzerland. Between 2004 and 2024, 1,722 cases were submitted to the Swiss Arbitration Centre. In 2024, 100 new cases were filed with the Swiss Arbitration Centre, 82% of which were international, which marked an increase of 4% compared to 2023. Parties to these proceedings came from 37 countries, and cases were administered in English, German, French, Italian, and other languages.

xxix. World Intellectual Property Organization

The World Intellectual Property Organization ("WIPO") Arbitration and Mediation Center was established in Geneva, Switzerland, in 1994. The WIPO Center has an additional office in Singapore and offers the WIPO Arbitration and Mediation Shanghai Service through WIPO's offices in China. WIPO and its Arbitration Rules, most recently revised in 2021, are designed particularly for intellectual property

("IP"), innovation, and technology disputes, although the WIPO Center has administered various types of commercial disputes under the WIPO Rules.

The WIPO Arbitration Rules contain detailed provisions dealing with issues that are of particular importance in IP, innovation, and technology disputes. These include provisions relating to disclosure, protection of trade secrets, confidentiality of arbitral proceedings, and the submission of technical evidence such as experiments, site visits and agreed primers and models.

As of 2023, WIPO has reportedly been involved in the resolution of over 3,700 IP, innovation, and technology disputes. These involved a range of IP, innovation and technology disputes, including IP infringements, IP licensing agreements, digital copyright and online content, software licenses and information technology agreements, distribution agreements, research and development and technology transfer agreements, and joint venture agreements.

c. *Selecting an International Arbitral Institution*

It is unwise to attempt to prescribe a single arbitral institution as the ideal choice for all transactions, disputes, or parties. Nevertheless, some general guidelines can be offered.

First, it is strongly advisable to avoid newly established institutions and institutions without proven track records. The risks that an institution will go out of existence or that it will make a disastrous appointment of an inappropriate or incompetent arbitrator are too great to justify experimenting with fledgling organizations. Likewise, extreme caution should be exercised before accepting arbitral institutions with track records of procedural complaints or lack of transparency (e.g., CIETAC). Events in the past decade, including instances of fraudulent "arbitral institutions," underscore these assessments, making it advisable in most cases for international parties not to resist the "flight to quality" and instead to select an established arbitral institution with a demonstrated track record and strong assurances of independence.

Second, it is prudent in most cases to rely on one of the relatively few leading international arbitral institutions with significant caseloads and experience. These include the ICC, LCIA, AAA/ICDR, SIAC, SCC and VIAC. If there are particular needs, they can also include established regional and national arbitral institutions, with either some or extensive experience in international disputes (such as the DIS, NAI, arbitrateAD, CRCICA, or SCAI). Arbitral institutions with particular international focuses include ICSID, WIPO, PCA and the International Institute for Conflict Prevention and Resolution ("CPR Institute"). As noted above, international parties should exercise caution in selecting CIETAC or HKIAC, including in China-related transactions.

Finally, choosing among these established institutions in particular cases requires considering the nature of the transaction, the identities of the parties, the likely nature of future disputes, and the parties' respective interests. As detailed above, each institution has its own distinct characteristics and predilections. These characteristics may or may not be desirable for a party in the disputes that are likely to arise under a given contract with a particular counterparty. For example, parties to contracts with German counterparties may be reluctant to agree to arbitration under the auspices of DIS (i.e., the German Institution of Arbitration), and parties to transactions with Saudi Arabian counterparties will be reluctant to agree to SCCA-administered arbitrations.

Absent contrary agreements by the parties, the characteristics of an arbitral institution affect matters such as the types of arbitrators the institution is likely to select, the general nature of the procedural rules, the probable arbitral seat, and the cost of the arbitration. These (and other) factors must be considered in light of a party's particular objectives in a given transaction. The effects and interplay of these considerations in individual cases can be subtle and complex. Nonetheless, there are many instances in which a party can gain distinct benefits or avoid distinct disadvantages through a prudent selection of an arbitral institution.

d. Incorporating Institutional Arbitration Rules

When parties have agreed upon an arbitral institution, it is important that their arbitration agreement correctly names that institution and effectively incorporates its rules. Although these points appear obvious, it is surprising how frequently in practice commercial contracts refer to an institution incorrectly, refer to an institution that no longer exists, or refer to an institution in a way that may confuse the selection of an arbitral seat (e.g., "the ICC Chamber in Geneva").

In general, it is wise to rely on the relevant institution's model arbitration clause, departing from it only with care and where necessary to achieve specifically desired results. In particular, care must be taken not to introduce conflicting or confusing language dealing with issues already addressed in institutional rules. Of course, this should not prevent parties from supplementing model clauses by addressing issues such as the arbitral seat, the number of arbitrators, the language of the arbitration, and the choice of applicable substantive law.

It is also important to refer correctly to the relevant institution's arbitration rules, and, in addition, it may be necessary to specify the relevant set of such rules. Most arbitral institutions periodically revise their arbitration rules, and disputes can arise over which set of rules (e.g., 1998 or 2012) applies to a particular dispute. Other arbitral institutions, such as the AAA/ICDR, have promulgated numerous sets of arbitration rules, designed for different types of disputes or industries. Except (arguably) where the relevant institutional rules address the issue, parties should make clear which set of rules they are selecting, and whether the relevant version of the rules is the version in force when their agreement was made or the version in force when their dispute arises.

e. *Modifying Institutional Arbitration Rules*

It is generally possible to modify aspects of an institution's arbitration rules by agreement. For example, parties can generally alter time limits, provide expressly for certain types of discovery (or for no discovery), prohibit the arbitrators from granting certain kinds of relief, and the like. Of course, parties can and should supplement model clauses by including provisions selecting an arbitral seat, designating the number of arbitrators, and specifying the applicable law. In general, it is prudent to seek specialized advice when altering or supplementing recommended model clauses.

Beyond this, however, great care should be exercised in adopting and drafting modifications to institutional rules. Leading institutional arbitration rules are the product of detailed consultation and review by experienced practitioners and institutional administrators, with provisions improved over the course of successive versions. Adopting changes to these provisions can either disrupt existing mechanisms or produce unforeseen results. Moreover, there are elements of institutional rules which may not be subject to modification by the parties' agreement (e.g., the role of the ICC Court of Arbitration); providing for such modifications may lead the institution to refuse to administer the arbitration, invalidate the parties' agreement to arbitrate, or produce other undesirable results. Finally, when drafting an arbitration clause that modifies institutional rules, care should be taken to ensure that the modifications produce a clear and specific change, rather than creating a confusing conflict between additional provisions and the text of the institutional rules themselves.

f. *Arbitral Institution and Seat of Arbitration*

All leading arbitral institutions are prepared to, and routinely do, administer arbitrations seated almost anywhere in the world, and not merely in the place where the institution is located. There is, therefore, no need to select an institution headquartered in the parties' desired arbitral seat (e.g., the LCIA or SIAC can readily administer arbitrations seated in New York, while the AAA can administer arbitrations seated in London or Singapore).

Many institutional rules include default provisions, providing a mechanism for selection of the arbitral seat if the parties' agreement does not specify a seat. As discussed below, however, the selection of an arbitral seat is a vitally important element of any agreement to arbitrate, and arbitration agreements should virtually always address this issue. (See pp. 81-84.)

g. *Ad Hoc Arbitration*

As noted above (See p. 47), ad hoc (or "non-administered") arbitration is not conducted with the support of an arbitral institution. Instead, the parties simply select an arbitrator or arbitrators who resolve the dispute without institutional support. Applicable national arbitration legislation and national courts will generally be available, as a last resort, to remedy procedural missteps in the arbitration (such as failure to agree upon arbitrators). In addition, the parties will sometimes also select a pre-existing set of procedural rules designed to govern ad hoc arbitrations. (such as the UNCITRAL Rules, discussed below at pp. 79-80.) Even in ad hoc arbitration agreements, parties should designate an "appointing authority" that is empowered to select the arbitrator(s), if the parties cannot agree upon their identity, and resolve challenges to them. (See pp. 95-98 below.)

If parties wish to adopt an ad hoc arbitration clause selecting the UNCITRAL Rules, UNCITRAL recommends the following clause:

> Any dispute, controversy, or claim arising out of or relating to this contract, or the breach, termination or invalidity thereof, shall be settled by arbitration in accordance with the UNCITRAL Arbitration Rules as at present in force.
>
> *Note. Parties should consider adding:*
>
> The appointing authority shall be [name of institution or person].
>
> The number of arbitrators shall be [one or three].
>
> The place of arbitration shall be [town and country].
>
> The language to be used in the arbitral proceedings shall be _________.

If, notwithstanding the considerations discussed above, parties desire a "pure" ad hoc clause, the following provision can be considered:

> All disputes, claims, controversies, and disagreements relating to or arising out of this Agreement, or the subject matter of this Agreement, shall be finally resolved by arbitration. The seat of the arbitration shall be _________. The language of the arbitration shall be _________.
>
> The arbitration shall be commenced by a request for arbitration delivered by the claimant to the respondent. The request for arbitration shall set out the parties to the arbitration, the agreement to arbitrate, the applicable law, the general nature of the claim(s), and the relief requested, and shall attach a copy of this Agreement. Within [30] days of receipt of the request for arbitration, the respondent shall deliver to the claimant an answer together with any counterclaim(s), setting out the nature of the counterclaim(s) and the relief requested.
>
> The number of arbitrators shall be three. The arbitrators shall be appointed as follows: (a) the claimant shall appoint an arbitrator in the request for arbitration, and the respondent shall appoint an arbitrator in the answer, and the two

arbitrators so appointed shall, within [30] days of delivery of the answer, appoint a third arbitrator who shall be the presiding arbitrator; (b) if either party fails to appoint an arbitrator within [the foregoing time limits], such arbitrator shall, at the written request of that other party, be appointed by [insert appointing authority]; (c) if the two arbitrators appointed by the parties fail to agree upon the presiding arbitrator within [30] days of the appointment of the second arbitrator, the third arbitrator shall be appointed at the written request of either party by [insert appointing authority]; (d) any challenge to an arbitrator for lack of independence or impartiality, or any other ground, shall be decided by [insert appointing authority]; and (e) if a vacancy arises on the arbitral tribunal, the vacancy shall be filled by the method by which that arbitrator was originally appointed. The presiding arbitrator shall not be of the same nationality as either of the two arbitrators or of the parties. The procedure to be followed during any arbitration under this Article [X] shall be agreed to by the parties or, failing such agreement, by the arbitral tribunal. Default by any party shall not prevent the arbitrators from proceeding to render an award.

The arbitral tribunal may make its decisions by a majority. In the event that no majority is possible, the presiding arbitrator may make the decision(s) as if acting as a sole arbitrator. If an arbitrator appointed by a party fails or refuses to participate, the two other arbitrators may proceed with the arbitration and render an award if they determine that the failure or refusal to participate was unjustified.

Any award(s) made by the arbitral tribunal under this Article [X] shall be final and binding on the parties, and each party waives to the fullest extent permitted by law any right it may otherwise have under the laws of any jurisdiction to any form of appeal, annulment, action to set-aside or vacate, collateral attack, or any other challenge to such award(s).

This provision addresses a number of issues that may arise in relation to the agreement to arbitrate, while not addressing numerous other issues (e.g., arbitrators' powers, provisional measures, separability, currency of awards, confidentiality, and interest). As both the length of the provision and its (inevitable) omissions suggest, it is ordinarily much more efficient and prudent to adopt a set of institutional arbitration rules or, failing that, a set of non-administered rules (such as the UNCITRAL Rules).

h. Choosing Between Ad Hoc and Institutional Arbitration

Notwithstanding the foregoing, ad hoc arbitration is occasionally considered in commercial arbitration agreements instead of institutional arbitration. Ad hoc arbitration may sometimes be less expensive than institutional arbitration, since there are no institutional staff or services to pay for. On the other hand, without an institutional administrator, the arbitrators themselves (or a secretary or registrar appointed by them) will need to perform basic administrative functions, which may entail equal or greater expense. Moreover, capable arbitral institutions take steps to ensure that the arbitrators' fees are kept within limits, which may not always happen in ad hoc arbitrations. Moreover, if judicial intervention is required to support the arbitral process (e.g., by appointing arbitrators), the costs of representation in national court proceedings may be substantial.

Ad hoc arbitration is arguably also somewhat more confidential than institutional arbitration, since it involves no institutional administrative staff. On the other hand, arbitral institutions are subject to confidentiality obligations, and the greatest risks of public disclosure ordinarily come from the parties and from post-award court enforcement proceedings. Ad hoc arbitration may also be slightly more flexible than institutional arbitration (assuming cooperation among the parties), but the differences in this regard are minimal.

Almost all international arbitration practitioners decisively prefer institutional arbitration to ad hoc arbitration. They do so primarily because of the enhanced predictability and regularity that institutional arbitration provides by virtue of professional case administration and the selection of arbitrators, as well as the benefits of incorporating institutional rules (e.g., provisions concerning the formation of the arbitral tribunal and limitations on judicial review). Particularly at the outset of an arbitration, between sometimes inexperienced parties from different legal cultures, an arbitral institution's role in moving proceedings along can be highly constructive and efficient.

For example, if the respondent fails to appoint an arbitrator (where a three-person tribunal is contemplated), an arbitral institution will generally do so under its institutional rules. This avoids the need for applications to national courts for judicial appointment of arbitrators, which virtually always takes more time and money to produce less appropriate results than would a competent arbitral institution. Likewise, the existence of an arbitral institution, whose rules address the question of the arbitrators' fees, avoids the problems that can result from the parties being required to deal directly with arbitrators on such issues.

Further, agreeing to institutional arbitration relieves the parties of the necessity of negotiating and drafting procedural rules for future arbitral proceedings. This can be a costly, slow, and uncertain effort, particularly without expert advice, for an eventuality that often never transpires. Parties who are intent upon an ad hoc arbitration agreement are usually well-advised to adopt a set of non-institutional arbitration rules, such as the UNCITRAL Rules. These are discussed briefly below.

Moreover, institutional arbitration rules include numerous default provisions addressing aspects of the arbitral process that can provide both predictability and sensible procedures. Furthermore, an award rendered under the auspices of a leading arbitral institution may carry greater weight in national court enforcement proceedings than an ad hoc award. U.S., English, and other courts have commented favorably on various arbitral institutions in enforcing their awards.

Finally, in some states (notably China), ad hoc arbitration agreements are unenforceable. Although the refusal to enforce ad hoc agreements to arbitrate violates the New York Convention, challenges to the enforceability of an ad hoc agreement can significantly delay and complicate the arbitral process, again providing good reason to prefer institutional arbitration.

In light of the foregoing, an ad hoc arbitration agreement ordinarily is advisable only where a dispute has already arisen and it is clear that all parties are prepared to proceed cooperatively with an arbitration. Even in these circumstances, and certainly when an ad hoc arbitration clause for future disputes is to be adopted, parties should ensure that an arbitral seat is designated and an appointing authority is specified for the selection of arbitrators. Failure to do so may result in significant delays, expense, and uncertainty, as well as potential invalidity of the arbitration agreement. Finally, parties are in principle free to amend an institutional arbitration clause (e.g., ICC, AAA/ICDR) after a dispute arises to instead provide for purely ad hoc arbitration; where both parties are cooperative and no external administration is necessary, this can of course be considered.

i. Procedural Rules for Ad Hoc Arbitration

There are several available sets of ad hoc or non-institutional arbitration rules that may be adopted for use in non-administered arbitrations. The advantages of adopting pre-existing procedural rules include the benefits of a set of procedural provisions drafted and revised by experts based upon decades of practical experience, and the avoidance of rule-by-rule bargaining over individual procedural points (which may be unsuccessful and is unrealistically expensive).

In international contracts, the most desirable ad hoc procedural rules are generally the UNCITRAL Arbitration Rules. These rules have the advantage of a U.N. imprimatur, having been approved by the U.N. General Assembly. This assists in making them broadly acceptable to parties (including states and state entities) from all geographic regions. There is also a substantial body of reported interpretations of the UNCITRAL Rules (principally by the Iran-U.S. Claims Tribunal, which adopted the Rules with minor modifications). The UNCITRAL Rules, as revised in 2010, 2013 and 2021, are reproduced in Appendix E. The latest revision in 2021 incorporates the UNCITRAL Expedited Arbitration Rules. The model UNCITRAL arbitration clause is set out above. (See pp. 76-78.)

The UNCITRAL Rules set forth a sound procedural basis for most ad hoc international commercial arbitrations, although they leave many details to be decided by the arbitral tribunal. The UNCITRAL Rules permit the parties to agree upon an appointing authority, empowered to select arbitrators in the absence of agreement by the parties. Where the parties have not, in their arbitration agreement or otherwise, designated an appointing authority, the UNCITRAL Rules provide a "fallback" solution—the Secretary-General of the PCA in The Hague. (See p. 60 above and p. 95 below.) The Secretary-General of the PCA will, upon request by a party, choose an appointing authority, which will then select the arbitrator(s). The PCA may select as appointing authority either an established arbitral institution (such as the ICC, SCC, AAA/ICDR, or LCIA) or an experienced arbitration practitioner.

Under the UNCITRAL Rules, the respondent must submit a "Response" to the Notice of Arbitration at the outset of the arbitral proceedings, and the tribunal must establish a provisional timetable shortly thereafter. The UNCITRAL Rules also allow for the joinder of parties and provide that the tribunal's power to order interim measures includes the authority to grant injunctions and order the preservation of evidence. In a departure from the approach of many other leading arbitration rules, the UNCITRAL Rules give the parties the option to waive any recourse against an arbitral award (while other rules, such as the ICC and LCIA Rules, include an automatic waiver).

The 2021 revision of the UNCITRAL Rules introduced a procedure for expedited arbitrations (paralleling similar provisions in many leading institutional arbitration rules). This procedure is only applicable where parties have agreed to its application and should ordinarily be used only for smaller-value disputes.

Although less well-known than the UNCITRAL Rules, the CPR Institute has published procedural rules for "non-administered" international arbitrations. The CPR Non-Administered Rules (most recently revised in 2018) have the potential to provide the basis for efficient, fair arbitrations, but have not been widely used.

4. Specifying the Seat or Place of Arbitration

A critically important element of any international arbitration agreement is the designation of the arbitral seat (or place of the arbitration). The arbitral seat is the place where the arbitral award will formally be made, and the jurisdiction whose laws will ordinarily govern the arbitral proceedings and actions to annul or set aside the arbitral award; likewise, the courts of the arbitral seat will have supervisory jurisdiction over the arbitration. The arbitral seat is also usually the geographical location where many or all of the hearings in the arbitration will be conducted, although the tribunal also typically has the authority to hold hearings elsewhere for reasons of convenience.

As discussed below, there are a number of legal and practical consequences that follow from the selection of an arbitral seat, making this one of the most important aspects of any international arbitration agreement. This contrasts with domestic arbitration in many countries, where the selection of an arbitral situs at a particular place within the country is much less important. Additionally, failure to specify the arbitral seat may result in a so-called "blank clause," whose validity or enforceability may be subject to challenge in some jurisdictions.

a. Importance of Arbitral Seat

There are a variety of reasons why it is critical in international arbitration both to specify a good arbitral seat and to avoid specifying a bad one. On a mundane level, the convenience of an arbitral seat can have material consequences for an arbitral proceeding. Travel time, flight connections, availability of meeting rooms, local support facilities (stenographers, interpreters, etc.), accommodations, and other amenities can have important practical effects on the conduct of an arbitration. Some jurisdictions have lengthy visa or work permit application procedures, or do not permit lawyers unlicensed at the place of arbitration to represent parties in arbitrations seated within the jurisdiction.

More importantly, as discussed below, the identity of the arbitral seat has significant legal effects. This is because a number of issues relating to judicial supervision of an arbitration will be subject to the law and courts of the arbitral seat, often regardless of the parties' choice of applicable substantive law. Recent international developments, including increasing risks of governmental or other influence on national court proceedings in some jurisdictions, underscore the importance of selecting an appropriate arbitral seat.

As discussed in detail below (See pp. 182-84), parties are ordinarily free to agree upon the substantive law that governs the merits of their dispute, as well as many issues relating to the procedural conduct of the arbitration itself. However, local law in many jurisdictions may not permit parties to contract out of various fundamental questions concerning judicial supervision of the arbitral process. These include:

- In most cases, whether an arbitral award is subject to the New York Convention's pro-arbitration enforcement regime depends on the award having been made in a state that is a party to the New York Convention. As a consequence, it is almost always critical to select such a nation as an arbitral seat. With some 172 Contracting States to the New York Convention, this is not ordinarily an issue.
- In most cases, the national courts that will hear actions to annul an arbitral award will be those of the arbitral seat (and not courts of other countries). That is, courts in England would ordinarily have jurisdiction over actions to annul awards made in London, and courts in the United States and France would not. Because of differing standards under national law for the annulment of arbitral awards, this can have very significant consequences. For example, absent contrary agreement, English courts will subject the arbitrators' decision to a measure of substantive review, while courts in Switzerland, France, and UNCITRAL Model Law jurisdictions will not. Similarly, there are some nations where the parties can exclude any local judicial review in certain international arbitrations (e.g., in Belgium, Switzerland, and Sweden), while other states permit limiting judicial review. (See pp. 130-31 below.)
- National courts in the arbitral seat will also potentially have the authority to appoint and remove arbitrators, resolve jurisdictional challenges to a tribunal's authority, grant provisional measures in aid of arbitration, and assist in the taking of evidence. It is critically important to select an arbitral seat whose courts are able to perform these functions well. In some cases, local courts may interfere in international arbitrations seated within their territory. Among other things, local courts may stay or enjoin arbitral proceedings, remove arbitrators, order or forbid discovery, limit a party's choice of

counsel, or require that some or all of the parties' disputes be resolved in national courts. Nations with interventionist or unreliable local courts should always be avoided as arbitral seats. Unfortunately, many countries outside a relatively limited group of major trading states must currently be considered as falling into this category of potentially interventionist or unreliable arbitral seats.
- In many cases, the question whether or not a particular claim is "arbitrable" will be determined by the laws of the arbitral seat. Agreements between the parties on this issue are generally of limited consequence in affecting local public policies or mandatory legal rules.

In addition to these issues, where local law may dictate certain results, there are other issues on which the arbitral seat has less direct consequences. These issues can nonetheless have considerable practical importance in particular cases. For example:

- The place of arbitration will influence the choice of arbitrators (including by many arbitral institutions), the procedural rules likely to be applied by the tribunal, and similar aspects of the arbitral process. The effects and interplay of these influences can be subtle, complex, and important. For example, if a U.S. and a Singaporean party agree to arbitrate in England, this substantially increases the likelihood that the presiding arbitrator will be English, rather than Swiss or Swedish. But, if one party selects an English co-arbitrator, and the other does not, this choice may well further affect the chairman's identity, by making appointment of an English chairman less likely (at least if the counterparty does not also select an English co-arbitrator). That is because many arbitral institutions will be reluctant to appoint a chairman of the same nationality as only one of the two co-arbitrators.
- The arbitral seat may affect or decide the law applicable to the validity and interpretation of the parties' arbitration agreement, at least where the parties have not agreed upon an applicable law. (See New York Convention, Articles II(3), V(1)(a)) The place of arbitration may also affect the law governing questions of non-arbitrability.
- The place of arbitration may affect the procedural rules adopted by the arbitrators (e.g., with respect to disclosure or cross-examination), at least in the absence of agreement between the parties. Most developed nations have rejected the view that arbitrators sitting there must apply local judicial procedural rules. There continues, however, to be a tendency, particularly among less experienced international arbitrators, to look to local judicial procedures as their starting point in determining arbitral procedures. For this reason, parties will sometimes include detailed procedural regimes in their arbitration agreements (See p. 118 below), but such efforts are both expensive and likely to leave gaps.
- The location of the arbitral seat may influence, in the absence of an express or implied choice of law by the parties, either the substantive or choice-of-law rules applied by the arbitrators. Historically, some authorities regarded

the selection of the arbitral seat as an implied choice of substantive law, or, at a minimum, an implied acceptance of the arbitral seat's conflict of laws rules. This view is sometimes rejected by modern authorities, but it may nonetheless be influential in particular cases.

As the foregoing suggests, it is highly desirable to specify the seat of the arbitration in any international arbitration agreement. If agreement cannot be reached between the parties, then most leading institutional rules provide for selection of a seat by the relevant administering institution or the arbitral tribunal. However, since the seat will not be known until after an arbitral proceeding has commenced, this produces uncertainty and may prompt actions in national courts that seek to override or preempt the institution's or tribunal's selection of a seat, or to challenge the validity of the arbitration clause.

Deciding what arbitral seat to specify in the parties' arbitration agreement involves a mixture of negotiating and technical issues. Both parties will generally be reluctant to agree to arbitration in their counterparty's domicile or principal place of business. For example, non-French companies would often be reluctant to agree to arbitrate with Total in France, while non-Korean companies would be reluctant to arbitrate against Samsung in Korea. This reluctance is sometimes exaggerated, since there is a material difference between an international arbitral tribunal having its seat in a particular jurisdiction and a local court (or jury) doing so. Nonetheless, the possibilities of judicial review of an award and other less tangible home-court advantages often rule out either party's principal place of business or domicile as an arbitral seat. Parties will, therefore, often seek to agree upon a suitable neutral arbitral seat.

b. Deciding What Arbitral Seat to Specify

In deciding what arbitral seat to specify in a particular transaction, several factors are important.

First, the seat must be a state that has acceded to the New York Convention (or, exceptionally, another comparable international instrument). This ensures that the parties' arbitration agreement and any resulting award will be maximally enforceable. With some 172 countries having ratified the New York Convention, there is no justification for ignoring this requirement. A list of the parties to the New York Convention is contained in Appendix A.

Second, and at least as important, the arbitral seat must have both national arbitration legislation and national courts that are hospitable to and supportive of international arbitration. Specifically, local arbitration law must provide unequivocally: (i) for the enforceability of arbitration agreements; (ii) for the parties to be able freely to choose their legal representatives and party-nominated arbitrators (e.g., not being limited to locally qualified lawyers); (iii) for minimal non-arbitrability exceptions; (iv) for minimal judicial review of the substance of arbitral awards; (v) for minimal judicial intervention in ongoing arbitrations (e.g., by considering interlocutory appeals from procedural orders by tribunals); and (vi) for a supportive approach by local courts to requests by arbitrators for judicial assistance in aid of the arbitration. More generally, local courts must not be susceptible to corruption or other biases and should be experienced in complex commercial matters, independent, and objective; regrettably, these qualities can be surprisingly difficult to find in many instances.

In general, states that clearly qualify under the foregoing standards include England (at least for institutional arbitration), Switzerland, France, Sweden, the United States, the Netherlands, Germany, Canada, Australia, and Singapore. Other states, including those which have adopted the UNCITRAL Model Law, may also be considered as arbitral seats, but caution should be exercised in doing so. A list of states that have adopted the UNCITRAL Model Law and its revisions is included in Appendix C.

It is critical, however, to distinguish between formal legislation and actual practice in real cases. That practice can only be demonstrated over time, and many states with theoretically satisfactory legislation have not yet accomplished this. Protectionist or partisan decisions in some jurisdictions during the past decade, including interference in pending arbitral proceedings, underscore the importance of selecting an arbitral seat with a demonstrated history of competence and judicial independence.

Third, as noted above (See pp. 81-84), the selection of an arbitral seat will often have a material influence upon the selection of the parties' arbitrators and the arbitral procedures. If an arbitration is seated in Switzerland, for example, it is likely that one or both parties will consider selecting a Swiss party-nominated arbitrator for reasons of convenience and familiarity with local arbitration law. Whether or not this is the case, the presiding arbitrator will often be selected based at least in part on the place of the arbitration.

Thus, choosing the arbitral seat often has an important effect on the nationality and legal training of the arbitrators (absent direct agreement between the parties). In turn, the nationality and legal training of the arbitrators will often influence their procedural and substantive approach to the arbitration. For example, the approach of civil law lawyers can be expected to reflect their training, thus making an inquisitorial approach, with less extensive disclosure (i.e., discovery) than in common law practice, more likely. Likewise, a U.S. or English trial lawyer's background will influence his or her perspectives on procedural questions.

Fourth, in some countries, the local law of the arbitral seat may have a material influence on the substantive or procedural issues. For example, local law may impose particular choice-of-law or statute of limitations provisions on arbitrators.

All of these factors should be taken into account in selecting an arbitral seat. Parties should take care to select a seat that ensures a reasonably predictable and efficient arbitration (e.g., England, Switzerland, France, Sweden, the United States, the Netherlands, Germany, Canada, Australia, New Zealand, or Singapore). In addition, where possible, a party should consider whether a particular seat offers systemic advantages to it (or its counterparty) in the kinds of disputes expected to arise under their agreement. For example, if broad, party-initiated discovery is desired but cannot be obtained directly through negotiations, the arbitration can be seated in the United States or England. If discovery is to be avoided, the arbitral seat might be in Switzerland or another civil law jurisdiction.

The ICC publishes annual statistics recording the seats in ICC arbitrations commenced the previous year. The table and graph below show, for selected countries, the seats in ICC arbitrations between 1995 and 2023, in cases where the parties selected the place of arbitration. These figures are weighted towards European seats, given the historic European orientation of the ICC and its users, with France and Switzerland accounting for nearly half the total among the top 15 seats.

Selection of Arbitral Seats by Parties in ICC Arbitrations (1995–2024)

	'95	'96	'97	'98	'99	'00	'01	'02	'03	'04	'05	'06	'07	'08	'09	'10	'11	'12	'13	'14	'15	'16	'17	'18	'19	'20	'21	'22	'23	'24	Total
France	80	81	90	51	89	56	103	72	97	75	69	81	86	73	94	109	92	80	93	84	78	76	111	121	97	80	81	71	90	79	2539
Switzerland	88	63	67	58	74	72	73	99	69	67	89	82	82	77	109	79	88	115	88	77	55	82	88	72	76	98	70	60	76	77	2370
U.K.	22	28	37	46	46	48	52	48	43	62	47	37	53	56	67	66	59	68	63	80	53	63	68	67	102	80	87	69	78	89	1784
U.S.A.	17	33	35	18	35	37	35	40	46	34	37	28	36	29	31	42	43	33	35	53	52	72	50	70	46	73	64	46	59	70	1299
Singapore	5	2	10	10	11	11	13	14	14	10	14	11	15	30	34	23	22	31	32	23	35	22	38	26	30	24	34	25	26	25	620
Germany	14	15	7	19	16	21	20	15	17	14	15	18	21	35	37	24	39	18	20	24	20	28	22	19	19	14	19	15	31	19	615
Brazil	0	1	0	0	1	1	1	0	4	10	1	12	14	8	11	11	14	14	22	20	19	22	28	27	24	29	31	32	34	30	421
Austria	14	11	12	7	10	11	8	10	7	10	5	2	13	14	22	11	11	13	10	19	15	11	11	11	5	11	23	13	17	14	351
Spain	1	2	3	2	4	3	3	6	8	7	17	7	10	13	11	8	15	7	8	18	15	15	13	13	16	11	15	19	18	32	320
Mexico	5	3	1	3	4	3	8	5	6	10	10	9	8	9	6	12	10	11	8	11	12	8	17	17	13	18	22	20	19	30	318
UAE	n/a	n/a	1	0	0	0	0	n/a	1	0	1	1	1	9	7	8	7	8	11	10	14	10	9	17	18	20	18	19	22	35	247
China/H.K.	3	5	6	6	3	5	3	6	4	6	5	9	5	11	8	11	5	10	14	16	10	8	15	10	13	16	3	7	5	8	236
Netherlands	4	0	4	3	6	4	10	12	9	6	5	10	9	8	6	5	5	4	4	5	4	14	8	12	4	19	6	3	8	4	201
Sweden	8	8	9	8	8	6	3	6	6	7	8	4	5	10	6	6	5	5	15	5	7	4	4	2	6	8	8	7	11	2	197
Italy	7	7	3	5	2	11	4	5	12	11	3	8	5	8	6	6	6	3	6	6	7	5	2	12	3	10	5	6	11	15	200
TOTAL	268	259	285	236	309	289	336	338	343	329	326	319	363	390	455	421	421	420	429	451	396	440	484	496	472	511	486	412	505	529	11718

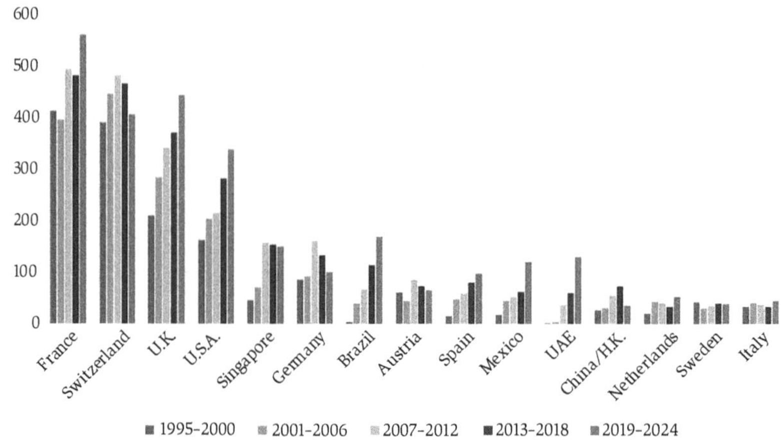

The highest-ranking choices (i.e., France, Switzerland, the United Kingdom, the United States, Germany, and Singapore) are often regarded as the most desirable and secure arbitral seats. Similarly, a 2018 Queen Mary University of London international arbitration survey reported that the most preferred seats were London, Paris, Singapore, Hong Kong, and Geneva. Agreements to arbitrate in these jurisdictions are generally subject to reasonably effective and reliable enforcement regimes, with substantial numbers of qualified local practitioners available to serve as arbitrators where this is desired.

c. *Potentially Problematic Arbitral Seats*

Parties are sometimes unable to agree to arbitration in an established and reliable arbitral seat. In particular, companies doing business in some emerging economies, including Brazil, Russia, India, China, Indonesia, the Philippines and parts of the Middle East and Africa, are sometimes confronted with requests to accept arbitral seats in jurisdictions that are ordinarily disfavored. International arbitration is in a state of early development in many developing countries, and it is almost always advisable for most parties to refuse such requests, often including when this means declining an otherwise attractive transaction. Nonetheless, there may be exceptional cases where a party is prepared to accept the (significant) risks of arbitrating in a potentially unfavorable jurisdiction in order to close a transaction.

i. Brazil

Although Brazil was historically hostile to international arbitration, there were indications that it was becoming a more arbitration-friendly jurisdiction, which is reflected in its ranking (5th) as the most popular seat of ICC arbitration between 2020 and 2023. Thus, Brazil has been more frequently selected by international businesses in recent years, in part because of perceptions about continuing reforms of its legal system. Among other things, Brazil ratified the Panama Convention in 1995 and adopted arbitration legislation based on the UNCITRAL Model Law in 1996 (which was recently amended in 2015), and ratified the New York Convention in 2002.

Nonetheless, there are still a number of significant risks associated with arbitrating in Brazil, particularly in cases involving local counterparties. Lower courts sometimes issue decisions, including with regard to international arbitration agreements and awards, which are unpredictable and difficult to reconcile with applicable legal rules. More general political uncertainties, serious doubts regarding judicial independence, and the lack of bilateral investment treaties protections underscore these risks. In general, sophisticated non-Brazilian parties resist seating international arbitrations, particularly against Brazilian counterparties, in Brazil. Brazilian companies, understandably, often have a different view, although even there, some sophisticated local parties have reservations about Brazil as an arbitral seat.

Non-Brazilian parties that do agree to Brazil as an arbitral seat often choose to use the rules of a leading international arbitral institution (e.g., ICC, SIAC, AAA/ICDR, LCIA) or ad hoc arbitration under the UNCITRAL Rules, rather than the rules of a Brazilian arbitral institution. There are several Brazilian arbitral institutions (e.g., CAM-CCBC (which updated its rules in 2022 to reflect best international practices) and the Brazilian Business Chamber of Commerce ("CAMARB")), but very few have significant experience with international arbitration and some have problematic arbitration rules (such as requirements that arbitrators be Brazilian nationals and that proceedings be in Portuguese).

ii. Russia

Russia is a party to the New York Convention, and the 1993 Russian Law on International Commercial Arbitration is based on the 1985 UNCITRAL Model Law. Moreover, some pro-arbitration decisions were issued by Russian appellate courts following adoption of the Model Law, including decisions refusing to review arbitral decisions on the merits and enforcing international arbitration agreements.

Nonetheless, Russia is at best a highly problematic choice as an arbitral seat for most foreign and international parties, albeit less so for Russian parties. Only four ICC arbitrations were seated in Russia between 2013 and 2019, reflecting continuing (and, given events since 2014, increasing) skepticism about legislative and judicial regimes for international arbitration.

Events over the past decade raise obvious, and very serious, questions regarding the objectivity and independence of Russian courts. In addition, three legislative developments in Russia are significant for international arbitration. First, in 2014, the Supreme Arbitrazh Court (which heard commercial cases, including cases relating to arbitral awards) and the Supreme Court (which heard civil, administrative and criminal cases) merged to become a unified Supreme Court. Since then, former Supreme Court judges (composing the majority of the new court and who generally have less commercial expertise) hearing arbitration-related cases have rendered thinly reasoned, less consistent decisions than the judges of the former Supreme Arbitrazh Court, causing concern among many Russian practitioners.

Second, in late 2015, new Russian arbitration legislation, replacing existing domestic arbitration law and amending international commercial arbitration law, was enacted. Under the new law, in force from September 2016, parties to international arbitration agreements selecting Russia as the seat of arbitration may, by express agreement, waive the right to set aside an award. Less desirably, the Russian legislation provides that so-called "corporate disputes" are arbitrable, but only in arbitrations administered by an arbitral institution approved by, and registered with, the Russian government.

Third, in June 2020, Russian legislative amendments granted Russian courts exclusive jurisdiction over all disputes involving Russian individuals and entities subject to foreign or international sanctions. The legislation applies notwithstanding the terms of either contractual arbitration agreements or international arbitration conventions or treaties.

Over the past decade, most foreign and international businesses have had very significant, and increasing, reservations about the experience, competence and reliability of Russian courts and similar concerns about Russia's legislative framework for arbitration. Virtually all foreign parties have therefore refused to accept Russia as an arbitral seat, even where this means walking away from an otherwise attractive transaction. Recent events underscore these concerns: as a consequence, in virtually no cases should foreign or international parties agree to a Russian arbitral seat.

The most well-established Russian arbitral institution is the International Commercial Arbitration Court at the Russian Federation Chamber of Commerce and Industry ("ICAC"), which is specifically endorsed by Russian arbitration legislation. ICAC's procedural rules and practices differ significantly, however, from those under most leading institutional arbitration rules. Moreover, the default language of ICAC arbitrations is Russian, the place of the arbitration is Moscow, and, unless the parties agree otherwise, ICAC appoints the presiding arbitrator from a list of approved arbitrators (largely Russian practitioners).

In 2013, a new arbitral institution, the Russian Arbitration Association (the "RAA"), was established by a number of leading Russian law firms and practitioners to bring arbitration in Russia more in line with international standards. The RAA administers arbitrations under the UNCITRAL Rules (instead of developing its own set of rules), maintains a database of arbitrators with extensive international arbitration experience, and offers online arbitration for small claims of up to USD 50,000.

iii. India

India was historically disfavored as an arbitral seat, owing to a tradition of interventionist judicial supervision and inefficient local courts. Although India ratified the

New York Convention in 1960, and the 1996 Indian Arbitration and Conciliation Act is based on the UNCITRAL Model Law, the enforcement of international arbitration agreements and arbitral awards in India has historically been unpredictable and difficult.

There have nonetheless been some positive developments with respect to arbitrating in India in recent years. The Indian Supreme Court and Indian appellate courts have issued a number of pro-arbitration decisions (although there are also inconsistent judgments), while efforts to reform procedures in lower courts are continuing. In line with this, the 2015 amendments to the Arbitration and Conciliation Act granted the Indian High Court exclusive supervisory jurisdiction over international commercial arbitrations, restricted judicial review of arbitral awards, and imposed time limits for applications under various provisions.

Although perceptions of the international arbitration regime in India have been materially improving, many international businesses remain skeptical about the risks of interference by lower courts in India-seated arbitrations and about the delays and unpredictability of Indian litigation. Indeed, many sophisticated Indian commercial parties prefer to arbitrate outside, rather than within, India.

When foreign parties are faced with no choice other than to agree to arbitrate in India, they tend to avoid local institutions in favor of arbitration under the rules of the ICC, SIAC, LCIA, or another international institution. India's best-known arbitral institution, the ICA, lacks extensive experience with international arbitration and, until amendments to the ICA Rules in 2016, arbitrators could only be chosen from its Panel of Arbitrators (which is composed largely of retired Indian judges and senior counsel).

A viable alternative to ICA is the MCIA. The MCIA Council is composed of approximately 20 prominent international and domestic arbitration practitioners, and the MCIA Rules are drafted in line with international best practices and the rules of leading international institutions.

iv. China

Other than Hong Kong (discussed separately below), China has also been disfavored as an arbitral seat by international businesses. China has taken steps over the past 15 years to reform its arbitration legislation, while CIETAC has also revised its institutional rules and practices. Nonetheless, foreign parties to arbitrations seated in China face a number of significant risks and uncertainties, including concerns regarding the independence of local courts and doubts about the enforceability of ad hoc arbitration agreements and agreements to arbitrate outside China in "domestic" contracts; similar concerns exist with regard to Chinese courts' exercise of authority to annul awards made in China-seated arbitrations, particularly in matters involving local and state-related parties. Continuing doubts about the transparency of CIETAC arbitrations and internal disputes between CIETAC Beijing and CIETAC Shenzhen, and CIETAC Shanghai have raised further concerns about arbitration under CIETAC Rules.

For the time being, these considerations counsel decisively against almost any foreign business agreeing to China as an arbitral seat or to arbitration under CIETAC Rules save in very unusual circumstances. If unusual circumstances do require arbitration in China, the least undesirable choice is currently to agree to HKIAC arbitration. In general, however, foreign and international parties should not agree to arbitrations seated in China, including where necessary to proceed with an otherwise attractive transaction.

Hong Kong was historically an acceptable arbitral seat in Asia. This was primarily due to HKIAC's past record of independence and competence, Hong Kong's UNCITRAL-based international arbitration law, an impartial and experienced judiciary, and the availability of well-trained common law lawyers. Among other things, Hong Kong also promulgated a revised Arbitration Ordinance in 2011, including amendments in 2013 which incorporate the 2006 revisions to the UNCITRAL Model Law.

The revised legislation permits arbitral tribunals to order interim measures and provides for the confidentiality of proceedings. Arbitral awards made in Hong Kong are enforceable in mainland China (and vice versa) pursuant to a 1999 Memorandum of Understanding. An Interim Measures Arrangement introduced in 2019 also enables parties to preserve assets and evidence in Hong Kong and/or mainland China in support of arbitration proceedings.

Since 1997, however, Hong Kong and HKIAC have been viewed with concern by many international businesses engaging in transactions with Chinese parties, particularly Chinese state-owned parties. Those concerns have been materially heightened by developments in recent years, as well as by the likely consequences for Hong Kong of the scheduled 2047 loss of all residual autonomy. Even with respect to cases that do not involve Chinese parties, Hong Kong and HKIAC have fallen significantly behind Singapore and SIAC as the premier seat and institution for international arbitration in Asia over the past decade; that trend appears likely to continue. Hong Kong should ordinarily be accepted by international parties as an arbitral seat in significant transactions with Chinese or Hong Kong parties only with caution and for compelling commercial reasons.

If an agreement cannot be reached on Hong Kong as a seat and mainland China is the only option, the available (but unattractive) choices are either arbitration under a foreign arbitral institution's rules or CIETAC arbitration. There have been a number of instances of HKIAC and ICC arbitrations seated in mainland China and awards rendered in such cases have been enforced by lower Chinese courts in several cases; nonetheless, the enforceability of non-CIETAC awards made in mainland China has not yet been clearly addressed by the Chinese courts and it remains a risk to agree to use a non-Chinese arbitral institution for an arbitration conducted in China. On the other hand, CIETAC arbitrations involve significant uncertainties and risks, leaving very few acceptable choices for foreign parties.

d. *Drafting Provisions Specifying an Arbitral Seat*

Once an arbitral seat has been selected, drafting a clause which properly specifies that seat is ordinarily not difficult. The following provisions are representative:

> The seat of the arbitration shall be [city/nation].

Alternatively, with essentially identical effect:

> The place of the arbitration shall be [city/nation].
>
> It is advisable to avoid formulations that provide: "The arbitrators shall conduct the arbitration hearings in ________" or "the arbitral proceeding will be located in ________."

These provisions do not expressly address the question of the arbitration's legal seat, and they constrain the tribunal's power to conduct hearings elsewhere, for reasons of convenience (e.g., a site inspection).

References to the arbitral seat should identify both a city and a nation. In some jurisdictions, reference to a nation, but not a specific city, may raise issues of enforceability.

Under most national laws and institutional rules, hearings may be conducted in places other than the arbitral seat for reasons of convenience; doing so does not ordinarily affect the location of the legal or juridical seat of the arbitration. For example, hearings might be held outside the arbitral seat in order to conduct site inspections, hear witnesses, accommodate travel schedules, reduce costs, or avoid unexpected events in the arbitral seat. Although this authority almost always exists without specific language in the arbitration agreement, some clauses specifying the arbitral seat go further and provide:

> The seat of the arbitration shall be ________. The arbitrators may hold hearings or meetings in any other locations for convenience.

This provision does not affect the juridical seat of the arbitration, and thus should not alter the various legal effects of selecting a seat, as discussed above. (See pp. 81-85.)

e. *Location of Arbitral Seat Based on Identity of Claimant*

As with forum selection clauses, arbitration agreements can make the location of the arbitral seat dependent upon the identity of the party that commences the arbitration. The rationale for such provisions is that they discourage recourse to formal dispute resolution and encourage negotiated settlements. A representative clause providing for this result is as follows:

> The seat of the arbitration shall be [identify Party B's principal place of business (e.g., Singapore)], if the arbitration is commenced by [Party A], and the place of arbitration shall be [identify Party A's principal place of business (e.g., Rome, Italy)] if the arbitration is commenced by [Party B].

Alternatively:

> Unless otherwise agreed in writing by the parties, the seat of the arbitration shall be either (a) in the case of claims initiated by Licensor, in the city with a population of 500,000 or more which is located nearest Licensee's main office, or (b) in the case of claims initiated by Licensee, in _________.

Ordinarily, the uncertainties and risks of procedural gamesmanship resulting from such provisions counsel decisively against adopting them.

5. Number, Method of Selection, and Qualifications of Arbitrators

It is also critical that the parties' arbitration agreement addresses the number, means of appointment, and qualifications of the arbitrators. Selection of the arbitrators is one of the most critical issues in any arbitration.

a. Specifically Named Arbitrators

The parties can agree in their arbitration agreement on the identity of individual arbitrators. The language accomplishing this is straightforward:

> The [arbitrator] [sole arbitrator] shall be Ms. Mila Born ...

Except in the case of submission agreements (covering existing disputes), it is generally not desirable to designate a specific individual as arbitrator in advance. That is because a named individual may acquire a conflict of interest or may turn out to be unsuitable for the disputes that ultimately arise.

If an individual is to be named in advance, it is critical for the parties to confirm formally before concluding the arbitration agreement that he or she is willing and able to serve. In addition, the arbitration clause should address the possibility that the named arbitrator will become unavailable, either by reason of conflicts, illness, or otherwise. This usually entails specifying a fallback appointing authority.

b. Number of Arbitrators

Arbitration clauses often specify the number of persons who will comprise an arbitral tribunal in the event of future disputes—typically either one or three arbitrators. For example, a typical clause would provide:

> Any dispute, claim, or controversy relating to, arising out of, or in connection with this agreement shall be finally resolved under the [Rules of Arbitration of the International Chamber of Commerce] by [three arbitrators] appointed in accordance with the said Rules.

Alternatively:

> Any dispute, claim, or controversy relating to, arising out of, or in connection with this agreement shall be finally resolved under the [Arbitration Rules of the Singapore International Arbitration Centre] by [a sole arbitrator] appointed in accordance with the said Rules.

If the parties do not agree upon the number of arbitrators, leading institutional arbitration rules generally grant the institution power to decide on it; otherwise, national courts will have the power to do so. Obtaining an institutional or judicial decision on the number of arbitrators can require time or give rise to jurisdictional disputes. As a consequence, it is virtually always best to specify the number of arbitrators in the parties' arbitration clause.

It is of course important to select an odd number of arbitrators. This is necessary to avoid deadlocks on the tribunal, and also to comply with mandatory requirements in some countries. As noted above, the two most frequently used numbers of arbitrators in international commercial arbitration are one and three; five-person tribunals are sometimes selected (ordinarily in state-to-state arbitrations), but the added cost and inconvenience are hardly ever justified. The general practice in international commercial arbitrations is to select three arbitrators, except where the amounts in dispute are too small to justify the cost.

In deciding how many arbitrators to select, the parties should consider cost, speed, expertise, consistency, and ease of communication. With respect to expense, three arbitrators cost roughly three times as much as a single arbitrator; there are some ministerial tasks which need to be performed only once, even with three arbitrators, but many efforts are tripled in a three-person tribunal. With respect to speed, there are inevitably greater difficulties in scheduling hearings with three arbitrators, where multiple busy calendars must be coordinated (sometimes to accommodate hearings of several weeks or more).

With respect to expertise and consistency, three arbitrators will have more skills, more varied backgrounds, and other resources than a sole arbitrator. Moreover, collegial interchange among the members of a tribunal materially reduces the likelihood of a fundamentally mistaken approach to a case. Finally, many parties draw substantial comfort from the right to appoint one of the tribunal's members, as a means of ensuring that their arguments will be fully considered in the tribunal's deliberations. This is particularly true in international disputes, where parties from different legal cultures may have dramatically differing procedural expectations.

When an experienced, competent arbitral institution is selected as an appointing authority, the parties' arbitration agreement can leave the number of arbitrators to the discretion of the institution. The ICC model arbitration clause adopts this approach:

> All disputes arising out of or in connection with the present contract shall be finally settled under the Rules of Arbitration of the International Chamber of Commerce by one or more arbitrators appointed in accordance with the said Rules.

This approach has the advantage of permitting the number of arbitrators to be tailored to particular disputes which are submitted to arbitration: smaller disputes can be resolved by a sole arbitrator, while larger ones can be heard by a three-person tribunal. This approach is only prudent, however, where an experienced and diligent appointing authority is used. In other cases, potential delays and uncertainties resulting from inexperienced selections or applications to national courts argue strongly in favor of specifying the number of arbitrators in the parties' arbitration agreement. It should also be noted that some institutional rules specify default choices regarding the number of arbitrators, with approaches varying under different institutional rules (e.g., one or three arbitrators).

c. *Methods of Selecting Arbitrators*

It is critical for an arbitration agreement to include some method for selecting the arbitrator(s) if the parties cannot agree upon their identities. The most common mechanism is the designation of an "appointing authority," which will select a sole arbitrator or presiding arbitrator in the event that the parties (or party-nominated arbitrators) cannot do so and which will select a co-arbitrator if a party fails or refuses to do so.

Parties typically select an appointing authority by incorporating a set of institutional arbitration rules in their agreement. All leading institutional rules provide for such a role by the administering institution when the parties agree to arbitrate under the institution's rules. (See 2021 ICC Rules, Articles 11–13; 2025 SIAC Rules, Rules 19–24; 2021 ICDR Rules, Article 13.) Where an arbitration agreement incorporates one of these sets of institutional rules, no additional provisions regarding the means of selecting the arbitrator(s) are ordinarily necessary.

In addition to appointing sole or presiding arbitrators, an institution will also appoint an arbitrator on behalf of a party which fails to exercise its right under the parties' arbitration agreement to do so. (See 2021 ICC Rules, Article 12; 2025 SIAC Rules, Rules 19–24; 2021 ICDR Rules, Article 13; 2020 LCIA Rules, Article 5(7).)

One significant consideration in selecting an arbitral institution is its means of, and track record in, appointing arbitrators. For example, when selecting a sole or presiding arbitrator, the ICC typically looks to the recommendation of a neutral "National Committee" that the ICC Court selects (often, but not always, the National Committee of the arbitral seat). It is relevant to consider, therefore, how that National Committee has fulfilled its functions in past cases. (The ICC Rules also grant the ICC Court power to directly appoint an arbitrator "that it considers to be appropriate" in circumstances where it disagrees with the proposal of the relevant

National Committee, or where the relevant National Committee has failed to make a proposal within the timeframe specified by the ICC Court.)

More generally, the ICC historically had a reputation (which it has partially shed) for appointing Continental European arbitrators. Conversely, the LCIA has had a reputation (which it continues to work to dispel) for favoring appointment of members of the English bar, or retired English judges, while the AAA historically was regarded as looking to U.S. practitioners and retired U.S. judges.

In arbitrations under the UNCITRAL Rules, parties may agree upon an appointing authority, with the Rules specifying the Secretary-General of the PCA as a "fallback" solution in the absence of agreement. (See p. 80 above.)

The UNCITRAL Rules recommend the following model clause:

> The appointing authority shall be [name of institution or person].
>
> Parties to agreements involving states, state-related entities, or international organizations often choose the Secretary-General of the PCA or of ICSID as the appointing authority under the UNCITRAL Rules.

When parties to an ad hoc arbitration agreement do not specify an appointing authority or other appointment mechanism in their arbitration agreement, many national arbitration statutes provide for judicial appointment of arbitrators by national courts in the country of the arbitral seat. (See, e.g., UNCITRAL Model Law, Article 11; Swiss Law on Private International Law, Article 179(2); English Arbitration Act 1996, §§16–18; U.S. Federal Arbitration Act, §§5, 206; French Code of Civil Procedure, Articles 1451–1454; German Code of Civil Procedure, §1035(3).) Although such appointment mechanisms can function well on occasion, they can also trigger multiple appointment actions in different states and can lead to the appointment of retired local judges or domestic practitioners without meaningful international arbitration experience.

If parties do not provide for either institutional arbitration or an appointing authority, then the following provision can be used to avoid disputes regarding the appropriate national court to appoint an arbitrator:

> If any arbitrator is not selected within the foregoing time limits, the [appropriate court (virtually always in arbitral seat)] will appoint such arbitrator(s).

Again, however, it is vastly preferable to provide for an appointing authority to select the arbitrator(s) if the parties are unable to do so themselves. Where three arbitrators are selected, each party usually selects one arbitrator (a so-called party-nominated arbitrator, party-appointed arbitrator, party-arbitrator, or co-arbitrator), with the third arbitrator (the "presiding arbitrator," "president," or "chair") being chosen by agreement between the two party-nominated arbitrators (or, failing agreement, by the administering institution). Under some institutional rules, the parties' arbitration agreement must confer power to select the presiding arbitrator on the co-arbitrators. Failing such agreement, the institution will select the presiding arbitrator itself. In such instances, the parties can agree during the arbitration to allow the co-arbitrators to select the chairman. By the time of a dispute, however, such cooperation may not be possible.

An example of language permitting the party-nominated arbitrators to propose a presiding arbitrator is:

> The arbitral tribunal shall be composed of three arbitrators. Each party shall appoint one arbitrator. The two arbitrators so appointed shall appoint the presiding arbitrator. If either party fails to appoint an arbitrator within [30] days of receiving written notice of the appointment of an arbitrator by the other party, such arbitrator shall be appointed by ________. If the two arbitrators to be appointed by the parties fail to agree upon a third arbitrator within [30] days of the appointment of the second arbitrator, the third arbitrator shall be appointed by ________.

An alternative formulation provides:

> The number of arbitrators shall be three. One arbitrator shall be [nominated] [selected] by the claimant in its [request for arbitration]. The second arbitrator shall be [nominated] [selected] by the respondent within [30] days of its receipt of the [request for arbitration]. The third arbitrator, who shall be the presiding arbitrator, shall be jointly [nominated] [selected] by the [two other arbitrators] [parties] within [30] days of the [nomination] [selection] [appointment] of the second arbitrator. If any arbitrator is not [nominated] [selected] within these time periods, the [appointing authority] shall appoint such arbitrator(s).

If the parties wish to attempt to select the presiding arbitrator themselves, rather than providing for the co-arbitrators to do so, the following language can be used:

> Within [30] days after the commencement of the arbitration, each party shall [appoint] [select] an arbitrator. The parties shall then [appoint] [select] the presiding arbitrator within [20] days after selection of the party-[appointed] [selected] arbitrators. If any arbitrators are not selected within these time periods, the [International Centre for Dispute Resolution] shall, at the written request of any party, complete the appointments that have not been made.

The foregoing provisions provide alternative language for the parties either to "nominate" or to "select" an arbitrator. Some institutional arbitration rules provide for parties to "nominate" the co-arbitrators, while other rules provide for their "appointment" or "selection." Use of the term "nominate" is appropriate where an appointing authority is required to confirm the parties' selection of an arbitrator; use of the term "appoint" or "select" (or "designate" or "name") is appropriate where no confirmation process exists. These sorts of provisions should not be used in conjunction with institutional rules without carefully considering their interaction.

It is possible for the parties to agree that an appointing authority shall select all three members of a three-person tribunal, rather than permitting each party to select a co-arbitrator, with only the presiding arbitrator then being chosen by the institution. Indeed, in multi-party cases, institutional rules sometimes require this result in order to avoid disputes between co-parties over jointly selecting a single party-nominated arbitrator and to avoid possible enforceability challenges (if one party, but not the others, were permitted to nominate a co-arbitrator). (See 2021 ICC Rules, Article 12(8); 2020 LCIA Rules, Article 8) The ICC Rules provide that, in the absence of a joint nomination pursuant to Article 12(6) or 12(7), and where all parties are unable to agree to a method for the constitution of the arbitral tribunal, the Court may appoint each member of the arbitral tribunal and shall designate one of them to act as presiding arbitrator.

In unusual cases, parties provide for simultaneous selection of the co-arbitrators by the claimant(s) and the respondent(s). The rationale for such provisions is to deny the respondent the tactical advantage of selecting "its" co-arbitrator with the knowledge of the claimant's choice of a co-arbitrator. A representative provision is as follows:

> The number of arbitrators shall be three.
>
> Each party shall [nominate/select] one co-arbitrator.
>
> On the [30th] day following receipt by the respondent(s) of the request for arbitration, the parties shall simultaneously exchange their respective [nomination/selections] of co-arbitrators.
>
> Within [30] days after [nomination/selection] of the two co-arbitrators, the co-arbitrators shall [nominate/select] a third arbitrator, who shall be the presiding arbitrator.
>
> If any arbitrator is not [nominated/selected] within these time periods, the [(add appointing authority)] shall appoint such arbitrator(s).

d. *Qualifications and Nationality of Arbitrators*

Arbitration agreements can either directly specify or indirectly influence the qualifications and characteristics of the arbitrators. For example, an arbitration agreement can expressly require (or prohibit) the appointment of persons with legal qualifications. In most international arbitrations, the parties and arbitral institutions will appoint legally qualified arbitrators, often with substantial arbitration experience. In general, given the potential legal complexity of most international arbitrations, it is unwise to preclude such appointments.

Arbitration clauses may also require particular types of linguistic or technical experience. Fluency in a particular language or an engineering or other professional degree are common examples. Such provisions can be useful in particular cases. A representative example provides:

> [Each arbitrator] [The presiding arbitrator] shall be an electrical engineer knowledgeable in ________.

Or:

> [Each arbitrator] [The presiding arbitrator] shall be fluent in written and spoken [English and German].

Nonetheless, it is often difficult to determine in advance what sorts of expertise will be genuinely relevant to a future dispute. Moreover, imposing advance requirements reduces the pool of available arbitrators—sometimes unacceptably, such as a "legally-qualified national of Bermuda with a civil engineering degree and fluency in Arabic." It can also indirectly influence the background and training of a potential presiding arbitrator (and the co-arbitrators), which may have consequences for the approach to both the procedures and the merits of the dispute in the arbitral proceedings. Despite these issues, for particular types of contracts or disputes, it can be worthwhile to require specific experience or qualifications. Such requirements should be stated objectively (e.g., a Certified Public Accountant), rather than subjectively (e.g., a distinguished geologist). A representative example of a provision regarding arbitrator qualifications is:

> [Each arbitrator] [The presiding arbitrator] shall be legally-qualified and experienced in [oil and gas contracts] [intellectual property] [construction projects].

Alternatively:

> Each arbitrator shall be [a Certified Public Accountant] [an electrical engineer].

Less risky are arbitration clauses that preclude the appointment of arbitrators with particular nationalities. Most leading institutional arbitration rules provide that a presiding or sole arbitrator shall not have the same nationality as that of any of the parties (unless otherwise agreed) (2021 ICC Rules, Articles 13(5)–(6); 2020 LCIA Rules, Article 6(1); compare 2013 AAA Rules, Rule 15). Some institutional rules give the appointing authority considerable discretion, increasing the likelihood that an arbitrator with the same nationality as that of the institution will be appointed unless otherwise agreed (e.g., 2023 CIETAC Rules, Articles 26–29).

Particularly in ad hoc arbitration clauses, parties should consider providing that the presiding arbitrator (or, alternatively, all arbitrators) shall not possess the nationality of any party. More elaborate provisions can require consideration of the nationalities of the shareholders or controlling persons of the parties:

> No arbitrator shall be of the nationality of the place of incorporation or principal place of business of any of the parties [or any shareholders holding more than [5%] of such party's shares].

Parties based outside the EU may also wish to consider issues relating to the presiding or sole arbitrator's nationality when contracting with an EU company. Under most arbitral institutions' rules and practices, the Member States of the EU are considered separate nations, and there is no provision for an EU nationality. Article 6(3) of the LCIA Rules is particularly explicit, and also unwise, on this subject, providing: "A person who is a citizen of two or more States shall be treated as a national of each State; citizens of the European Union shall be treated as nationals of its different Member States and shall not be treated as having the same nationality; a citizen of a State's overseas territory shall be treated as a national of that territory and not of that State; and a legal person incorporated in a State's overseas territory shall be treated as such and not (by such fact alone) as a national of or a legal person incorporated in that State."

The practice under other leading institutional arbitration rules is similar. In principle, this approach is unwarranted, at least for non-EU companies. At least in some cases, it can give rise to potentially unanticipated and unsatisfactory results (if, for example, the sole arbitrator in a dispute between Japanese and French parties is Belgian or Swiss-French). Although leading institutions seek to avoid such results in their appointment practices, non-EU parties should consider including additional protections in their arbitration agreement. Such protections may include a prohibition on specified nationalities:

> The presiding [or sole] arbitrator shall not be a national of ________.

Alternatively, provisions may include a contractual definition of nationality intended to address issues arising from EU nationality:

> In ascertaining an arbitrator's or proposed arbitrator's nationality for purposes of this Article [X], any national of a Member State of the European Union shall be deemed to have the nationalities of both the European Union and each of its Member States.

This type of provision is advisable for North American, Asian, African, and other non-EU enterprises contracting with parties from EU states.

e. Independence and Impartiality of Arbitrators

The independence and impartiality of arbitrators are a subject of great importance and some controversy. Leading institutional arbitration rules require that all arbitrators be and remain "independent" of the parties or "independent and impartial." (See 2021 ICC Rules, Articles 11(1)–(2); 2021 ICDR Rules, Article 14(1); 2020 LCIA

Rules, Article 5(3)). Under most institutional rules, arbitrators are required to submit statements at the time of their nomination formally certifying their independence, and to update these declarations during the course of the arbitration if circumstances change. The ICC Rules include amended disclosure requirements for arbitrators, requiring statements of "acceptance, availability, impartiality and independence."

In ad hoc arbitrations (or institutional arbitrations where the applicable institutional rules do not satisfactorily address the issue), parties can agree contractually to require the arbitrators to be independent and impartial. For example:

> Each of the arbitrators shall be and remain impartial and independent of the parties.

Occasionally, arbitration agreements require more formal assurances of impartiality:

> Prior to commencement of the arbitral proceedings, each of the arbitrators shall provide an oath or undertaking of impartiality.

The precise meanings of "independence" and "impartiality" are much-debated topics, with answers varying in different legal systems and contexts. At a minimum, arbitrators are generally forbidden in developed legal regimes from having direct financial, business, or professional relations with one of the parties to the arbitration. Arguably, more attenuated connections, such as prior legal representations on unrelated matters, positional conflicts, or conceivably social ties to a party or counsel, may also be relevant to an arbitrator's independence. In addition, the 2021 ICC Rules also highlight the relevance of third-party funding; Article 11(7) requires parties to disclose the existence and identity of third-party funders to assist prospective arbitrators and arbitrators in complying with their duties of independence and impartiality.

There is a consensus that all arbitrators in international commercial arbitrations must be independent. This contrasts with practice in some domestic arbitration systems, where "party-nominated" arbitrators are expected to be quasi-advocates for the party which appointed them. In most international contexts, party-nominated arbitrators are required to be independent and to refrain from ex parte contacts with any of the parties about the dispute. At the same time, co-arbitrators are also often expected actively to ensure that the arguments and evidence of the party which nominated them are fully considered and taken into account by the tribunal.

It is generally possible (although rare) for parties to an international arbitration to agree upon an arbitral process that includes overtly predisposed party-nominated arbitrators. For example, the current AAA Rules permit parties to agree to non-neutral party-nominated arbitrators.

National arbitration legislation in some states may impose mandatory constraints, beyond the parties' agreement, which could preclude such arrangements. In most leading arbitral seats, however, courts will accord substantial deference to the parties' chosen mechanism for dispute resolution and to an arbitral institution's appointments. Nonetheless, the legal and practical difficulties that arise from partisan party-appointed arbitrators ordinarily argue against adopting such a course in international transactions.

f. IBA Guidelines on Conflicts of Interest in International Arbitration

The IBA published detailed guidelines in 2004 concerning the impartiality and independence of international arbitrators (the "IBA Guidelines on Conflicts of Interest in International Arbitration" or "IBA Guidelines"), which supplemented the IBA's more general 1987 Rules of Ethics for International Arbitrators. The IBA Guidelines were revised in 2014 and, most recently, in 2024; they detail circumstances which are customarily considered to raise doubts regarding an arbitrator's independence or impartiality and, therefore, require disclosure to the parties by arbitrators.

The IBA Guidelines categorize such circumstances into those matters that give rise to justifiable doubts concerning independence (a so-called red list), matters that require disclosure and that may give rise to justifiable doubts as to an arbitrator's independence (a lengthy, so-called orange list), and matters that do not ordinarily give rise to doubts regarding independence (a so-called green list). Among other things, the 2024 version of the IBA Guidelines provides that advance declarations and waivers of arbitrators in relation to possible future conflicts of interests do not discharge the arbitrator's ongoing duty of disclosure, makes clear that the IBA Guidelines apply to arbitral secretaries and assistants, and requires parties to disclose any direct or indirect relationship between a third-party funder and an arbitrator.

The IBA Guidelines are not binding on either national courts or arbitral institutions, and have been the subject of some criticism, on the grounds that they are needlessly detailed and susceptible to encouraging challenges to both arbitrators and awards. They nonetheless provide one perspective on customary attitudes towards an arbitrator's obligations of independence and impartiality. If parties desire, they can incorporate the IBA Guidelines by reference in their arbitration agreement, although this is ordinarily not advisable. An example of how the parties may do so is as follows:

> The parties agree to comply with the IBA Guidelines on Conflicts of Interest in Arbitration in matters concerning prospective arbitrator appointments and disclosure of relationships between parties, party representatives and arbitrators.

6. Language of the Arbitration

Arbitration clauses in international agreements should always specify the language (or languages) of the arbitral proceedings and award. Although sometimes overlooked, this is a point of vital importance, which can have a profound practical effect on the selection of the arbitrators and the character of the arbitral proceedings.

Ordinarily, it will be sensible for the language of the arbitration to be the same as that of the contract.

Representative examples of clauses dealing with the language of the arbitration include:

> The language of the arbitration shall be ________.

Or, if a more detailed (if less flexible) provision is desired:

> The arbitration proceedings shall be conducted in the ________ language. All written submissions shall be made in the ________ language. All evidence, including all witness statements, shall be submitted in the ________ language, or with a translation into the ________ language. Oral testimony shall be in the ________ language or shall be simultaneously translated into the ________ language by a translator. Each party shall bear its own translation costs.

Absent the parties' agreement, institutional arbitration rules usually expressly authorize the arbitral tribunal to select a language (or languages) of the arbitration. (2021 UNCITRAL Rules, Article 19; 2021 ICC Rules, Article 20; 2025 SIAC Rules, Rule 37(1); 2021 ICDR Rules, Article 20.) This will often be the language of the underlying contract or arbitration agreement. (See 2021 ICC Rules, Article 20; 2021 ICDR Rules, Article 20.) Nonetheless, there is seldom any reason to leave this issue to chance, particularly because some institutional rules may default to the institution's local language in the absence of contrary agreement (e.g., 2023 CIETAC Rules, Article 84(2) (Chinese); 2017 ICAC Rules, §22 (Russian)).

Some international arbitration clauses provide that one language (e.g., English) shall be the language of the arbitration, but that all the arbitrators shall be fluent in a second language (e.g., Spanish). Such provisions are most often used where one party wishes to ensure that the tribunal can understand its likely witnesses in their native tongue. Provisions of this nature can significantly limit or distort the pool of possible arbitrators and should therefore be used with caution.

7. Choice-of-Law Clauses: Law Applicable to Arbitration Agreement and to Arbitral Proceedings

International arbitration can give rise to tortuous choice-of-law questions. As a consequence, almost any international arbitration agreement should be accompanied by a choice-of-law clause, specifying the substantive law applicable to the parties' underlying contract and related disputes. The drafting of choice-of-law provisions is discussed below. (See pp. 179-90.)

In general, a choice-of-law provision should be included in a separate and independent clause of the parties' contract rather than as a sub-part of an arbitration or choice of forum clause. This serves to avoid confusion as to whether the parties' choice of law is also intended to designate a procedural law for the arbitration, which it ordinarily should not be. (As discussed below, it is possible (although virtually never desirable) for the parties to designate a foreign procedural law, different from the law of the seat.) A separate choice-of-law clause helps to make clear that the parties' choice of law is freestanding and operates independently of their dispute resolution procedures, and that it specifies the law applicable to the parties' underlying commercial contract.

In addition to the substantive law governing the parties' underlying agreement, other questions of applicable law frequently arise in connection with international arbitrations.

First, a different law may apply to the arbitration agreement (as distinguished from the parties' underlying contract); this is because most legal systems will treat the arbitration agreement as a separable contract, which may not be subject to a substantive choice-of-law clause in the underlying contract. It is possible, and occasionally advisable, to adopt a choice-of-law clause that specifically addresses the law applicable to the arbitration agreement, as distinct from the parties' underlying contract. An example of a provision dealing specifically with the law applicable to the arbitration agreement is:

> This Article [X] shall be governed by the laws of ________.

Second, the law governing the arbitral proceedings (including actions to annul awards and remove arbitrators) will almost always be that of the arbitral seat. (See pp. 81-83 above.) In turn, this will almost always be that of the place of arbitration selected by the parties. It is possible (but very rare) for parties to select a separate body of procedural law to apply to the procedural conduct of the arbitration itself, different from that of the place of arbitration. If parties wish to do so, they must include choice-of-law provisions that specifically designate the procedural law applicable to future arbitral proceedings.

Such provisions can give rise to significant uncertainties and should virtually never be used. A provision specifying the applicable procedural law can arguably discourage judicial intervention in the conduct of an arbitration by foreign courts. Judicial decisions and other authority in some states (including Pakistan, Indonesia, and Tanzania) permit local courts to issue orders regarding arbitrations seated abroad (e.g., Switzerland), on the theory that the procedural law applicable to the Swiss arbitration is, for example, Pakistani. A choice-of-law clause, making clear the procedural law applicable in the arbitration is that of the arbitral seat, provides at least some protection against this risk. An example of a provision dealing specifically with the procedural law of the arbitration provides:

> The arbitration agreement and the arbitral proceedings shall be governed by the laws of ________.

Despite their benefits, provisions addressing the law applicable to the arbitration agreement or the law applicable to the arbitral proceedings can produce significant complexities, particularly where parties select a different law to govern the arbitral proceedings than that of the arbitral seat. Such provisions should be adopted only where compelling justification exists—for example, to prevent application of a foreign procedural law by courts in a jurisdiction such as Indonesia or Pakistan—and should be drafted with great caution and specialized advice. In particular, parties should be alert to the possibility that agreement to a foreign procedural law or arbitration statute may affect the identity of the national courts that will consider annulment challenges to any arbitral award, select arbitrators (in an ad hoc arbitration), decide challenges to arbitrators, and otherwise have primary supervisory jurisdiction over the arbitral proceedings. In virtually no circumstances should parties agree to a provision selecting a foreign procedural law different from that of the arbitral seat.

8. Formalities, Capacity, and Validity

It is critical to ensure that a proposed arbitration clause satisfies applicable formal requirements. The New York Convention is generally applicable only to arbitration agreements in "writing" (New York Convention, Article II(1)), and many national arbitration statutes contain similar limitations. (See 1985 UNCITRAL Model Law, Article 7(2); U.S. Federal Arbitration Act, §2; Swiss Law on Private International Law, Article 178.) Although oral agreements to arbitrate may be enforceable in some jurisdictions, there is virtually no justification for failing to commit such an undertaking to writing, and doing so can deny the agreement the protections of the New York Convention on national arbitration legislation.

Beyond the writing requirement, national law in different jurisdictions may impose additional formal requirements. These should be identified and complied with when the law of a certain jurisdiction applies to the arbitration or when enforcement in that jurisdiction is contemplated. Among other things, as discussed below, particular care should be used when incorporating an arbitration clause by reference from another document (e.g., another contract or a set of trade association rules). For U.S.-related transactions, an entry-of-judgment clause (See p. 125 below) should also generally be included.

It is also vital to ensure that parties to a proposed arbitration agreement have the capacity to enter into the agreement. Questions of capacity raise choice-of-law issues, with the law of each party's domicile or place of organization and the law applicable to the arbitration agreement all being potentially applicable.

In general, the laws of most developed legal systems give rise to only limited risks that corporate entities lack the capacity to enter into binding arbitration agreements. There are nonetheless circumstances where particular formal requirements (e.g., a specific board resolution approving the arbitration agreement) may be required by applicable law. It is essential to ascertain the existence of such requirements and to ensure that they are complied with. It is also prudent to ensure that the parties' contract contains representations and warranties that include issues of capacity to enter into the arbitration agreement. Questions of capacity where state entities or foreign states themselves are involved can raise particularly difficult questions, sometimes requiring formal opinions on foreign law or compliance with foreign administrative or other requirements. For example, in some states, state entities arguably cannot validly agree to international arbitration without specific legislative or other governmental approval.

Finally, and more generally, it is important to confirm that a proposed arbitration agreement will be a valid and binding contract. Again, this raises choice-of-law questions, which can be partially (but not entirely) dealt with by agreement. As discussed below in Chapter 5, international arbitration agreements are readily enforceable under the laws of most developed jurisdictions, subject to a fairly limited number of generally applicable contract law principles of invalidity (e.g., unconscionability, fraud, mistake). Nonetheless, it is sometimes appropriate to consider specifically a proposed arbitration agreement's validity under all applicable laws.

Also, as discussed below (See p. 170), there are various categories of claims which may be deemed "non-arbitrable" under national law in some jurisdictions. It is advisable to consider what types of future claims, likely to arise under an agreement, would fall within non-arbitrability exceptions in potentially relevant states (e.g., the arbitral seat, the jurisdictions where the contract is performed, and potential enforcement fora). There may be little that can be done to contract out of such mandatory national laws, but it is still worth being aware of the consequences that would follow from certain disputes being non-arbitrable. (As a practical matter, non-arbitrability exceptions are usually narrower, and less likely to be invoked, than similar public policy issues that arise in the context of forum selection clauses.)

9. Representative Institutional and Ad Hoc Arbitration Clauses

The considerations discussed above produce recommended institutional and ad hoc arbitration clauses which can be considered for use in many cases. These clauses contain the critical elements for an international arbitration agreement. Additional elements, which also may be desirable in particular cases, are discussed below (See pp. 109-149), but are not ordinarily essential.

A representative ad hoc arbitration agreement provides:

> All disputes, claims, controversies, and disagreements relating to or arising out of this Agreement (including the formation, existence, validity, enforceability, performance, or termination of this Agreement) or the subject matter of this Agreement shall be finally resolved by arbitration [in accordance with the UNCITRAL Arbitration Rules].
>
> The number of arbitrators shall be [one] [three].
>
> The appointing authority shall be ________.

> The arbitral tribunal shall be composed of three arbitrators.
>
> Each party shall appoint one arbitrator. The two arbitrators so appointed shall appoint the presiding arbitrator. If either party fails to appoint an arbitrator within [30] days of receiving written notice of the appointment of an arbitrator by the other party, such arbitrator shall be appointed by ________. If the two arbitrators to be appointed by the parties fail to agree upon a third arbitrator within [30] days of the appointment of the second arbitrator, the third arbitrator shall be appointed by ________.
>
> The seat of the arbitration shall be ________.
>
> The language of the arbitration shall be ________.
>
> This Agreement will be governed by, and all disputes relating to or arising in connection with this Agreement [or the subject matter of this Agreement] shall be resolved in accordance with, the laws of ________.

An alternative ad hoc agreement, from the IBA Guidelines for Drafting International Arbitration Clauses:

> All disputes arising out of or in connection with this agreement, including any question regarding its existence, validity or termination, shall be finally resolved by arbitration.
>
> The place of arbitration shall be [city, country].
>
> The language of the arbitration shall be [...].
>
> The arbitration shall be commenced by a request for arbitration by the claimant, delivered to the respondent. The request for arbitration shall set out the nature of the claim(s) and the relief requested.
>
> The arbitral tribunal shall consist of three arbitrators, one selected by the claimant in the request for arbitration, the second selected by the respondent within [30] days of receipt of the request for arbitration, and the third, who shall act as presiding arbitrator, selected by the two parties within [30] days of the selection of the second arbitrator. If any arbitrators are not selected within these time periods, [the designated appointing authority] shall, upon the request of any party, make the selection(s).
>
> If a vacancy arises, the vacancy shall be filled by the method by which that arbitrator was originally appointed, provided, however, that if a vacancy arises

during or after the hearing on the merits, the remaining two arbitrators may proceed with the arbitration and render an award.

The arbitrators shall be independent and impartial. Any challenge of an arbitrator shall be decided by [the designated appointing authority].

The procedure to be followed during the arbitration shall be agreed upon by the parties or, failing such agreement, determined by the arbitral tribunal after consultation with the parties.

The arbitral tribunal shall have the power to rule on its own jurisdiction, including any objections with respect to the existence, validity or effectiveness of the arbitration agreement. The arbitral tribunal may make such ruling in a preliminary decision on jurisdiction or in an award on the merits, as it considers appropriate in the circumstances.

Default by any party shall not prevent the arbitral tribunal from proceeding to render an award.

The arbitral tribunal may make its decisions by a majority. In the event that no majority is possible, the presiding arbitrator may make the decision(s) as if acting as a sole arbitrator.

If the arbitrator appointed by a party fails or refuses to participate, the two other arbitrators may proceed with the arbitration and render an award if they determine that the failure or refusal to participate was unjustified.

Any award of the arbitral tribunal shall be final and binding on the parties. The parties undertake to carry out any award without delay and shall be deemed to have waived their right to any form of recourse insofar as such waiver can validly be made. Enforcement of any award may be sought in any court of competent jurisdiction.

The same principles apply generally to institutional arbitration agreements, which are often materially preferred over ad hoc arbitration clauses. In addition, as mentioned above (See pp. 39-40), and subject to the needs of specific cases, the preferable course is ordinarily to use one of the model arbitration clauses of a leading arbitral institution. Specifically:

ICC Model Clause:

All disputes arising out of or in connection with the present contract shall be finally settled under the Rules of Arbitration of the International Chamber of Commerce by one or more arbitrators appointed in accordance with the said Rules.

ICDR Standard Clause:

Any controversy or claim arising out of or relating to this contract, or the breach thereof, shall be determined by arbitration administered by the International Centre for Dispute Resolution in accordance with its International Arbitration Rules.

The number of arbitrators shall be [one or three];

The place of arbitration shall be [city, (province or state), country];

The language of the arbitration shall be ________.

LCIA Model Clause:

Any dispute arising out of or in connection with this contract, including any question regarding its existence, validity or termination, shall be referred to and finally resolved by arbitration under the LCIA Rules, which Rules are deemed to be incorporated by reference into this clause.

The number of arbitrators shall be [one/three].

The seat, or legal place, of arbitration shall be [City and/or Country].

The language to be used in the arbitral proceedings shall be [].

The governing law of the contract shall be the substantive law of [].

SIAC Model Clause:

Any dispute arising out of or in connection with this contract, including any question regarding its existence, validity or termination, shall be referred to and finally resolved by arbitration administered by the Singapore International Arbitration Centre ("SIAC") in accordance with the Arbitration Rules of the Singapore International Arbitration Centre ("SIAC Rules") for the time being in force, which Rules are deemed to be incorporated by reference in this clause.

The seat of the arbitration shall be [City, Country].

The Tribunal shall consist of [one] [three] arbitrator(s).

The language of the arbitration shall be ________.

This contract is governed by the laws of [Country or Jurisdiction].

As discussed above (See pp. 75-76), individual circumstances may warrant modifying or supplementing model arbitration clauses in particular cases. Care should be exercised, however, in making such modifications (again, for the reasons detailed above). (See p. 76 above.)

B. POTENTIALLY DESIRABLE ELEMENTS OF INTERNATIONAL ARBITRATION AGREEMENTS

In addition to the foregoing necessary elements of international arbitration agreements, there are a number of other provisions which are sometimes desirable and occasionally necessary. This is particularly true where ad hoc, rather than institutional, arbitration has been agreed. These additional elements are detailed below.

1. Provisions Allocating Legal Costs

A material issue in many international commercial disputes is liability for the legal and related costs of resolving the dispute. Under most international arbitration agreements and institutional arbitration rules, the parties are initially responsible for paying their own litigation expenses (e.g., costs and expenses of counsel, producing evidence, etc.). They are also responsible for sharing equally in advance deposits and payments of the arbitrators' and arbitral institution's fees and costs.

In many international arbitrations, the parties' initial payments of legal costs are ordinarily subject to subsequent reallocation by either the tribunal or the arbitral institution. Under most institutional rules and national laws, the fees of the tribunal and legal costs of the adverse party can be reallocated by the tribunal in its award(s). (See 2021 UNCITRAL Rules, Article 42(1); 2021 ICC Rules, Article 38(4); 2025 SIAC Rules, Rules 57, 58; 2020 LCIA Rules, Article 28; 2006 ICSID Rules, Rule 28(1).) Under these rules, the prevailing party in many international arbitrations will be entitled to recover its reasonable legal expenses from its unsuccessful adversary. This is in contrast to the "American Rule," under which the parties usually bear their own costs and expenses. Under the ICC Rules, the arbitral tribunal may, in making decisions as to costs, take into account such circumstances as it considers relevant, including the extent to which each party has conducted the arbitration in an expeditious and cost-effective manner (2021 ICC Rules, Article 38(5)).

Where awards of arbitration expenses and costs of legal representation are strongly desired or opposed by a party, that party should address this issue in the arbitration agreement. It can do so directly, by including a provision expressly dealing with the issue, which will ordinarily be interpreted as overriding inconsistent provisions in institutional arbitration rules; to avoid uncertainty, parties can expressly provide that their provision regarding legal costs prevails over the institutional rules they have adopted. Care should be taken in drafting provisions dealing with legal costs because they may raise questions of enforceability under the laws of the arbitral seat.

Examples of provisions allocating legal costs include:

> The prevailing party shall be entitled to recover its [reasonable] costs, including administrative fees and expenses, arbitrators' fees and expenses, and fees and expenses of legal representation, incurred in the arbitration proceedings.

Or:

> The arbitral tribunal shall award to the prevailing party, if any, all of its costs and fees. "Costs and fees" means all reasonable pre-award expenses of the arbitration, including the arbitrators' fees, administrative fees, travel expenses, out-of-pocket expenses such as copying and telephone, court costs, witness fees, and costs of legal representation in the arbitration.

An alternative formulation, extending to both arbitral and judicial proceedings, provides:

> The prevailing party may recover its reasonable fees for legal representation and related costs in any arbitration under this Article [X] and in any action to enforce this Article [X] or any award made under this Article [X] in any judicial or arbitration proceeding.

Given uncertainties that exist under many legal systems about the recovery of time spent by in-house counsel, experts, and management, parties wishing to ensure recovery of such amounts should include specific reference to:

> ... including all costs of in-house or internal lawyers, legal staff, experts, or management in connection with these arbitral proceedings.

Alternatively, provisions may be drafted to preclude any award of legal costs:

> Notwithstanding any provision to the contrary in the [ICC Arbitration Rules], each party shall bear its own costs and expenses, including fees for legal representation.

Or:

> The fees and expenses of the arbitrators shall be borne in equal shares by the parties. Each party shall bear the fees and expenses of its legal representation in the arbitration. The arbitral tribunal shall not reallocate the fees and expenses of either the arbitrators or the parties' legal representation.

Alternatively:

> Each party shall bear its own costs and expenses (including costs and expenses of legal representation in the arbitration) and an equal share of the arbitrators' fees and expenses and all administrative fees and expenses of the arbitration.

These formulations all use the term "legal representation" rather than domestic phrases such as "costs," "attorneys' fees," and the like, which may be subject to misinterpretation.

Finally, an arbitration clause may grant the arbitrators discretion to award costs of legal representation, without defining how that power should be exercised:

> The arbitrators shall have the power to make an award allocating the costs of the arbitration between the parties, including administrative fees and expenses, arbitrators' fees and expenses, and the fees and expenses of legal representation.

Alternatively, the arbitral tribunal may be authorized to award the costs of the arbitration, but not the costs of legal representation:

> The arbitral tribunal may include in any award an allocation of the costs and expenses of the arbitration, but it shall not have the authority to allocate or award costs of legal representation in the arbitration.

ICSID recommends a provision that addresses expenses relating to the Tribunal and the administrative services of the arbitral institution, but does not specifically refer to the costs of legal representation:

> In any arbitration proceeding conducted pursuant to this agreement, the fees and expenses of the members of the Arbitral Tribunal as well as the charges for the use of the facilities of the Centre shall be [borne equally by the parties hereto]/[divided between the parties hereto as follows: ...].

If a party does not wish to raise the question of legal costs directly, it can seek to influence fee-shifting through the selection of institutional rules or arbitral seat. Different institutional rules and national legal regimes adopt different approaches to legal representation costs. For example, an LCIA arbitration in London is very likely to result in legal representation costs being awarded to the prevailing party, while an arbitration conducted under the AAA Rules in Pennsylvania would likely produce the opposite result (by reason of the tribunal's tendency to apply the "American Rule" in the absence of contrary agreement).

Where the arbitration agreement is silent in respect to costs, many institutional rules grant wide latitude to the arbitrators. (See, e.g., 2021 ICC Rules, Article 38(4); 2025 SIAC Rules, Article 58; 2020 LCIA Rules, Articles 28(3)–(4); 2006 ICSID Rules, Rule 28(1).) Where the parties require a greater certainty of recoverability of costs, it is advisable to include language directing the tribunal to award, for example, all reasonably incurred costs (as in the model clauses above).

2. Award of Interest

Some international arbitration agreements address the question of whether interest (both pre-award interest and post-award interest) is to be awarded in respect to any damages that may ultimately be awarded. Many national laws and institutional rules expressly confer upon arbitrators the discretion to award interest. (See English Arbitration Act 1996, §49; 2021 ICDR Rules, Article 34(4); 2020 LCIA Rules, Article 26(4); 2025 SIAC Rules, Rule 51.5.) Nonetheless, it is possible, and in some instances advisable, for the parties to add a specific provision for the payment of interest in their arbitration agreement. For example, an arbitration clause can provide:

> Any monetary award shall include interest from the date of any breach or violation of this agreement. The arbitrator(s) shall fix the appropriate rate of interest from the date of the breach or other violation to the date when the award is paid in full.

Alternatively, the subject of interest may be addressed in greater detail:

> The arbitral tribunal shall include in any award of monetary damages interest from the date of loss or default until the date of payment of the award in full, at the prime commercial lending rate published by the [name of bank] at its principal office in [city, country] for [90-day commercial loans to substantial borrowers] averaged over the period from the date of the loss or default until the date of the award.

Or:

> The arbitral tribunal shall include in any award of monetary damages interest (including, if appropriate, compound interest) from the date of loss or default until the date of payment of the award.

Or:

> The arbitral tribunal may order that simple or compound interest shall be paid by any party on any monetary amounts awarded at such rates as the arbitral tribunal determines to be appropriate without being bound by legal rates of interest applicable in any national courts.

Care should be taken in drafting such provisions to ensure that they are consistent with otherwise applicable legislation in the arbitral seat.

3. Currency of Award

It can be useful for the parties to specify the currency in which the award may be expressed. A provision dealing with the currency of the award can be drafted along the following lines:

> Any award shall be made payable in [Euros] [U.S. Dollars].

Or, in order to grant the tribunal discretion:

> An award may be expressed in [any currency] [any freely-convertible currency].

To require award of pre-award interest against the breaching party:

> Any monetary award in an arbitration initiated under this Article [X] shall include pre-award interest [(including compound interest [compounded [daily] [monthly] [annually]])] at the rate of ___% from the time of the act or acts giving rise to the award.

4. No Set-Off

Parties may agree that the arbitral award shall be paid in full, without any set-off or deduction. Although this result may follow from generally applicable legal rules, parties desiring greater certainty may provide:

> Any award of monetary relief shall be promptly paid, without any set-off, allowance for tax, or other deduction.

5. Disclosure

There is no general legal regime governing disclosure (or discovery) of documents and other evidentiary materials in international arbitration. The extent to which disclosure may be obtained from an adverse party depends on the terms of the parties' arbitration agreement, the applicable law, the seat of the arbitration, and the identities and legal backgrounds of the arbitrators.

An arbitration agreement may address the subject of disclosure in the arbitral proceedings. It can do so by expressly providing for specified modes of disclosure, by expressly forbidding discovery, or by specifying some alternative. The arbitration clause may do so either directly or by incorporating institutional rules that address the tribunal's disclosure (or discovery) authority.

Given the lack of any fixed legal regime governing disclosure in international arbitration, a party that desires a particular approach to disclosure should ordinarily address this issue in its arbitration agreement. Some examples of disclosure provisions which may be included in international arbitration agreements are set forth below:

> The parties shall be entitled to engage in reasonable discovery, including requests for the production of relevant documents. [Depositions may be ordered by the arbitrator upon a showing of need.]

Or:

> The parties shall be entitled to engage in discovery as provided for by the [U.S. Federal Rules of Civil Procedure] [other procedural rules, with or without modification].

Or:

> At the request of a party, the arbitral tribunal shall have the discretion to order the disclosure of specified documents by the parties. Such a request shall identify the document(s) with a reasonable degree of specificity and establish the relevance of the document(s) to the arbitration.

At the request of a party, the arbitral tribunal shall have the discretion to order the disclosure of specified documents by the parties. Such a request shall identify the document(s) with a reasonable degree of specificity and establish the relevance of the document(s) to the arbitration.

An alternative formulation, with less specific provisions, is as follows:

> The arbitral tribunal shall have the authority to order the parties to produce such [documents] [categories of documents] as are reasonably requested by another party or by the arbitral tribunal.

A more limited grant of authority provides:

> The arbitral tribunal shall have the authority to order production of documents relevant and material to the issues in dispute, upon the showing by either party of a justifiable need for such document(s).

Although it is unusual in international practice, parties can agree on the possibility of "oral depositions" by inserting the following provision:

> The arbitral tribunal shall have the authority to order the examination by deposition of any witness [or officer or director of any party]. No party shall request more than ___ depositions.

A more detailed provision is as follows:

> After the arbitrators are selected, the parties shall confer jointly with the arbitral tribunal at the earliest convenient date (not to exceed [30] days after selection of the last arbitrator) to determine the discovery that shall take place. Each party shall have the right to take no more than ___ depositions of potential witnesses, and each

> shall have the right to serve no more than ___ sets of interrogatories, none of which shall include more than ___ interrogatories. Additional discovery shall be in the discretion of the arbitral tribunal. All discovery shall be completed within ___ months after the selection of the last arbitrator, unless this period of time is extended by the arbitral tribunal for good cause.

On the other hand, the parties may exclude disclosure or discovery:

> The parties shall not be entitled to discovery, and the arbitrators shall have no power to order discovery or disclosure of documents, oral testimony, or other materials.

The efficacy and application of disclosure provisions may be affected by several factors. First, they may be affected by the national law of the arbitral seat. Some developed national laws leave the parties free to agree upon the appropriate scope and manner of disclosure and evidence-taking. (See, e.g., UNCITRAL Model Law, Article 19; Swiss Law on Private International Law, Article 182; German Code of Civil Procedure, §1042(3)) However, other jurisdictions forbid arbitrators from ordering disclosure or discovery, and instead require application to national courts.

Second, the availability and scope of disclosure or discovery may be affected by the institutional rules under which an arbitration is conducted. All leading institutional rules contain provisions dealing generally with the subject of disclosure, although some are less explicit (2021 UNCITRAL Rules, Article 27(3); 2021 ICC Rules, Article 25) than others (2025 SIAC Rules, Rule 50.2(f); 2020 LCIA Rules, Article 22(1)(v); 2020 WIPO Rules, Article 50). In general, if the parties agree to a specific form of disclosure, applicable institutional rules and national laws will provide for the tribunal to proceed in accordance with the parties' agreement.

Third, as a practical matter, disclosure will be affected by the nationalities and legal backgrounds of the arbitrators. This is true whether or not the parties have agreed upon a particular approach to disclosure in their arbitration agreement. In general, lawyers from civil law jurisdictions will be less likely to order broad, party-initiated disclosure than lawyers from common law backgrounds. Of course, where the parties' arbitration agreement provides for disclosure or discovery, or for a specified form of discovery, tribunals will ordinarily give effect to the provision. Even here, however, an arbitrator's interpretation of a provision for disclosure will be influenced by his or her legal background; most Continental European arbitrators will have different approaches to applying an agreement for "document discovery" from those of common law arbitrators.

Fourth, although some U.S.-oriented arbitration clauses provide for "depositions," this form of discovery is rarely ordered in international arbitration outside the United States. Most arbitrators will be very reluctant to order oral depositions or similar procedures because of concerns about the tribunal's ability to effectively supervise such proceedings and resolve disputes arising from them. Moreover, few jurisdictions provide procedures like oral depositions (where counsel for the party is permitted to question the opposing party's witnesses/employees, under oath, prior to a full evidentiary hearing). As a result, non-U.S. arbitrators generally find the process unnecessary and unlikely to be workable.

Fifth, disclosure frequently involves electronic communications and documents, which raises particular issues. Some guidelines have addressed them, including the ICDR's 2008 Guidelines for Arbitrators Concerning Exchanges of Information, the Chartered Institute of Arbitrators' 2008 Protocol for E-disclosure in Arbitration, and the IBA's 2020 Rules on the Taking of Evidence in International Arbitration (discussed below). Parties concerned about the breadth or method of electronic disclosure might refer to these guidelines in their arbitration clauses.

Finally, if a party refuses to comply with disclosure ordered by an arbitral tribunal, the question of remedies and/or sanctions arises. Arbitrators sometimes lack the direct contempt authority of national courts and cannot themselves impose coercive sanctions (e.g., fines) to compel compliance. Depending upon the laws of the arbitral seat, however, the tribunal (or a party) may be able to apply to local courts for enforcement of its disclosure orders. Alternatively, and of substantial practical importance, a tribunal can draw adverse factual inferences from a party's non-compliance with disclosure or discovery orders. This can be a potent remedy.

6. IBA Rules on the Taking of Evidence in International Arbitration

A useful perspective on disclosure in contemporary international arbitration is contained in the IBA Rules on the Taking of Evidence in International Arbitration. The IBA Rules provide for a measure of document disclosure (where specific documents or defined categories of documents are material to the issues in dispute) that reflects a blend of common and civil law approaches. The IBA Rules also contain useful provisions regarding written witness statements (and expert reports), direct examination, cross-examination, and similar evidentiary matters; these provisions are consistent with customary practice and provide a constructive starting point for procedural orders in individual arbitrations.

The IBA Rules were revised in 2010 and, subsequently, in 2020 to provide generally for greater case management by tribunals. The revisions obligate arbitrators to consult the parties early in arbitral proceedings, with a view to agreeing on a process for taking evidence; expand confidentiality protections; provide specific guidance regarding privilege issues and so-called "e-disclosure"; identify data protection as a relevant evidentiary issue; provide for the possibility of virtual hearings; and empower the tribunal to exclude illegally obtained evidence.

An arbitration clause may incorporate the IBA Rules. Absent such incorporation (or adoption by a tribunal's procedural order), the IBA Rules do not have binding effects on parties to individual arbitrations; they may provide guidance to arbitral tribunals, but will not have independent force.

The following provision is recommended by the IBA to incorporate the IBA Rules:

> The IBA Rules of Evidence shall apply together with the ________ Rules governing any submission to arbitration incorporated in this contract. Where they are inconsistent with the before said ________ Rules, these IBA Rules of Evidence shall prevail but solely as regards the presentation and reception of evidence.

Where parties wish to define in advance procedural matters such as the scope of disclosure or discovery and the mode of evidentiary presentations, the IBA Rules provide a reasonable, neutral choice.

Alternatively, parties may wish to provide for only some aspects of the IBA Rules' procedures (e.g., written witness statements) and not the entire framework. The following provision is an example of how this can be accomplished:

> Direct testimony of fact or expert witnesses shall be submitted in any arbitration pursuant to this Article [X] through written witness statements made in accordance with the procedures set forth in the IBA Rules on the Taking of Evidence in International Arbitration, as such procedures may be varied by the arbitral tribunal.

Alternatively, a provision that does not refer to the IBA Rules could provide:

> Direct testimony of fact or expert witnesses shall be submitted in any arbitration pursuant to this Article [X] through written witness statements made in accordance with the procedures directed by the arbitral tribunal. Any party submitting a written witness statement shall make the witness providing any such statement available for cross-examination as directed by the arbitral tribunal. If cross-examination is requested by another party and the witness is not made available, the written witness statement will be excluded from evidence except for good cause shown.

An alternative to the IBA Rules are the Prague Rules on the Efficient Conduct of Proceedings in International Arbitration, published in December 2018. The Prague Rules forbid or narrowly limit the scope of disclosure in international arbitration, particularly e-disclosure. Like the IBA Rules, the Prague Rules can be incorporated into arbitration agreements, although this occurs relatively infrequently. A representative formulation provides:

> The Prague Rules on the Efficient Conduct of Proceedings in International Arbitration shall apply to any arbitration conducted under this Article [X].

It is also possible to provide for optional procedures with regard to witness statements:

> Either party may submit direct testimony through written witness statements (in accordance with procedures directed by the arbitral tribunal). Any party submitting a written witness statement shall make the witness providing any such statement available for cross-examination as directed by the arbitral tribunal. If cross-examination is requested by another party and the witness is not made available, the written witness statement shall be excluded from evidence except for good cause shown.

The arbitration agreement can also address the arbitral tribunal's right to appoint experts. Absent such provisions, arbitrators will ordinarily have such authority, but the following clause removes any question:

> The arbitral tribunal shall have the authority, [after consulting the parties], to appoint experts to advise it with respect to any issue in the arbitration. If the arbitral tribunal appoints an expert, such expert shall render a report in writing, and the parties shall have the right to examine such expert at a hearing before the arbitral tribunal.

7. Contractually Specified Procedural Regimes

Some arbitration agreements attempt to prescribe fairly detailed procedural rules for future arbitral proceedings. For example, the agreement can prescribe timetables for initial written submissions, types of allowable discovery and an accompanying timetable, the length and timing of hearings, the mode of witness testimony, and the like. In general, it is not productive to attempt such detail in an arbitration agreement for future disputes. The best-intentioned plans will often be inappropriate for particular future disputes and may unwisely constrain the arbitrators' procedural discretion or render the arbitral process unworkable.

8. Pre-Arbitration Notice and/or Consultation

Some arbitration clauses contain provisions requiring the parties to provide specified periods of notice, or engage in consultation or negotiations for specified periods, prior to commencing arbitral proceedings. A representative example of such a provision is as follows:

> All disputes relating to this Agreement shall be referred to management representatives of the parties for resolution. If such representatives are unable to resolve any dispute(s) referred to them within [30] days of referral, either party may submit such dispute(s) to arbitration in accordance with the provisions of Article [X] hereof.

Alternatively:

> The parties shall endeavor in good faith to resolve any dispute, claim, controversy, or disagreement relating to or arising out of this Agreement, or the subject matter of this Agreement ("Dispute"), by negotiation. Any Dispute which remains unresolved [45] days after either party gives written notice of the existence of such Dispute shall be finally resolved by arbitration.

A variation on this approach is to include "multi-step" levels of negotiation between designated representatives of the parties (also discussed below). The theory underlying such provisions is that elevating disputes through the parties' respective corporate hierarchies increases the likelihood of and pressure for settlement. A representative example is:

> The parties shall use their best efforts to resolve all disputes relating to this Agreement by amicable negotiations. If either party gives notice to the other party that a dispute has arisen, and the parties are unable within 30 days of such notice to resolve the dispute, then it shall be referred to [the Vice-President for Sales] of Seller and [the Vice-President for Quality Control] of Buyer. If these officers are unable within 30 days to resolve the dispute, then it shall be referred to the [Chief Executive Officers] of Seller and Buyer. If the Chief Executive Officers of Seller and Buyer are unable within 30 days to resolve the dispute, then either party may submit the dispute to arbitration in accordance with the provisions of Article [X] hereof.

A shorter alternative, with variations that either permit arbitration at any time or that delay it until after negotiations are completed, is:

> The parties shall attempt to settle any dispute relating to this Agreement amicably. Nothing in this Article shall preclude either party from commencing arbitration in accordance with the provisions of Article [X] hereof [at any time] [within ___ days after written notice that efforts to amicably settle any dispute have commenced].

These provisions can provide an impetus for the parties to reach a negotiated resolution of the dispute. At the same time, they can create procedural confusion and opportunities for dilatory behavior. For example, questions may arise as to whether genuine efforts at settlement have been made or exhausted and whether particular disputes were included in discussions aimed at amicable settlement.

In general, it is safer to avoid requirements for pre-arbitration negotiations and to draft notice provisions with care. This avoids procedural disputes over what sorts of notices must be given to permit arbitration, what disputes these notices cover, and the like. If provisions for pre-dispute negotiations are used, the descriptions of disputes which are referred to negotiation, and subsequently, arbitration, should be identical. There should also be very clear specification of the date on which consultation should begin and when arbitration may be commenced.

9. Multi-Tiered Dispute Resolution Clauses

Arbitration clauses can be combined with provisions for other means of alternative dispute resolution ("ADR"). Such provisions are often referred to as "multi-tiered dispute resolution clauses" because they provide for initial stages of less formal dispute resolution (such as ADR) before arbitration is commenced.

These provisions have been popular in the United States, with parties in some European and Asian jurisdictions also showing interest. Typically, such clauses involve various sorts of pre-arbitration consultation, sometimes followed by mediation or a similar ADR mechanism, pursuant to a specified timetable. If these efforts fail, resort may be had to arbitration. A sample clause, recommended by the AAA, provides:

> If a dispute arises from or relates to this contract or the breach thereof, and if the dispute cannot be settled through direct discussions, the parties agree to endeavor first to settle the dispute by mediation administered by the American Arbitration Association under its Commercial Mediation Procedures before resorting to arbitration. Any unresolved controversy or claim arising from or relating to this contract or breach thereof shall be settled by arbitration administered by the American Arbitration Association in accordance with its Commercial Arbitration Rules, and judgment on the award rendered by the arbitrator may be entered in any court having jurisdiction thereof. If all parties to the dispute agree, a mediator involved in the parties' mediation may be asked to serve as the arbitrator.

An alternative clause providing for mediation under the auspices of the Centre for Effective Dispute Resolution ("CEDR") in London states:

> If any dispute arises in connection with this agreement, the parties agree to enter into mediation in good faith to settle such a dispute and will do so in accordance with the CEDR Model Mediation Procedure. Unless otherwise agreed between the parties within 14 [working] days of notice of the dispute, the mediator will be nominated by CEDR. To initiate the mediation a party must give notice in writing ("ADR notice") to the other party[ies] to the dispute, referring the dispute to mediation. A copy of the referral should be sent to CEDR. Unless otherwise agreed, the mediation will start not later than [28] days after the date of the ADR notice. No party may commence any court proceedings/arbitration in relation to any dispute arising out of this agreement until it has attempted to settle the dispute by mediation and either the mediation has terminated or the other party has failed to participate in the mediation, provided that the right to issue proceedings is not prejudiced by a delay.

An alternative formulation, based on the CPR model clause, provides:

> *Negotiation Between Executives (A)*: The parties shall attempt to resolve any dispute arising out of or relating to this [Agreement] [Contract] promptly by

negotiation between executives who have authority to settle the controversy and who are at a higher level of management than the persons with direct responsibility for administration of this contract. To initiate a negotiation, a party shall give the other party written notice of any dispute not resolved in the normal course of business. Within [30] days after delivery of the notice, the executives of both parties shall meet at a mutually acceptable time and place, and thereafter as often as they reasonably deem necessary, to attempt to resolve the dispute. All negotiations pursuant to this clause are confidential and shall be treated as compromise and settlement negotiations for purposes of applicable rules of evidence.

Mediation (B): If the dispute has not been resolved by negotiation as provided herein within [45] days after delivery of the initial notice of negotiation, [or if the parties failed to meet within [20] days,] the parties shall endeavor to settle the dispute by mediation under the International Institute for Conflict Prevention & Resolution ("CPR") Mediation Procedure [currently in effect OR in effect on the date of this Agreement], [provided, however, that if one party fails to participate in the negotiation as provided herein, the other party can initiate mediation prior to the expiration of the [45] days.] Unless otherwise agreed, the parties will select a mediator from the CPR Panels of Distinguished Neutrals.

Arbitration (C): Any dispute arising out of or relating to this [Agreement] [Contract], including the breach, termination or validity thereof, which has not been resolved by mediation as provided herein [within [45] days after initiation of the mediation procedure] [within [30] days after appointment of a mediator], shall be finally resolved by arbitration in accordance with the International Institute for Conflict Prevention and Resolution ("CPR") Rules for Administered Arbitration [currently in effect OR in effect on the date of this Agreement], by [a sole arbitrator] [three independent and impartial arbitrators, of whom each party shall designate one] [three arbitrators to be appointed in accordance with the "screened" appointment procedure provided in Rule 5(4)] [three independent and impartial arbitrators, none of whom shall be appointed by either party]; [provided, however, that if one party fails to participate in either the negotiation or mediation as agreed herein, the other party can commence arbitration prior to the expiration of the time periods set forth above.] Judgment upon the award rendered by the arbitrator(s) may be entered by any court having jurisdiction thereof. The place of the arbitration shall be [city, country]. The language of the arbitration shall be [language].

The ICDR's model clause provides for optional mediation, in parallel to arbitration (and not as a prior condition):

> Any controversy or claim arising out of or related to this contract, or a breach thereof, shall be resolved by arbitration administered by the International Centre for Dispute Resolution in accordance with its International Arbitration Rules. Once the demand for arbitration is initiated, the parties agree to attempt to settle any controversy or claim arising out of or relating to this contract or a breach thereof by mediation administered by the International Centre for Dispute Resolution under its International Mediation Rules. Mediation will proceed concurrently with arbitration and shall not be a condition precedent to any stage of the arbitration process.

A revised ICC model clause imposes an obligation to submit the dispute to ADR, followed by arbitration:

> In the event of any dispute arising out of or in connection with the present contract, the parties shall first refer the dispute to proceedings under the ICC Mediation Rules. If the dispute has not been settled pursuant to the said Rules within [45] days following the filing of a Request for Mediation or within such other period as the parties may agree in writing, such dispute shall thereafter be finally settled under the Rules of Arbitration of the International Chamber of Commerce by one or more arbitrators appointed in accordance with the said Rules of Arbitration.

Care must be exercised in drafting such provisions to avoid overly cumbersome procedures or planting the seeds of jurisdictional disputes. Care should also be taken in specifying whether a mediation procedure prior to arbitration is optional or mandatory. Some national court decisions have held that where a mediation provision is phrased in mandatory language, it can be a condition precedent to arbitration. In these instances, there is a risk that no arbitration can properly commence until after the stipulated mediation procedures have been exhausted, with the possibility of both procedural disputes in arbitral proceedings and, potentially, parallel litigation in national courts and challenges to arbitral awards.

In addition, enforcement issues may arise from multi-tiered arbitration clauses. Some national courts have suggested that multi-tiered arbitration clauses may not fall within the New York Convention because the clause is not an agreement to submit disputes to arbitration, but rather an agreement providing for the resolution of disputes by a procedure other than arbitration, with the possibility of arbitration if the dispute cannot be resolved through the earlier procedures. In order to minimize these risks, where a multi-tiered arbitration clause is used, it is vital to clearly define the procedure in each tier and the point at which one stage terminates and the next may be undertaken.

ADR provisions often contemplate mediation or conciliation. Most leading arbitral institutions, including the ICC, AAA/ICDR, LCIA, SIAC, and UNCITRAL, have published rules that establish mechanisms for non-binding conciliation or mediation. Under all of these rules, a neutral mediator or conciliator conducts meetings (both ex parte and otherwise), shuttle diplomacy, and the like. In some cases, the neutral arbitrator may issue a non-binding report or recommendation. Drafters and users of mediation/conciliation provisions must consider the possibility of discovery into the neutral arbitrator's notes, the parties' presentations, and similar materials. The risk of such discovery varies among jurisdictions, and usually can be addressed through confidentiality provisions.

10. Fast-Track Arbitration and Contractual Time Limits

Some arbitration agreements establish "fast-track" procedures or impose specific contractual time limits on the arbitral process. These can require an award to be made by the arbitral tribunal within a specified time period, or can set out a more detailed procedural timetable, with short deadlines for each step of the proceedings. The following examples are representative:

> The arbitral tribunal shall make a final award within ___ months from the date of [the respondent's receipt of the claimant's notice of arbitration] [appointment of the [sole] [presiding] arbitrator].

Alternatively:

> The arbitrators shall conclude the arbitration no later than ___ days from the date that the claimant's statement of claim is received by the arbitrators. Unless the parties otherwise agree, a single hearing (lasting no more than ___ days) shall be conducted commencing no later than ___ days from the date that the claimant's statement of claim is received by the arbitrators. If the arbitrators determine that the interests of justice so require, they may extend the dates for the hearing and/or for conclusion of the arbitration by up to a total of ___ days.

Although fast-track arbitrations can be desirable in some cases, there is a risk of imposing unworkable or unrealistic constraints on the arbitral tribunal and counsel, particularly if disputes prove to be more complex or important than anticipated. Additionally, if the contractual deadlines are not complied with, the validity of the tribunal's award, and the agreement to arbitrate, may be challenged.

An alternative formulation, leaving the arbitrators greater discretion to exceed the parties' agreed time limit, is as follows:

> The final award in any arbitration under this Article [X] shall be made by the arbitral tribunal within [180] days from the appointment of the [sole arbitrator] [presiding arbitrator], unless the arbitral tribunal concludes that the interest of justice requires that such limit be extended [by an additional period not to exceed [45] days].

Or:

> The parties mutually desire and intend that, barring exceptional and unforeseen circumstances, the final award of any arbitration under this Article [X] shall be made ___ days from the appointment of the [sole arbitrator] [presiding arbitrator]. The parties may extend this time limit by written agreement. The arbitral tribunal may extend this time limit in its discretion if it considers that the interest of justice so requires. The arbitral tribunal shall use its best efforts to issue the final award within such time period. The arbitral tribunal's failure to make a final award within this time limit shall not be a basis for refusing to comply with or for challenging or resisting enforcement of any such award.

11. Expedited Procedures

Many arbitral institutions, including the SIAC, ACICA, HKIAC, ICDR, KLRCA, SCC, Swiss Chambers, and WIPO, have adopted rules providing for fast-track or "expedited" arbitrations. For example, the Expedited Procedure under the SIAC Rules provides for a fast-track arbitration before a sole arbitrator, who is ordinarily required to make a final award within six months of appointment (2025 SIAC Rules, Rule 14). SIAC's fast-track procedure is available in (i) cases involving less than approximately USD 7.5 million but more than USD 750,000 in dispute; (ii) cases involving less than USD 750,000 where SIAC has determined that its new "Streamlined Procedure" shall not apply; or (iii) cases where the circumstances "warrant the application" of the procedure.

Parties may agree to apply the Streamlined Procedure at any time prior to the constitution of the tribunal. The procedure is also applicable (unless otherwise determined by the President of the SIAC or on an application by a party) for claims below USD 750,000. Under the Streamlined Procedure, an award is made within three months from the date of constitution of the tribunal.

Parties are free, under the SIAC Rules and otherwise, to exclude the possibility of expedited procedures. A representative formulation provides:

> Unless otherwise agreed, no arbitration conducted pursuant to this Article [X] shall be subject to expedited procedures under [Rule 14 of the SIAC Arbitration Rules] or otherwise.

Alternatively, parties can exclude the possibility of appointment of a sole arbitrator (rather than a three-person tribunal) even if an arbitration is expedited. A suitable provision is:

> The number of arbitrators shall be three, including in any arbitration conducted pursuant to the Expedited Procedures under [Rule 14 of the SIAC Arbitration Rules].

12. *Amiable Compositeur* or *Ex Aequo et Bono*

Parties can grant the arbitral tribunal the power to decide their dispute either as "*amiable compositeur*" or "*ex aequo et bono.*" Broadly speaking, either formulation allows the arbitrators to resolve the parties' dispute without being required to apply rules of law, and instead being free to reach an "equitable" or "fair" result. Institutional arbitration rules and national arbitration statutes generally make it clear that an arbitral tribunal does not enjoy these powers except where the parties have specifically agreed. (See 2021 UNCITRAL Rules, Article 35(2); 2021 ICC Rules, Article 21(3); ICSID Convention, Article 42(3).) Parties that wish to give an arbitral tribunal *ex aequo et bono* authority may consider the following:

> The Arbitral Tribunal shall have the power to decide a dispute *ex aequo et bono.*

There is uncertainty under some national laws about the enforceability of *amiable compositeur* or *ex aequo et bono* clauses. Most legal advisers are rightly wary about the wide degree of largely unreviewable discretion that such provisions grant to an arbitrator. *Amiable compositeur* or *ex aequo et bono* provisions should be used by commercial parties with caution and only in rare cases.

13. Entry-of-Judgment Clauses

It is customary to include "entry-of-judgment" or "enforcement-of-judgment" clauses in domestic U.S. arbitration agreements. The purpose of these provisions is to ensure the enforceability of arbitral awards in U.S. courts. The following language is representative:

> Judgment upon any award made by the arbitrator(s) may be entered in any state or federal court having jurisdiction thereof.

Entry-of-judgment clauses are desirable in domestic U.S. arbitration agreements due to language in §9 of Chapter 1 of the U.S. Federal Arbitration Act ("FAA"), which has been interpreted as requiring contractual agreement on judicial enforcement of any arbitral award. This requirement is very likely not applicable to international arbitration agreements, which are governed by Chapters 2 and 3 of the FAA.

Developed legal systems outside of the United States generally do not require entry-of-judgment provisions as a condition for enforcing arbitral awards. Nonetheless, prudence counsels for inclusion of an entry-of-judgment clause where a U.S.-related party or transaction is involved, or where enforcement of an award in the United States is a possibility.

14. Multi-Party Contracts and Arbitrations

Multi-party contracts raise special issues for dispute resolution, planning, and drafting. Most international arbitration clauses, and some institutional arbitration rules, are drafted with two-party disputes in mind. Use of such provisions where three or more parties are involved can produce cumbersome or unworkable results. For example, the usual formula that "each" party may nominate one arbitrator is not easily applied to contracts with three or more parties with differing interests.

A multi-party arbitration clause should be drafted to ensure that all parties to the underlying contract can be included within a single arbitration, and that the appointment of arbitrators can proceed smoothly. The latter usually can be accomplished by providing for the appointing authority to appoint either a sole arbitrator or all three members of a three-person tribunal; alternatively, efforts can be made to align the parties on two "sides," each of which may appoint a single arbitrator by joint action of all parties on that "side."

A multi-party arbitration agreement can also permit any party to assert claims against any other party, for any respondent to add additional parties, and for any party to have the right to intervene in an arbitration initiated among other parties (all subject to procedural controls). Such an agreement may also permit the arbitrators to consolidate two or more pending arbitrations among the same parties. The provisions allowing for these possibilities require careful drafting and tailoring to particular circumstances.

A relatively simple clause addressing issues of consolidation provides:

> Each Party agrees that it may be joined as an additional Party to an arbitration involving other Parties under this Agreement. If more than one arbitration is begun under this Agreement and any Party contends that two or more arbitrations are substantially related and that the issues should be heard in one proceeding, the arbitral tribunal appointed in the first-filed of such proceedings shall have the power to determine whether, in the interests of justice and efficiency, the proceedings should be consolidated before that arbitral tribunal.

Alternatively, a more detailed and comprehensive provision for multi-party disputes is as follows (with "Parties" being parties to the underlying commercial contract):

> Any Party may, either separately or together with any other Party, initiate arbitration pursuant to this Article [X] by sending a request for arbitration to all other Parties. In any arbitration pursuant to this Article [X], any Party may submit claims, counterclaims, or cross-claims against any other Party, regardless whether such Party was named as a respondent in a request for arbitration, counterclaim, or cross-claim, provided that (A) each such new claim, counterclaim, or cross-claim is substantially related to the dispute, claim, controversy or disagreement in a previously submitted request for arbitration, counterclaim or cross-claim, and (B) such new claims, counterclaims, or cross-claims are submitted by written notice to all other Parties within [30] days from the receipt by such Party of the relevant request for arbitration, counterclaim, or cross-claim.

Or:

> Any Party against whom claims, counterclaims, or cross-claims are submitted may submit counterclaims or cross-claims against any Party, provided that (A) each such new counterclaim or cross-claim is substantially related to the dispute, claim, controversy, or disagreement in a previously submitted request for arbitration, counterclaim, or cross-claim, and (B) such new counterclaim or cross-claim is submitted by written notice to the other Parties within [30] days from the receipt by such Party of the relevant notice of arbitration, counterclaim, or cross-claim.
>
> Any joined or intervening Party shall be bound by any award rendered by the arbitral tribunal even if such Party chooses not to participate in the arbitral proceedings.

This provision can be modified for use in situations involving multiple contracts. (See pp. 128-29 below.)

The ICC, LCIA, SIAC, ICDR, HKIAC, and other arbitral institutions have revised their respective institutional rules to address multi-party arbitrations. These provisions allow for consolidation of arbitrations, and joinder and intervention of parties, in a variety of circumstances.

The 2021 ICC Rules also provide that, where there are multiple claimants (or respondents), they will "jointly" nominate an arbitrator (2021 ICC Rules, Article 12(6)); if the multiple claimants (or respondents) cannot agree upon a nomination, then the ICC International Court of Arbitration will ordinarily appoint all of the members of the tribunal (2021 ICC Rules, Article 12(8)). Similarly, the LCIA Rules provide that where an arbitration involves three or more parties, who are unable to agree upon their respective roles for purposes of nominating an arbitrator, the LCIA will appoint all of the members of the tribunal (2020 LCIA Rules, Article 8). Other institutional arbitration rules are generally similar.

15. Non-Signatories

Questions not infrequently arise concerning the application of arbitration agreements to putative third parties, such as affiliates, successors, and assigns to the formal signatories of the agreement. It is of course possible, as a drafting matter, for an arbitration clause to purport to bind the signatories' respective affiliates, successors, and assigns. The enforceability of an arbitration agreement against such third parties depends on applicable national law and will not infrequently be subject to challenge. Moreover, insofar as permitted successors and assigns are concerned, applicable law will, in any event, often bind these parties to the arbitration clause contained within an agreement which has been otherwise validly assigned or transferred. Nonetheless, parties may wish to include a clause providing that:

> This agreement to arbitrate shall be binding upon the parties and their successors, assigns, and affiliates.

Alternatively, to limit the scope and transferability of an arbitration agreement:

> This agreement to arbitrate is binding only upon the signatories hereto and not, unless otherwise agreed in writing by the signatories hereto, their successors, assigns, or affiliates.

Or:

> The arbitration agreement contained in this Article [X] binds only the signatories to this Agreement.

As noted above, these provisions can give rise to more questions than they resolve, and should be used with care.

In addition, when parties intend to bind all companies in a corporate group to an arbitration agreement, each company in the group should generally execute the agreement, or, at least, one company should expressly sign on behalf of all of its subsidiaries and affiliates. Although the former approach is preferable, the latter will permit arguments that all companies in the group are bound by principles of agency and related doctrines.

16. Multi-Contract Arbitrations

Many commercial undertakings involve multiple contractual instruments, sometimes with different contracting parties under each agreement. Representative examples include project finance transactions, construction projects, and joint ventures. These arrangements can raise difficult drafting and planning issues for dispute resolution mechanisms.

In these cases, it may be undesirable to have separate dispute resolution mechanisms for each agreement (even if each one is drafted in identical terms) because this may artificially fragment a dispute and its parties. A frequently employed means of providing a single contractual dispute resolution mechanism where there are multiple contractual instruments is to use a "Master Dispute Resolution Agreement" or a dispute clause in a framework agreement that is then incorporated by reference into all of the individual project contracts concluded thereafter. On the other hand, designing a single, consolidated mechanism for disputes under all the parties' agreements raises its own drafting and other technical problems.

Depending on the size and complexity of the transactions in question, the issues arising from multiple contracts may best be addressed by appropriately drafted individual arbitration agreements with provisions for consolidation (also discussed above at pp. 125-27). An example of a clause providing for consolidation provides:

> If more than one arbitration is begun under this Agreement, the [second Agreement], and/or the [third Agreement] and any party contends that two or more arbitrations are substantially related and that the issues should be heard in one proceeding, the arbitral tribunal appointed in the first-filed of such proceedings shall have the power to determine whether, in the interests of justice and efficiency, the proceedings should be consolidated before that arbitral tribunal.

Alternatively:

> An arbitral tribunal constituted pursuant to this Article [X] may consolidate an arbitration hereunder with an arbitration (or arbitrations) under Article [XX] of [insert related agreement(s)], provided that the arbitrations involve common questions of law or fact. If two or more arbitral tribunals constituted under this Article [X] or under Article [XX] of [insert related agreement(s)] issue decisions providing for consolidation of different arbitrations, the order issued first shall prevail.

A less detailed formulation provides:

> The parties shall agree to join any dispute resolution proceeding under this Agreement with any other dispute resolution pending in respect of any other Project Contract relating to substantially the same matter.

The AAA's model clause for consolidation of construction disputes provides:

> The owner, the contractor, and all subcontractors, specialty contractors, material suppliers, engineers, designers, architects, construction lenders, bonding companies, and other parties concerned with the construction of the structure are bound, each to each other, by this arbitration clause, provided that they have signed this contract or a contract that incorporates this contract by reference or signed any other agreement to be bound by this arbitration clause. Each such party agrees that it may be joined as an additional party to an arbitration involving other parties under any such agreement. If more than one arbitration is begun under any such agreement and any party contends that two or more arbitrations are substantially related and that the issues should be heard in one proceeding, the arbitrator(s) selected in the first-filed of such proceedings shall determine whether, in the interests of justice and efficiency, the proceedings should be consolidated before that (those) arbitrator(s).

The efficacy of consolidation provisions under applicable law and institutional arbitration rules must be carefully considered in individual cases. Some national laws impose mandatory restrictions on such provisions (relating to the protection of a party's right to participate in the selection of an arbitral tribunal).

17. Exclusion of Judicial Review

Many nations' arbitration statutes provide for very limited judicial review of international arbitral awards in annulment actions. This is generally true under the laws of leading arbitral seats, including Switzerland, France, the United States, Canada, Sweden, the Netherlands, the UAE, and Singapore. In many of these countries, judicial review is ordinarily limited to questions of public policy, jurisdiction of the arbitrators, and the procedural regularity of the arbitration. In most cases, judicial review of arbitral awards is limited by operation of law, without the need for an express limitation of judicial review in the parties' arbitration agreement. In other states, such as England, applicable law continues (unless contractually excluded) to provide for a measure of judicial review of the merits of the arbitrators' decision in annulment actions, making a contractual limitation of review important.

Most institutional arbitration rules contain limitations on judicial review of arbitral awards. (See 2021 ICC Rules, Article 35(6); 2025 SIAC Rules, Rule 51.6; 2020 LCIA Rules, Article 26(8).) Alternatively, or additionally, parties can include provisions in their arbitration agreement limiting or excluding judicial review of the arbitrators' award. Care must be taken in drafting such clauses to ensure that they are enforceable under local arbitration legislation in the arbitral seat; in some countries, only some forms of judicial review of international arbitral awards can be excluded. In other countries, such as Belgium, Switzerland, and Sweden, virtually all judicial review can be excluded, at least if only foreign parties are involved. A representative provision limiting judicial review is as follows:

> The arbitrators' award will be final and binding. The parties expressly exclude any and all rights to appeal, set aside, or otherwise challenge any award by the arbitrators, insofar as such exclusion can validly be made.

Alternatively:

> Any award(s) made by the arbitral tribunal under this Article [X] shall be final and binding on the parties, and each party waives to the fullest extent permitted by law any right it may otherwise have under the laws of any jurisdiction to any form of appeal, annulment, action to set aside or vacate, collateral attack, or any other form of recourse against or challenge to such award(s).

The 2021 UNCITRAL Rules include a model provision for the waiver of rights to seek to annul any award by the arbitral tribunal:

> The parties hereby waive their right to any form of recourse against an award to any court or other competent authority, insofar as such waiver can validly be made under the applicable law.

In some jurisdictions, express reference to local statutory provisions concerning an appeal may be advisable. That may be necessary, for example, in England and India.

Thus, parties agreeing to arbitrate in England may elect to opt out of substantive review of the arbitrators' decision under section 69 of the English Arbitration Act 1996. A sample provision is as follows:

> The parties expressly agree that leave to appeal under section 69 of the English Arbitration Act 1996 shall not be sought with respect to any question of law arising during the course of the arbitration or with respect to any award made.

A provision to this effect is particularly appropriate in ad hoc agreements to arbitrate in England (where no waiver of judicial review is included by the incorporation of institutional rules).

18. Heightened Judicial Review

It is also possible to draft an arbitration agreement to provide for heightened judicial review of any arbitral award. Although many international arbitration practitioners are skeptical about such provisions, they seek to address parties' concerns about the absence of any meaningful appellate review of arbitrators' decisions. An example of such a clause is as follows:

> The arbitrators' award shall be final and binding, but any party hereto shall have the right to seek judicial review of such award in the courts of the place where the award is made in accordance with the standards of appellate review applicable to decisions of courts of first instance in that place.

Importantly, such provisions raise significant enforceability issues on the grounds that they purportedly interfere with statutory regimes specifying the permissible grounds for judicial review of arbitral awards. U.S. courts have held such clauses to be unenforceable, and similar conclusions may be reached in other jurisdictions.

It is also possible to draft an arbitration agreement so as to provide for review of an arbitral award by a second arbitral tribunal. This is unusual and can create significant practical and drafting issues. Parties should not pursue such a course without special circumstances justifying its use and specialized advice. There are also some institutional arbitration rules that provide for a measure of "internal" (e.g., non-judicial) review of awards. ICSID is one leading example of such an arrangement; some specialized trade arbitration mechanisms adopt similar approaches.

Should parties desire a more comprehensive appeal mechanism within the arbitration process, they may agree, either in their arbitration agreement or otherwise, to permit the appeal of an underlying award under the AAA Optional Appellate Arbitration Rules (the CPR and JAMS also contain similar rules). Notably, parties may agree to apply the AAA Optional Appellate Arbitration Rules regardless of whether the underlying award is governed by the AAA or ICDR Rules. The AAA has provided the following language to include in a contract with a standard arbitration clause:

> Notwithstanding any language to the contrary in the contract documents, the parties hereby agree: that the Underlying Award may be appealed pursuant to the AAA's Optional Appellate Arbitration Rules ("Appellate Rules"); that the Underlying Award rendered by the arbitrator(s) shall, at a minimum, be a reasoned award; and that the Underlying Award shall not be considered final until after the time for filing the notice of appeal pursuant to the Appellate Rules has expired. Appeals must be initiated within 30 days of receipt of an Underlying Award, as defined by Rule A-3 of the Appellate Rules, by filing a Notice of Appeal with any AAA office. Following the appeal process, the decision rendered by the appeal tribunal may be entered in any court having jurisdiction thereof.

Under the AAA Optional Appellate Arbitration Rules, an appeal must be submitted not later than 30 days after the award has been notified to the parties. After an appeal is submitted, the underlying award is not to be considered as final for purposes of actions to modify, enforce, correct, or vacate the award in national courts. Parties may appeal on two grounds: that the award is based upon (1) an error of law that is material and prejudicial; or (2) determinations of fact that are clearly erroneous. Upon the conclusion of the appeal process and after delivery of the appeal tribunal's decision to the parties, the appeal tribunal's decision shall become the final award for purposes of enforcement proceedings.

19. "Documents Only" Arbitration

Many national arbitration statutes and institutional arbitration rules provide that the arbitral tribunal shall conduct a hearing if requested by either of the parties. Parties are, however, generally free to waive their right to a hearing, including by agreeing to a "documents only" arbitration in which the parties' dispute will be resolved without an evidentiary hearing, solely on the basis of documentary evidence.

A representative clause provides:

> The arbitration shall be conducted on a documents only basis and no party shall have the right to a hearing.

Alternatively, the arbitral tribunal can be given discretion to conduct (or not to conduct) a hearing:

> Neither party shall have the right to request or require a hearing before the arbitral tribunal. The arbitral tribunal shall have the power to decide, in its discretion, whether or not to conduct a hearing.

The European Court of Arbitration has published "documents only" arbitration rules and an arbitration clause, which provides:

> Any dispute arising from the relationships between the parties to this Agreement shall be subject to determination by a sole arbitrator selected and appointed by the European Court of Arbitration being part of the European Centre of Arbitration having its seat in Strasbourg in accordance with the Documents Only Arbitration Rules of the Court in force at the time the application for arbitration is filed.

20. Remote Hearings and Testimony

Most national arbitration statutes are silent regarding the use of telephonic or videoconferencing in arbitral proceedings. The same was true for institutional arbitration rules until recent additions to some rules, precipitated by the COVID-19 pandemic, were adopted. (See 2021 ICC Rules, Article 26(1); 2020 LCIA Rules, Article 19(2).) Nonetheless, both before and after COVID-19, arbitral tribunals generally permitted examination of witnesses by videoconference or telephone, and conducted "remote hearings" entirely by videoconference.

Although arbitral tribunals very likely have the authority under most national arbitration statutes to order remote testimony or a remote hearing, including over one party's objection, parties can also provide expressly in their arbitration agreement that the arbitral tribunal has the power to order examination of witnesses by telephone or videoconference technology and to conduct hearings "remotely" (using the same technology). The following are sample provisions expressly granting such authority:

> The Arbitral Tribunal shall have the power to either hear witness evidence by [telephone or] videoconference or conduct hearings by [telephone or] videoconference. No party shall have the right to either in-person examination of any witness or an in-person hearing in the physical presence of the arbitral tribunal.

Or:

> The Arbitral Tribunal shall have the power to establish the conduct of a hearing, including whether it may take place physically or remotely (including by video or telephone conference) or a combination thereof.

Alternatively:

> At a request of a Party or on its own motion, the Arbitral Tribunal, after having heard the Parties, may decide to conduct a hearing either physically or remotely (including by video or telephone conference) or a combination thereof.

Parties may also agree that remote hearings should be held where the tribunal believes possible, placing the burden on the party resisting remote hearings to show why a physical hearing is necessary. An example of such a provision is as follows:

> The Arbitral Tribunal should consider conducting hearings remotely where possible, and unless there are good reasons why a physical hearing is necessary, taking into account all circumstances of the case.

Alternatively, parties might wish to require in-person hearings (unless otherwise agreed):

> Any examination of witnesses or hearing shall be in person in the physical presence of the arbitral tribunal, unless otherwise agreed by the parties.

21. Provisional and Interim Relief by Arbitral Tribunal

It is possible for arbitration agreements to expressly grant the arbitral tribunal power to award interim or conservatory measures. Such provisions are seldom necessary because many national arbitration laws contain provisions permitting the parties to seek interim or conservatory measures from either a national court or the arbitrators themselves in advance of a final award. (See English Arbitration Act 1996, 2025, §§38, 44.) In addition, most institutional rules empower arbitral tribunals constituted under those rules to grant provisional or interim measures. (See 2021 UNCITRAL Rules, Article 26; 2021 ICC Rules, Article 28; 2025 SIAC Rules, Rule 45.1; 2020 LCIA Rules, Article 25.)

In addition, however, it is also possible to expressly provide the arbitral tribunal with the power to grant interim measures in the agreement to arbitrate. A representative provision is as follows:

> Any provisional, interim, or conservatory measures which would be available from a court of law shall be available from the arbitral tribunal.

Alternatively:

> Without prejudice to the parties' right to seek provisional measures from any court of competent jurisdiction, the arbitral tribunal shall have the power to grant provisional, interim, or conservatory measures, including, but not limited to, provisional injunctive relief. The parties undertake to comply forthwith with any such provisional, interim, or conservatory measures ordered by the arbitral tribunal and agree that such measures may, to the extent not precluded by applicable law, be enforceable as a final award in any court of competent jurisdiction.

The enforceability of the final clause of the foregoing provision is subject to doubt: some jurisdictions treat arbitral decisions granting interim or provisional relief as "non-final" and do not provide for judicial enforcement of them. In these cases, it is uncertain whether the parties' contrary agreement would permit an alternative result. Nonetheless, such provisions do little or no harm and may enhance the enforceability of provisional measures.

It is also possible to specify or limit the scope of provisional relief that may be sought by the parties from the arbitral tribunal:

> Without prejudice to the parties' right to seek provisional measures from any court of competent jurisdiction, the arbitral tribunal shall have the power to grant provisional, interim, or conservatory measures, but only in order to maintain the status quo until either a final award is made by the arbitral tribunal or the dispute is otherwise resolved.

An alternative and more expansive clause provides:

> Each party hereby acknowledges that it would not have an adequate remedy at law for money damages in the event that this Agreement was not performed in accordance with its terms and therefore agrees that each party shall be entitled to specific performance and/or interim relief. The parties hereby acknowledge and agree that they may apply to the arbitral tribunal [or to any court of competent jurisdiction] for conservatory or interim measures.

22. Provisional and Interim Relief by National Court

In most jurisdictions, parties ordinarily have the right to seek provisional relief from a national court, notwithstanding their agreement to arbitrate. Nonetheless, some national courts hold that the availability of provisional measures from the arbitral tribunal (or an emergency arbitrator) precludes parties from also seeking provisional relief from a court. In these instances, parties can seek to preserve the right to seek court-ordered provisional relief by including a provision to that effect in their arbitration agreement. A representative example of such a clause provides:

> Nothing in this provision shall prevent any party from seeking conservatory or interim measures, including, but not limited to, temporary retaining orders or preliminary injunctions or their equivalent, from any court of competent jurisdiction before the arbitral tribunal is constituted or, thereafter, upon the order of the arbitral tribunal.

There may be circumstances counselling for expanded rights to seek provisional relief from national courts. For example, in the context of a contract for the development of software, there may be a compelling commercial case for ensuring the availability of as broad a range of interim measures as possible, in order to prevent one party from irreversibly appropriating to itself jointly developed technologies in advance of any arbitral award. A representative provision is as follows:

> Nothing in this Article [X] shall prevent any party from seeking provisional, interim, or conservatory measures from any court of competent jurisdiction at any

> time. Any such request by a party to a court for provisional, interim, or conservatory measures shall not be deemed incompatible with the agreement to arbitrate in this Article [X] or a waiver of the right to arbitrate.

Under Rule 39(6) of the ICSID Convention, parties to ICSID arbitration agreements must expressly provide that they retain the right to seek provisional measures from judicial or other authorities. ICSID recommends that parties wishing to provide for the possibility of seeking court-ordered provisional measures include a clause such as the following:

> Without prejudice to the power of the Arbitral Tribunal to recommend provisional measures, either party hereto may request any judicial or other authority to order any provisional or conservatory measure, including attachment, prior to the institution of the arbitration proceeding, or during the proceeding, for the preservation of its rights and interests.

It is theoretically possible, although unlikely and generally inadvisable in practice, for parties to exclude the right to seek provisional measures from either the arbitral tribunal or national courts or both. A provision to this effect is as follows:

> Notwithstanding any other provision of this Article [X] or the [applicable institutional rules], [the arbitral tribunal shall not have the power to order any provisional, interim, or conservatory measures] [and] [the parties irrevocably undertake and agree not to seek any provisional, interim, or conservatory measures from any court or judicial authority].

It is very doubtful that such provisions should be used. Interim and provisional measures are exceptional remedies, but waiving any right to seek such relief in any circumstance is ordinarily imprudent.

23. Emergency Arbitration

A number of arbitral institutions, including the ICC, LCIA, ICDR, SIAC, and SCC, have adopted so-called emergency arbitrator provisions in recent years. These provisions are intended to provide a means of obtaining immediate interim relief, prior to the constitution of an arbitral tribunal, without the need for recourse to national courts.

The ICC Rules include a provision that permits the parties to request an "emergency arbitrator" to grant urgent interim or conservatory measures prior to the transmission of the arbitration file to the arbitral tribunal. (See 2021 ICC Rules, Article 29 & Appendix V.)

Although the parties are required to comply with any order made by the emergency arbitrator, the emergency arbitrator's order is not binding on the arbitral tribunal after it is appointed. The ICC's emergency arbitrator procedure is available to parties unless the dispute is treaty-based or if the parties expressly opt out of it, using a clause such as the following:

> All disputes arising out of or in connection with the present contract shall be finally settled under the Rules of Arbitration of the International Chamber of Commerce by one or more arbitrators appointed in accordance with the said Rules. The Emergency Arbitrator Provisions shall not apply.

As noted above, most leading institutional arbitration rules now include emergency arbitrator provisions comparable to those of the ICC Rules. (See 2025 SIAC Rules, Schedule 1; 2020 LCIA Rules, Article 9B; 2013 AAA Rules, Article 38.) In drafting arbitration clauses selecting these institutional arbitration rules, parties should consider whether or not to opt out of such emergency arbitrator provisions.

24. E-Commerce Arbitration

The rapid growth of the internet has brought with it an increasing number of cross-border disputes involving electronic commerce. Many of these disputes are small and better suited for dispute settlement that is quicker and more cost-effective than ordinary international arbitration, such as documents only and online arbitration.

Some institutions have published rules for online dispute resolution, including through electronic submissions and web conferencing. For example, the WIPO Arbitration and Mediation Center has processed more than 30,000 domain name disputes under the WIPO-initiated Uniform Domain Name Dispute Resolution Policy procedure.

25. Limitations on Arbitrators' Remedial Authority

An arbitration clause can be specifically worded so as to limit the remedial powers of the arbitrator. For example, an arbitration agreement may forbid the arbitral tribunal from awarding particular categories of relief, such as punitive, exemplary or consequential damages. A representative formulation provides:

> The arbitrator(s) shall not award consequential damages in any arbitration initiated under this section.

Or:

> The arbitrator(s) will have no authority to award punitive, exemplary, or other damages not measured by the prevailing party's actual damages, except as may be required by statute.

Alternatively, an arbitration clause may limit a tribunal's authority to order non-monetary relief:

> Any award in an arbitration initiated under this clause shall be limited to monetary damages and shall include no injunction or direction to any party other than the direction to pay a monetary amount.

Apart from limitations on awards of punitive, exemplary, or consequential damages, restrictions on the tribunal's remedial authority should be used with caution and only in special circumstances.

26. "High-Low" and "Baseball" Arbitration

An arbitration agreement may, in principle, expressly state a range of monetary awards and provide that the arbitrator(s) may only grant an award of damages within that range. This is sometimes referred to as "high-low" arbitration. A typical "high-low" arbitration clause provides:

> Any award of the arbitration in favor of [X], but against [Y], shall be at least [specify amount] but shall not exceed [specify amount]. [X] expressly waives any claim in excess of [specify amount] and agrees that its recovery shall not exceed that amount. Any award of damages shall be in satisfaction of all claims by [X] against [Y].

Some such agreements provide that the arbitral tribunal will not be informed of the parties' "high-low" agreement:

> In the event the arbitral tribunal denies the claim or awards an amount less than the minimum amount of [specify], then this minimum amount shall be paid to claimant. Should the arbitral tribunal's award exceed the maximum amount of [specify], then only this maximum amount shall be paid to the claimant. It is further understood between the parties that if the arbitral tribunal awards an amount between the minimum and the maximum stipulated range, then the exact awarded amount will be paid to the claimant. The parties further agree that this agreement is private between them and will not be disclosed to the arbitral tribunal.

Another possibility is for an arbitration agreement to provide that the parties shall negotiate their final positions, that each party shall submit its "last best offer," and that the arbitrators must select the "last best offer" of one party or the other (with no power to grant any award of damages between, above, or below the "last best offers" of the parties). This approach is called "last best offer" or "baseball" arbitration. A typical "baseball" arbitration clause provides:

> Each party shall submit to the arbitrator and exchange with each other in advance of their hearing their last best offers. The arbitrator shall be limited to awarding only one or the other of the figures submitted by the parties.

Alternatively:

> The parties agree that the arbitration to be employed by the arbitral tribunal shall be "baseball" arbitration. On a date specified by the arbitrators, each party shall submit to the arbitrators and to each other its proposed valuation of all the claims before the arbitrators, as an aggregate amount. The parties shall include any specifics or breakdown of the amounts included within their respective figures, as they may desire. The arbitrators shall be limited to awarding only one or the other of the two proposed aggregate figures, being the amount closest to the arbitrators' own valuation of the aggregate of all submitted claims.

In general, it is not often advisable to limit the arbitrators' remedial powers in this way except after careful consideration of the commercial consequences. The intention behind "high-low" and "baseball" arbitration clauses is to provide a financial incentive for compromise and negotiation in the event of a dispute. However, the imposition of limitations in advance of the arbitrators' remedial discretion may produce results that are arbitrary and unintended, and can raise enforceability issues in some jurisdictions.

27. Expert Determination

Parties occasionally wish to provide for expert determination, rather than arbitration. This is most commonly done with regard to highly technical issues such as purchase price accounting provisions, calculations of oil and gas reserves, quality of goods, and the like. A sample clause providing for expert determination is as follows:

> If the parties are unable to agree on [identify issue(s)], either party may request that the matter be referred for decision to [identify individual or company to serve as expert] OR [the expert selected by the [ICC Centre for Expertise] (the "Expert")]. The Expert shall attempt to agree with the parties upon the procedure and timetable to be followed in the expert determination. If and to the extent that any such matter cannot be agreed upon, the Expert may in its sole discretion adopt such procedures and timetables as it shall consider appropriate and these shall be binding on the parties.

Alternatively, an expert determination clause based in part on WIPO's model provision is as follows:

> Any dispute or difference between the parties arising under [describe matter referred to expert determination] shall be referred to expert determination in accordance with the WIPO Expert Determination Rules. The determination made by the expert shall [not] be binding upon the parties. The language to be used in the expert determination shall be [specify language].

Another example of an expert determination clause, appropriate for use in a corporate acquisition, is as follows:

> If the Vendors and the Purchasers are unable to agree on [the Completion Accounts and calculation of Net Current Assets as at the Completion Date] by [date], the matter in dispute shall be referred, at the request of either the Vendors or the Purchasers, for decision to an Independent Chartered Accountant (the "Independent Accountant") who shall be appointed by agreement between the Vendors and the Purchasers, or, if they have not agreed within 14 days of the [first date above or date of request to refer by one of the parties], by the President for the time being of the Institute of Chartered Accountants in England and Wales ("the President") on the application of either party. If an Independent Accountant has been appointed but is unable to complete the reference, another independent accountant shall be appointed by the parties, or if they have not agreed on the appointment within 14 days of the request to do so by one of the parties, by the President.

Care should be taken in drafting expert determination clauses that provide only for a non-binding expert determination. In such cases, the expert determination procedure may be used to delay the dispute resolution process, rather than to facilitate it; equally, if an expert determination is not binding, then the parties must provide for an alternative means of dispute resolution which is binding (either an arbitration clause or forum selection agreement).

Some clauses provide that expert determination is binding, unless it is followed by a request for arbitration (or, alternatively, expedited arbitration). For example:

> The determination made by the expert shall be binding upon the parties, unless within [30] days of the communication of the determination to the parties, the matter referred to expert determination is, upon the filing of a Request for Arbitration by either party, referred to arbitration in accordance with the WIPO [Expedited] Arbitration Rules. [The arbitral tribunal shall consist of [a sole arbitrator] [three arbitrators].] The place of arbitration shall be [specify place]. The language to be used in the arbitral proceedings shall be [specify language]. The dispute or difference referred to arbitration shall be decided in accordance with the law of [specify jurisdiction].

To provide for mediation followed, in the absence of a settlement, by expert determination, a clause along the following lines can be used:

> Any dispute or difference between the parties arising under [describe matter referred to expert determination] shall be submitted to mediation in accordance with the [WIPO Mediation Rules]. The place of mediation shall be [specify place]. The language to be used in the mediation shall be [specify language].
>
> If, and to the extent that, any such dispute or difference has not been settled pursuant to the mediation within [60] [90] days of the commencement of the mediation, it shall, upon the filing of a Request for Expert Determination by either party, be referred to expert determination in accordance with the WIPO Expert Determination Rules. Alternatively, if, before the expiration of the said period of [60] [90] days, either party fails to participate or to continue to participate in the mediation, the dispute or difference shall, upon the filing of a Request for Expert Determination by the other party, be referred to expert determination in accordance with the WIPO Expert Determination Rules. The determination made by the expert shall [not] be binding upon the parties. The language to be used in the expert determination shall be [specify language].

As with arbitration agreements, provisions for expert determinations can also address issues of fees. For example:

> Each party shall bear all costs (internal and external) that it incurs in the course of the expert determination unless the expert determines otherwise. If any party does not pay its share of the expert's fees and costs, the other part(y)/(ies) may advance such share of the expert's fees and costs on the defaulting party's behalf, and the expert determination shall proceed. The part(y)/(ies) which pay the defaulting party's share of the expert's fees and costs shall have the right to request that the expert or an arbitral tribunal constituted under Article [X] of this Agreement direct the defaulting party to reimburse such fees and costs.

An expert determination clause can also expressly address the possibility that a party refuses to comply with the expert's determination. For example:

> The expert determination shall be final and binding, and each party undertakes to comply forthwith with such expert determination. If a party does not comply fully with an expert determination, the other party may refer this failure to arbitration under Article [X] of this Agreement [or, at its sole option, seek to enforce its rights under such expert determination in any court of competent jurisdiction].

Ordinarily, the latter alternative in this model provision is preferable: a further arbitration, involving failure to comply with an expert determination, is generally not the most effective way of enforcing a party's rights under such a determination.

The ICC's International Centre for ADR appoints and proposes technical, financial, and legal experts to make factual or technical findings or recommendations. Apart from proposal and appointment where the role of the ICC Centre ends upon the appointment/proposal, the ICC Centre also offers the service of administering the entire expert proceedings. The subject matter of such appointments ranges from accounting to construction and information technology. The technical expert's conclusions can, subject to enforceability considerations, be either binding or advisory. The ICC Centre's model clause for optional use of the administered expert proceedings provides:

> The parties may at any time, without prejudice to any other proceedings, agree to submit any dispute arising out of or in connection with [clause X of the present contract] to administered expert proceedings in accordance with the Rules for the Administration of Expert Proceedings of the International Chamber of Commerce.

The ICC's model clause for mandatory submission of disputes for resolution in accordance with the ICC Rules for the Administration of Expert Proceedings provides as follows:

> In the event of any dispute arising out of or in connection with [clause X of the present contract], the parties agree to submit the dispute to administered expert proceedings in accordance with the Rules for the Administration of Expert Proceedings of the International Chamber of Commerce. [The parties agree that the findings of the expert shall be contractually binding upon them.]

The ICC's Expert Rules can, but need not, be used in conjunction with the ICC's Arbitration Rules. If the Rules for the Administration of Expert Proceedings are adopted, the parties' agreement should specify the binding effect (or lack thereof) of a technical expert's report.

Other institutions, such as the CEDR, have also published model agreements to submit disputes for expert determination. Under the CEDR model expert determination agreement, the CEDR will appoint the expert. The CEDR model agreement also requires parties to agree on a window within which the expert decision is to be implemented:

> **1. Appointment of Expert** CEDR will appoint an Expert to resolve the Dispute and has exclusive rights to do so under this Procedure. The Parties agree that the Expert will resolve the Dispute by Expert Determination. The Expert will act as an expert and not as an arbitrator or legal adviser.
>
> **2. Purpose of Expert Determination** Unless the Parties subsequently agree otherwise, this Expert Determination leads to a decision ("the Decision") being issued by the Expert via CEDR. The Decision will be final and binding on the Parties ...
>
> **11. Implementation of the Decision** The Parties agree to implement the Decision within [e.g., seven] days of the Decision being published to them.

> **12. Challenge to the Decision** The Parties agree that the Decision of the Expert is final and binding and that the Dispute cannot be referred to a subsequent tribunal …

28. Confidentiality of Arbitral Proceedings

In some transactions or industries, parties desire maximum confidentiality for arbitral proceedings, submissions and awards. This is often the case, for example, with intellectual property disputes, where one or both parties wish to avoid public disclosure of trade secrets or technical information.

Some institutional arbitration rules include confidentiality provisions. For example, the WIPO Arbitration Rules contain relatively detailed confidentiality provisions. (See 2020 WIPO Arbitration Rules, Articles 75–78.) Unlike many other institutional rules, the WIPO Rules impose an affirmative duty of confidentiality with respect to the existence of the arbitration, address the treatment of disclosures made during the proceeding, and provide for the confidentiality of the award. Other institutional rules also contain express confidentiality provisions. (See 2025 SIAC Rules, Rule 59; 2020 LCIA Rules, Article 30; 2012 Swiss Rules, Article 44; 2023 CIETAC Rules, Article 38; 2018 DIS Rules, §44.)

Some institutional arbitration rules impose no general duty of confidentiality; parties can only ensure confidentiality through agreement or as provided by the applicable law. For example, the ICC Rules do not impose an express duty of confidentiality on the parties. Instead, Article 22(3) of the 2021 ICC Rules authorizes the tribunal to make a confidentiality order that is responsive to the needs of the parties in the particular arbitration. Both arbitration agreements selecting these rules and ad hoc arbitration clauses can ordinarily be usefully supplemented by including confidentiality provisions in the parties' arbitration agreement. The following example is representative of such a provision:

> The parties to any arbitration under this Article [X] shall keep the arbitration confidential and shall not disclose to any person, other than those necessary to the proceedings, the existence of the arbitration, any information submitted during the arbitration, any documents submitted in connection with it, any oral submissions or testimony, transcripts, or any award unless disclosure is required by law or is necessary for permissible court proceedings, such as proceedings to recognize or enforce an award.

An alternative formulation provides:

> The parties agree to keep confidential all awards in any arbitration conducted under this Article [X], together with all materials submitted or exchanged in any such arbitration (including all documents and other materials produced by another

> party in such arbitration), except insofar as such documents are already in the public domain or to the extent that disclosure may be required by legal duty, to protect or pursue a legal right, or to recognize, enforce, or challenge an award in legal proceedings before a court or other judicial authority.

A more expansive confidentiality provision provides:

> The arbitrators, any party, any witness, and any other participant in the arbitration shall not disclose, transmit, or disseminate (a) anything said or done in the arbitration, (b) any documents disclosed or provided during or in connection with the arbitration, (c) any information disclosed during or in connection with the arbitration, and (d) the existence or result of the arbitration, including, without limitation, the arbitration award and any explanations or reasons for the award.

The ICDR's model confidentiality clause provides:

> Except as may be required by law, neither a party nor its representatives may disclose the existence, content, or results of any arbitration hereunder without the prior written consent of (all/both) parties.

Although it is relatively unusual, parties may also agree that their arbitration will not be confidential. Appropriate language is as follows:

> Neither party shall be under any confidentiality obligations with respect to any arbitration pursuant to this Article [X], and either party shall be free to publicly disclose any award made in any such arbitration and any materials submitted or exchanged in any such arbitration (including all documents and other materials produced by another party in such arbitration).

An alternative formulation provides:

> Any award made by the arbitrators pursuant to this Article [X] may be disclosed by either party (including to non-parties to this Agreement or to any arbitration conducted pursuant to this Article [X]).

29. Incorporation of Arbitration Agreement by Reference

Under most national laws, it is in principle possible to incorporate an arbitration agreement into a contract by reference, rather than setting it out in full in the contract. Although this may save space and avoid duplication, it should be done with caution. National law frequently limits the circumstances when or manner in which this can be done (e.g., by requiring a specific and express reference) or imposes notice or other requirements. Any space or time saved by an incorporation by reference would seldom warrant the uncertainties and litigation expenses that subsequent disputes over an incorporated clause may produce.

30. Asymmetrical Arbitration Clauses

As with forum selection clauses (See pp. 27-29 above), international arbitration agreements may be drafted to be one-sided or asymmetrical, allowing one party, but not the other, to elect to initiate arbitration of the parties' disputes. A representative clause is as follows:

> All disputes, claims, controversies, and disagreements relating to or arising out of this Agreement, or the subject matter of this Agreement, shall be finally resolved by arbitration in accordance with [institutional arbitration rules]. Notwithstanding the foregoing, [Party A] shall be free at its sole option to seek judicial or non-judicial relief to enforce [specified provisions imposing monetary obligations or specified agreements]. [Party A]'s request for judicial or non-judicial relief pursuant to the foregoing sentence shall not constitute a waiver of its right to arbitrate under this Article [X] or to enforce the arbitration agreement contained in this Article [X]. If an arbitration has been initiated by [Party B] prior to or at the time that [Party A] elects to pursue judicial or non-judicial remedies, then [Party B] shall forthwith take all necessary steps to discontinue and dismiss such arbitration and shall in no event proceed with such arbitral proceedings.

Alternatively:

> The courts of England shall have jurisdiction to settle any disputes which may arise out of or in connection with this Agreement but [Party A] shall have the option of bringing any dispute hereunder to arbitration. ... Any dispute arising from the provisions of this Agreement or its performance which cannot be resolved by mutual agreement which [Party A] determines to resolve by arbitration shall be referred to arbitration. ...

Provisions for asymmetrical rights to demand arbitration raise enforceability issues under some national laws and should be used only with the benefit of specialized advice.

31. Preliminary Decision of Dispositive Issues

It is sometimes said that arbitration is less efficient than (some) national court litigation because arbitrators either lack authority, or will not exercise the authority, to decide potentially dispositive issues at a preliminary stage of the arbitral proceedings. Many leading institutional arbitration rules provide specifically for the possibility of such early determinations. (See 2025 SIAC Rules, Rule 46; 2020 LCIA Rules,

Article 22.1(viii).) Moreover, in practice, arbitrators are often willing to address and sometimes decide preliminary disputes such as statute of limitations or prescription defenses, jurisdictional objections, and formal matters. Nonetheless, parties may wish to confirm the existence of such authority (and encourage its exercise in appropriate cases).

A provision along the following lines confirms the arbitral tribunal's authority to make preliminary decisions of dispositive issues:

> The arbitral tribunal shall have the authority to decide at any stage of the arbitration any issue claimed by a party to be dispositive of any claim or counterclaim, in whole or in part, in accordance with such procedures as the arbitral tribunal prescribes. The arbitral tribunal shall have the authority to make a partial, final, or other award with respect to any such issue.

In most cases, the arbitral tribunal will already possess the power referred to in such provisions; nonetheless, expressly identifying that authority may make the arbitrators more receptive to requests that the authority be exercised.

32. Decisions Regarding Time Bars and Similar Defenses

In some jurisdictions, there are doubts about the arbitrators' authority to decide issues of timeliness (e.g., was the claim asserted within statutory time periods?). Although the better view is that arbitrators may decide such issues without special authorization, the following provision removes any doubt:

> The arbitral tribunal shall have the authority to decide any defense that any claim or counterclaim is not timely by reason of contractual limitations period, statute of limitations, prescriptive periods, laches, or any similar defense.

Conversely, parties could (usually ill-advisedly) provide for a national court to decide issues of timeliness. The following provision is representative:

> Any decision of whether a claim or counterclaim is timely under this Agreement or applicable law shall be determined by a court of competent jurisdiction, and not by the arbitral tribunal. The parties irrevocably consent to the exclusive jurisdiction of ________ for the decision of any such issue of timeliness.

Alternatively:

> Notwithstanding [the arbitration agreement], determination of whether a dispute is timely under this Agreement or the applicable law shall be determined by a court of competent jurisdiction, and not by the arbitral tribunal.

Or:

> If a claim sought to be arbitrated would be barred by limitation of time had the claim sought to be arbitrated been asserted in a court under the law applicable to the arbitration, a party may apply to a court of competent jurisdiction—and not to the arbitral tribunal—to stay arbitration or to vacate any award as untimely.

The following clause (again, ill-advisedly) provides that an issue of timeliness may be raised before either a national court or the arbitrators:

> If, at the time that a demand for arbitration was made or a notice of intention to arbitrate was served, the claim sought to be arbitrated would have been barred by limitation of time or other time bar had it been asserted in a court under the law applicable to the arbitration, a party may assert the limitation as a bar to the arbitration on an application to a court of competent jurisdiction. The failure to make such an application in court shall not preclude a party from subsequently asserting it before an arbitral tribunal.

It is very unlikely, however, that sophisticated commercial parties would wish to use such a clause: among other things, it invites parallel proceedings and delays in the arbitral process.

33. Jurisdictional Decisions

Virtually all developed jurisdictions, including those that have adopted the UNCITRAL Model Law, recognize the arbitral tribunal's authority (so-called "competence-competence") to consider and decide objections to its own jurisdiction, subject to subsequent judicial review in an annulment or recognition proceeding. In some other legal systems (notably the United States), an arbitral tribunal may also be granted the authority to decide jurisdictional disputes, concerning the validity of the parties' agreement to arbitrate, in a final manner. In order to permit this, the parties must ordinarily have agreed clearly and unmistakably to permit the arbitral tribunal to finally resolve jurisdictional objections. If this is what the parties desire, the following provision is designed, particularly for use in ad hoc arbitration provisions, to accomplish it by expressly granting the arbitral tribunal power to finally resolve jurisdictional disputes:

> The arbitral tribunal shall have the authority to rule upon its own jurisdiction, including any objection to the formation, existence, validity, or effectiveness of the arbitration agreement in this Article [X]. The arbitral tribunal's decision on any such jurisdictional matter shall be final and binding and the parties agree not to apply to any national court or other judicial authority to annul or deny recognition to any such decision.

The enforceability of such provisions is subject to doubt in some jurisdictions.

Alternatively, the parties may wish to provide for the opposite result (i.e., that all jurisdictional disputes are resolved by national courts, rather than the arbitrators):

> Any objection to the jurisdiction of the arbitral tribunal shall be submitted exclusively to the courts of ________ [ordinarily the courts of the arbitral seat].

In general, it is unwise to provide that the arbitral tribunal shall not have the authority to consider jurisdictional objections. Even if parties do not wish to grant the arbitral tribunal authority to decide jurisdictional disputes in a final and binding manner, it is ordinarily appropriate for the arbitrators to have the authority (acknowledged by most institutional arbitration rules and national laws) to consider and resolve jurisdictional disputes, subject to subsequent judicial review in an annulment or recognition action. If the parties wish to specify a judicial forum for considering actions to enforce or challenge their agreement to arbitrate, the following provision is representative:

> Without prejudice to the arbitral tribunal's authority to consider challenges to its jurisdiction, the courts of ________ [ordinarily the courts of the arbitral seat] shall have exclusive jurisdiction over any judicial action to enforce or challenge the agreement to arbitrate contained in this Article [X], and each of the parties irrevocably submits to the exclusive jurisdiction of such courts for such purpose. [Notwithstanding the preceding sentence, any party may apply to any court or other judicial authority seeking recognition or enforcement of any award(s) made by the arbitral tribunal under this Article [X]].

34. Submission Agreement

As noted above (See p. 39), parties may agree to submit an existing dispute to arbitration. A model submission agreement is contained in Appendix H. Alternatively, the parties could use a less elaborate provision to submit an existing dispute to arbitration:

> This agreement is between [Party A] and [Party B] as of [date]. A dispute has arisen between the parties concerning ________ (the "Dispute"). The parties agree to submit such Dispute, and all claims, controversies, disputes, or differences in connection with such Dispute, for final resolution by arbitration in accordance with this Agreement. The seat of the arbitration shall be ________. The language of the arbitration shall be ________.
>
> There shall be three arbitrators. [Party A] hereby designates ________ as one of the arbitrators. [Party B] hereby designates ________ as the second of the

> arbitrators. The two arbitrators so designated shall, within [30] days of the effective date of this agreement, jointly designate in writing a third arbitrator, who shall be the presiding arbitrator. If the two arbitrators fail jointly to designate in writing the presiding arbitrator within such period, then, on the application of either party, the presiding arbitrator shall be selected within [30] days by [appointing authority].
>
> The procedures to be applied in the arbitration shall be agreed upon by the parties or, failing such agreement, shall be directed by the arbitral tribunal. Default by any party shall not prevent the arbitrators from proceeding to render an award.

As with other types of agreements to arbitrate, it is usually wiser to incorporate a set of institutional arbitration rules into a submission agreement (to provide default rules on procedural issues arising in the arbitration and institutional mechanisms for challenges to arbitrators or fixing of the arbitrators' fees and expenses).

35. Class Action Arbitration Waivers

In a few jurisdictions (in particular, the United States and Canada), it is possible to pursue a "class action" arbitration. A class action arbitration involves claims brought on behalf of a large number of similarly situated claimants (e.g., all purchasers of a particular security during a stated period; all users of a specified credit card or service during a stated period) who are too numerous to be specifically identified. The claimant class is represented by a class representative and, often more importantly, class action plaintiffs' lawyers who pursue claims on behalf of the entire class; if a class is certified, then the resulting award (or, in court, judgment) will both benefit and bind all members of the class.

In the United States, class action waivers are commonly included in consumer and related transactions (e.g., credit card agreements, mobile or other telephone services, securities transactions) and employment agreements. A representative example of language waiving the right to bring class action claims in arbitration is as follows:

> All claims shall be arbitrated on an individual basis and no party shall have any right or authority to assert or pursue any claims subject to this agreement to arbitrate as a class action of any sort.

Alternatively:

> All claims arising out of or relating to this Agreement, or the subject matter of this Agreement ("Claims") must be brought in the name of an individual person or entity and must proceed on an individual (non-class, non-representative) basis. The arbitrator shall not be authorized to, and shall not, award relief for or against

> anyone who is not a party to this Agreement and to an individual arbitration. If any party requires arbitration of any Claim, no party nor any other person may pursue any such Claims in arbitration as a class action, private attorney general action, or other representative action, [nor may such Claim be pursued on behalf of any party in any court]. Claims, including any assigned Claims, of two or more persons or entities may not be joined or consolidated in the same arbitration.

Although some doubt existed in the past, U.S. case law now clearly affirms the enforceability of class action arbitration waivers.

C. ARBITRATION AGREEMENTS IN CONTRACTS WITH STATES

As discussed above (See p. 31), international businesses frequently conclude commercial contracts with foreign states or foreign state-related entities. Many of the same considerations apply to international arbitration agreements with states as those that apply to agreements with commercial parties. In addition, however, a number of special considerations, summarized below, also arise in connection with agreements involving states or state-related entities.

As in commercial settings, parties considering arbitration provisions in state contracts must select an arbitral institution. It is also possible to provide for ad hoc arbitration in state contracts, but this is generally disfavored for many of the same reasons that apply in commercial arbitration agreements. In selecting an arbitral institution, parties to state contracts often wish (or are required) to choose from among a different set of arbitral institutions than in purely commercial settings.

1. ICSID Arbitration

The ICSID Convention provides a specialized legal regime for ICSID arbitrations between foreign investors and host states, with a number of distinctive features. Among other things:

- there is no right to set aside an ICSID award in national courts, and review of an award can only be sought before an ad hoc annulment committee, selected by ICSID, on narrow grounds set out in the ICSID Convention;
- an ICSID award is binding and enforceable with the same effect as a final local court judgment in each of the state parties to the ICSID Convention, without any possibility of denying recognition under the New York Convention; and
- the appointment, removal, and replacement of arbitrators is the responsibility of the parties and ICSID, with no role for national courts.

These provisions result in arbitrations which are almost entirely detached from national legal systems and that are instead subject exclusively to the ICSID Convention's specialized legal and procedural regime. These features arguably make ICSID awards relatively more enforceable than other international arbitral awards and provide ICSID arbitrations with particular insulation from national legal systems. At the same time, ICSID's selections of arbitrators and annulment committee members are sometimes questioned. As a consequence, at least until recent years, most commercial parties have tended to prefer other arbitral mechanisms (UNCITRAL, ICC, SCC, SIAC, LCIA, PCA) to ICSID.

a. ICSID Arbitration Clause

Nonetheless, parties are not infrequently prepared to accept, or for particular reasons prefer, ICSID arbitration. If so, then a model ICSID arbitration clause, which can be included in a state contract, provides:

> The [Government]/[name of constituent subdivision or agency] of [name of Contracting State] (hereinafter the "Host State") and [name of investor] (hereinafter the "Investor") hereby consent to submit to the International Centre for Settlement of Investment Disputes (hereinafter the "Centre") any dispute arising out of or relating to this agreement for settlement by [conciliation]/[arbitration]/[conciliation followed, if the dispute remains unresolved within time limit of the communication of the report of the Conciliation Commission to the parties, by arbitration] pursuant to the Convention on the Settlement of Investment Disputes between States and Nationals of Other States (hereinafter the "Convention").

ICSID also suggests that parties consider including a number of other potentially desirable elements in their arbitration clauses, which are discussed below. (See pp. 151-153.)

b. ICSID Jurisdictional Requirements

In considering ICSID arbitration, particular care should be taken to ensure that the ICSID Convention's jurisdictional limits are satisfied. These include the requirement that the investor's home state and the host state have both ratified the ICSID Convention and the requirement that an "investment dispute" will be involved. These requirements can be highly technical, and specialized advice is advisable when seeking to satisfy them.

i. "Investment" Dispute

In particular, Article 25(1) of the ICSID Convention requires that a dispute arise "directly out of an investment." The ICSID Convention does not, however, define "investment," and after disputes arise, states very frequently argue that no investment exists. While agreeing to ICSID arbitration implies that the parties believe that an investment is involved, an investor may wish to strengthen this presumption by including a clause making it explicit. ICSID suggests that the following clause be included for that purpose:

> It is hereby stipulated that the transaction to which this agreement relates is an investment.

ii. Nationality of Investor

Arbitration under the ICSID Convention is available only for disputes between Contracting States to the Convention (and their state-related entities), on the one hand, and investors who are nationals of other ICSID Contracting States, on the other hand. ICSID suggests a clause to record the investor's nationality (although it is unclear whether this will affect the investor's actual nationality for jurisdictional purposes):

> It is hereby stipulated by the parties that the Investor is a national of [name of another Contracting State].

ICSID also recommends including a provision to make clear that the local subsidiary of a foreign company has the nationality of its parent (and therefore satisfies the ICSID Convention's nationality requirement):

> It is hereby agreed that, although the Investor is a national of the Host State, it is controlled by nationals of [name(s) of other Contracting State(s)] and shall be treated as a national of [that]/[those] State[s] for the purposes of the Convention.

iii. Host State Entities

Under Article 25 of the ICSID Convention, ICSID jurisdiction only extends to state-related entities of a Contracting State that have been designated to ICSID as such and have consented to ICSID jurisdiction. The Contracting State must approve of the state entity consenting to ICSID jurisdiction or indicate to the Centre that no such approval is necessary. ICSID suggests that parties to contracts with state entities include the following provision in their arbitration agreement:

> The [name of constituent subdivision or agency] is [a constituent subdivision]/[an agency] of the Host state, which has been designated to the Centre by the Government of that State in accordance with Article 25(1) of the ICSID Convention. In accordance with Article 25(3) of the ICSID Convention, the Host State [hereby gives its approval to this consent agreement (if this government is also a party to the agreement)] [has given its approval to this consent agreement in [citation of

> instrument in which approval is expressed]]/[has notified the Centre that no approval of [this type of consent agreement]/[of consent agreements by the [name of constituent subdivision or agency] is required]].

To address the attribution issue, investors who are contracting with a state entity, rather than directly with a Contracting State, may also wish to include a clause along the following lines:

> The parties agree that, for the purposes of Article 25(1) of the ICSID Convention, the acts of [State entity] are attributable to [the State] within the meaning of the ILC Articles on State Responsibility.

c. *Preservation of Other Remedies*

Article 26 of the ICSID Convention provides that consent to ICSID arbitration "shall, unless otherwise stated, be deemed consent to such arbitration to the exclusion of any other remedy." Should an investor (or Contracting State) wish to "state otherwise" for some reason, ICSID suggests the following provision:

> The consent to the jurisdiction of the Centre recorded in [citation of basic clause] above shall not preclude either party hereto from resorting to the following alternative remedy: [identification of other type of proceeding]. While such other proceeding is pending, no arbitration proceeding pursuant to the Convention shall be instituted.

d. *Exhaustion of Local Remedies*

The second sentence of Article 26 of the ICSID Convention permits a Contracting State to "require the exhaustion of local administrative or judicial remedies as a condition of its consent to arbitration under this Convention." An investor will ordinarily oppose the inclusion of such a provision in a state contract. If a host state requires such a clause, the following can be considered:

> Before either party hereto institutes an arbitration proceeding under the ICSID Convention with respect to a particular dispute, that party must have taken all steps necessary to exhaust the [following] [administrative] [and] [judicial] remedies available under the laws of the Host State with respect to that dispute [list of

> required remedies], unless the other party hereto waives that requirement in writing.

e. *Waivers of State Immunity*

In transactions with states or state entities, it is almost always advisable to include waivers of state immunity from jurisdiction and/or execution and enforcement. ICSID recommends that parties use the following provision as a waiver of sovereign immunity with respect to enforcement:

> The Host State hereby waives any right of sovereign immunity as to it and its property in respect of the enforcement and execution of any award rendered by an Arbitral Tribunal constituted pursuant to this agreement.

Additional waivers of state immunity are provided above and can be readily used in conjunction with an arbitration agreement. (See pp. 31-32 above.) Note that it may be necessary, and is generally advisable, to separately provide for waivers of immunity from both recognition and enforcement of arbitration agreements and awards and execution against property of the state.

2. ICSID Additional Facility

ICSID's "Additional Facility" is an option for contracts or parties that cannot meet the ICSID Convention's jurisdictional requirements. Arbitration under the ICSID Additional Facility is available for the settlement of those disputes which do not fall within the ICSID Convention's jurisdiction, as they do not directly arise out of an investment, and/or because one of the investor's home states and the host state is not an ICSID Contracting State.

The Additional Facility enables parties to select ICSID as appointing authority, but without arbitrating under the ICSID Convention's legal regime. Instead, Additional Facility awards are subject to possible set-aside proceedings in national court (in the arbitral seat) and non-recognition (under the New York Convention). It nonetheless may be preferred over other available options in particular cases.

ICSID's Secretary-General must approve any agreement providing for arbitration under the Additional Facility; in practice, an application for approval can be made prior to or contemporaneously with a request for conciliation or arbitration. The ICSID's recommended clause for arbitration pursuant to the Additional Facility is as follows:

> ICSID Additional Facility Arbitration:
>
> The Government of [name of host State] (hereinafter the "Host State") and [name of investor] (hereinafter the "Investor"), a national of [name of home State] (hereinafter the "Home State"), hereby consent to submit to the International Centre for Settlement of Investment Disputes (hereinafter the "Centre") any dispute arising out of or relating to this agreement for settlement by arbitration pursuant to:
>
> (a) the Convention on the Settlement of Investment Disputes between States and Nationals of Other States (hereinafter the "Convention") if the Host State and the Home State have both become parties to the Convention at the time when any proceeding hereunder is instituted, or
> (b) the Arbitration (Additional Facility) Rules of the Centre if the jurisdictional requirements *ratione personae* of Article 25 of the Convention remain unfulfilled at the time specified in (a) above.

As with other arbitration clauses, parties should consider supplementing each of these basic arbitration provisions in state contracts with additional provisions concerning procedural and other matters. (See pp. 91-103 above.)

3. Alternatives to ICSID Arbitration

Parties to state contracts that cannot meet ICSID's jurisdictional requirements or that do not wish to select ICSID arbitration may choose among a number of other alternatives. The primary disadvantage of non-ICSID arbitration is that the enforcement regime for awards made under other international arbitration rules is arguably less effective than the enforcement regime for awards made under the ICSID Convention. As discussed above (See pp. 163-168), non-ICSID awards are subject to set-aside proceedings in the arbitral seat and to non-recognition under the New York Convention. Conversely, the primary advantage of non-ICSID arbitration mechanisms is that they are likely to be more expeditious and efficient and arguably to provide a less politicized means of appointing the arbitral tribunal.

a. UNCITRAL Arbitration

Arbitration under the UNCITRAL Arbitration Rules is the most frequently chosen alternative to ICSID arbitration for state contracts. A model UNCITRAL arbitration clause is set out above. (See pp. 76-78.) The advantages and disadvantages of ad hoc UNCITRAL arbitration are also discussed above. (See pp. 78-79.) If an UNCITRAL arbitration clause is used, it is advisable to include provisions regarding waivers of state immunity from both jurisdiction and execution. (See pp. 31-32, 153] above.)

b. *ICC, SIAC, SCC, and LCIA Arbitration*

Arbitral institutions that are generally used for international commercial disputes, such as the ICC, LCIA, SCC, and SIAC, are frequently used for arbitrations arising under state contracts. According to the ICC, approximately 20% of its cases in recent years involved a state or state entity. Model arbitration clauses for a variety of commercial arbitration institutions are set out above (See pp. 108-109) and in Appendix I. These provisions are generally appropriate for state contracts, although, again, it is advisable to include waivers of state immunity from both jurisdiction and execution.

c. *Permanent Court of Arbitration*

Another option for contracts with states or state entities is arbitration under the PCA's Optional Rules for Arbitrating Disputes Between Two Parties of Which Only One Is A State. The jurisdiction of the PCA is not restricted to disputes directly arising out of an investment. The PCA's selections of arbitrators are generally well-considered. A model PCA arbitration clause is set out above. (See p. 52.)

The PCA also recommends the following waiver of state immunity for contracts including arbitration provisions:

> This agreement to arbitrate constitutes a waiver of any right to sovereign immunity from execution to which a party might otherwise be entitled with respect to the enforcement of any award rendered by an arbitral tribunal constituted pursuant to this agreement.

Alternative provisions for the waiver of state immunity are also provided above. (See pp. 31-32, 153.)

D. INTERNATIONAL ARBITRATION AGREEMENTS IN ROUTINE TRANSACTIONS

As discussed above, smaller, repetitive transactions seldom warrant individually tailored dispute resolution provisions. (See p. 35) In some cases, there may be an industry standard for dispute resolution (e.g., maritime or commodities arbitration). If not, a reasonable approach is to include a model institutional arbitration clause, providing for arbitration before a sole arbitrator in a specified language in a neutral, reliable, legally beneficial, and convenient place (e.g., London, Paris, Geneva, Stockholm, New York, Miami, Singapore). The temptation to include other provisions, which may well be useful, should be resisted in order to preserve the simplicity of the clause and to minimize points of disagreement.

Where consumer transactions, or transactions with very small individual monetary values, are involved, arbitration agreements may encounter significant enforceability obstacles under some national laws. As noted above, they may also give rise to the possibility of "class arbitrations" among multiple, similarly situated parties, at least in the United States. (See pp. 149-50.)

Chapter 4

Enforcing International Forum Selection Agreements

The utility of an international dispute resolution mechanism may depend on the mechanism's ultimate enforceability. After disputes arise, a party may reconsider its original willingness to accept a forum selection or arbitration agreement. This can result in proceedings in national courts or elsewhere to enforce or interpret the clause.

Significantly different bodies of legal rules govern the interpretation and enforceability of international forum selection clauses on the one hand, and international arbitration agreements on the other. The former are governed largely by national legislation or, in limited instances, regional treaties. In many cases, there is a substantial possibility that an international forum selection clause will be denied effect by national courts, either partially or wholly. In contrast, international arbitration agreements are governed primarily by the New York Convention and by supportive national arbitration statutes which implement the New York Convention. This enforcement regime generally renders international arbitration agreements more readily enforceable than forum selection clauses.

As discussed above, the 2005 Convention (reproduced in Appendix B) might render forum selection agreements somewhat more enforceable in the future, provided that it is ratified by a significant number of states. (See pp. 23-24.) It appears unlikely, however, that such ratifications will occur. At least for the foreseeable future, international arbitration agreements will retain a significant "enforceability premium" as compared to many forum selection clauses.

A. PRESUMPTIVE ENFORCEABILITY OF FORUM SELECTION CLAUSES

Like other contractual provisions, forum selection clauses raise issues of validity and enforceability. Most developed countries are not party to any international treaty or other agreement relating to the enforcement of forum selection clauses. There are some bilateral and regional treaties governing international forum agreements, such as the Lugano Convention and the former Brussels Convention (replaced by the Brussels I Regulation (EC Regulation 44/2001) and now by the recast Brussels I Regulation (EU Regulation 1215/2012)). Nonetheless, most international forum selection clauses are governed in most national courts by domestic law.

Historically, courts in some states regarded forum selection agreements as violative of public policy and unenforceable. That approach has been abandoned in most developed jurisdictions, which now generally hold that international forum selection clauses are presumptively enforceable. There are still important variations between the treatment of forum clauses in different nations, but the general approach in many jurisdictions is broadly similar.

1. EU Approach to Enforceability of Forum Selection Clauses

In Europe, the recast Brussels I Regulation (EU Regulation 1215/2012) governs the enforceability of many international forum selection clauses involving one or more European parties. As discussed above, the Brussels I Regulation is applicable only to "civil and commercial" matters, which exclude questions of personal status, matrimonial issues, succession, and bankruptcy. (See pp. [20–21].) The Brussels I Regulation is not by its terms applicable in the courts of the United States or other non-EU nations.

The recast Brussels I Regulation (in Article 25) provides that forum selection clauses specifying the courts of any EU Member State as the contractual forum are presumptively enforceable. This rule is subject to a number of significant exceptions, which are reviewed above. (See pp. [159–161].) European Court of Justice decisions have also materially weakened the enforcement mechanisms in EU courts for agreements selecting such courts (by preventing issuance of anti-suit injunctions).

2. U.S. Approach to Enforceability of Forum Selection Clauses

Forum selection agreements in U.S. courts are generally governed by common law principles. Following a classic U.S. Supreme Court decision in *Bremen v. Zapata Off-Shore Co.*, most U.S. courts have held that forum clauses between sophisticated corporate entities are presumptively enforceable, with only limited exceptions. Those exceptions concern challenges to the initial validity of the clause, to the "reasonableness" of the selected forum, and to "mandatory law" or "public policy" limits.

A few U.S. jurisdictions continue to hold forum selection clauses unenforceable. It also appears that courts in some states will, applying local state statutes, refuse to enforce forum selection clauses that select an out-of-state forum, either generally or in specific types of agreements (e.g., franchise or insurance contracts). In a few other U.S. jurisdictions, forum selection agreements are treated as one factor in an open-ended "reasonableness" or "*forum non conveniens*" analysis, rather than as binding contractual commitments. Nonetheless, in the vast majority of cases, U.S.

courts will treat international forum selection clauses as presumptively enforceable, subject only to limited exceptions.

3. Other Approaches to Enforceability of Forum Selection Clauses

Many other national courts take approaches that are broadly similar to those in the United States and the EU. That is, in most developed jurisdictions, there is a presumptive willingness to enforce forum selection clauses, subject to various, limited, but unpredictable, exceptions.

B. EXCEPTIONS TO PRESUMPTIVE ENFORCEABILITY OF FORUM SELECTION CLAUSES

Different jurisdictions take different approaches to the exceptions to the presumptive enforceability of a forum clause. In most instances, the existence and scope of these exceptions are defined by national law. Nonetheless, some general observations about categories of exceptions are useful. These exceptions can be broadly categorized as concerning the initial validity of the forum clause (e.g., mistake, fraudulent inducement, unconscionability), the "reasonableness" or "fairness" of the forum clause, and mandatory law or public policy protections for specific classes of parties (e.g., consumers, employees, insureds) or types of claims (e.g., real estate or competition law).

1. Initial Invalidity of Forum Selection Clause

Authorities in many jurisdictions have held that forum selection clauses may be denied enforcement by reason of initial invalidity. In summary:

- A forum selection clause may generally be challenged on the grounds that it does not exist (i.e., the parties' alleged agreement contains no forum clause) or does not bind a particular party thereto.
- A forum selection clause may generally be challenged on the grounds that it is invalid (i.e., it is unconscionable, fraudulent, or the product of mistake). Some courts have invalidated forum clauses on the grounds that they were not the product of sufficient arm's-length negotiation.
- One party's lack of awareness of a forum selection clause is sometimes a basis for denying enforcement. Particularly where consumers or similar parties are involved, some courts have held forum selection clauses unenforceable on the grounds that they were in fine print, were ineffectively incorporated by reference, or were otherwise not readily ascertainable.

Although few national courts have addressed the question, it is likely that challenges to the initial validity of forum selection agreements must be directed specifically to the forum clause *itself*, rather than to the parties' underlying contract. This parallels the treatment of arbitration agreements, which are generally regarded as "separable" from the underlying contract in which they appear. (See pp. 168-169 above.) However, unlike arbitration agreements, the separability of which is generally well-established and expressly guaranteed by both national arbitration statutes and institutional arbitration rules, forum selection clauses seldom enjoy the benefit of national legislation specifically providing for separability.

2. Enforcement of Forum Selection Clause Would Be Unreasonable or Unjust

Authorities in some jurisdictions have held that forum selection clauses will not be enforced where doing so would be "unreasonable" or "unjust." This potentially broad exception has included claims that the contractual forum would be a substantially less convenient place for legal proceedings, or that the contractually chosen courts cannot grant effective relief or are closed to one party.

Some courts have also refused to enforce forum selection clauses designating a forum that lacks any "reasonable relationship" to the parties' dispute. Other courts treat forum clauses as merely one factor in a more generalized inquiry into what forum is most convenient. Under this approach, a forum clause is not enforced as a contract; rather, it is merely an indication of the parties' intentions at one time, which is to be weighed together with considerations of convenience, fairness, judicial economy, and other factors in deciding what forum is "appropriate." It is unlikely that this view would ultimately prevail in most developed legal systems where two sophisticated commercial parties from different nations selected a third country's courts in order to obtain a neutral and competent forum.

3. Public Policy or Illegality

National courts may refuse to uphold a forum selection clause that violates applicable mandatory law or overrides the public policy of the forum. Many countries have enacted legislation expressly invalidating forum selection agreements with respect to certain substantive causes of action. For example, forum selection clauses are sometimes unenforceable in connection with franchise, employment, insurance, consumer, securities, and real estate transactions.

Illustrative examples of claims which may not validly be subject to exclusive forum selection clauses in various jurisdictions include:

- *Consumer contracts*—Recast Brussels I Regulation (EU Regulation 1215/2012, Articles 17–19) (consumer may commence action in his or her domicile); Swiss Law on Private International Law, Article 114(1) (consumer may rescind agreement to litigate disputes in court outside his or her domicile).
- *Employees' claims against employers*—Recast Brussels I Regulation, Articles 20–23 (employee may commence action in his or her domicile); U.K. Employment Rights Act 1996.

- *In rem actions concerning real property*—Recast Brussels I Regulation, Article 24.1; Swiss Law on Private International Law, Article 98.
- *Certain intellectual property rights, including the validity of patents and trademarks*—Recast Brussels I Regulation, Article 24.4.
- *Distribution or franchise agreements*—Michigan Compiled Laws Annotated §445.1527(f) (West 1998) ("A provision requiring that arbitration or litigation be conducted outside this state" is "void and unenforceable if contained in any documents relating to a franchise"); Puerto Rican Law 85 (prohibiting enforcement of clauses in distribution agreements selecting foreign fora).
- *Certain protections for securities investors*—California Corporation Code §25701; Swiss Law on Private International Law, Article 151(3) (claims arising from public offerings of securities).

In many jurisdictions, specific statutory restrictions on forum clauses are coupled with a general "public policy" exception. The public policy exception is notoriously difficult to define, and creates the possibility of expansive and unpredictable grounds for resisting the enforceability of forum selection agreements. These vary from state to state, often depending on local history and concerns (e.g., restrictions on interest, protections for local natural resources).

C. CHOICE-OF-LAW ISSUES RELATING TO FORUM SELECTION CLAUSES

Like other aspects of international contracts, it is necessary to determine what body of law governs the validity, enforceability, and interpretation of a forum selection agreement. The most likely choices are: (a) the law of the forum where litigation is proceeding (on the theory that choice of forum is a procedural issue, subject to the forum's rules); (b) the law governing the parties' underlying contract (on the theory that enforcing a forum selection agreement is a question of substantive law, no different from other questions of contract interpretation and validity); or (c) the law of the contractually specified forum (on the theory that the parties impliedly intended this forum's rules to govern their forum selection agreement). Of course, different national courts may reach different conclusions as to the law governing the same forum selection clause in parallel proceedings in the same dispute. Most national courts have devoted little attention to the question of which of these laws governs forum selection agreements.

In some instances, the foregoing choice-of-law issues are academic because of the general similarity of the rules governing forum clauses in different developed jurisdictions. As discussed elsewhere, however, there remain states that consider forum selection clauses per se unenforceable, that accord them less weight than other contractual terms, or that subject them to materially different exceptions to enforceability. As a consequence, these relatively unexplored choice-of-law issues may assume importance in particular cases.

One approach to reducing the uncertainty surrounding these choice-of-law issues would be to include a choice-of-law clause that expressly designates the law applicable to the parties' forum selection clause. It is not clear, however, that this contractual choice of law would prevail over local law in jurisdictions that consider forum selection to be procedural or remedial, and therefore subject to the *lex fori*. Moreover, a choice-of-law provision will seldom affect issues of public policy or mandatory law, such as those summarized above. (See pp. [160–161].) Nonetheless, as discussed above (See pp. [179–180]), a broadly worded choice-of-law clause, which includes within its scope the parties' forum selection agreement, may be advisable.

Chapter 5

Enforcing International Arbitration Agreements

After disputes have arisen, parties frequently disagree over the interpretation and enforceability of the international arbitration agreements they have signed, just as disagreements arise concerning forum selection clauses. The rules governing the enforcement of international arbitration agreements differ, however, in vital respects from those governing forum selection clauses.

In general, international arbitration agreements are more readily enforceable, and more expansively interpreted, than forum selection clauses. This is largely a consequence of a framework of "pro-arbitration" international conventions and national laws which apply to international arbitration agreements, but not to choice of forum clauses.

A. LEGAL FRAMEWORK FOR ENFORCING INTERNATIONAL ARBITRATION AGREEMENTS

1. New York Convention

As discussed above, the centerpiece of the legal regime governing international arbitration agreements is the New York Convention. The New York Convention was drafted under U.N. auspices in 1958, and, as noted above, has been ratified by some 172 countries, including virtually all significant trading states. A list of the New York Convention's parties is included at the end of Appendix A.

The New York Convention was designed to enhance the enforceability of international arbitration agreements and awards. It is widely regarded as having contributed to the significant increase in the use and efficacy of international commercial arbitration in recent decades. The English language text of the New York Convention is reprinted in Appendix A.

In broad outline, the New York Convention requires national courts in Contracting States to: (a) recognize and enforce international arbitration agreements, subject to certain exceptions (Articles II(1), II(3)); and (b) recognize and enforce foreign arbitral awards, again subject to specified exceptions (Articles III, V). As a consequence of these provisions, and of national arbitration legislation implementing them, international arbitration agreements and awards are typically subject to an avowedly pro-enforcement international legal regime. As detailed below, this specialized regime materially increases the likelihood that international arbitration agreements will be given effect in the courts of Contracting States.

2. Other International Arbitration Conventions

Although the New York Convention is the most important international treaty affecting commercial arbitration, there are other more specialized treaties that are also of importance.

a. ICSID Convention

The ICSID Convention was drafted under the auspices of the United Nations and World Bank in 1965. The ICSID Convention has been ratified by 158 states (as of June 2025).

As discussed above (See pp. [150–153]), the ICSID Convention provides a specialized arbitration regime for "investment disputes" between states and foreign investors that agree to arbitrate pursuant to the ICSID Convention. Where an arbitration agreement or award is subject to the ICSID Convention, the ICSID Convention's regime overrides inconsistent provisions of other treaties, including the New York Convention.

The ICSID Convention contains a variety of unusual provisions. These include provisions regarding choice-of-law (providing, absent contrary choice, for application of the host state's laws and "such rules of international law as may be applicable"), an internal process for reviewing and potentially annulling arbitral awards, and theoretically direct enforceability of ICSID arbitral awards in Member States' courts without judicial review.

b. Panama Convention

The Panama Convention, drafted in 1975, has been ratified by the United States and 20 South and Central American states. The Panama Convention was conceived at a time when long-standing distrust of international arbitration made many South American states reluctant to ratify the New York Convention, and it was intended as a more acceptable regional alternative.

The interplay between the Panama Convention and the New York Convention is complex. In acceding to the Panama Convention, the United States adopted a reservation according to which, if an agreement or award was otherwise subject to both the Panama and New York Conventions, the former would control where a majority of the parties involved were citizens of states that ratified the Panama Convention; this rule can be altered by agreement among the parties. The New York

Convention is the subject of a larger, more developed body of precedent than the Panama Convention, which generally counsels in favor of selecting it when a choice is available.

The Panama Convention largely parallels the New York Convention in its treatment of international arbitration agreements and awards. In addition, however, the Panama Convention also provides that, where the parties' arbitration agreement does not incorporate any specific institutional arbitration rules, then the rules of procedure of the "Inter-American Commercial Arbitration Commission" will govern, and the Commission will act as the appointing authority with respect to arbitrators. This can be useful in cases where the parties have not agreed upon an appointing authority, by reducing the likelihood of resort to local courts for the appointment of arbitrators.

c. *European Convention on International Commercial Arbitration*

The European Convention on International Commercial Arbitration ("European Convention") was drafted in 1961 and entered into force in October 1965. The European Convention has now been ratified by over 30 countries (the majority of which are in Europe), including a significant number of countries in Eastern Europe and the former Soviet Union. The European Convention imposes a variety of obligations upon signatory states, many of which mirror the New York Convention.

d. *Bilateral Investment Treaties*

BITs became common during the 1980s and 1990s, as a means of encouraging capital investment in developing markets. Most capital-exporting states (including the United States and many EU states) have entered into numerous BITs with countries in developing regions. There are currently approximately 2,200 BITs in force.

Virtually all BITs provide substantive international protections for specified classes of foreign investors and their investments. In a typical BIT, the host state undertakes not to expropriate investments except for a public purpose and on payment of prompt, adequate, and effective compensation; to accord fair and equitable treatment to investments; to treat protected investors and investments as favorably as investors and investments from the host state or any third state; and to guarantee unrestricted transfer of funds and returns.

In addition, the overwhelming majority of BITs provide for some form of arbitration of disputes under the BIT. Under most BITs, the host state ordinarily extends a generic invitation (or "standing offer to arbitrate") to all investors who are nationals of the other Contracting State to submit investment disputes to arbitration—even in the absence of an arbitration agreement in the contract(s) giving rise to the dispute. ICSID is the favored forum for this form of arbitration, although some BITs permit ad hoc arbitration under the UNCITRAL Rules or specified institutional arbitration rules on an equal footing with ICSID. The possibility of "arbitration without privity" under a BIT is often an option to consider in international commercial disputes. For this reason, careful attention should be paid to whether disputes under a particular contract may fall within an applicable BIT and the effect that this may have upon the available dispute resolution procedures. A list of websites containing links to applicable BITs is included in Appendix G.

3. National Arbitration Legislation

The existence of the nearly universal New York Convention enhances the likelihood that international arbitration agreements and arbitral awards will be enforceable. At the end of the day, however, it may well be necessary in particular cases for either arbitration agreements or arbitral awards to be judicially enforced. In some countries, these international treaties are directly applicable in national courts. In other nations, however, the New York Convention and other treaties are not automatically applicable in domestic courts, but must be implemented by national legislation.

Different nations have adopted widely differing types of arbitration legislation. Among other things, different countries apply varying standards to such matters as resolution of challenges to the arbitrators' jurisdiction, judicial review of arbitral awards made within national territory, and the availability of effective procedural mechanisms to support enforcement efforts (e.g., attachment). These differences can have substantial practical consequences for parties seeking to enforce an international arbitral award.

During the late 20th and early 21st centuries, there was a strong trend towards uniformity of national arbitration statutes, in part by virtue of the UNCITRAL Model Law. This trend somewhat reduced the disparities among the international arbitration regimes of different states. Nonetheless, the practical realities of arbitration and judicial responses to arbitration in different countries still vary widely; these differences have become more pronounced over the past decade, with the risks of parochial or partisan local court decisions increasing. As a practical matter, this has significant effects on the enforceability of arbitration agreements and awards in different jurisdictions.

4. UNCITRAL Model Law

More than 90 states, including many major trading states, have adopted national arbitration legislation based on the UNCITRAL Model Law on International Commercial Arbitration. UNCITRAL Model Law countries include Australia, Austria, Bahrain, Bermuda, Canada, Egypt, England (to an extent), Germany, Hong Kong, India, Mexico, New Zealand, Russia, Singapore, Spain, Turkey, and the UAE. The UNCITRAL Model Law, which was first released in 1985, is reproduced in Appendix C. The purpose of the Model Law is to make international arbitration agreements and awards more readily, predictably, and uniformly enforceable. The Model Law also seeks to minimize the potential for judicial interference in international arbitral proceedings.

A number of provisions of the Model Law were revised in 2006; the 2006 revisions, which have only recently started to be adopted by some jurisdictions, are included in Appendix D. A list of countries that have adopted legislation based on the UNCITRAL Model Law and its revisions is also included in Appendix D.

The 1985 UNCITRAL Model Law contains 36 articles which deal comprehensively with the issues that arise in national courts in connection with international arbitration. Among other things, the Model Law contains provisions concerning the enforcement of arbitration agreements (Articles 7–9), appointment of and challenges to arbitrators (Articles 10–15), jurisdiction of arbitrators (Article 16), provisional measures (Article 17), conduct of the arbitral proceedings (including language, seat, and procedures) (Articles 18–26), evidence-taking and disclosure (Article 27), applicable law (Article 28), awards (Articles 29–33), setting aside or annulling awards (Article 34), and recognition and enforcement of awards, including bases for non-recognition (Articles 35–36).

Under the UNCITRAL Model Law, written international arbitration agreements are presumptively valid and enforceable, subject to limited, specified exceptions. Article 8 of the Model Law provides for the enforcement of valid arbitration agreements, regardless of the arbitral seat, by way of a dismissal or stay of national court litigation. The Model Law also adopts the separability presumption (Article 16) and grants arbitrators authority (competence-competence) to consider their own jurisdiction (also in Article 16).

Article 5 of the UNCITRAL Model Law prescribes a principle of judicial non-intervention in arbitral proceedings. The Model Law also affirms the parties' autonomy (subject to due process limits) with regard to the arbitral procedures (Article 19(1)) and, absent agreement between the parties, the arbitral tribunal's authority to prescribe such procedures (Article 19(2)). The approach of the Model Law to the arbitral proceedings is to define a basic set of procedural rules which—subject to a very limited number of mandatory principles of fairness, due process, and equality of treatment—the parties are free to alter or supplement by agreement. The Model Law also provides for judicial assistance to the arbitral process in prescribed and limited respects, including provisional measures, constitution of a tribunal, and evidence-taking (Articles 9, 11–13 and 27).

Article 34 of the UNCITRAL Model Law mandates the presumptive validity of international arbitral awards, subject to a limited, exclusive list of grounds for annulment of awards in the arbitral seat; these grounds parallel those available under the New York Convention for non-recognition of an award (i.e., lack or excess of jurisdiction, non-compliance with arbitration agreement, due process violations, public policy, and non-arbitrability). In a parallel provision, Articles 35 and 36 of the Model Law require the recognition and enforcement of foreign awards (made in arbitral seats located outside the recognizing state), again on terms identical to those prescribed in the New York Convention.

The 2006 revisions to the Model Law made only modest changes. These included a revised (and significantly reduced) form requirement for arbitration agreements (in Article 7), revised provisions regarding interim measures (in Article

17), including allowing a party to seek orders from the tribunal ex parte, and a limited number of additional provisions (including technical amendments and statements of principle regarding interpretation of the Model Law).

B. PRESUMPTIVE VALIDITY AND ENFORCEABILITY OF INTERNATIONAL ARBITRATION AGREEMENTS

One of the central purposes of the New York Convention was to make international arbitration agreements more readily enforceable. Article II of the Convention provides:

> "1. Each Contracting State shall recognize an agreement in writing under which the parties undertake to submit to arbitration all or any differences which have arisen or which may arise between them in respect of a defined legal relationship, whether contractual or not, concerning a subject matter capable of settlement by arbitration. ...
>
> 3. The court of a Contracting State, when seized of an action in a matter in respect of which the parties have made an agreement within the meaning of this article, shall, at the request of one of the parties, refer the parties to arbitration, unless it finds that the said agreement is null and void, inoperative or incapable of being performed."

Article II supersedes provisions, still extant in a few countries, that rendered arbitration agreements invalid or unenforceable. Under Article II, international arbitration agreements are generally valid and enforceable, save where a party can demonstrate that they are null and void, inoperative, or incapable of being performed.

Most national arbitration statutes contain provisions parallel to those of Article II of the New York Convention. In particular, Article 8 of the UNCITRAL Model Law provides for the presumptive validity and enforceability of international arbitration agreements.

C. SEPARABILITY OF INTERNATIONAL ARBITRATION AGREEMENTS

In many nations, including all major trading states, an arbitration agreement is presumptively "separable" from the underlying contract in which it appears. National arbitration legislation often expressly so provides. (See UNCITRAL Model Law, Article 16(1); Swiss Law on Private International Law, Article 178(3); U.S. Federal Arbitration Act §2; German Civil Procedure Act, Article 1040(1); Chinese Arbitration Law, Article 19.) Most leading institutional arbitration rules do so as well. (See 2021 UNCITRAL Rules, Article 23(1); 2021 ICC Rules, Article 6(9); 2021 ICDR Rules, Article 21(2); 2020 LCIA Rules, Article 23(2).)

The separability presumption has important practical consequences. It means that challenges to the parties' underlying contract will generally not be regarded as affecting or vitiating the parties' "separate" or "autonomous" arbitration agreement.

Specifically, if a party alleges that the parties' underlying contract was fraudulently induced or is invalid for lack of consideration, this will not provide a basis for challenging the validity of the arbitration agreement or for refusing to arbitrate. The theory is that the arbitration clause is a separate and independent agreement that validly exists even if the underlying contract is invalid. Nonetheless, in some jurisdictions, the separability presumption may not provide grounds for upholding the validity of the arbitration agreement where the very existence of the underlying contract is challenged.

Another consequence of the separability presumption is that a different law may apply to the parties' arbitration agreement than to their underlying contract. This has been relied upon by some national courts (e.g., French and U.S.) to embrace avowedly "international" rules of substantive law that significantly limit the grounds for challenging the validity of international arbitration agreements. In other jurisdictions, the separability presumption can give rise to complex choice-of-law issues (whose practical importance should ordinarily be limited by the trend towards uniform, pro-enforcement national arbitration laws).

D. INTERPRETATION OF INTERNATIONAL ARBITRATION AGREEMENTS

Many national courts adopt a "pro-arbitration" approach to the interpretation of the scope of arbitration agreements. For example, U.S. courts apply a strong presumption favoring the interpretation of arbitration agreements to extend to disputed issues. In case of doubt regarding the scope of an arbitration clause and its coverage of particular disputes, courts must resolve the issue in favor of arbitration. Swiss, English, Singaporean, and some other national courts also interpret international arbitration agreements relatively expansively. Although other national courts approach the task of interpreting an arbitration agreement as one of objectively ascertaining the parties' intent, as a practical matter, doubts about the scope of a concededly valid agreement are often resolved in favor of arbitration.

E. EXCEPTIONS TO PRESUMPTIVE ENFORCEABILITY OF INTERNATIONAL ARBITRATION AGREEMENTS

1. Invalidity of Arbitration Agreements

National courts have typically interpreted Article II in an avowedly "pro-arbitration" fashion. Generally applicable contract rules govern most questions regarding the validity of arbitration agreements, including doctrines such as mistake, fraud, unconscionability, duress, and lack of capacity. Most courts in developed states have been reluctant to invoke such defenses to invalidate international arbitration agreements subject to the New York Convention. Moreover, very few courts have been willing to entertain objections (such as those sometimes available in resisting forum selection clauses) that an arbitration agreement is "unreasonable" or "unjust" or that it selects an "inconvenient" arbitral seat.

In many cases, challenges to the validity of an international arbitration agreement are presented first to the arbitrators themselves. This may result from a party's unwillingness to incur the costs or other consequences of commencing litigation in national courts to challenge an agreement because of concerns about alienating a tribunal, or otherwise. Although a tribunal's jurisdictional rulings are usually subject to eventual judicial review, they will often have substantial practical weight, either because many disputes settle before ultimate judicial review or because of deference to arbitral rulings.

2. "Non-Arbitrability" Exceptions

Virtually all nations treat some categories of claims as incapable of resolution by arbitration—that is, "non-arbitrable." Consistent with this, Articles II(1) and V(2)(a) of the New York Convention do not require enforcement of arbitration agreements concerning a subject matter not "capable of settlement by arbitration."

The types of claims that are "non-arbitrable" are defined primarily by national law and differ from nation to nation. Among other things, various nations refuse to permit arbitration of disputes concerning labor or employment grievances, intellectual property, competition (antitrust) claims, real estate, consumer claims, and franchise relations. These categories of non-arbitrable disputes are roughly comparable to, if more limited than, those claims as to which forum selection clauses may be unenforceable. (See pp. [160–161] above.) As a practical matter, however, non-arbitrability exceptions are often more narrowly applied, in part because they frequently are considered first by arbitral tribunals. Moreover, there are substantial arguments that the New York Convention limits the extent to which local public policy or legislation may be invoked to deny effect to an otherwise valid arbitration clause.

Chapter 6

Recognizing and Enforcing Foreign Judgments

The ultimate test of an international dispute resolution mechanism is the enforceability of the result that it produces. That is true whether the result is a national court judgment or an arbitral award. In many international disputes, a judgment or award may be rendered in a forum where one or both parties have no assets. That judgment or award will therefore need to be taken elsewhere, either for recognition (to preclude assertion of inconsistent claims or defenses in other legal proceedings) or for enforcement (to collect a money debt or obtain specific performance).

The legal rules governing the enforceability of foreign judgments and foreign arbitral awards differ significantly. The former are governed largely by national legislation or, in limited circumstances, regional treaty arrangements such as the Brussels I Regulation and the Lugano Convention. The latter are governed primarily by the New York Convention, or other multilateral conventions, and secondarily by supportive national arbitration statutes. As discussed above (See pp. [175–176]), the enforcement regime applicable to arbitral awards makes such awards more readily enforceable, in most cases, than national court judgments.

A. NO WORLDWIDE CONVENTION ON FOREIGN JUDGMENTS

There is no universal international treaty governing the recognition and enforcement of foreign court judgments. Nothing equivalent to the New York Convention's essentially global enforcement regime for arbitral awards exists with respect to national court judgments.

As discussed above, the Member States of the Hague Conference on Private International Law finalized the text of the 2005 Convention, and Albania, the European Union, Mexico, Montenegro, North Macedonia, Moldova, Switzerland, Ukraine and the United Kingdom have ratified the 2005 Convention. (See p. 24.) Thus far, however, other states have (advisedly) declined to ratify the 2005 Convention, and it appears doubtful that it will provide an effective mechanism for recognizing and enforcing national court judgments in the foreseeable future. At present, the enforcement of foreign judgments is therefore still governed by either bilateral or regional treaties, or by domestic national law. Under these legal regimes, there are significant obstacles to obtaining effective enforcement of foreign court judgments in many cases.

B. PRESUMPTIVE ENFORCEABILITY OF FOREIGN MONEY JUDGMENTS IN MOST MAJOR TRADING STATES

Under the laws of many states, foreign money judgments are presumptively enforceable, subject to a variety of exceptions. This basic rule has been adopted in a substantial number of jurisdictions, including most EU states, the United States, developed Asian states, and elsewhere. In the United States, for example, both common law and statutory rules (based on the Uniform Foreign Money Judgments Recognition Act) treat foreign money judgments as presumptively enforceable. Applicable rules in many other nations, and in a number of bilateral judgments treaties, are broadly similar.

Nonetheless, a substantial number of jurisdictions will generally not enforce foreign court judgments. Some states apply rules which deny recognition to any foreign judgment absent a treaty relationship with the rendering state (or "state of origin") providing for mutual recognition and enforcement of judgments. This includes a number of European states, principally Nordic and Eastern European countries. Other countries simply refuse to recognize any foreign judgments, or admit foreign judgments solely as evidence in support of a party's substantive claims, which must then be relitigated.

Even in jurisdictions where it is theoretically possible, the recognition and enforcement of foreign judgments is infrequently sought and even less frequently obtained. This is particularly true with respect to judgments against local nationals—against whom enforcement is typically most likely to be sought.

The enforcement of foreign judgments can be subject to procedural delays and other shortcomings, especially in states where courts lack experience with such efforts. The absence of treaty commitments means that there are few external checks on parochial obstacles to enforcement against local nationals. Additionally, as a practical matter, effective enforcement of money judgments often requires speedy and effective actions to attach assets. In many legal systems, this is not a realistic expectation for foreign judgment creditors, particularly those holding judgments against local parties.

The treatment of foreign judgments granting injunctive or other non-monetary relief is even less favorable in most states than the treatment of money judgments. In many jurisdictions, precedents or legislation according presumptive validity to foreign money judgments do not apply to equitable decrees, injunctions, and similar orders.

C. EXCEPTIONS TO PRESUMPTIVE ENFORCEABILITY OF FOREIGN MONEY JUDGMENTS

Even in jurisdictions which provide for the presumptive enforceability of foreign money judgments, this presumption is subject to a variety of important exceptions. These exceptions can pose significant obstacles to enforcing foreign judgments:

- *Inconvenient Forum*—Some states will refuse to recognize judgments rendered by a court that was unduly inconvenient. Inconvenience is often assessed by the standards of the enforcement forum, and can be a relatively malleable standard.
- *Conflicting Judgment*—Many states will refuse to recognize foreign judgments if they conflict with a local judgment. That is sometimes true regardless of the timing of the two judgments, or of the commencement of the two sets of proceedings, as in the case of Japan.
- *Procedural Regularity*—Many states will not recognize foreign judgments unless they were the result of judicial proceedings which satisfy local standards of procedural fairness. Given the wide disparity of procedural rules around the world, this requirement provides ample grounds for non-recognition.
- *Lack of Notice*—Courts in almost all jurisdictions will refuse to recognize foreign judgments where the judgment debtor did not receive adequate notice of the foreign proceedings. Differences in approaches to the service of process in different legal systems make this a more serious obstacle than might appear. A judgment debtor's participation in foreign proceedings will sometimes waive its objections to service in subsequent enforcement actions.
- *Personal Jurisdiction* (*Rationae Personae*)—Courts in almost all states will refuse to recognize foreign judgments rendered by courts which lacked jurisdiction over the person of the judgment debtor. Personal jurisdiction is usually determined in accordance with the standards of the enforcement forum, not the rendering court. Where a valid contractual forum selection clause exists, and is complied with, jurisdictional challenges will be more difficult. In other circumstances, personal jurisdiction is often a significant hurdle to enforcing judgments abroad.
- *Subject Matter Jurisdiction* (*Rationae Materiae*)—Many nations treat various categories of disputes as falling within the exclusive competence of local courts. In some countries, for example, foreign judgments in disputes between nationals are unenforceable, on the grounds that such disputes are subject to the exclusive jurisdiction of local courts. In other states, disputes concerning matters such as real property, employment relations, certain questions of corporate affairs and the like, are regarded as within the exclusive jurisdiction of particular local courts.
- *Mandatory Laws or Public Policy*—Almost all states refuse to recognize foreign judgments that violate local public policy or mandatory laws.

Examples of such laws and policies are set forth above (See pp. [160–161]), but in many countries, public policy will permit novel and expansive arguments that a foreign judgment should not be enforced.
- *Reciprocity*—A number of states deny recognition to foreign judgments rendered in nations that will not recognize their local judgments.
- *Revenue and Penal Judgments*—Many jurisdictions adhere to the historic rule that foreign "revenue" *and* "penal" judgments will not be recognized. These exceptions are directed primarily at judgments obtained by foreign governmental and administrative entities, but they can also extend to judgments based on quasi-public law protections (arguably, such as competition law).

The cumulative impact of these exceptions makes it difficult to seek the enforcement of foreign money or other judgments with any degree of confidence, at least where no bilateral or regional treaty governs the subject. The relative infrequency of efforts to enforce foreign judgments in many countries exacerbates the uncertainties that accompany such efforts. Even in developed jurisdictions with a substantial record of enforcing foreign judgments (e.g., Switzerland, France, Germany, Canada, England, United States), questions of jurisdiction, procedural regularity, and public policy can present very substantial problems. Of course, where there are developed bilateral or regional arrangements for the mutual recognition of foreign judgments, such as the Brussels I Regulation and the Lugano Convention, enforcement will be much less complex.

Chapter 7

Recognizing and Enforcing International Arbitral Awards

Parties sometimes refuse to honor international arbitral awards against them, although anecdotal evidence indicates that this occurs much less frequently than with foreign court judgments. As outlined above, international arbitral awards are subject to a significantly different legal framework for recognition and enforcement than foreign court judgments. (See pp. 163–168.) In general, this regime makes international arbitral awards significantly more enforceable than foreign court judgments.

A. PRESUMPTIVE VALIDITY AND ENFORCEABILITY OF INTERNATIONAL ARBITRAL AWARDS

A central purpose of the New York Convention is to facilitate the recognition and enforcement of foreign and non-domestic arbitral awards. Article III of the New York Convention imposes a general requirement that Contracting States recognize arbitral awards made in other countries:

> "Each Contracting State shall recognize arbitral awards as binding and enforce them in accordance with the rules of procedure of the territory where the award is relied upon, under the conditions laid down in the following articles. There shall not be imposed substantially more onerous conditions or higher fees or charges on the recognition or enforcement of arbitral awards to which the Convention applies than are imposed on the recognition or enforcement of domestic arbitral awards."

The New York Convention's provisions regarding the enforceability of foreign arbitral awards are binding on some 172 jurisdictions, including almost all major trading states. (See Appendix A.)

Nonetheless, the recognition and enforcement of an international arbitral award often requires proceeding under local arbitration legislation in the enforcement forum. Many states have enacted legislation that faithfully implements the New York Convention and provides a favorable statutory regime for enforcement. In practice, of course, the application of such regimes can vary significantly from one country to another, with these variations having become somewhat more frequent in recent years.

In most developed states, there is substantial practical experience with the enforcement of foreign arbitral awards. In the vast majority of reported decisions under Article V of the New York Convention, courts have recognized and enforced foreign arbitral awards. In so doing, they have frequently rejected arguments by local defendants challenging the fairness or correctness of the arbitral award or raising arguments under one of Article V's exceptions. Although there are instances where international arbitral awards have been denied enforcement, these cases are unusual exceptions, rather than the rule.

Outside the developed world, the likelihood of effective enforcement of a foreign arbitral award, particularly against a local national, can sometimes be less certain. Not all states have enacted "pro-arbitration" national arbitration legislation, such as the UNCITRAL Model Law, and some jurisdictions have instead adopted local statutes that limit the recognition of foreign arbitral awards; even in the absence of such provisions, some domestic courts may be reluctant to enforce awards against local nationals. Nonetheless, in a number of developing states, the prospect of successfully enforcing a foreign arbitral award can be realistically expected. In any event, whatever the relevant jurisdiction, it is clear that there will usually be a greater likelihood that a foreign arbitral award will be enforced than a foreign court judgment.

B. EXCEPTIONS TO PRESUMPTIVE VALIDITY AND ENFORCEABILITY OF INTERNATIONAL ARBITRAL AWARDS

Article V of the New York Convention identifies a limited number of grounds for non-recognition of foreign arbitral awards. These include claims that the award was rendered pursuant to an invalid arbitration agreement; that the losing party "was not given proper notice of the appointment of the arbitrator or of the arbitration proceedings or was otherwise unable to present his case"; that the arbitral award deals with a dispute that was not subject to the parties' arbitration agreement; that the composition of the arbitral tribunal or its procedures violated either the parties' arbitration agreement or (absent such agreement) the law of the arbitral seat; that the award concerns a dispute which is "not capable of settlement by arbitration" under the law of the enforcing state; or that recognition or enforcement of the award would be contrary to the public policy of the enforcing state. Once a party seeking to enforce an award has produced a copy of it (under Article IV of the New York Convention), the burden is on the other party to demonstrate that one of Article V's exceptions is applicable.

1. Arbitrators' Lack of Jurisdiction

National courts will refuse to enforce foreign arbitral awards where there was no valid arbitration agreement or where the arbitral tribunal exceeded the scope of its jurisdiction. (See New York Convention, Articles V(1)(a), (c).) Jurisdictional issues are sometimes reviewed de novo, except where the parties' arbitration agreement, a party's unreserved participation in arbitral proceedings to determine jurisdiction, or other actions submit such issues to the arbitrators for final decision. Challenges to a tribunal's jurisdiction can involve the validity of the parties' arbitration agreement (e.g., raising issues of contract formation, mistake, duress, fraud, capacity, and the like) or the issues submitted to the tribunal (e.g., whether the arbitral award exceeded the scope of the parties' submissions).

2. Procedural Irregularity

Among the most frequently invoked exceptions to the enforceability of foreign arbitral awards is Article V(1)(b)'s exception for lack of notice and/or procedural irregularity. Article V(1)(d) provides a related exception, applicable where the arbitral procedures did not comply with the parties' agreement regarding such procedures or, in the absence of any agreement by the parties, the law of the arbitral seat. Although national courts generally accord substantial deference to procedural decisions of international arbitrators, some New York Convention awards have been denied enforcement based on perceived procedural unfairness. The risk of such results is heightened somewhat by the significant differences in judicial procedures which exist in different states.

3. Public Policy and "Non-Arbitrability"

Parties seeking to resist enforcement of international arbitral awards frequently invoke the "public policy" exception under Article V(2)(b). Closely related to the public policy exception is the rule that certain disputes are "non-arbitrable," and that awards on these questions need not be enforced (Article V(2)(a)).

Most national courts have adopted narrow definitions of "public policy" and "non-arbitrability" as bases for denying enforcement to foreign arbitral awards. Some courts have held that only truly "international" public policies will permit non-recognition of an award. Other courts have rejected a variety of proffered public policies, either on the grounds that they were not sufficiently serious or that they were not in fact affected by the arbitral award. Nonetheless, creative counsel can sometimes construct public policy or non-arbitrability arguments, which can delay enforcement efforts. In countries with comparatively little exposure to international arbitration, these defenses can present issues of first impression, with some uncertainty existing as to their judicial reception. The elasticity of "public policies" in some states heightens this uncertainty. Despite this, and although they are frequently invoked, in most cases, neither the public policy nor the non-arbitrability exception has proved a significant practical obstacle to the effective enforcement of international arbitral awards.

Chapter 8

Drafting and Enforcing Choice-of-Law Clauses

Forum selection and arbitration agreements are frequently accompanied by choice-of-law clauses, specifying the substantive law applicable to the parties' contractual and other relations. A choice-of-law clause provides enhanced predictability, security, and efficiency with respect to the interpretation and enforcement of the parties' contractual obligations, and is ordinarily a critical aspect of any international transaction. A choice-of-law clause should generally be a separate, stand-alone provision, rather than incorporated as a sub-section within an arbitration or forum selection clause. As discussed above (See pp. 103-104), this minimizes the risk of claims that the provision includes, or is limited to, essentially procedural matters.

Contracting parties are not always able to agree on what body of law should govern their contractual and other relations. There are circumstances where the parties' inability to agree upon an applicable substantive law can satisfactorily be resolved through the omission of a choice-of-law clause from the parties' contract. This results in a measure of uncertainty as to the likely governing law, since there will often be doubt as to the conclusion that contemporary conflict of laws rules will produce. Nonetheless, where the substantive laws which will likely apply are all neutral and developed, this uncertainty will not necessarily warrant abandoning an otherwise desirable transaction. In contrast, if an undeveloped law is potentially applicable, a transaction involves a foreign state, or there are particular needs for certainty or enforceability, then an express choice-of-law clause will often be an essential prerequisite for proceeding with a transaction.

A. PLANNING AND DRAFTING CHOICE-OF-LAW CLAUSES

1. Scope of Choice-of-Law Clauses

In practice, choice-of-law clauses are sometimes drafted in narrower terms than forum selection or arbitration agreements. As discussed above, forum selection and arbitration provisions often (and prudently) extend to all disputes "relating to" or "arising in connection with" the parties' contractual relationship. (See pp. 25–26,

41–42.) These reach non-contractual claims, such as those sounding in tort, as well as contractual ones.

In contrast, choice-of-law clauses are not infrequently drafted more narrowly, along the following lines:

> This agreement shall be interpreted in accordance with, and governed by, the laws of ________.

Such formulations can be interpreted as extending solely to the parties' contractual rights and duties, and not to questions of tort or other non-contractual rights.

Alternatively, choice-of-law clauses can be drafted even more narrowly, such as:

> This agreement shall be construed in accordance with the laws of ________.

This formulation should generally be avoided. It arguably applies only to questions of contract interpretation and construction, and not to issues of validity, enforceability, excuses for non-performance, and capacity, much less to questions of tort or other non-contractual rights.

It is generally advisable to draft choice-of-law clauses with a scope that is identical to the parties' contractual dispute resolution mechanism. This enhances predictability by increasing the likelihood that quasi-contractual, tort, or statutory claims will also be resolved according to the parties' chosen law. As discussed below, there are issues regarding the enforceability of choice-of-law clauses, particularly where non-contractual claims are concerned. (See pp. 189–190.) These issues should generally not detract from the wisdom of attempting to achieve uniformity between choice-of-law and dispute resolution provisions.

A suitable formulation for choice-of-law clauses, designed to track an appropriate dispute resolution provision, is as follows:

> This Agreement will be governed by, and all disputes relating to or arising in connection with this Agreement [or the subject matter of this Agreement] shall be resolved in accordance with, the laws of ________.

Whatever formulation is utilized, the important point is that—in contrast with what is sometimes encountered in practice—the scope of the parties' choice-of-law clause should ordinarily parallel that of the parties' forum selection or arbitration agreement.

2. *Renvoi* Versus "Whole Law"

It ordinarily should not be necessary, but parties frequently include a provision in their choice-of-law clause excluding the possibility of "*renvoi*." That is, the choice-of-law clause will make it clear that the *substantive* laws of the chosen jurisdiction, and not its *conflict of laws rules*, are applicable. A suitable formulation is as follows:

> This Agreement will be governed by, and all disputes relating to or arising in connection with this Agreement shall be resolved in accordance with, the laws of _________ (to the exclusion of its conflict of laws rules).

International instruments and authorities in many developed jurisdictions will interpret choice-of-law clauses as accomplishing this result, even if an anti-*renvoi* provision is not included in the choice-of-law clause.

3. "Procedural" Issues

Choice-of-law clauses are often not interpreted as extending to "procedural" issues, which are instead considered to be subject to the generally applicable rules of civil procedure of the parties' contractual forum. For example, most choice-of-law clauses would not be regarded as extending to pleading requirements, discovery mechanisms, and joinder of parties. Other questions, such as statutes of limitations, burdens of proof, rights to legal expenses, and interest, raise more difficult issues; they are sometimes regarded as substantive (and thus arguably subject to commonly used choice-of-law provisions) and sometimes treated as procedural (and thus arguably subject to the forum's rules).

Even if parties extend their choice-of-law clause to "procedural" issues, this may raise issues of enforceability, particularly in national court (as distinct from arbitral) proceedings. Procedural issues may be bound up with questions of judicial administration, as to which local public policy will require application of the forum's law. Moreover, the application of foreign law to some procedural issues will often be regarded as impracticable (e.g., pleading requirements).

4. Choice-of-Law Clauses in Investment Contracts

Choice-of-law clauses in investment contracts are sometimes drafted broadly to allow for the application of both national and international law to disputes relating to the agreement. An example of such a clause is as follows:

> For purposes of this Contract, the laws of _________ existing and in force on the Effective Date of this Contract and generally accepted principles of international law shall govern this Contract.

ICSID suggests that the following model provision serves as a basis for a choice-of-law clause in an investment agreement:

> Any Arbitral Tribunal constituted pursuant to this agreement shall apply [specification of system of law] [subject to the following modifications: _________].

5. Which Law Should Be Chosen?

There is no single, simple answer to the question of what substantive law a party should seek to make applicable to a particular international commercial relationship. The answer to this question is influenced by a variety of considerations that are dependent on the parties' identities, the nature of the transaction, and the potentially applicable national laws. Nonetheless, several general guidelines are useful.

a. *Developed, Stable, and Commercially Sophisticated Law*

A party should generally seek agreement upon a law that is developed, stable, and well-adapted to sophisticated commercial dealings. Parties should pay particular attention to the existence of a well-articulated body of commercial, contractual, and corporate law. The laws of England, New York, Singapore, France, and Switzerland meet this criterion. Some other developed jurisdictions also have suitable commercial and other laws.

Parties should ordinarily avoid the law of a state that is newly formed, that has not yet formulated significant areas of law, or that appears to be exposed to significant political changes. This includes many of the recently emergent states that established market economies during the late 1980s and 1990s. Equally important, parties should avoid jurisdictions which are potentially subject to future sea changes in legal order. These radical transformations can have unpredictable and undesirable consequences for pre-existing contractual relations.

b. *Familiarity and Ease of Access*

It is important to insist on a law with which the parties are either familiar or whose content they can ascertain with reasonable ease. That typically means the laws of a jurisdiction where a party conducts business, or where it can consult reliable counsel efficiently. Parties should select a law from a state which offers a substantial corpus of published statutes, judicial decisions, and commentaries, rather than only conclusory expert opinion.

c. *Enforceability*

Counsel should ensure that the search for a neutral, predictable body of law is not inconsistent with mandatory national law applicable to local aspects of a transaction. Issues relating to real estate, corporate organization, and security interests are examples of matters which ordinarily cannot be contracted out of by means of a choice-of-law clause. Particular care must be devoted to this issue in joint venture or similar transactions, where the local law of the place where the parties' corporate vehicle is incorporated will frequently apply with mandatory force to certain matters relating to corporate organization.

d. "Favorable" Laws

Parties sometimes try to bargain for the application of a law that they expect to be "favorable" to them. This effort is often chimerical because of the difficulty of predicting in advance what issues will arise in some future dispute and on what side of these issues a party may be. Nonetheless, in specialized fields, such an effort can be worthwhile. The laws of financial centers, such as New York and London, are frequently desirable for lenders or creditors.

Parties will often wish to avoid the law of the place where their counterparty has its principal place of operations. That predisposition frequently rests on the assumption that this law may be favorable to that party. In reality, this often will not be the case, although a party can be presumed to be reasonably well informed about its law and to have advantages in the future in ascertaining its content and pursuing legal proceedings (by reason of established relations with counsel).

In dealings with foreign states, parties will generally insist, rightly, on application of the laws of another jurisdiction. This reduces risks that the foreign state will enact legislation or other measures that are designed to improve its position in a contractual dispute.

e. Literal Language Versus Equity

It is often said that the laws of England and most U.S. jurisdictions are especially likely to give effect to the literal language of the parties' agreement. This is in contrast to the laws of civil law (and other) jurisdictions, which are said to be more likely to import general principles of good faith and reasonableness into contractual relations. Although this observation is difficult to confirm, it is consistent with the anecdotal experience of most experienced international practitioners. Which approach is more appropriate, or more advantageous for a particular party, depends on the character of the transaction and potential future disputes.

f. Interaction with Dispute Resolution Provisions

It is important to consider how the parties' choice-of-law clause will interact with their dispute resolution provisions. Specifically, if the parties agree to a judicial forum for dispute resolution, they need to take into account the legal and linguistic capabilities of the tribunals in the chosen forum.

For example, if the parties agree upon an exclusive Swiss forum selection clause, is it desirable to select New York law to govern their dealings? Doing so will require a Swiss judge to apply New York law, derived from expert legal opinions and source materials in English. This can impose expense and inconvenience, particularly when translations are required. There is also the distinct possibility that the contractual forum's judges will see the parties' chosen law through the prism of familiar local doctrine. Much may be lost, or changed, in the translation.

One of the attractive features of international arbitration is that it permits tribunals with differing legal backgrounds, and with legal backgrounds that are different from that of the arbitral seat. That is, parties can agree upon the application of New York law, in an arbitration seated in Switzerland, with the expectation that one or more members of the tribunal will be familiar with New York law (and, of course, fluent in English).

Nonetheless, there are certain efficiencies and benefits from having the parties' chosen law coincide with the law of the forum for dispute resolution. This reduces the likelihood of disputes over what issues are "substantive" or "procedural," it increases the pool of local arbitrators that would be suitable for future disputes, and it makes subsequent judicial proceedings (including review of arbitral awards) more predictable. Thus, a common approach in international transactions is for the parties to agree upon dispute resolution in a neutral forum and to the application of the laws of that forum to their dispute. England, Switzerland, New York, Paris, and Singapore are the most commonly chosen fora and legal systems for this approach.

Questions also arise as to whether it is wiser to obtain a favorable law, or a favorable forum, in contractual negotiations. Ordinarily, obtaining a satisfactory forum is significantly more important: as one experienced European practitioner puts it, "better a French arbitration with Bolivian law, than a Bolivian arbitration with French law."

6. Non-National Legal Systems

Parties sometimes propose choice-of-law clauses selecting "general principles of law" or some similar reference to rules not derived from a specific national legal system. The following examples are common: general principles of law; *lex mercatoria* or law merchant; the International Institute for the Unification of Private Law ("UNIDROIT") Principles of Contract Law; "principles common to the laws of states A and B"; "principles of international law"; or "the laws of state A, to the extent not inconsistent with international law." Provisions to this effect are only infrequently litigated, although they have been considered in several major arbitral awards involving oil concessions.

Except in unusual cases, which almost always involve state contracts, these formulations should be resisted. There is much academic debate, but little judicial authority, about what such clauses mean, and there are doubts about how widely they are enforceable (e.g., English courts in particular have expressed reservations). Save where there is some powerful countervailing reason, business enterprises should not expose themselves to the uncertainties or expenses that participation in this scholastic debate could entail.

a. General Principles of Law

Parties sometimes consider choice-of-law provisions requiring application of "general principles of law," either alone or in conjunction with some national system or international body of law. The meaning of this formula is controversial, but it is generally understood as referring to principles of law common to leading legal systems (e.g., *pacta sunt servanda*, the principle that contracts should be performed in good faith). There are inevitable difficulties in identifying the contents of such principles, particularly with sufficient specificity to provide meaningful guidance in commercial contexts. Because of these difficulties, provisions choosing "general principles of law" as the applicable "law" should generally be avoided, save in exceptional cases involving state contracts.

An example of a provision selecting general principles of law is as follows:

> This contract, and all disputes arising out of a relating to this contract, shall be governed by general principles of law, to the exclusion of any rules of national law.

Some contracts include a tiered choice-of-law clause referring to both national law and general principles of law, introducing complexity that is ordinarily unnecessary; only where it is essential to permit an otherwise favorable transaction, without alternatives, should such formulations be adopted. An example of such a provision is as follows:

> This concession shall be governed by and interpreted in accordance with the principles of Libya common to the principles of international law, and in the absence of such common principles then by and in accordance with the general principles of law as may have been applied by international tribunals.

b. UNIDROIT Principles of International Commercial Contracts

Choice-of-law provisions occasionally specify the "Principles of International Commercial Contracts" published by UNIDROIT. The UNIDROIT Principles were designed to establish a neutral set of international rules of contract law and cover interpretation, validity, performance, and negotiation of contracts. A representative clause selecting the UNIDROIT Principles provides:

> This contract shall be governed by the UNIDROIT Principles (2016) [except as to Articles _____], supplemented when necessary by the law of [jurisdiction X].

Commercial parties should be cautious about adopting the UNIDROIT Principles as the only "law" governing their contract. The Principles inevitably lack the detail and supporting judicial precedent of leading national legal systems. Questions also arise about the interaction between a consensually selected legal system (addressing matters of validity and similar issues) and generally applicable national law.

c. *"Concurrent" Choice-of-Law Clause*

Parties sometimes consider "concurrent" choice-of-law clauses, which select both a national law and international law; these provisions are most likely to be considered in state contracts. An example of such a clause provides:

> The laws of [State] will apply, insofar as they are consistent with international law.

Such a formulation permits the state party's law to apply to the transaction, while still affording the commercial party a measure of protection if legislative actions by the state violate international law. The content of international law restraints on state actions in these circumstances remains a subject of controversy, but "internationalizing" a contract provides at least a degree of protection against unilateral state actions.

7. Stabilization Clauses

In some transactions, parties may seek protection against future changes in the applicable law. This protection can take the form of "freezing," "stabilization," or "economic equilibrium" clauses, which fix, for contractual purposes, the legal system applicable to the parties' agreement as that system stands at a specified date (without regard to subsequent legislative or other developments) or that, alternatively, either forbid giving effect to specified legislative changes, as between the parties, or require compensation to one party if such changes occur. Such provisions are generally used only in agreements between foreign investors and states or state-owned entities, where the possibilities for legislative interference are most substantial.

A representative example of a simple stabilization clause provides:

> No new laws, regulations, modifications or interpretation which could be conflicting or incompatible with the provisions of this Agreement shall be applicable.

Some stabilization provisions take the form of "economic equilibrium clauses." Under these provisions, the state party is required either to restore the economic equilibrium prevailing at the time of the contract or to compensate the commercial party for any adverse consequences of such changes.
An example of such an economic equilibrium clause provides:

> In the event that any provisions contained in the laws, rules or regulations of the Government are inconsistent with the terms and conditions of this Agreement, the Government shall take such action as is necessary to relieve the Company from any loss, liability or jeopardy as a result of such inconsistency and shall also take such

> action as may be necessary to maintain the economic equilibrium existing between the Parties on the Effective Date of this Agreement.

Another example of such a clause provides:

> The Government guarantees to the Contractor, for the entire duration of this Agreement, that it will maintain the stability of the fiscal and economic conditions of this Agreement, as they result from this Agreement and as they result from the Laws in force on the Effective Date. The Contractor has entered into this Agreement on the basis of the legal, fiscal and economic framework prevailing at the Effective Date. If there are any changes with respect to any provisions of any Law which may detrimentally and unfairly affect the Contractor's economic position during the Stability Period, this Agreement shall be amended as may be necessary to restore the Contractor to the economic position it would have enjoyed during the Stability Period but for such changes.

An example of a hybrid freezing and economic equilibrium clause is as follows:

> If any Change of Law has the effect of impairing, conflicting or interfering with the implementation of the Project, or limiting, abridging or adversely affecting the value of the Project or any of the rights, indemnifications or protections granted or arising under this Agreement or any Project Agreement, or of imposing (directly or indirectly) any Costs on any Project Investor, the Project Investor shall, within [one year] of the date when it could with reasonable diligence have become aware of the effect of the Change of Law upon the project as aforesaid, give notice thereof in writing to the Host Government. During the [90 days] following the Host Government's receipt of this notice, the Project Investor and the Host Government shall endeavour to resolve the matter through amicable negotiations. Failing such a resolution, the Host Government shall, by the end of this [90-day] period, do one of the following:
>
> (a) take all actions available to it to reverse the effect of that Change of Law upon the Project, the value of the Project or the relevant rights, indemnifications or protections. The foregoing obligation shall include the obligation to take all appropriate measures to resolve promptly by whatever means may be necessary, including by way of exemption, legislation, decree and/or other authoritative acts, any conflict or anomaly between this Agreement and any Project Agreement and [insert name of State] law; or
>
> (b) compensate the Project Investor for the Costs incurred by that Project Investor as a result of the Change of Law. Such compensation shall, if the

> relevant Project Investor so requires, be paid in Convertible Currency and shall, at the option of the Host Government, take the form of:
> - reimbursement by the Host Government of the Costs incurred by the Project Investor as a result of the Change of Law, promptly as and when such Costs are incurred;
> - reimbursement by the Host Government of the Costs incurred by the Project Investor as a result of the Change of Law, in the form of equal annual payments to the Project Investor during the remaining expected life of the Project ...;
>
> provided, however, that the obligation to take one of the actions referred to above shall not apply in relation to a Change of Law if the Host Government establishes that that Change of Law reflects a change in standards generally applicable in relation to standards of environmental protection, safety, employment, training, social impact or security in the [petroleum] [gas] industry internationally.

Stabilization clauses can raise questions of enforceability in some jurisdictions and should be used with care. They nonetheless contribute important stability and commercial bargaining power to investors in contracts with host state authorities.

8. Exclusion of CISG

A substantial number of international sale of goods contracts are subject to the provisions of the 1980 United Nations Convention on Contracts for the International Sale of Goods ("CISG"). The CISG applies to contracts for the sale of goods between parties whose places of business are in different Contracting States (or when applicable conflict of laws rules lead to the application of the law of a Contracting State). Parties are free to opt out of the substantive provisions (CISG, Article 6), but a number of authorities hold that such provision must be express.

The following provision is a representative example of such an opt-out clause under the CISG:

> The Parties agree that this Agreement, and any disputes, claims, controversies, or disagreements relating to or arising under this Agreement, shall not be subject to the 1980 United Nations Convention on Contracts for the International Sale of Goods ("CISG") and that the provisions of the CISG are hereby excluded. This Agreement, and any disputes, claims, controversies, or disagreements relating to or arising under this Agreement, shall be governed by the law of ________ (without regard to its conflict of laws rules and without regard to the CISG).

A simple choice-of-law provision, selecting a national law (e.g., "This agreement shall be governed by the law of New York.") may not be sufficient to opt out of the

CISG; rather, express language opting out of the CISG, and selecting an alternative law, may be necessary in some jurisdictions.

9. *Amiable Composition* and *Ex Aequo et Bono*

As discussed above (See p. 321), parties sometimes consider granting arbitrators the power to decide disputes "*ex aequo et bono*" or as "*amiable compositeur.*" These formulations permit the arbitrator to decide disputes based on equitable considerations and without reference to or compliance with strict principles of law. In general, *ex aequo et bono* and *amiable composition* provisions give rise to significant risks and are almost always (advisably) disfavored by commercial parties.

B. ENFORCEABILITY OF CHOICE-OF-LAW CLAUSES

1. Presumptive Enforceability of Choice-of-Law Clauses

In some countries, early authorities held that choice-of-law clauses were unenforceable. That view has been largely rejected by more recent authorities. It is now well settled under the laws of most jurisdictions, including almost all major trading states, that choice-of-law clauses are presumptively valid and enforceable, subject to important exceptions. This basic principle of party autonomy is recognized in sources such as the CISG and the Rome I Regulation (Regulation (EC) 593/2008 on the Law Applicable to Contractual Obligations).

2. Exceptions to Presumptive Enforceability of Choice-of-Law Clauses

The general enforceability of choice-of-law clauses under the laws of most jurisdictions is subject to several significant exceptions. These exceptions are broadly similar to those applicable to forum selection clauses. (See pp. 160–161 above.)

a. Reasonable Relationship Requirement

Some courts will not enforce a choice-of-law clause unless the parties' chosen law bears a "reasonable relationship" to the parties or their transaction. Section 1-105(1) of the original Uniform Commercial Code ("UCC"), applicable in most U.S. states, provides that:

> "When a transaction bears a reasonable relationship to this state and also to another state or nation the parties may agree that the law of either of this state or of such other state or nation shall govern their rights and duties."

In drafting documentation for a transaction which will include a choice-of-law clause, counsel should structure the transaction (and draft recitals and other provisions) with the reasonable relationship requirement in mind.

The reasonable relationship requirement has been criticized more frequently than it has been applied. Regrettably, the requirement gives rise to questions about whether the choice of a "neutral" state's law is effective. Typically, however, parties select the law of a "neutral" jurisdiction precisely because it lacks any connection to either them or their transaction; by raising doubts regarding the validity of such choices, the reasonable relationship requirement impedes the formation of stable, predictable commercial relations.

Fortunately, the legal regimes in many countries recognize that parties may validly select the laws of a neutral state that have no other material relationship to the parties' transaction. Many other jurisdictions are rethinking and/or abandoning the reasonable relationship requirement. As a practical matter, international arbitrators, as distinguished from national courts, are more likely to give effect to choices of substantive law without a material relation to the parties or their dealings.

b. Public Policy or Mandatory Law

A choice-of-law clause will not generally permit parties to avoid the application of otherwise applicable principles of public policy or mandatory rules of national law. In international commercial settings, the most likely instances in which public policies or mandatory laws will be relevant involve competition (antitrust) law, securities, bankruptcy, employment relations, consumer protection, certain matters of corporate organization, real property, and security interests. It is important to obtain local advice on the existence and effect of such exceptions in individual transactions. Again, as a practical matter, international arbitral tribunals are somewhat more likely than national courts to take a pragmatic and balanced approach to issues of public policy and to accord substantial weight to principles of party autonomy.

Appendix A

United Nations Convention on the Recognition and Enforcement of Foreign Arbitral Awards (New York Convention)

Article I

(1) This Convention shall apply to the recognition and enforcement of arbitral awards made in the territory of a State other than the State where the recognition and enforcement of such awards are sought, and arising out of differences between persons, whether physical or legal. It shall also apply to arbitral awards not considered as domestic awards in the State where their recognition and enforcement are sought.

(2) The term "arbitral awards" shall include not only awards made by arbitrators appointed for each case but also those made by permanent arbitral bodies to which the parties have submitted.

(3) When signing, ratifying or acceding to this Convention, or notifying extension under article X hereof, any State may on the basis of reciprocity declare that it will apply the Convention to the recognition and enforcement of awards made only in the territory of another Contracting State. It may also declare that it will apply the Convention only to differences arising out of legal relationships, whether contractual or not, which are considered as commercial under the national law of the State making such declaration.

Article II

(1) Each Contracting State shall recognize an agreement in writing under which the parties undertake to submit to arbitration all or any differences which have arisen or which may arise between them in respect of a defined legal relationship, whether contractual or not, concerning a subject matter capable of settlement by arbitration.

(2) The term "agreement in writing" shall include an arbitral clause in a contract or an arbitration agreement, signed by the parties or contained in an exchange of letters or telegrams.

(3) The court of a Contracting State, when seized of an action in a matter in respect of which the parties have made an agreement within the meaning of this article, shall, at the request of one of the parties, refer the parties to arbitration, unless it finds that the said agreement is null and void, inoperative or incapable of being performed.

Article III

Each Contracting State shall recognize arbitral awards as binding and enforce them in accordance with the rules of procedure of the territory where the award is relied upon, under the conditions laid down in the following articles. There shall not be imposed substantially more onerous conditions or higher fees or charges on the recognition or enforcement of arbitral awards to which this Convention applies than are imposed on the recognition or enforcement of domestic arbitral awards.

Article IV

(1) To obtain the recognition and enforcement mentioned in the preceding article, the party applying for recognition and enforcement shall, at the time of application, supply:
   (a) The duly authenticated original award or a duly certified copy thereof;
   (b) The original agreement referred to in article II or a duly certified copy thereof.
(2) If the said award or agreement is not made in an official language of the country in which the award is relied upon, the party applying for recognition and enforcement of the award shall produce a translation of these documents into such language. The translation shall be certified by an official or sworn translator or by a diplomatic or consular agent.

Article V

(1) Recognition and enforcement of the award may be refused, at the request of the party against whom it is invoked, only if that party furnishes to the competent authority where the recognition and enforcement is sought, proof that:
   (a) The parties to the agreement referred to in article II were, under the law applicable to them, under some incapacity, or the said agreement is not valid under the law to which the parties have subjected it or, failing any indication thereon, under the law of the country where the award was made; or
   (b) The party against whom the award is invoked was not given proper notice of the appointment of the arbitrator or of the arbitration proceedings or was otherwise unable to present his case; or
   (c) The award deals with a difference not contemplated by or not falling within the terms of the submission to arbitration, or it contains decisions on matters beyond the scope of the submission to arbitration, provided that, if the decisions on matters submitted to arbitration can be separated from those

not so submitted, that part of the award which contains decisions on matters submitted to arbitration may be recognized and enforced; or

(d) The composition of the arbitral authority or the arbitral procedure was not in accordance with the agreement of the parties, or, failing such agreement, was not in accordance with the law of the country where the arbitration took place; or

(e) The award has not yet become binding on the parties or has been set aside or suspended by a competent authority of the country in which, or under the law of which, that award was made.

(2) Recognition and enforcement of an arbitral award may also be refused if the competent authority in the country where recognition and enforcement is sought finds that:

(a) The subject matter of the difference is not capable of settlement by arbitration under the law of that country; or

(b) The recognition or enforcement of the award would be contrary to the public policy of that country.

Article VI

If an application for the setting aside or suspension of the award has been made to a competent authority referred to in Article V (1) (e), the authority before which the award is sought to be relied upon may, if it considers it proper, adjourn the decision on the enforcement of the award and may also, on the application of the party claiming enforcement of the award, order the other party to give suitable security.

Article VII

(1) The provisions of the present Convention shall not affect the validity of multilateral or bilateral agreements concerning the recognition and enforcement of arbitral awards entered into by the Contracting States nor deprive any interested party of any right he may have to avail himself of an arbitral award in the manner and to the extent allowed by the law or the treaties of the country where such award is sought to be relied upon.

(2) The Geneva Protocol on Arbitration Clauses of 1923 and the Geneva Convention on the Execution of Foreign Arbitral Awards of 1927 shall cease to have effect between Contracting States on their becoming bound and to the extent that they become bound, by this Convention.

Article VIII

(1) This Convention shall be open until 31 December 1958 for signature on behalf of any Member of the United Nations and also on behalf of any other State which is or hereafter becomes a member of any specialized agency of the United Nations, or which is or hereafter becomes a party to the Statute of the International Court of Justice, or any other State to which an invitation has been addressed by the General Assembly of the United Nations.

(2) This Convention shall be ratified and the instrument of ratification shall be deposited with the Secretary-General of the United Nations.

Article IX

(1) This Convention shall be open for accession to all States referred to in article VIII.
(2) Accession shall be effected by the deposit of an instrument of accession with the Secretary-General of the United Nations.

Article X

(1) Any State may, at the time of signature, ratification or accession, declare that this Convention shall extend to all or any of the territories for the international relations of which it is responsible. Such a declaration shall take effect when the Convention enters into force for the State concerned.
(2) At any time thereafter any such extension shall be made by notification addressed to the Secretary-General of the United Nations and shall take effect as from the ninetieth day after the day of receipt by the Secretary-General of the United Nations of this notification, or as from the date of entry into force of the Convention for the State concerned, whichever is the later.
(3) With respect to those territories to which this Convention is not extended at the time of signature, ratification or accession, each State concerned shall consider the possibility of taking the necessary steps in order to extend the application of this Convention to such territories, subject, where necessary for constitutional reasons, to the consent of the Governments of such territories.

Article XI

In the case of a federal or non-unitary State, the following provisions shall apply:

(a) With respect to those articles of this Convention that come within the legislative jurisdiction of the federal authority, the obligations of the federal Government shall to this extent be the same as those of Contracting States which are not federal States;
(b) With respect to those articles of this Convention that come within the legislative jurisdiction of constituent states or provinces which are not, under the constitutional system of the federation, bound to take legislative action, the federal Government shall bring such articles with a favourable recommendation to the notice of the appropriate authorities of constituent states or provinces at the earliest possible moment;
(c) A federal State Party to this Convention shall, at the request of any other Contracting State transmitted through the Secretary-General of the United Nations, supply a statement of the law and practice of the federation and its constituent units in regard to any particular provision of this Convention,

showing the extent to which effect has been given to that provision by legislative or other action.

Article XII

(1) This Convention shall come into force on the ninetieth day following the date of deposit of the third instrument of ratification or accession.
(2) For each State ratifying or acceding to this Convention after the deposit of the third instrument of ratification or accession, this Convention shall enter into force on the ninetieth day after deposit by such State of its instrument of ratification or accession.

Article XIII

(1) Any Contracting State may denounce this Convention by a written notification to the Secretary-General of the United Nations. Denunciation shall take effect one year after the date of receipt of the notification by the Secretary-General.
(2) Any State which has made a declaration or notification under article X may, at any time thereafter, by notification to the Secretary-General of the United Nations, declare that this Convention shall cease to extend to the territory concerned one year after the date of the receipt of the notification by the Secretary-General.
(3) This Convention shall continue to be applicable to arbitral awards in respect of which recognition and enforcement proceedings have been instituted before the denunciation takes effect.

Article XIV

A Contracting State shall not be entitled to avail itself of the present Convention against other Contracting States except to the extent that it is itself bound to apply the Convention.

Article XV

The Secretary-General of the United Nations shall notify the States contemplated in article VIII of the following:

(a) Signatures and ratifications in accordance with article VIII;
(b) Accessions in accordance with article IX;
(c) Declarations and notifications under articles I, X, and XI;
(d) The date upon which this Convention enters into force in accordance with article XII;
(e) Denunciations and notifications in accordance with article XIII.

Article XVI

(1) This Convention, of which the Chinese, English, French, Russian and Spanish texts shall be equally authentic, shall be deposited in the archives of the United Nations.
(2) The Secretary-General of the United Nations shall transmit a certified copy of this Convention to the States contemplated in article VIII.

STATUS

Authoritative information on the status of the treaties deposited with the Secretary-General of the United Nations, including historical status information, may be obtained by consulting the United Nations Treaty Collection (treaties.un.org).

The UNCITRAL Secretariat also prepares yearly a document containing the Status of Conventions and Enactments of UNCITRAL Model Laws, which is available on the web page of the corresponding UNCITRAL Commission Session.

All dates: DD/MM/YYYY

State	Notes	Signature	Ratification, Accession(*), Approval(†), Acceptance(‡) or Succession(§)	Entry into force
Afghanistan	(a), (c)		30/11/2004(*)	28/02/2005
Albania			27/06/2001(*)	25/09/2001
Algeria	(a), (c)		07/02/1989(*)	08/05/1989
Andorra	(a)		19/06/2015(*)	17/09/2015
Angola			06/03/2017(*)	04/06/2017
Antigua and Barbuda	(a), (c)		02/02/1989(*)	03/05/1989
Argentina	(a), (c)	26/08/1958	14/03/1989	12/06/1989
Armenia	(a), (c)		29/12/1997(*)	29/03/1998
Australia			26/03/1975(*)	24/06/1975
Austria			02/05/1961(*)	31/07/1961
Azerbaijan			29/02/2000(*)	29/05/2000
Bahamas			20/12/2006(*)	20/03/2007
Bahrain	(a), (c)		06/04/1988(*)	05/07/1988
Bangladesh			06/05/1992(*)	04/08/1992
Barbados	(a), (c)		16/03/1993(*)	14/06/1993
Belarus	(b)	29/12/1958	15/11/1960	13/02/1961
Belgium	(a)	10/06/1958	18/08/1975	16/11/1975
Benin			16/05/1974(*)	14/08/1974

State	Notes	Signature	Ratification, Accession(*), Approval(†), Acceptance(‡) or Succession(§)	Entry into force
Bhutan	(a), (c)		25/09/2014(*)	24/12/2014
Bolivia (Plurinational State of)			28/04/1995(*)	27/07/1995
Bosnia and Herzegovina	(a), (c), (i)		01/09/1993(§)	06/03/1992
Botswana	(a), (c)		20/12/1971(*)	19/03/1972
Brazil			07/06/2002(*)	05/09/2002
Brunei Darussalam	(a)		25/07/1996(*)	23/10/1996
Bulgaria	(a), (b)	17/12/1958	10/10/1961	08/01/1962
Burkina Faso			23/03/1987(*)	21/06/1987
Burundi	(c)		23/06/2014(*)	21/09/2014
Cabo Verde			22/03/2018(*)	20/06/2018
Cambodia			05/01/1960(*)	04/04/1960
Cameroon			19/02/1988(*)	19/05/1988
Canada	(d)		12/05/1986(*)	10/08/1986
Central African Republic	(a), (c)		15/10/1962(*)	13/01/1963
Chile			04/09/1975(*)	03/12/1975
China	(a), (c), (h)		22/01/1987(*)	22/04/1987
Colombia			25/09/1979(*)	24/12/1979
Comoros			28/04/2015(*)	27/07/2015
Cook Islands			12/01/2009(*)	12/04/2009
Costa Rica		10/06/1958	26/10/1987	24/01/1988
Côte d'Ivoire			01/02/1991(*)	02/05/1991
Croatia	(a), (c), (i)		26/07/1993(§)	08/10/1991
Cuba	(a), (c)		30/12/1974(*)	30/03/1975
Cyprus	(a), (c)		29/12/1980(*)	29/03/1981
Czechia	(a), (b)		30/09/1993(§)	01/01/1993

State	Notes	Signature	Ratification, Accession(*), Approval(†), Acceptance(‡) or Succession(§)	Entry into force
Democratic Republic of the Congo			05/11/2014(*)	03/02/2015
Denmark	(a), (c), (f)		22/12/1972(*)	22/03/1973
Djibouti	(a), (c)		14/06/1983(§)	27/06/1977
Dominica			28/10/1988(*)	26/01/1989
Dominican Republic			11/04/2002(*)	10/07/2002
Ecuador	(a), (c)	17/12/1958	03/01/1962	03/04/1962
Egypt			09/03/1959(*)	07/06/1959
El Salvador		10/06/1958	26/02/1998	27/05/1998
Estonia			30/08/1993(*)	28/11/1993
Ethiopia	(a), (c), (i)		24/08/2020(*)	22/11/2020
Fiji			27/09/2010(*)	26/12/2010
Finland		29/12/1958	19/01/1962	19/04/1962
France	(a)	25/11/1958	26/06/1959	24/09/1959
Gabon			15/12/2006(*)	15/03/2007
Georgia			02/06/1994(*)	31/08/1994
Germany		10/06/1958	30/06/1961	28/09/1961
Ghana			09/04/1968(*)	08/07/1968
Greece	(a), (c)		16/07/1962(*)	14/10/1962
Guatemala	(a), (c)		21/03/1984(*)	19/06/1984
Guinea			23/01/1991(*)	23/04/1991
Guyana			25/09/2014(*)	24/12/2014
Haiti			05/12/1983(*)	04/03/1984
Holy See	(a), (c)		14/05/1975(*)	12/08/1975
Honduras	(a), (c)		03/10/2000(*)	01/01/2001
Hungary	(a), (c)		05/03/1962(*)	03/06/1962
Iceland			24/01/2002(*)	24/04/2002
India	(a), (c)	10/06/1958	13/07/1960	11/10/1960
Indonesia	(a), (c)		07/10/1981(*)	05/01/1982

State	Notes	Signature	Ratification, Accession(*), Approval(†), Acceptance(‡) or Succession(§)	Entry into force
Iran (Islamic Republic of)	(a), (c)		15/10/2001(*)	13/01/2002
Iraq	(a),(c),(i)		11/11/2021(*)	09/02/2022
Ireland	(a)		12/05/1981(*)	10/08/1981
Israel		10/06/1958	05/01/1959	07/06/1959
Italy			31/01/1969(*)	01/05/1969
Jamaica	(a), (c)		10/07/2002(*)	08/10/2002
Japan	(a)		20/06/1961(*)	18/09/1961
Jordan		10/06/1958	15/11/1979	13/02/1980
Kazakhstan			20/11/1995(*)	18/02/1996
Kenya	(a)		10/02/1989(*)	11/05/1989
Kuwait	(a)		28/04/1978(*)	27/07/1978
Kyrgyzstan			18/12/1996(*)	18/03/1997
Lao People's Democratic Republic			17/06/1998(*)	15/09/1998
Latvia			14/04/1992(*)	13/07/1992
Lebanon	(a)		11/08/1998(*)	09/11/1998
Lesotho			13/06/1989(*)	11/09/1989
Liberia			16/09/2005(*)	15/12/2005
Liechtenstein	(a)		07/07/2011(*)	05/10/2011
Lithuania	(b)		14/03/1995(*)	12/06/1995
Luxembourg	(a)	11/11/1958	09/09/1983	08/12/1983
Madagascar	(a), (c)		16/07/1962(*)	14/10/1962
Malawi	(a),(c),(i)		04/03/2021(*)	02/06/2021
Malaysia	(a), (c)		05/11/1985(*)	03/02/1986
Maldives			17/09/2019(*)	16/12/2019
Mali			08/09/1994(*)	07/12/1994
Malta	(a), (i)		22/06/2000(*)	20/09/2000
Marshall Islands			21/12/2006(*)	21/03/2007
Mauritania			30/01/1997(*)	30/04/1997
Mauritius			19/06/1996(*)	17/09/1996
Mexico			14/04/1971(*)	13/07/1971

State	Notes	Signature	Ratification, Accession(*), Approval(†), Acceptance(‡) or Succession(§)	Entry into force
Monaco	(a), (c)	31/12/1958	02/06/1982	31/08/1982
Mongolia	(a), (c)		24/10/1994(*)	22/01/1995
Montenegro	(a), (c), (i)		23/10/2006(§)	03/06/2006
Morocco	(a)		12/02/1959(*)	07/06/1959
Mozambique	(a)		11/06/1998(*)	09/09/1998
Myanmar			16/04/2013(*)	15/07/2013
Nepal	(a), (c)		04/03/1998(*)	02/06/1998
Netherlands	(a), (e)	10/06/1958	24/04/1964	23/07/1964
New Zealand	(a)		06/01/1983(*)	06/04/1983
Nicaragua			24/09/2003(*)	23/12/2003
Niger			14/10/1964(*)	12/01/1965
Nigeria	(a), (c)		17/03/1970(*)	15/06/1970
North Macedonia	(c), (i)		10/03/1994(§)	17/11/1991
Norway	(a), (j)		14/03/1961(*)	12/06/1961
Oman			25/02/1999(*)	26/05/1999
Pakistan	(a)	30/12/1958	14/07/2005	12/10/2005
Palau	(a), (c)		31/03/2020	29/06/2020
Panama			10/10/1984(*)	08/01/1985
Papua New Guinea			17/07/2019(*)	15/10/2019
Paraguay			08/10/1997(*)	06/01/1998
Peru			07/07/1988(*)	05/10/1988
Philippines	(a), (c)	10/06/1958	06/07/1967	04/10/1967
Poland	(a), (c)	10/06/1958	03/10/1961	01/01/1962
Portugal	(a)		18/10/1994(*)	16/01/1995
Qatar			30/12/2002(*)	30/03/2003
Republic of Korea	(a), (c)		08/02/1973(*)	09/05/1973
Republic of Moldova	(a), (i)		18/09/1998(*)	17/12/1998
Romania	(a), (b), (c)		13/09/1961(*)	12/12/1961

State	Notes	Signature	Ratification, Accession(*), Approval(†), Acceptance(‡) or Succession(§)	Entry into force
Russian Federation	(b)	29/12/1958	24/08/1960	22/11/1960
Rwanda			31/10/2008(*)	29/01/2009
Saint Vincent and the Grenadines	(a), (c)		12/09/2000(*)	11/12/2000
San Marino			17/05/1979(*)	15/08/1979
São Tomé and Príncipe			20/11/2012(*)	18/02/2013
Saudi Arabia	(a)		19/04/1994(*)	18/07/1994
Sierra Leone	(a), (c), (i)		28/10/2020(*)	26/01/2021
Senegal			17/10/1994(*)	15/01/1995
Serbia	(a), (c), (i)		12/03/2001(§)	27/04/1992
Seychelles	(a), (c), (i)		03/02/2020(*)	03/05/2020
Singapore	(a)		21/08/1986(*)	19/11/1986
Slovakia	(a), (b)		28/05/1993(§)	01/01/1993
Slovenia	(i)		06/07/1992(§)	25/06/1991
South Africa			03/05/1976(*)	01/08/1976
Spain			12/05/1977(*)	10/08/1977
Sri Lanka		30/12/1958	09/04/1962	08/07/1962
State of Palestine			02/01/2015(*)	02/04/2015
Sudan			26/03/2018(*)	24/06/2018
Suriname	(a), (c)		10/11/2022(*)	08/02/2023
Sweden		23/12/1958	28/01/1972	27/04/1972
Switzerland		29/12/1958	01/06/1965	30/08/1965
Syrian Arab Republic			09/03/1959(*)	07/06/1959
Tajikistan	(a), (i), (j)		14/08/2012(*)	12/11/2012
Thailand			21/12/1959(*)	20/03/1960
Timor-Leste			17/01/2023(*)	17/04/2023

State	Notes	Signature	Ratification, Accession(*), Approval(†), Acceptance(‡) or Succession(§)	Entry into force
Tonga	(c)		12/06/2020(*)	10/09/2020
Trinidad and Tobago	(a), (c)		14/02/1966(*)	15/05/1966
Tunisia	(a), (c)		17/07/1967(*)	15/10/1967
Turkey	(a), (c)		02/07/1992(*)	30/09/1992
Uganda	(a)		12/02/1992(*)	12/05/1992
Ukraine	(b)	29/12/1958	10/10/1960	08/01/1961
United Arab Emirates			21/08/2006(*)	19/11/2006
United Kingdom of Great Britain and Northern Ireland	(a), (g)		24/09/1975(*)	23/12/1975
United Republic of Tanzania	(a)		13/10/1964(*)	11/01/1965
United States of America	(a), (c)		30/09/1970(*)	29/12/1970
Uruguay			30/03/1983(*)	28/06/1983
Uzbekistan			07/02/1996(*)	07/05/1996
Venezuela (Bolivarian Republic of)	(a), (c)		08/02/1995(*)	09/05/1995
Viet Nam	(a), (b), (c)		12/09/1995(*)	11/12/1995
Zambia			14/03/2002(*)	12/06/2002
Zimbabwe			29/09/1994(*)	28/12/1994

Parties: 172

Notes

(a) This State will apply the Convention only to recognition and enforcement of awards made in the territory of another contracting State.

(b) With regard to awards made in the territory of non-contracting States, this State will apply the Convention only to the extent to which those States grant reciprocal treatment.

(c) This State will apply the Convention only to differences arising out of legal relationships, whether contractual or not, that are considered commercial under the national law.
(d) Canada declared that it would apply the Convention only to differences arising out of legal relationships, whether contractual or not, that were considered commercial under the laws of Canada, except in the case of the Province of Quebec, where the law did not provide for such limitation.
(e) On 24 April 1964, the Netherlands declared that the Convention shall apply to the Netherlands Antilles.
(f) On 10 February 1976, Denmark declared that the Convention shall apply to the Faeroe Islands and Greenland.
(g) On 24 February 2014, the United Kingdom submitted a notification to extend territorial application of the Convention to the British Virgin Islands. For the following territories, the United Kingdom has submitted notifications extending territorial application and declaring that the Convention shall apply only to the recognition and enforcement of awards made in the territory of another Contracting State: Gibraltar (24 September 1975), Isle of Man (22 February 1979), Bermuda (14 November 1979), Cayman Islands (26 November 1980), Guernsey (19 April 1985), and Bailiwick of Jersey (28 May 2002).
(h) Upon resumption of sovereignty over Hong Kong on 1 July 1997, the Government of China extended the territorial application of the Convention to Hong Kong, Special Administrative Region of China, subject to the statement originally made by China upon accession to the Convention. On 19 July 2005, China declared that the Convention shall apply to the Macao Special Administrative Region of China, subject to the statement originally made by China upon accession to the Convention. Reservations or other notifications.
(i) This State formulated a reservation with regard to retroactive application of the Convention.
(j) This State formulated a reservation with regard to the application of the Convention in cases concerning immovable property.

Appendix B

Hague Choice of Court Convention 2005

The States Parties to the present Convention,
Desiring to promote international trade and investment through enhanced judicial co-operation,
Believing that such co-operation can be enhanced by uniform rules on jurisdiction and on recognition and enforcement of foreign judgments in civil or commercial matters,
Believing that such enhanced co-operation requires in particular an international legal regime that provides certainty and ensures the effectiveness of exclusive choice of court agreements between parties to commercial transactions and that governs the recognition and enforcement of judgments resulting from proceedings based on such agreements,
Have resolved to conclude this Convention and have agreed upon the following provisions:

CHAPTER I: SCOPE AND DEFINITIONS

Article 1: Scope

(1) This Convention shall apply in international cases to exclusive choice of court agreements concluded in civil or commercial matters.
(2) For the purposes of Chapter II, a case is international unless the parties are resident in the same Contracting State and the relationship of the parties and all other elements relevant to the dispute, regardless of the location of the chosen court, are connected only with that State.
(3) For the purposes of Chapter III, a case is international where recognition or enforcement of a foreign judgment is sought.

Article 2: Exclusions from scope

(1) This Convention shall not apply to exclusive choice of court agreements:
  (a) to which a natural person acting primarily for personal, family or household purposes (a consumer) is a party;
  (b) relating to contracts of employment, including collective agreements.

(2) This Convention shall not apply to the following matters:
  (a) the status and legal capacity of natural persons;
  (b) maintenance obligations;
  (c) other family law matters, including matrimonial property regimes and other rights or obligations arising out of marriage or similar relationships;
  (d) wills and succession;
  (e) insolvency, composition and analogous matters;
  (f) the carriage of passengers and goods;
  (g) marine pollution, limitation of liability for maritime claims, general average, and emergency towage and salvage;
  (h) anti-trust (competition) matters;
  (i) liability for nuclear damage;
  (j) claims for personal injury brought by or on behalf of natural persons;
  (k) tort or delict claims for damage to tangible property that do not arise from a contractual relationship;
  (l) rights in rem in immovable property, and tenancies of immovable property;
  (m) the validity, nullity, or dissolution of legal persons, and the validity of decisions of their organs;
  (n) the validity of intellectual property rights other than copyright and related rights;
  (o) infringement of intellectual property rights other than copyright and related rights, except where infringement proceedings are brought for breach of a contract between the parties relating to such rights, or could have been brought for breach of that contract;
  (p) the validity of entries in public registers.

(3) Notwithstanding paragraph 2, proceedings are not excluded from the scope of this Convention where a matter excluded under that paragraph arises merely as a preliminary question and not as an object of the proceedings. In particular, the mere fact that a matter excluded under paragraph 2 arises by way of defence does not exclude proceedings from the Convention, if that matter is not an object of the proceedings.

(4) This Convention shall not apply to arbitration and related proceedings.

(5) Proceedings are not excluded from the scope of this Convention by the mere fact that a State, including a government, a governmental agency or any person acting for a State, is a party thereto.

(6) Nothing in this Convention shall affect privileges and immunities of States or of international organisations, in respect of themselves and of their property.

Article 3: Exclusive choice of court agreements

For the purposes of this Convention:

(a) "exclusive choice of court agreement" means an agreement concluded by two or more parties that meets the requirements of paragraph c) and designates, for the purpose of deciding disputes which have arisen or may arise in connection with a particular legal relationship, the courts of one Contracting State or one or more specific courts of one Contracting State to the exclusion of the jurisdiction of any other courts;

(b) a choice of court agreement which designates the courts of one Contracting State or one or more specific courts of one Contracting State shall be deemed to be exclusive unless the parties have expressly provided otherwise;

(c) an exclusive choice of court agreement must be concluded or documented:
   (i) in writing; or
   (ii) by any other means of communication which renders information accessible so as to be usable for subsequent reference;

(d) an exclusive choice of court agreement that forms part of a contract shall be treated as an agreement independent of the other terms of the contract. The validity of the exclusive choice of court agreement cannot be contested solely on the ground that the contract is not valid.

Article 4: Other definitions

(1) In this Convention, "judgment" means any decision on the merits given by a court, whatever it may be called, including a decree or order, and a determination of costs or expenses by the court (including an officer of the court), provided that the determination relates to a decision on the merits which may be recognised or enforced under this Convention. An interim measure of protection is not a judgment.

(2) For the purposes of this Convention, an entity or person other than a natural person shall be considered to be resident in the State:
   (a) where it has its statutory seat;
   (b) under whose law it was incorporated or formed;
   (c) where it has its central administration; or
   (d) where it has its principal place of business.

CHAPTER II: JURISDICTION

Article 5: Jurisdiction of the chosen court

(1) The court or courts of a Contracting State designated in an exclusive choice of court agreement shall have jurisdiction to decide a dispute to which the agreement applies, unless the agreement is null and void under the law of that State.

(2) A court that has jurisdiction under paragraph 1 shall not decline to exercise jurisdiction on the ground that the dispute should be decided in a court of another State.

(3) The preceding paragraphs shall not affect rules:
   (a) on jurisdiction related to subject matter or to the value of the claim;
   (b) on the internal allocation of jurisdiction among the courts of a Contracting State. However, where the chosen court has discretion as to whether to

transfer a case, due consideration should be given to the choice of the parties.

Article 6: Obligations of a court not chosen

A court of a Contracting State other than that of the chosen court shall suspend or dismiss proceedings to which an exclusive choice of court agreement applies unless:

(a) the agreement is null and void under the law of the State of the chosen court;
(b) a party lacked the capacity to conclude the agreement under the law of the State of the court seised;
(c) giving effect to the agreement would lead to a manifest injustice or would be manifestly contrary to the public policy of the State of the court seised;
(d) for exceptional reasons beyond the control of the parties, the agreement cannot reasonably be performed; or
(e) the chosen court has decided not to hear the case.

Article 7: Interim measures of protection

Interim measures of protection are not governed by this Convention. This Convention neither requires nor precludes the grant, refusal or termination of interim measures of protection by a court of a Contracting State and does not affect whether or not a party may request or a court should grant, refuse or terminate such measures.

CHAPTER III: RECOGNITION AND ENFORCEMENT

Article 8: Recognition and enforcement

(1) A judgment given by a court of a Contracting State designated in an exclusive choice of court agreement shall be recognised and enforced in other Contracting States in accordance with this Chapter. Recognition or enforcement may be refused only on the grounds specified in this Convention.
(2) Without prejudice to such review as is necessary for the application of the provisions of this Chapter, there shall be no review of the merits of the judgment given by the court of origin. The court addressed shall be bound by the findings of fact on which the court of origin based its jurisdiction, unless the judgment was given by default.
(3) A judgment shall be recognised only if it has effect in the State of origin, and shall be enforced only if it is enforceable in the State of origin.
(4) Recognition or enforcement may be postponed or refused if the judgment is the subject of review in the State of origin or if the time limit for seeking ordinary review has not expired. A refusal does not prevent a subsequent application for recognition or enforcement of the judgment.
(5) This Article shall also apply to a judgment given by a court of a Contracting State pursuant to a transfer of the case from the chosen court in that Contracting State as permitted by Article 5, paragraph 3. However, where the chosen court had

discretion as to whether to transfer the case to another court, recognition or enforcement of the judgment may be refused against a party who objected to the transfer in a timely manner in the State of origin.

Article 9: Refusal of recognition or enforcement

(1) Recognition or enforcement may be refused if:
  (a) the agreement was null and void under the law of the State of the chosen court, unless the chosen court has determined that the agreement is valid;
  (b) a party lacked the capacity to conclude the agreement under the law of the requested State;
  (c) the document which instituted the proceedings or an equivalent document, including the essential elements of the claim,
    (i) was not notified to the defendant in sufficient time and in such a way as to enable him to arrange for his defence, unless the defendant entered an appearance and presented his case without contesting notification in the court of origin, provided that the law of the State of origin permitted notification to be contested; or
    (ii) was notified to the defendant in the requested State in a manner that is incompatible with fundamental principles of the requested State concerning service of documents;
  (d) the judgment was obtained by fraud in connection with a matter of procedure;
  (e) recognition or enforcement would be manifestly incompatible with the public policy of the requested State, including situations where the specific proceedings leading to the judgment were incompatible with fundamental principles of procedural fairness of that State;
  (f) the judgment is inconsistent with a judgment given in the requested State in a dispute between the same parties; or
  (g) the judgment is inconsistent with an earlier judgment given in another State between the same parties on the same cause of action, provided that the earlier judgment fulfils the conditions necessary for its recognition in the requested State.

Article 10: Preliminary questions

(1) Where a matter excluded under Article 2, paragraph 2, or under Article 21, arose as a preliminary question, the ruling on that question shall not be recognised or enforced under this Convention.
(2) Recognition or enforcement of a judgment may be refused if, and to the extent that, the judgment was based on a ruling on a matter excluded under Article 2, paragraph 2.
(3) However, in the case of a ruling on the validity of an intellectual property right other than copyright or a related right, recognition or enforcement of a judgment may be refused or postponed under the preceding paragraph only where:

(a) that ruling is inconsistent with a judgment or a decision of a competent authority on that matter given in the State under the law of which the intellectual property right arose; or

(b) proceedings concerning the validity of the intellectual property right are pending in that State.

(4) Recognition or enforcement of a judgment may be refused if, and to the extent that, the judgment was based on a ruling on a matter excluded pursuant to a declaration made by the requested State under Article 21.

Article 11: Damages

(1) Recognition or enforcement of a judgment may be refused if, and to the extent that, the judgment awards damages, including exemplary or punitive damages, that do not compensate a party for actual loss or harm suffered.

(2) The court addressed shall take into account whether and to what extent the damages awarded by the court of origin serve to cover costs and expenses relating to the proceedings.

Article 12: Judicial settlements (transactions judiciaires)

Judicial settlements (*transactions judiciaires*) which a court of a Contracting State designated in an exclusive choice of court agreement has approved, or which have been concluded before that court in the course of proceedings, and which are enforceable in the same manner as a judgment in the State of origin, shall be enforced under this Convention in the same manner as a judgment.

Article 13: Documents to be produced

(1) The party seeking recognition or applying for enforcement shall produce:

(a) a complete and certified copy of the judgment;

(b) the exclusive choice of court agreement, a certified copy thereof, or other evidence of its existence;

(c) if the judgment was given by default, the original or a certified copy of a document establishing that the document which instituted the proceedings or an equivalent document was notified to the defaulting party;

(d) any documents necessary to establish that the judgment has effect or, where applicable, is enforceable in the State of origin;

(e) in the case referred to in Article 12, a certificate of a court of the State of origin that the judicial settlement or a part of it is enforceable in the same manner as a judgment in the State of origin.

(2) If the terms of the judgment do not permit the court addressed to verify whether the conditions of this Chapter have been complied with, that court may require any necessary documents.

(3) An application for recognition or enforcement may be accompanied by a document, issued by a court (including an officer of the court) of the State of

origin, in the form recommended and published by the Hague Conference on Private International Law.

(4) If the documents referred to in this Article are not in an official language of the requested State, they shall be accompanied by a certified translation into an official language, unless the law of the requested State provides otherwise.

Article 14: Procedure

The procedure for recognition, declaration of enforceability or registration for enforcement, and the enforcement of the judgment, are governed by the law of the requested State unless this Convention provides otherwise. The court addressed shall act expeditiously.

Article 15: Severability

Recognition or enforcement of a severable part of a judgment shall be granted where recognition or enforcement of that part is applied for, or only part of the judgment is capable of being recognised or enforced under this Convention.

CHAPTER IV: GENERAL CLAUSES

Article 16: Transitional provisions

(1) This Convention shall apply to exclusive choice of court agreements concluded after its entry into force for the State of the chosen court.

(2) This Convention shall not apply to proceedings instituted before its entry into force for the State of the court seised.

Article 17: Contracts of insurance and reinsurance

(1) Proceedings under a contract of insurance or reinsurance are not excluded from the scope of this Convention on the ground that the contract of insurance or reinsurance relates to a matter to which this Convention does not apply.

(2) Recognition and enforcement of a judgment in respect of liability under the terms of a contract of insurance or reinsurance may not be limited or refused on the ground that the liability under that contract includes liability to indemnify the insured or reinsured in respect of:

   (a) a matter to which this Convention does not apply; or

   (b) an award of damages to which Article 11 might apply.

Article 18: No legalisation

All documents forwarded or delivered under this Convention shall be exempt from legalisation or any analogous formality, including an Apostille.

Article 19: Declarations limiting jurisdiction

A State may declare that its courts may refuse to determine disputes to which an exclusive choice of court agreement applies if, except for the location of the chosen court, there is no connection between that State and the parties or the dispute.

Article 20: Declarations limiting recognition and enforcement

A State may declare that its courts may refuse to recognise or enforce a judgment given by a court of another Contracting State if the parties were resident in the requested State, and the relationship of the parties and all other elements relevant to the dispute, other than the location of the chosen court, were connected only with the requested State.

Article 21: Declarations with respect to specific matters

(1) Where a State has a strong interest in not applying this Convention to a specific matter, that State may declare that it will not apply the Convention to that matter. The State making such a declaration shall ensure that the declaration is no broader than necessary and that the specific matter excluded is clearly and precisely defined.

(2) With regard to that matter, the Convention shall not apply:
   (a) in the Contracting State that made the declaration;
   (b) in other Contracting States, where an exclusive choice of court agreement designates the courts, or one or more specific courts, of the State that made the declaration.

Article 22: Reciprocal declarations on non-exclusive choice of court agreements

(1) A Contracting State may declare that its courts will recognise and enforce judgments given by courts of other Contracting States designated in a choice of court agreement concluded by two or more parties that meets the requirements of Article 3, paragraph *c)*, and designates, for the purpose of deciding disputes which have arisen or may arise in connection with a particular legal relationship, a court or courts of one or more Contracting States (a non-exclusive choice of court agreement).

(2) Where recognition or enforcement of a judgment given in a Contracting State that has made such a declaration is sought in another Contracting State that has made such a declaration, the judgment shall be recognised and enforced under this Convention, if:
   (a) the court of origin was designated in a non-exclusive choice of court agreement;
   (b) there exists neither a judgment given by any other court before which proceedings could be brought in accordance with the non-exclusive choice of court agreement, nor a proceeding pending between the same parties in any other such court on the same cause of action; and
   (c) the court of origin was the court first seised.

Article 23: Uniform interpretation

In the interpretation of this Convention, regard shall be had to its international character and to the need to promote uniformity in its application.

Article 24: Review of operation of the Convention

The Secretary General of the Hague Conference on Private International Law shall at regular intervals make arrangements for:

(a) review of the operation of this Convention, including any declarations; and
(b) consideration of whether any amendments to this Convention are desirable.

Article 25: Non-unified legal systems

(1) In relation to a Contracting State in which two or more systems of law apply in different territorial units with regard to any matter dealt with in this Convention:
  (a) any reference to the law or procedure of a State shall be construed as referring, where appropriate, to the law or procedure in force in the relevant territorial unit;
  (b) any reference to residence in a State shall be construed as referring, where appropriate, to residence in the relevant territorial unit;
  (c) any reference to the court or courts of a State shall be construed as referring, where appropriate, to the court or courts in the relevant territorial unit;
  (d) any reference to a connection with a State shall be construed as referring, where appropriate, to a connection with the relevant territorial unit.
(2) Notwithstanding the preceding paragraph, a Contracting State with two or more territorial units in which different systems of law apply shall not be bound to apply this Convention to situations which involve solely such different territorial units.
(3) A court in a territorial unit of a Contracting State with two or more territorial units in which different systems of law apply shall not be bound to recognise or enforce a judgment from another Contracting State solely because the judgment has been recognised or enforced in another territorial unit of the same Contracting State under this Convention.
(4) This Article shall not apply to a Regional Economic Integration Organisation.

Article 26: Relationship with other international instruments

(1) This Convention shall be interpreted so far as possible to be compatible with other treaties in force for Contracting States, whether concluded before or after this Convention.
(2) This Convention shall not affect the application by a Contracting State of a treaty, whether concluded before or after this Convention, in cases where none of the parties is resident in a Contracting State that is not a Party to the treaty.

(3) This Convention shall not affect the application by a Contracting State of a treaty that was concluded before this Convention entered into force for that Contracting State, if applying this Convention would be inconsistent with the obligations of that Contracting State to any non-Contracting State. This paragraph shall also apply to treaties that revise or replace a treaty concluded before this Convention entered into force for that Contracting State, except to the extent that the revision or replacement creates new inconsistencies with this Convention.
(4) This Convention shall not affect the application by a Contracting State of a treaty, whether concluded before or after this Convention, for the purposes of obtaining recognition or enforcement of a judgment given by a court of a Contracting State that is also a Party to that treaty. However, the judgment shall not be recognised or enforced to a lesser extent than under this Convention.
(5) This Convention shall not affect the application by a Contracting State of a treaty which, in relation to a specific matter, governs jurisdiction or the recognition or enforcement of judgments, even if concluded after this Convention and even if all States concerned are Parties to this Convention. This paragraph shall apply only if the Contracting State has made a declaration in respect of the treaty under this paragraph. In the case of such a declaration, other Contracting States shall not be obliged to apply this Convention to that specific matter to the extent of any inconsistency, where an exclusive choice of court agreement designates the courts, or one or more specific courts, of the Contracting State that made the declaration.
(6) This Convention shall not affect the application of the rules of a Regional Economic Integration Organisation that is a Party to this Convention, whether adopted before or after this Convention:
   (a) where none of the parties is resident in a Contracting State that is not a Member State of the Regional Economic Integration Organisation;
   (b) as concerns the recognition or enforcement of judgments as between Member States of the Regional Economic Integration Organisation.

CHAPTER V: FINAL CLAUSES

Article 27: Signature, ratification, acceptance, approval or accession

(1) This Convention is open for signature by all States.
(2) This Convention is subject to ratification, acceptance or approval by the signatory States.
(3) This Convention is open for accession by all States.
(4) Instruments of ratification, acceptance, approval or accession shall be deposited with the Ministry of Foreign Affairs of the Kingdom of the Netherlands, depositary of the Convention.

Article 28: Declarations with respect to non-unified legal systems

(1) If a State has two or more territorial units in which different systems of law apply in relation to matters dealt with in this Convention, it may at the time of signature, ratification, acceptance, approval or accession declare that the Convention shall extend to all its territorial units or only to one or more of them and may modify this declaration by submitting another declaration at any time.
(2) A declaration shall be notified to the depositary and shall state expressly the territorial units to which the Convention applies.
(3) If a State makes no declaration under this Article, the Convention shall extend to all territorial units of that State.
(4) This Article shall not apply to a Regional Economic Integration Organisation.

Article 29: Regional Economic Integration Organisations

(1) A Regional Economic Integration Organisation which is constituted solely by sovereign States and has competence over some or all of the matters governed by this Convention may similarly sign, accept, approve or accede to this Convention. The Regional Economic Integration Organisation shall in that case have the rights and obligations of a Contracting State, to the extent that the Organisation has competence over matters governed by this Convention.
(2) The Regional Economic Integration Organisation shall, at the time of signature, acceptance, approval or accession, notify the depositary in writing of the matters governed by this Convention in respect of which competence has been transferred to that Organisation by its Member States. The Organisation shall promptly notify the depositary in writing of any changes to its competence as specified in the most recent notice given under this paragraph.
(3) For the purposes of the entry into force of this Convention, any instrument deposited by a Regional Economic Integration Organisation shall not be counted unless the Regional Economic Integration Organisation declares in accordance with Article 30 that its Member States will not be Parties to this Convention.
(4) Any reference to a "Contracting State" or "State" in this Convention shall apply equally, where appropriate, to a Regional Economic Integration Organisation that is a Party to it.

Article 30: Accession by a Regional Economic Integration Organisation without its Member States

(1) At the time of signature, acceptance, approval or accession, a Regional Economic Integration Organisation may declare that it exercises competence over all the matters governed by this Convention and that its Member States will not be Parties to this Convention but shall be bound by virtue of the signature, acceptance, approval or accession of the Organisation.
(2) In the event that a declaration is made by a Regional Economic Integration Organisation in accordance with paragraph 1, any reference to a "Contracting

State" or "State" in this Convention shall apply equally, where appropriate, to the Member States of the Organisation.

Article 31: Entry into force

(1) This Convention shall enter into force on the first day of the month following the expiration of three months after the deposit of the second instrument of ratification, acceptance, approval or accession referred to in Article 27.
(2) Thereafter this Convention shall enter into force:
   (a) for each State or Regional Economic Integration Organisation subsequently ratifying, accepting, approving or acceding to it, on the first day of the month following the expiration of three months after the deposit of its instrument of ratification, acceptance, approval or accession;
   (b) for a territorial unit to which this Convention has been extended in accordance with Article 28, paragraph 1, on the first day of the month following the expiration of three months after the notification of the declaration referred to in that Article.

Article 32: Declarations

(1) Declarations referred to in Articles 19, 20, 21, 22 and 26 may be made upon signature, ratification, acceptance, approval or accession or at any time thereafter, and may be modified or withdrawn at any time.
(2) Declarations, modifications and withdrawals shall be notified to the depositary.
(3) A declaration made at the time of signature, ratification, acceptance, approval or accession shall take effect simultaneously with the entry into force of this Convention for the State concerned.
(4) A declaration made at a subsequent time, and any modification or withdrawal of a declaration, shall take effect on the first day of the month following the expiration of three months after the date on which the notification is received by the depositary.
(5) A declaration under Articles 19, 20, 21 and 26 shall not apply to exclusive choice of court agreements concluded before it takes effect.

Article 33: Denunciation

(1) This Convention may be denounced by notification in writing to the depositary. The denunciation may be limited to certain territorial units of a non-unified legal system to which this Convention applies.
(2) The denunciation shall take effect on the first day of the month following the expiration of twelve months after the date on which the notification is received by the depositary. Where a longer period for the denunciation to take effect is specified in the notification, the denunciation shall take effect upon the expiration of such longer period after the date on which the notification is received by the depositary.

Article 34: Notifications by the depositary

The depositary shall notify the Members of the Hague Conference on Private International Law, and other States and Regional Economic Integration Organisations which have signed, ratified, accepted, approved or acceded in accordance with Articles 27, 29 and 30 of the following:

(a) the signatures, ratifications, acceptances, approvals and accessions referred to in Articles 27, 29 and 30;
(b) the date on which this Convention enters into force in accordance with Article 31;
(c) the notifications, declarations, modifications and withdrawals of declarations referred to in Articles 19, 20, 21, 22, 26, 28, 29 and 30;
(d) the denunciations referred to in Article 33.

In witness whereof the undersigned, being duly authorised thereto, have signed this Convention.

Done at The Hague, on 30 June 2005, in the English and French languages, both texts being equally authentic, in a single copy which shall be deposited in the archives of the Government of the Kingdom of the Netherlands, and of which a certified copy shall be sent, through diplomatic channels, to each of the Member States of the Hague Conference on Private International Law as of the date of its Twentieth Session and to each State which participated in that Session.

STATUS

Contracting Party*	**S1**	**R/A/Ap/Su2**	**Type3**	**EIF4**	**EXT5**	**Auth6**	**Res/D/N/DC7**
Albania	13-II-2024	25-VI-2024	R	1-X-2024			
Austria			Ap*	1-X-2015			D
Belgium			Ap*	1-X-2015			D
Bulgaria			Ap*	1-X-2015			D
China, People's Republic of	12-IX-2017						
Croatia			Ap*	1-X-2015			D
Cyprus			Ap*	1-X-2015			D
Czech Republic			Ap*	1-X-2015			D
Denmark		30-V-2018	A	1-IX-2018			D
Estonia			Ap*	1-X-2015			D
European Union	1-IV-2009	11-VI-2015	Ap	1-X-2015			D, N
Finland			Ap*	1-X-2015			D

Contracting Party*	**S1**	**R/A/Ap/ Su2**	**Type3**	**EIF4**	**EXT5**	**Auth6**	**Res/D/ N/DC7**
France			Ap*	1-X-2015			D
Germany			Ap*	1-X-2015			D
Greece			Ap*	1-X-2015			D
Hungary			Ap*	1-X-2015			D
Ireland			Ap*	1-X-2015			D
Israel	3-III-2021						
Italy			Ap*	1-X-2015			D
Kosovo	19-IX-2024						
Latvia			Ap*	1-X-2015			D
Lithuania			Ap*	1-X-2015			D
Luxembourg			Ap*	1-X-2015			D
Malta			Ap*	1-X-2015			D
Mexico		26-IX-2007	A	1-X-2015			
Montenegro	5-X-2017	18-IV-2018	R	1-VIII-2018			
Netherlands			Ap*	1-X-2015			D
Poland			Ap*	1-X-2015			D
Republic of Moldova		14-III-2024	A	1-VII-2024			D
Portugal			Ap*	1-X-2015			D
Republic of North Macedonia	9-XII-2019						
Romania			Ap*	1-X-2015			D
Singapore	25-III-2015	2-VI-2016	R	1-X-2016			
Slovakia			Ap*	1-X-2015			D
Slovenia			Ap*	1-X-2015			D
Spain			Ap*	1-X-2015			D
Sweden			Ap*	1-X-2015			D
Switzerland		18-IX-2024	A	1-I-2025			D
Ukraine	21-III-2016						
United Kingdom of Great Britain and Northern Ireland		28-IX-2020	A	1-X-2015			D, Res, DC
United States of America	19-I-2009						

* (incl. REIOs and States bound by its approval).
Contracting Parties that are not Members of the HCCH are in *italics*.

(1) S = Signature
(2) R/A/Su = Ratification, Accession or Succession
(3) Type =

R: Ratification;
A: Accession;
A*: Accession giving rise to an acceptance procedure; click on A* for details of acceptances of the accession;
Ap: Approval by an REIO
Ap*: State bound as a result of an approval by an REIO
C: Continuation;
Su: Succession;
Den: Denunciation;

(4) EIF = Entry into force
(5) EXT = Extensions of application
(6) Authorities per Convention = Designation of Authorities
(7) Res/D/N/DC = Reservations, declarations, notifications or depositary communications

Appendix C

UNCITRAL Model Law on International Commercial Arbitration (1985)

CHAPTER I: GENERAL PROVISIONS

Article 1: Scope of Application

(1) This Law applies to international commercial arbitration, subject to any agreement in force between this State and any other State or States.
(2) The provisions of this Law, except articles 8, 9, 17 H, 17 I, 17 J, 35 and 36, apply only if the place of arbitration is in the territory of this State.
(3) An arbitration is international if:
   (a) the parties to an arbitration agreement have, at the time of the conclusion of that agreement, their places of business in different States; or
   (b) one of the following places is situated outside the State in which the parties have their places of business:
      (i) the place of arbitration if determined in, or pursuant to, the arbitration agreement;
      (ii) any place where a substantial part of the obligations of the commercial relationship is to be performed or the place with which the subject-matter of the dispute is most closely connected; or
   (c) the parties have expressly agreed that the subject matter of the arbitration agreement relates to more than one country.
(4) For the purposes of paragraph (3) of this article:
   (a) if a party has more than one place of business, the place of business is that which has the closest relationship to the arbitration agreement;
   (b) if a party does not have a place of business, reference is to be made to his habitual residence.
(5) This Law shall not affect any other law of this State by virtue of which certain disputes may not be submitted to arbitration or may be submitted to arbitration only according to provisions other than those of this Law.

Article 2: Definitions and Rules of Interpretation

For the purposes of this Law:

(a) "arbitration" means any arbitration whether or not administered by a permanent arbitral institution;
(b) "arbitral tribunal" means a sole arbitrator or a panel of arbitrators;
(c) "court" means a body or organ of the judicial system of a State;
(d) where a provision of this Law, except article 28, leaves the parties free to determine a certain issue, such freedom includes the right of the parties to authorize a third party, including an institution, to make that determination;
(e) where a provision of this Law refers to the fact that the parties have agreed or that they may agree or in any other way refers to an agreement of the parties, such agreement includes any arbitration rules referred to in that agreement;
(f) where a provision of this Law, other than in articles 25(*a*) and 32(2)(*a*), refers to a claim, it also applies to a counter-claim, and where it refers to a defence, it also applies to a defence to such counter-claim.

Article 3: Receipt of Written Communications

(1) Unless otherwise agreed by the parties:
  (a) any written communication is deemed to have been received if it is delivered to the addressee personally or if it is delivered at his place of business, habitual residence or mailing address; if none of these can be found after making a reasonable inquiry, a written communication is deemed to have been received if it is sent to the addressee's last-known place of business, habitual residence or mailing address by registered letter or any other means which provides a record of the attempt to deliver it;
  (b) the communication is deemed to have been received on the day it is so delivered.
(2) The provisions of this article do not apply to communications in court proceedings.

Article 4: Waiver of Right to Object

A party who knows that any provision of this Law from which the parties may derogate or any requirement under the arbitration agreement has not been complied with and yet proceeds with the arbitration without stating his objection to such non-compliance without undue delay or, if a time limit is provided therefore, within such period of time, shall be deemed to have waived his right to object.

Article 5: Extent of Court Intervention

In matters governed by this Law, no court shall intervene except where so provided in this Law.

Article 6: Court or Other Authority for Certain Functions of Arbitration Assistance and Supervision

The functions referred to in articles 11(3), 11(4), 13(3), 14, 16(3) and 34(2) shall be performed by ... [Each State enacting this Model law specifies the court, courts or, where referred to therein, other authority competent to perform these functions.]

CHAPTER II: ARBITRATION AGREEMENT

Article 7: Definition and Form of Arbitration Agreement

(1) "Arbitration agreement" is an agreement by the parties to submit to arbitration all or certain disputes which have arisen or which may arise between them in respect of a defined legal relationship, whether contractual or not. An arbitration agreement may be in the form or an arbitration clause in a contract or in the form of a separate agreement.

(2) The arbitration agreement shall be in writing. An agreement is in writing if it is contained in a document signed by the parties or in an exchange of letters, telex, telegrams or other means of telecommunications which provide a record of the agreement, or in an exchange of statements of claim and defence in which the existence of an agreement is alleged by one party and not denied by another. The reference in a contract to a document containing an arbitration clause constitutes an arbitration agreement provided that the contract is in writing and the reference is such as to make that clause part of the contract.

Article 8: Arbitration Agreement and Substantive Claim Before Court

(1) A court before which an action is brought in a matter which is the subject of an arbitration agreement shall, if a party so requests not later than when submitting his first statement on the substance of the dispute, refer the parties to arbitration unless if finds that the agreement is null and void, inoperative or incapable of being performed.

(2) Where an action referred to in paragraph (1) of this article has been brought, arbitral proceedings may nevertheless be commenced or continued, and an award may be made, while the issue is pending before the court.

Article 9: Arbitration Agreement and Interim Measures by Court

It is not incompatible with an arbitration agreement for a party to request, before or during arbitral proceedings, from a court an interim measure of protection and for a court to grant such measure.

CHAPTER III: COMPOSITION OF ARBITRAL TRIBUNAL

Article 10: Number of Arbitrators

(1) The parties are free to determine the number of arbitrators.

(2) Failing such determination, the number of arbitrators shall be three.

Article 11: Appointment of Arbitrators

(1) No person shall be precluded by reason of his nationality from acting as an arbitrator, unless otherwise agreed by the parties.
(2) The parties are free to agree on a procedure of appointing the arbitrator or arbitrators, subject to the provisions of paragraphs (4) and (5) of this article.
(3) Failing such agreement,
   (a) in an arbitration with three arbitrators, each party shall appoint one arbitrator, and the two arbitrators thus appointed shall appoint the third arbitrator; if a party fails to appoint the arbitrator within thirty days of receipt of a request to do so from the other party, or if the two arbitrators fail to agree on the third arbitrator within thirty days of their appointment, the appointment shall be made, upon request of a party, by the court or other authority specified in article 6;
   (b) in an arbitration with a sole arbitrator, if the parties are unable to agree on the arbitrator, he shall be appointed, upon the request of a party, by the court or other authority specified in article 6.
(4) Where, under an appointment procedure agreed upon by the parties,
   (a) a party fails to act as required under such procedure, or
   (b) the parties, or two arbitrators, are unable to reach an agreement expected of them under such procedure, or
   (c) a third party, including an institution, fails to perform any function entrusted to it under such procedure,

any party may request the court or other authority specified in article 6 to take the necessary measure, unless the agreement on the appointment procedure provides other means for securing the appointment.

(5) A decision on a matter entrusted by paragraph (3) or (4) of this article to the court or other authority specified in article 6 shall be subject to no appeal. The court or other authority, in appointing an arbitrator, shall have due regard to any qualifications required of the arbitrator by the agreement of the parties and to such considerations as are likely to secure the appointment of an independent and impartial arbitrator and, in the case of a sole or third arbitrator, shall take into account as well the advisability of appointing an arbitrator of a nationality other than those of the parties.

Article 12: Grounds for Challenge

(1) When a person is approached in connection with his possible appointment as an arbitrator, he shall disclose any circumstances likely to give rise to justifiable doubts as to his impartiality or independence. An arbitrator, from the time of his appointment and throughout the arbitral proceedings, shall without delay disclose any such circumstances to the parties unless they have already been informed of them by him.

(2) An arbitrator may be challenged only if circumstances exist that give rise to justifiable doubts as to his impartiality or independence, or if he does not possess qualifications agreed to by the parties. A party may challenge an arbitrator appointed by him, or in whose appointment he has participated, only for reasons of which he becomes aware after the appointment has been made.

Article 13: Challenge Procedure

(1) The parties are free to agree on a procedure for challenging an arbitrator, subject to the provisions of paragraph (3) of this article.
(2) Failing such agreement, a party who intends to challenge an arbitrator shall, within fifteen days after becoming aware of the constitution of the arbitral tribunal or after becoming aware of any circumstance referred to in article 12(2), send a written statement of the reasons for the challenge to the arbitral tribunal. Unless the challenged arbitrator withdraws from his office or the other party agrees to the challenge, the arbitral tribunal shall decide on the challenge.
(3) If a challenge under any procedure agreed upon by the parties or under the procedure of paragraph (2) of this article is not successful, the challenging party may request, within thirty days after having received notice of the decision rejecting the challenge, the court or other authority specified in article 6 to decide on the challenge, which decision shall be subject to no appeal; while such a request is pending, the arbitral tribunal, including the challenged arbitrator, may continue the arbitral proceedings and make an award.

Article 14: Failure or Impossibility to Act

(1) If an arbitrator becomes de jure or de facto unable to perform his functions or for other reasons fails to act without undue delay, his mandate terminates if he withdraws from his office or if the parties agree on the termination. Otherwise, if a controversy remains concerning any of these grounds, any party may request the court or other authority specified in article 6 to decide on the termination of the mandate, which decision shall be subject to no appeal.
(2) If, under this article or article 13(2), an arbitrator withdraws from his office or a party agrees to the termination of the mandate of an arbitrator, this does not imply acceptance of the validity of any ground referred to in this article or article 12(2).

Article 15: Appointment of Substitute Arbitrator

Where the mandate of an arbitrator terminates under article 13 or 14 or because of his withdrawal from office for any other reason or because of the revocation of his mandate by agreement of the parties or in any other case of termination of his mandate, a substitute arbitrator shall be appointed according to the rules that were applicable to the appointment of the arbitrator being replaced.

CHAPTER IV: JURISDICTION OF ARBITRAL TRIBUNAL

Article 16: Competence of Arbitral Tribunal to Rule on Its Jurisdiction

(1) The arbitral tribunal may rule on its own jurisdiction, including any objections with respect to the existence or validity of the arbitration agreement. For that purpose, an arbitration clause which forms part of a contract shall be treated as an agreement independent of the other terms of the contract. A decision by the arbitral tribunal that the contract is null and void shall not entail *ipso jure* the invalidity of the arbitration clause.
(2) A plea that the arbitral tribunal does not have jurisdiction shall be raised not later than the submission of the statement of defence. A party is not precluded from raising such a plea by the fact that he has appointed, or participated in the appointment of, an arbitrator. A plea that the arbitral tribunal is exceeding the scope of its authority shall be raised as soon as the matter alleged to be beyond the scope of its authority is raised during the arbitral proceedings. The arbitral tribunal may, in either case, admit a later plea if it considers the delay justified.
(3) The arbitral tribunal may rule on a plea referred to in paragraph (2) of this article either as a preliminary question or in an award on the merits. If the arbitral tribunal rules as a preliminary question that it has jurisdiction, any party may request, within thirty days after having received notice of that ruling, the court specified in article 6 to decide the matter, which decision shall be subject to no appeal; while such a request is pending, the arbitral tribunal may continue the arbitral proceedings and make an award.

Article 17: Power of Arbitral Tribunal to Order Interim Measures

Unless otherwise agreed by the parties, the arbitral tribunal may, at the request of a party, order any party to take such interim measure of protection as the arbitral tribunal may consider necessary in respect of the subject-matter of the dispute. The arbitral tribunal may require any party to provide appropriate security in connection with such measure.

CHAPTER V: CONDUCT OF ARBITRAL PROCEEDINGS

Article 18: Equal Treatment of Parties

The parties shall be treated with equality and each party shall be given a full opportunity of presenting his case.

Article 19: Determination of Rules of Procedure

(1) Subject to the provisions of this Law, the parties are free to agree on the procedure to be followed by the arbitral tribunal in conducting the proceedings.
(2) Failing such agreement, the arbitral tribunal may, subject to the provisions of this Law, conduct the arbitration in such a manner as it considers appropriate. The power conferred upon the arbitral tribunal includes the power to determine the admissibility, relevance, materiality and weight of any evidence.

Article 20: Place of Arbitration

(1) The parties are free to agree on the place of arbitration. Failing such agreement, the place of arbitration shall be determined by the arbitral tribunal having regard to the circumstances of the case, including the convenience of the parties.
(2) Notwithstanding the provisions of paragraph (1) of this article, the arbitral tribunal may, unless otherwise agreed by the parties, meet at any place it considers appropriate for consultation among its members, for hearing witnesses, experts or the parties, or for inspection of goods, other property or documents.

Article 21: Commencement of Arbitral Proceedings

Unless otherwise agreed by the parties, the arbitral proceedings in respect of a particular dispute commence on the date on which a request for that dispute to be referred to arbitration is received by the respondent.

Article 22: Language

(1) The parties are free to agree on the language or languages to be used in the arbitral proceedings. Failing such agreement, the arbitral tribunal shall determine the language or languages to be used in the proceedings. This agreement or determination, unless otherwise specified therein, shall apply to any written statement by a party, any hearing and any award, decision or other communication by the arbitral tribunal.
(2) The arbitral tribunal may order that any documentary evidence shall be accompanied by a translation into the language or languages agreed upon by the parties or determined by the arbitral tribunal.

Article 23: Statements of Claim and Defence

(1) Within the period of time agreed by the parties or determined by the arbitral tribunal, the claimant shall state the facts supporting his claim, the points at issue and the relief or remedy sought, and the respondent shall state his defence in respect of these particulars, unless the parties have otherwise agreed as to the required elements of such statements. The parties may submit with their statements all documents they consider to be relevant or may add a reference to the documents or other evidence they will submit.
(2) Unless otherwise agreed by the parties, either party may amend or supplement his claim or defence during the course of the arbitral proceedings, unless the arbitral tribunal considers it inappropriate to allow such amendment having regard to the delay in making it.

Article 24: Hearings and Written Proceedings

(1) Subject to any contrary agreement by the parties, the arbitral tribunal shall decide whether to hold oral hearings for the presentation of evidence or for oral

argument, or whether the proceedings shall be conducted on the basis of documents and other materials. However, unless the parties have agreed that no hearings shall be held, the arbitral tribunal shall hold such hearings at an appropriate stage of the proceedings, if so requested by a party.

(2) The parties shall be given sufficient advance notice of any hearing and of any meeting of the arbitral tribunal for the purposes of inspection of goods, other property or documents.

(3) All statements, documents or other information supplied to the arbitral tribunal by one party shall be communicated to the other party. Also, any expert report or evidentiary document on which the arbitral tribunal may rely in making its decision shall be communicated to the parties.

Article 25: Default of a Party

Unless otherwise agreed by the parties, if, without showing sufficient cause,

(a) the claimant fails to communicate his statement of claim in accordance with article 23(1), the arbitral tribunal shall terminate the proceedings;

(b) the respondent fails to communicate his statement of defence in accordance with article 23(1), the arbitral tribunal shall continue the proceedings without treating such failure in itself as an admission of the claimant's allegations;

(c) any party fails to appear at a hearing or to produce documentary evidence, the arbitral tribunal may continue the proceedings and make the award on the evidence before it.

Article 26: Expert Appointed by Arbitral Tribunal

(1) Unless otherwise agreed by the parties, the arbitral tribunal

  (a) may appoint one or more experts to report to it on specific issues to be determined by the arbitral tribunal;

  (b) may require a party to give the expert any relevant information or to produce, or to provide access to, any relevant documents, goods or other property for his inspection.

(2) Unless otherwise agreed by the parties, if a party so requests or if the arbitral tribunal considers it necessary, the expert shall, after delivery of his written or oral report, participate in a hearing where the parties have the opportunity to put questions to him and to present expert witnesses in order to testify on the points at issue.

Article 27: Court Assistance in Taking Evidence

The arbitral tribunal or a party with the approval of the arbitral tribunal may request from a competent court of this State assistance in taking evidence. The court may execute the request within its competence and according to its rules on taking evidence.

CHAPTER VI: MAKING OF AWARD AND TERMINATION OF PROCEEDINGS

Article 28: Rules Applicable to Substance of Dispute

(1) The arbitral tribunal shall decide the dispute in accordance with such rules of law as are chosen by the parties as applicable to the substance of the dispute. Any designation of the law or legal system of a given State shall be construed, unless otherwise expressed, as directly referring to the substantive law of that State and not to its conflict of laws rules.
(2) Failing any designation by the parties, the arbitral tribunal shall apply the law determined by the conflict of laws rules which it considers applicable.
(3) The arbitral tribunal shall decide *ex aequo et bono* or as *amiable compositeur* only if the parties have expressly authorized it to do so.
(4) In all cases, the arbitral tribunal shall decide in accordance with the terms of the contract and shall take into account the usages of the trade applicable to the transaction.

Article 29: Decision Making by Panel of Arbitrators

In arbitral proceedings with more than one arbitrator, any decision of the arbitral tribunal shall be made, unless otherwise agreed by the parties, by a majority of all its members. However, questions of procedure may be decided by a presiding arbitrator, if so authorized by the parties or all members of the arbitral tribunal.

Article 30: Settlement

(1) If, during arbitral proceedings, the parties settle the dispute, the arbitral tribunal shall terminate the proceedings and, if requested by the parties and not objected to by the arbitral tribunal, record the settlement in the form of an arbitral award on agreed terms.
(2) An award on agreed terms shall be made in accordance with the provisions of article 31 and shall state that it is an award. Such an award has the same status and effect as any other award on the merits of the case.

Article 31: Form and Contents of Award

(1) The award shall be made in writing and shall be signed by the arbitrator or arbitrators. In arbitral proceedings with more than one arbitrator, the signatures of the majority of all members of the arbitral tribunal shall suffice, provided that the reason for any omitted signature is stated.
(2) The award shall state the reasons upon which it is based, unless the parties have agreed that no reasons are to be given or the award is an award on agreed terms under article 30.
(3) The award shall state its date and the place of arbitration as determined in accordance with article 20(1). The award shall be deemed to have been made at that place.

(4) After the award is made, a copy signed by the arbitrators in accordance with paragraph (1) of this article shall be delivered to each party.

Article 32: Termination of Proceedings

(1) The arbitral proceedings are terminated by the final award or by an order of the arbitral tribunal in accordance with paragraph (2) of this article.
(2) The arbitral tribunal shall issue an order for the termination of the arbitral proceedings when:
  (a) the claimant withdraws his claim, unless the respondent objects thereto and the arbitral tribunal recognizes a legitimate interest on his part in obtaining a final settlement of the dispute;
  (b) the parties agree on the termination of the proceedings;
  (c) the arbitral tribunal finds that the continuation of the proceedings has for any other reason become unnecessary or impossible.
(3) The mandate of the arbitral tribunal terminates with the termination of the arbitral proceedings, subject to the provisions of articles 33 and 34(4).

Article 33: Correction and Interpretation of Award; Additional Award

(1) Within thirty days of receipt of the award, unless another period of time has been agreed upon by the parties:
  (a) a party, with notice to the other party, may request the arbitral tribunal to correct in the award any errors in computation, any clerical or typographical errors or any errors of similar nature;
  (b) if so agreed by the parties, a party, with notice to the other party, may request the arbitral tribunal to give an interpretation of a specific point or part of the award.
  (c) If the arbitral tribunal considers the request to be justified, it shall make the correction or give the interpretation within thirty days of receipt of the request. The interpretation shall form part of the award.
(2) The arbitral tribunal may correct any error of the type referred to in paragraph (l)(a) of this article on its own initiative within thirty days of the date of the award.
(3) Unless otherwise agreed by the parties, a party, with notice to the other party, may request, within thirty days of receipt of the award, the arbitral tribunal to make an additional award as to claims presented in the arbitral proceedings but omitted from the award. If the arbitral tribunal considers the request to be justified, it shall make the additional award within sixty days.
(4) The arbitral tribunal may extend, if necessary, the period of time within which it shall make a correction, interpretation or an additional award under paragraph (1) or (3) of this article.
(5) The provisions of article 31 shall apply to a correction or interpretation of the award or to an additional award.

CHAPTER VII: RECOURSE AGAINST AWARD

Article 34: Application for Setting Aside as Exclusive Recourse against Arbitral Award

(1) Recourse to a court against an arbitral award may be made only by an application for setting aside in accordance with paragraphs (2) and (3) of this article.
(2) An arbitral award may be set aside by the court specified in article 6 only if:
  (a) the party making the application furnishes proof that:
    (i) a party to the arbitration agreement referred to in article 7 was under some incapacity; or the said agreement is not valid under the law to which the parties have subjected it or, failing any indication thereon, under the law of this State; or
    (ii) the party making the application was not given proper notice of the appointment of an arbitrator or of the arbitral proceedings or was otherwise unable to present his case; or
    (iii) the award deals with a dispute not contemplated by or not falling within the terms of the submission to arbitration, or contains decisions on matters beyond the scope of the submission to arbitration, provided that, if the decisions on matters submitted to arbitration can be separated from those not so submitted, only that part of the award which contains decisions on matters not submitted to arbitration may be set aside; or
    (iv) the composition of the arbitral tribunal or the arbitral procedure was not in accordance with the agreement of the parties, unless such agreement was in conflict with a provision of this Law from which the parties cannot derogate, or, failing such agreement, was not in accordance with this Law; or
  (b) the court finds that:
    (i) the subject-matter of the dispute is not capable of settlement by arbitration under the law of this State; or
    (ii) the award is in conflict with the public policy of this State.
(3) An application for setting aside may not be made after three months have elapsed from the date on which the party making that application had received the award or, if a request had been made under article 33, from the date on which that request had been disposed of by the arbitral tribunal.
(4) The court, when asked to set aside an award, may, where appropriate and so requested by a party, suspend the setting aside proceedings for a period of time determined by it in order to give the arbitral tribunal an opportunity to resume the arbitral proceedings or to take such other action as in the arbitral tribunal's opinion will eliminate the grounds for setting aside.

CHAPTER VIII: RECOGNITION AND ENFORCEMENT OF AWARDS

Article 35: Recognition and Enforcement

(1) An arbitral award, irrespective of the country in which it was made, shall be recognized as binding and, upon application in writing to the competent court, shall be enforced subject to the provisions of this article and of article 36.
(2) The party relying on an award or applying for its enforcement shall supply the duly authenticated original award or a duly certified copy thereof, and the original arbitration agreement referred to in article 7 or a duly certified copy thereof. If the award or agreement is not made in an official language of this State, the party shall supply a duly certified translation thereof into such language.

Article 36: Grounds for Refusing Recognition or Enforcement

(1) Recognition or enforcement of an arbitral award, irrespective of the country in which it was made, may be refused only:
  (a) at the request of the party against whom it is invoked, if that party furnishes to the competent court where recognition or enforcement is sought proof that:
    (i) a party to the arbitration agreement referred to in article 7 was under some incapacity; or the said agreement is not valid under the law to which the parties have subjected it or, failing any indication thereon, under the law of the country where the award was made; or
    (ii) the party against whom the award is invoked was not given proper notice of the appointment of an arbitrator or of the arbitral proceedings or was otherwise unable to present his case; or
    (iii) the award deals with a dispute not contemplated by or not falling within the terms of the submission to arbitration, or it contains decisions on matters beyond the scope of the submission to arbitration, provided that, if the decisions on matters submitted to arbitration can be separated from those not so submitted, that part of the award which contains decisions on matters submitted to arbitration may be recognized and enforced; or
    (iv) the composition of the arbitral tribunal or the arbitral procedure was not in accordance with the agreement of the parties or, failing such agreement, was not in accordance with the law of the country where the arbitration took place; or
    (v) the award has not yet become binding on the parties or has been set aside or suspended by a court of the country in which, or under the law of which, that award was made; or
  (b) if the court finds that:
    (i) the subject-matter of the dispute is not capable of settlement by arbitration under the law of this State; or

(ii) the recognition or enforcement of the award would be contrary to the public policy of this State.

(2) If an application for setting aside or suspension of an award has been made to a court referred to in paragraph (1)(a)(v) of this article, the court where recognition or enforcement is sought may, if it considers it proper, adjourn its decision and may also, on the application of the party claiming recognition or enforcement of the award, order the other party to provide appropriate security.

Appendix D

UNCITRAL Model Law on International Commercial Arbitration (2006 Revisions)

Amendments by the United Nations Commission on International Trade Law, 7 July 2006

Article 1: Scope of application[1]

(Art. 1(2) has been amended by the Commission at its thirty-ninth session, in 2006)

(1) This Law applies to international commercial[2] arbitration, subject to any agreement in force between this State and any other State or States.
(2) The provisions of this Law, except articles 8, 9, 17H, 17I, 17J, 35 and 36, apply only if the place of arbitration is in the territory of this State.

...

Article 2 A: International origin and general principles

(As adopted by the Commission at its thirty-ninth session, in 2006)

(1) In the interpretation of this Law, regard is to be had to its international origin and to the need to promote uniformity in its application and the observance of good faith.

1. Article headings are for reference purposes only and are not to be used for purposes of interpretation.
2. The term "commercial" should be given a wide interpretation so as to cover matters arising from all relationships of a commercial nature, whether contractual or not. Relationships of a commercial nature include, but are not limited to, the following transactions: any trade transaction for the supply or exchange or goods or services; distribution agreement; commercial representation or agency; factoring; leasing; construction of works; consulting; engineering; licensing; investment; financing; banking; insurance; exploitation agreement or concession; joint venture and other forms or industrial or business cooperation; and carriage of goods or passengers by air, sea, rail or road.

(2) Questions concerning matters governed by this Law which are not expressly settled in it are to be settled in conformity with the general principles on which this Law is based.

CHAPTER II: ARBITRATION AGREEMENT

Option I

Article 7: Definition and form of arbitration agreement

(As adopted by the Commission at its thirty-ninth session, in 2006)

(1) "Arbitration agreement" is an agreement by the parties to submit to arbitration all or certain disputes which have arisen or which may arise between them in respect of a defined legal relationship, whether contractual or not. An arbitration agreement may be in the form of an arbitration clause in a contract or in the form of a separate agreement.
(2) The arbitration agreement shall be in writing.
(3) An arbitration agreement is in writing if its content is records in any form, whether or not the arbitration agreement or contract has been concluded orally, by conduct, or by other means.
(4) The requirement that an arbitration agreement be in writing is met by an electronic communication if the information contained therein is accessible so as to be useable for subsequent reference; "electronic communication" means any communication that the parties make by means of data messages; "data message" means information generated, sent, received or stored by electronic magnetic, optical or similar means, including, but not limited to, electronic data interchange (EDI), electronic mail, telegram, telex or telecopy.
(5) Furthermore, an arbitration agreement is in writing if it is contained in an exchange of statements of claim and defence in which the existence of an agreement is alleged by one party and not denied by the other.
(6) The reference in a contract to any document containing an arbitration clause constitutes an arbitration agreement in writing, provided that the reference is such as to make that clause part of the contract.

Option II

Article 7: Definition of arbitration agreement

(As adopted by the Commission at its thirty-ninth session, in 2006)

"Arbitration agreement" is an agreement by the parties to submit to arbitration all or certain disputes which have arisen or which may arise between them in respect of a defined legal relationship, whether contractual or not.

CHAPTER IV A: INTERIM MEASURES AND PRELIMINARY ORDERS

(As adopted by the Commission at its thirty-ninth session, in 2006)

Section 1: Interim measures

Article 17: Power of arbitral tribunal to order interim measures

(1) Unless otherwise agreed by the parties, the arbitral tribunal may, at the request of a party, grant interim measures.
(2) An interim measure is any temporary measure, whether in the form of an award or in another form, but which, at any time prior to the issuance of the award by which the dispute is finally decided, the arbitral tribunal orders a party to:
  (a) Maintain or restore the status quo pending determination of the dispute;
  (b) Take action that would prevent, or refrain from taking action that is likely to cause, current or imminent harm or prejudice to the arbitral process itself;
  (c) Provide a means of preserving assets out of which a subsequent award may be satisfied; or
  (d) Preserve evidence that may be relevant and material to the resolution of the dispute.

Article 17 A: Conditions for granting interim measures

(1) The party requesting an interim measure under article 17(2) (a), (b) and (c) shall satisfy the arbitral tribunal that:
  (a) Harm not adequately reparable by an award of damages is likely to result if the measure is not ordered, and such harm substantially outweighs the harm that is likely to result to the party against whom the measure is directed if the measure is granted; and
  (b) There is a reasonable possibility that the requesting party will succeed on the merits of the claim. The determination on this possibility shall not affect the discretion of the arbitral tribunal in making any subsequent determination.
(2) With regard to a request for an interim measure under article 17(2)(d), the requirements in paragraphs (1)(a) and (b) of this article shall apply only to the extent the arbitral tribunal considers appropriate.

Section 2: Preliminary Orders

Article 17 B: Applications for preliminary orders and conditions for granting preliminary orders

(1) Unless otherwise agreed by the parties, a party may, without notice to any other party, make a request for an interim measure together with an application for a preliminary order directing a party not to frustrate the purpose of the interim measure requested.
(2) The arbitral tribunal may grant a preliminary order provided it considers that prior disclosure of the request for the interim measure to the party against whom it is directed risks frustrating the purpose of the measure.

(3) The conditions defined under article 17A apply to any preliminary order, provided that the harm to be assessed under article 17A(1)(a), is the harm likely to result from the order being granted or not.

Article 17 C: Specific regime for preliminary orders

(1) Immediately after the arbitral tribunal has made a determination in respect of an application for a preliminary order, the arbitral tribunal shall give notice to all parties of the request for the interim measure, the application for the preliminary order, the preliminary order, if any, and all other communications, including by indicating the content of any oral communication, between any party and the arbitral tribunal in relation thereto.
(2) At the same time, the arbitral tribunal shall give an opportunity to any party against whom a preliminary order is directed to present its case at the earliest practicable time.
(3) The arbitral tribunal shall decide promptly on any objection to the preliminary order.
(4) A preliminary order shall expire after twenty days from the date on which it was issued by the arbitral tribunal. However, the arbitral tribunal may issue an interim measure adopting or modifying the preliminary order, after the party against whom the preliminary order is directed has been given notice and an opportunity to present its case.
(5) A preliminary order shall be binding on the parties but shall not be subject to enforcement by a court. Such a preliminary order does not constitute an award.

Section 3: Provisions applicable to interim measures and preliminary orders

Article 17 D: Modification, suspension, termination

The arbitral tribunal may modify, suspend or terminate an interim measure or a preliminary order it has granted, upon application of any party or, in exceptional circumstances and upon prior notice to the parties, on the arbitral tribunal's own initiative.

Article 17 E: Provision of security

(1) The arbitral tribunal may require the party requesting an interim measure to provide appropriate security in connection with the measure.
(2) The arbitral tribunal shall require the party applying for a preliminary order to provide security in connection with the order unless the arbitral tribunal considers it inappropriate or unnecessary to do so.

Article 17 F: Disclosure

(1) The arbitral tribunal may require any party promptly to disclose any material change in the circumstances on the basis of which the measure was requested or granted.

(2) The party applying for a preliminary order shall disclose to the arbitral tribunal all circumstances that are likely to be relevant to the arbitral tribunal's determination whether to grant or maintain the order, and such obligation shall continue until the party against whom the order has been requested has had an opportunity to present its case. Thereafter, paragraph (1) of this article shall apply.

Article 17 G: Costs and damages

The party requesting an interim measure or applying for a preliminary order shall be liable for any costs and damages caused by the measure or the order to any party if the arbitral tribunal later determines that, in the circumstances, the measure or the order should not have been granted. The arbitral tribunal may award such costs and damages at any point during the proceedings.

Section 4: Recognition and enforcement of interim measures

Article 17 H: Recognition and enforcement

(1) An interim measure issued by an arbitral tribunal shall be recognized as binding and, unless otherwise provided by the arbitral tribunal, enforced upon application to the competent court, irrespective of the country in which it was issued, subject to the provisions of article 17 I.

(2) The party who is seeking or has obtained recognition or enforcement of an interim measure shall promptly inform the court of any termination, suspension or modification of that interim measure.

(3) The court of the State where recognition or enforcement is sought may, if it considers it proper, order the requesting party to provide appropriate security if the arbitral tribunal has not already made a determination with respect to security or where such a decision is necessary to protect the rights of third parties.

Article 17 I: Grounds for refusing recognition or enforcement[3]

(1) Recognition or enforcement of an interim measure may be refused only:
   (a) At the request of the party against whom it is invoked if the court is satisfied that:
      (i) Such refusal is warranted on the grounds set forth in article 36(1)(a)(i), (ii), (iii) or (iv); or
      (ii) The arbitral tribunal's decision with respect to the provision of security in connection with the interim measure issued by the arbitral tribunal has not been complied with; or

3. The conditions set forth in Article 17 I are intended to limit the number of circumstances in which the court may refuse to enforce an interim measure. It would not be contrary to the level of harmonization sought to be achieved by these model provisions if a State were to adopt fewer circumstances in which enforcement may be refused.

(iii) The interim measure has been terminated or suspended by the arbitral tribunal or, where so empowered, by the court of the State in which the arbitration takes place or under the law of which that interim measure was granted; or

(b) If the court finds that:

(i) The interim measure is incompatible with the powers conferred upon the court unless the court decides to reformulate the interim measure to the extent necessary to adapt it to its own powers and procedures for the purposes of enforcing that interim measure and without modifying its substance; or

(ii) Any of the grounds set forth in article 36(1)(b)(i) or (ii), apply to the recognition and enforcement of the interim measure.

(2) Any determination made by the court on any ground in paragraph (1) of this article shall be effective only for the purposes of the application to recognize and enforce the interim measure. The court where recognition or enforcement is sought shall not, in making that determination, undertake a review of the substance of the interim measure.

Section 5: Court-ordered interim measures

Article 17 J: Court-ordered interim measures

A court shall have the same power of issuing an interim measure in relation to arbitration proceedings, irrespective of whether their place is in the territory of this State, as it has in relation to proceedings in courts. The court shall exercise such power in accordance with its own procedures in consideration of the specific features of international arbitration.

CHAPTER VIII: RECOGNITION AND ENFORCEMENT OF AWARDS

Article 35: Recognition and enforcement

(Article 35(2) has been amended by the Commission at its thirty-ninth session, in 2006)

(1) ...

(2) The party relying on an award or applying for its enforcement shall supply the original award or a copy thereof. If the award is not made in an official language of this State, the court may request the party to supply a translation thereof into such language.[4]

4. The conditions set forth in this paragraph are intended to set maximum standards. It would, thus, not be contrary to the harmonization to be achieved by the model law if a State retained even less onerous conditions.

STATUS

The UNCITRAL Secretariat also prepares yearly a document containing the Status of Conventions and Enactments of UNCITRAL Model Laws, which is available on the web page of the corresponding UNCITRAL Commission session.

Legislation based on the Model Law has been adopted in 93 States in a total of 126 jurisdictions:

State	Year	Notes
Albania	2023	(b)
Argentina	2018	
Armenia	2006	
Australia	2010	(a), (b)
Australian Capital Territory	2017	(b)
New South Wales	2010	(b)
Northern Territory	2011	(b)
Queensland	2013	(b)
South Australia	2011	(b)
Tasmania	2011	(b)
Victoria	2011	(b)
Western Australia	2012	(b)
Austria	2006	
Azerbaijan	2024	(b)
Bahrain	2015	(a), (b)
Bangladesh	2001	
Barbados	2007	(b)
Belarus	1999	
Belgium	2013	(b)
Bhutan	2013	(b)
Brunei Darussalam	2009	(b)
Bulgaria	2002	(a)
Cambodia	2006	
Canada	1986	
Alberta	1986	
British Columbia	2018	(a), (b)
Manitoba	1986	
New Brunswick	1986	
Newfoundland and Labrador	1986	
Northwest Territories	1986	

State	**Year**	**Notes**
Nova Scotia	1986	
Nunavut	1999	
Ontario	1987	(a), (b)
Prince Edward Island	1986	
Quebec	1986	
Saskatchewan	1988	
Yukon	1986	
Chile	2004	
China		
Hong Kong, China	2010	(a), (b)
Macao, China	2019	(a), (b)
Costa Rica	2011	(b)
Croatia	2001	
Cyprus	1987	
Denmark	2005	
Dominican Republic	2008	
Egypt	1994	
Estonia	2006	
Fiji	2017	(b)
Georgia	2009	(b)
Germany	1998	
Greece	2023	(b)
Guatemala	1995	
Guyana	2024	(b)
Honduras	2000	
Hungary	1994	
India	1996	
Iran (Islamic Republic of)	1997	
Ireland	2010	(a), (b)
Israel	2024	(b)
Jamaica	2017	(b)
Japan	2023	(b)
Jordan	2001	
Kenya	1995	
Liechtenstein	2010	
Lithuania	2012	(a), (b)

State	Year	Notes
Madagascar	1998	
Malawi	2024	(b)
Malaysia	2018	(a), (b)
Maldives	2013	
Malta	1996	
Marshall Islands	2018	(b)
Mauritius	2008	(b)
Mexico	1993	
Mongolia	2017	(b)
Montenegro	2015	
Myanmar	2016	
New Zealand	2007	(a), (b)
Nicaragua	2005	
Nigeria	2023	(b)
North Macedonia	2006	
Norway	2004	
Oman	1997	
Paraguay	2002	
Peru	2008	(a), (b)
Philippines	2004	
Poland	2005	
Qatar	2017	
Republic of Korea	2016	(a), (b)
Russian Federation	1993	
Rwanda	2008	(b)
Saudi Arabia	2012	
Serbia	2006	
Sierra Leone	2022	(b)
Singapore	1994	(a)
Slovakia	2014	
Slovenia	2008	(b)
South Africa	2017	(b)
Spain	2003	
Sri Lanka	1995	
Thailand	2002	
Tonga	2020	(b)

State	Year	Notes
Trinidad and Tobago	2023	(b)
Tunisia	1993	
Turkey	2001	
Turkmenistan	2016	(b)
Uganda	2000	
Ukraine	1994	
United Arab Emirates	2018	
Dubai International Financial Centre	2013	
Abu Dhabi Global Market	2015	
United Kingdom of Great Britain and Northern Ireland		
Bermuda	1993	(c)
British Virgin Islands	2013	(b), (c)
Scotland	1990	
United States of America		
California	1988	
Connecticut	1989	
Florida	2010	(b)
Georgia	2012	
Illinois	1998	
Louisiana	2006	
Oregon	1991	
Texas	1989	
Uruguay	2018	
Uzbekistan	2021	(b)
Venezuela (Bolivarian Republic of)	1998	
Zambia	2000	
Zimbabwe	1996	

Notes

(a) The legislation amends previous legislation based on the Model Law.
(b) Indicates legislation based on the text of the UNCITRAL Model Law on International Commercial Arbitration with amendments as adopted in 2006.
(c) Overseas territory of the United Kingdom of Great Britain and Northern Ireland.

Disclaimer: A model law is created as a suggested pattern for lawmakers to consider adopting as part of their domestic legislation. Since States enacting legislation based upon a model law have the flexibility to depart from the text, the above list is only indicative of the enactments that were made known to the UNCITRAL Secretariat.

The legislation of each State should be considered in order to identify the exact nature of any possible deviation from the model in the legislative text that was adopted. The year of enactment indicated above is the year the legislation was passed by the relevant legislative body, as indicated to the UNCITRAL Secretariat; it does not address the date of entry into force of that piece of legislation, the procedures for which vary from State to State, and could result in entry into force some time after enactment.

Appendix E

UNCITRAL Arbitration Rules 2021 (with Article 1, Paragraph 4, as Adopted in 2013 and Article 1, Paragraph 5, as Adopted in 2021)

SECTION I: INTRODUCTORY RULES

Article 1

(1) Where parties have agreed that disputes between them in respect of a defined legal relationship, whether contractual or not, shall be referred to arbitration under the UNCITRAL Arbitration Rules, then such disputes shall be settled in accordance with these Rules subject to such modification as the parties may agree.

(2) The parties to an arbitration agreement concluded after 15 August 2010 shall be presumed to have referred to the Rules in effect on the date of commencement of the arbitration, unless the parties have agreed to apply a particular version of the Rules. That presumption does not apply where the arbitration agreement has been concluded by accepting after 15 August 2010 an offer made before that date.

(3) These Rules shall govern the arbitration except that where any of these Rules is in conflict with a provision of the law applicable to the arbitration from which the parties cannot derogate, that provision shall prevail.

(4) For investor-State arbitration initiated pursuant to a treaty providing for the protection of investments or investors, these Rules include the UNCITRAL Rules on Transparency in Treaty-based Investor-State Arbitration ("Rules on Transparency"), subject to article 1 of the Rules on Transparency.

(5) The Expedited Arbitration Rules in the appendix shall apply to the arbitration where the parties so agree.

* A model arbitration clause for contracts can be found in the annex to the Rules.

Article 2

(1) A notice, including a notification, communication or proposal, may be transmitted by any means of communication that provides or allows for a record of its transmission.
(2) If an address has been designated by a party specifically for this purpose or authorized by the arbitral tribunal, any notice shall be delivered to that party at that address, and if so delivered shall be deemed to have been received. Delivery by electronic means such as facsimile or e-mail may only be made to an address so designated or authorized.
(3) In the absence of such designation or authorization, a notice is:
  (a) Received if it is physically delivered to the addressee; or
  (b) Deemed to have been received if it is delivered at the place of business, habitual residence or mailing address of the addressee.
(4) If, after reasonable efforts, delivery cannot be effected in accordance with paragraphs 2 or 3, a notice is deemed to have been received if it is sent to the addressee's last-known place of business, habitual residence or mailing address by registered letter or any other means that provides a record of delivery or of attempted delivery.
(5) A notice shall be deemed to have been received on the day it is delivered in accordance with paragraphs 2, 3 or 4, or attempted to be delivered in accordance with paragraph 4. A notice transmitted by electronic means is deemed to have been received on the day it is sent, except that a notice of arbitration so transmitted is only deemed to have been received on the day when it reaches the addressee's electronic address.
(6) For the purpose of calculating a period of time under these Rules, such period shall begin to run on the day following the day when a notice is received. If the last day of such period is an official holiday or a non-business day at the residence or place of business of the addressee, the period is extended until the first business day which follows. Official holidays or non-business days occurring during the running of the period of time are included in calculating the period.

Article 3

(1) The party or parties initiating recourse to arbitration (herein after called the "claimant") shall communicate to the other party or parties (hereinafter called the "respondent") a notice of arbitration.
(2) Arbitral proceedings shall be deemed to commence on the date on which the notice of arbitration is received by the respondent.
(3) The notice of arbitration shall include the following:
  (a) A demand that the dispute be referred to arbitration
  (b) The names and contact details of the parties;
  (c) Identification of the arbitration agreement that is invoked;

(d) Identification of any contract or other legal instrument out of or in relation to which the dispute arises or, in the absence of such contract or instrument, a brief description of the relevant relationship;
(e) A brief description of the claim and an indication of the amount involved, if any;
(f) The relief or remedy sought;
(g) A proposal as to the number of arbitrators, language and place of arbitration, if the parties have not previously agreed thereon.

(4) The notice of arbitration may also include:
(a) A proposal for the designation of an appointing authority referred to in article 6, paragraph 1;
(b) A proposal for the appointment of a sole arbitrator referred to in article 8, paragraph 1;
(c) Notification of the appointment of an arbitrator referred to in article 9 or 10.

(5) The constitution of the arbitral tribunal shall not be hindered by any controversy with respect to the sufficiency of the notice of arbitration, which shall be finally resolved by the arbitral tribunal.

Article 4

(1) Within 30 days of the receipt of the notice of arbitration, the respondent shall communicate to the claimant a response to the notice of arbitration, which shall include:
(a) The name and contact details of each respondent;
(b) A response to the information set forth in the notice of arbitration, pursuant to article 3, paragraphs 3 (c) to (g).

(2) The response to the notice of arbitration may also include:
(a) Any plea that an arbitral tribunal to be constituted under these Rules lacks jurisdiction;
(b) A proposal for the designation of an appointing authority referred to in article 6, paragraph 1;
(c) A proposal for the appointment of a sole arbitrator referred to in article 8, paragraph 1;
(d) Notification of the appointment of an arbitrator referred to in article 9 or 10;
(e) A brief description of counterclaims or claims for the purpose of a set-off, if any, including where relevant, an indication of the amounts involved, and the relief or remedy sought;
(f) A notice of arbitration in accordance with article 3 in case the respondent formulates a claim against a party to the arbitration agreement other than the claimant.

(3) The constitution of the arbitral tribunal shall not be hindered by any controversy with respect to the respondent's failure to communicate a response to the notice of arbitration, or an incomplete or late response to the notice of arbitration, which shall be finally resolved by the arbitral tribunal.

Article 5

Each party may be represented or assisted by persons chosen by it. The names and addresses of such persons must be communicated to all parties and to the arbitral tribunal. Such communication must specify whether the appointment is being made for purposes of representation or assistance. Where a person is to act as a representative of a party, the arbitral tribunal, on its own initiative or at the request of any party, may at any time require proof of authority granted to the representative in such a form as the arbitral tribunal may determine.

Article 6

(1) Unless the parties have already agreed on the choice of an appointing authority, a party may at any time propose the name or names of one or more institutions or persons, including the Secretary-General of the Permanent Court of Arbitration at The Hague (hereinafter called the "PCA"), one of whom would serve as appointing authority.
(2) If all parties have not agreed on the choice of an appointing authority within 30 days after a proposal made in accordance with paragraph 1 has been received by all other parties, any party may request the Secretary-General of the PCA to designate the appointing authority.
(3) Where these Rules provide for a period of time within which a party must refer a matter to an appointing authority and no appointing authority has been agreed on or designated, the period is suspended from the date on which a party initiates the procedure for agreeing on or designating an appointing authority until the date of such agreement or designation.
(4) Except as referred to in article 41, paragraph 4, if the appointing authority refuses to act, or if it fails to appoint an arbitrator within 30 days after it receives a party's request to do so, fails to act within any other period provided by these Rules, or fails to decide on a challenge to an arbitrator within a reasonable time after receiving a party's request to do so, any party may request the Secretary-General of the PCA to designate a substitute appointing authority.
(5) In exercising their functions under these Rules, the appointing authority and the Secretary-General of the PCA may require from any party and the arbitrators the information they deem necessary and they shall give the parties and, where appropriate, the arbitrators, an opportunity to present their views in any manner they consider appropriate. All such communications to and from the appointing authority and the Secretary-General of the PCA shall also be provided by the sender to all other parties.
(6) When the appointing authority is requested to appoint an arbitrator pursuant to articles 8, 9, 10 or 14, the party making the request shall send to the appointing authority copies of the notice of arbitration and, if it exists, any response to the notice of arbitration.
(7) The appointing authority shall have regard to such considerations as are likely to secure the appointment of an independent and impartial arbitrator and shall take

into account the advisability of appointing an arbitrator of a nationality other than the nationalities of the parties.

SECTION II. COMPOSITION OF THE ARBITRAL TRIBUNAL

Article 7

(1) If the parties have not previously agreed on the number of arbitrators, and if within 30 days after the receipt by the respondent of the notice of arbitration the parties have not agreed that there shall be only one arbitrator, three arbitrators shall be appointed.

(2) Notwithstanding paragraph 1, if no other parties have responded to a party's proposal to appoint a sole arbitrator within the time limit provided for in paragraph 1 and the party or parties concerned have failed to appoint a second arbitrator in accordance with article 9 or 10, the appointing authority may, at the request of a party, appoint a sole arbitrator pursuant to the procedure provided for in article 8, paragraph 2, if it determines that, in view of the circumstances of the case, this is more appropriate.

Article 8

(1) If the parties have agreed that a sole arbitrator is to be appointed and if within 30 days after receipt by all other parties of a proposal for the appointment of a sole arbitrator the parties have not reached agreement thereon, a sole arbitrator shall, at the request of a party, be appointed by the appointing authority.

(2) The appointing authority shall appoint the sole arbitrator as promptly as possible. In making the appointment, the appointing authority shall use the following list-procedure, unless the parties agree that the list-procedure should not be used or unless the appointing authority determines in its discretion that the use of the list-procedure is not appropriate for the case:

  (a) The appointing authority shall communicate to each of the parties an identical list containing at least three names;
  (b) Within 15 days after the receipt of this list, each party may return the list to the appointing authority after having deleted the name or names to which it objects and numbered the remaining names on the list in the order of its preference;
  (c) After the expiration of the above period of time the appointing authority shall appoint the sole arbitrator from among the names approved on the lists returned to it and in accordance with the order of preference indicated by the parties;
  (d) If for any reason the appointment cannot be made according to this procedure, the appointing authority may exercise its discretion in appointing the sole arbitrator.

Article 9

(1) If three arbitrators are to be appointed, each party shall appoint one arbitrator. The two arbitrators thus appointed shall choose the third arbitrator who will act as the presiding arbitrator of the arbitral tribunal.
(2) If within 30 days after the receipt of a party's notification of the appointment of an arbitrator the other party has not notified the first party of the arbitrator it has appointed, the first party may request the appointing authority to appoint the second arbitrator.
(3) If within 30 days after the appointment of the second arbitrator the two arbitrators have not agreed on the choice of the presiding arbitrator, the presiding arbitrator shall be appointed by the appointing authority in the same way as a sole arbitrator would be appointed under article 8.

Article 10

(1) For the purposes of article 9, paragraph 1, where three arbitrators are to be appointed and there are multiple parties as claimant or as respondent, unless the parties have agreed to another method of appointment of arbitrators, the multiple parties jointly, whether as claimant or as respondent, shall appoint an arbitrator.
(2) If the parties have agreed that the arbitral tribunal is to be composed of a number of arbitrators other than one or three, the arbitrators shall be appointed according to the method agreed upon by the parties.
(3) In the event of any failure to constitute the arbitral tribunal under these Rules, the appointing authority shall, at the request of any party, constitute the arbitral tribunal and, in doing so, may revoke any appointment already made and appoint or reappoint each of the arbitrators and designate one of them as the presiding arbitrator.

Article 11

When a person is approached in connection with his or her possible appointment as an arbitrator, he or she shall disclose any circumstances likely to give rise to justifiable doubts as to his or her impartiality or independence. An arbitrator, from the time of his or her appointment and throughout the arbitral proceedings, shall without delay disclose any such circumstances to the parties and the other arbitrators unless they have already been informed by him or her of these circumstances.

Article 12

(1) Any arbitrator may be challenged if circumstances exist that give rise to justifiable doubts as to the arbitrator's impartiality or independence.
(2) A party may challenge the arbitrator appointed by it only for reasons of which it becomes aware after the appointment has been made.

(3) In the event that an arbitrator fails to act or in the event of the de jure or de facto impossibility of his or her performing his or her functions, the procedure in respect of the challenge of an arbitrator as provided in article 13 shall apply.

Article 13

(1) A party that intends to challenge an arbitrator shall send notice of its challenge within 15 days after it has been notified
(2) The notice of challenge shall be communicated to all other parties, to the arbitrator who is challenged and to the other arbitrators. The notice of challenge shall state the reasons for the challenge.
(3) When an arbitrator has been challenged by a party, all parties may agree to the challenge. The arbitrator may also, after the challenge, withdraw from his or her office. In neither case does this imply acceptance of the validity of the grounds for the challenge.
(4) If, within 15 days from the date of the notice of challenge, all parties do not agree to the challenge or the challenged arbitrator does not withdraw, the party making the challenge may elect to pursue it. In that case, within 30 days from the date of the notice of challenge, it shall seek a decision on the challenge by the appointing authority.

** Model statements of independence pursuant to article 11 can be found in the annex to the Rules.

Article 14

(1) Subject to paragraph 2, in any event where an arbitrator has to be replaced during the course of the arbitral proceedings, a substitute arbitrator shall be appointed or chosen pursuant to the procedure provided for in articles 8 to 11 that was applicable to the appointment or choice of the arbitrator being replaced. This procedure shall apply even if during the process of appointing the arbitrator to be replaced, a party had failed to exercise its right to appoint or to participate in the appointment.
(2) If, at the request of a party, the appointing authority determines that, in view of the exceptional circumstances of the case, it would be justified for a party to be deprived of its right to appoint a substitute arbitrator, the appointing authority may, after giving an opportunity to the parties and the remaining arbitrators to express their views: (a) appoint the substitute arbitrator; or (b) after the closure of the hearings, authorize the other arbitrators to proceed with the arbitration and make any decision or award.

Article 15

If an arbitrator is replaced, the proceedings shall resume at the stage where the arbitrator who was replaced ceased to perform his or her functions, unless the arbitral tribunal decides otherwise.

Article 16

Save for intentional wrongdoing, the parties waive, to the fullest extent permitted under the applicable law, any claim against the arbitrators, the appointing authority and any person appointed by the arbitral tribunal based on any act or omission in connection with the arbitration.

SECTION III. ARBITRAL PROCEEDINGS

Article 17

(1) Subject to these Rules, the arbitral tribunal may conduct the arbitration in such manner as it considers appropriate, provided that the parties are treated with equality and that at an appropriate stage of the proceedings each party is given a reasonable opportunity of presenting its case. The arbitral tribunal, in exercising its discretion, shall conduct the proceedings so as to avoid unnecessary delay and expense and to provide a fair and efficient process for resolving the parties' dispute.
(2) As soon as practicable after its constitution and after inviting the parties to express their views, the arbitral tribunal shall establish the provisional timetable of the arbitration. The arbitral tribunal may, at any time, after inviting the parties to express their views, extend or abridge any period of time prescribed under these Rules or agreed by the parties.
(3) If at an appropriate stage of the proceedings any party so requests, the arbitral tribunal shall hold hearings for the presentation of evidence by witnesses, including expert witnesses, or for oral argument. In the absence of such a request, the arbitral tribunal shall decide whether to hold such hearings or whether the proceedings shall be conducted on the basis of documents and other materials.
(4) All communications to the arbitral tribunal by one party shall be communicated by that party to all other parties. Such communications shall be made at the same time, except as otherwise permitted by the arbitral tribunal if it may do so under applicable law.
(5) The arbitral tribunal may, at the request of any party, allow one or more third persons to be joined in the arbitration as a party provided such person is a party to the arbitration agreement, unless the arbitral tribunal finds, after giving all parties, including the person or persons to be joined, the opportunity to be heard, that joinder should not be permitted because of prejudice to any of those parties. The arbitral tribunal may make a single award or several awards in respect of all parties so involved in the arbitration.

Article 18

(1) If the parties have not previously agreed on the place of arbitration, the place of arbitration shall be determined by the arbitral tribunal having regard to the circumstances of the case. The award shall be deemed to have been made at the place of arbitration.

(2) The arbitral tribunal may meet at any location it considers appropriate for deliberations. Unless otherwise agreed by the parties, the arbitral tribunal may also meet at any location it considers appropriate for any other purpose, including hearings.

Article 19

(1) Subject to an agreement by the parties, the arbitral tribunal shall, promptly after its appointment, determine the language or languages to be used in the proceedings. This determination shall apply to the statement of claim, the statement of defence, and any further written statements and, if oral hearings take place, to the language or languages to be used in such hearings.
(2) The arbitral tribunal may order that any documents annexed to the statement of claim or statement of defence, and any supplementary documents or exhibits submitted in the course of the proceedings, delivered in their original language, shall be accompanied by a translation into the language or languages agreed upon by the parties or determined by the arbitral tribunal.

Article 20

(1) The claimant shall communicate its statement of claim in writing to the respondent and to each of the arbitrators within a period of time to be determined by the arbitral tribunal. The claimant may elect to treat its notice of arbitration referred to in article 3 as a statement of claim, provided that the notice of arbitration also complies with the requirements of paragraphs 2 to 4 of this article.
(2) The statement of claim shall include the following particulars:
  (a) The names and contact details of the parties;
  (b) A statement of the facts supporting the claim;
  (c) The points at issue;
  (d) The relief or remedy sought;
  (e) The legal grounds or arguments supporting the claim.
(3) A copy of any contract or other legal instrument out of or in relation to which the dispute arises and of the arbitration agreement shall be annexed to the statement of claim.
(4) The statement of claim should, as far as possible, be accompanied by all documents and other evidence relied upon by the claimant, or contain references to them.

Article 21

(1) The respondent shall communicate its statement of defence in writing to the claimant and to each of the arbitrators within a period of time to be determined by the arbitral tribunal. The respondent may elect to treat its response to the notice of arbitration referred to in article 4 as a statement of defence, provided

that the response to the notice of arbitration also complies with the requirements of paragraph 2 of this article.

(2) The statement of defence shall reply to the particulars (b)to (e) of the statement of claim (art. 20, para. 2). The statement of defence should, as far as possible, be accompanied by all documents and other evidence relied upon by the respondent, or contain references to them.

(3) In its statement of defence, or at a later stage in the arbitral proceedings if the arbitral tribunal decides that the delay was justified under the circumstances, the respondent may make a counterclaim or rely on a claim for the purpose of a set-off provided that the arbitral tribunal has jurisdiction over it.

(4) The provisions of article 20, paragraphs 2 to 4, shall apply to a counterclaim, a claim under article 4, paragraph 2 (f), and a claim relied on for the purpose of a set-off.

Article 22

During the course of the arbitral proceedings, a party may amend or supplement its claim or defence, including a counterclaim or a claim for the purpose of a set-off, unless the arbitral tribunal considers it inappropriate to allow such amendment or supplement having regard to the delay in making it or prejudice to other parties or any other circumstances. However, a claim or defence, including a counterclaim or a claim for the purpose of a set-off, may not be amended or supplemented in such a manner that the amended or supplemented claim or defence falls outside the jurisdiction of the arbitral tribunal.

Article 23

(1) The arbitral tribunal shall have the power to rule on its own jurisdiction, including any objections with respect to the existence or validity of the arbitration agreement. For that purpose, an arbitration clause that forms part of a contract shall be treated as an agreement independent of the other terms of the contract. A decision by the arbitral tribunal that the contract is null shall not entail automatically the invalidity of the arbitration clause.

(2) A plea that the arbitral tribunal does not have jurisdiction shall be raised no later than in the statement of defence or, with respect to a counterclaim or a claim for the purpose of a set-off, in the reply to the counterclaim or to the claim for the purpose of a set-off. A party is not precluded from raising such a plea by the fact that it has appointed, or participated in the appointment of, an arbitrator. A plea that the arbitral tribunal is exceeding the scope of its authority shall be raised as soon as the matter alleged to be beyond the scope of its authority is raised during the arbitral proceedings. The arbitral tribunal may, in either case, admit a later plea if it considers the delay justified.

(3) The arbitral tribunal may rule on a plea referred to in paragraph 2 either as a preliminary question or in an award on the merits. The arbitral tribunal may continue the arbitral proceedings and make an award, notwithstanding any pending challenge to its jurisdiction before a court.

Article 24

The arbitral tribunal shall decide which further written statements, in addition to the statement of claim and the statement of defence, shall be required from the parties or may be presented by them and shall fix the periods of time for communicating such statements.

Article 25

The periods of time fixed by the arbitral tribunal for the communication of written statements (including the statement of claim and statement of defence)should not exceed 45 days. However, the arbitral tribunal may extend the time limits if it concludes that an extension is justified.

Article 26

(1) The arbitral tribunal may, at the request of a party, grant interim measures.

(2) An interim measure is any temporary measure by which, at any time prior to the issuance of the award by which the dispute is finally decided, the arbitral tribunal orders a party, for example and without limitation, to:
   (a) Maintain or restore the status quo pending determination of the dispute;
   (b) Take action that would prevent, or refrain from taking action that is likely to cause,
      (i) current or imminent harm or
      (ii) prejudice to the arbitral process itself;
   (c) Provide a means of preserving assets out of which a subsequent award may be satisfied; or
   (d) Preserve evidence that may be relevant and material to the resolution of the dispute.

(3) The party requesting an interim measure under paragraphs 2 (a) to (c) shall satisfy the arbitral tribunal that:
   (a) Harm not adequately reparable by an award of damages is likely to result if the measure is not ordered, and such harm substantially outweighs the harm that is likely to result to the party against whom the measure is directed if the measure is granted; and
   (b) There is a reasonable possibility that the requesting party will succeed on the merits of the claim. The determination on this possibility shall not affect the discretion of the arbitral tribunal in making any subsequent determination.

(4) With regard to a request for an interim measure under paragraph 2 (d), the requirements in paragraphs 3 (a) and (b)shall apply only to the extent the arbitral tribunal considers appropriate.

(5) The arbitral tribunal may modify, suspend or terminate an interim measure it has granted, upon application of any party or, in exceptional circumstances and upon prior notice to the parties, on the arbitral tribunal's own initiative.

(6) The arbitral tribunal may require the party requesting an interim measure to provide appropriate security in connection with the measure.

(7) The arbitral tribunal may require any party promptly to disclose any material change in the circumstances on the basis of which the interim measure was requested or granted.
(8) The party requesting an interim measure may be liable for any costs and damages caused by the measure to any party if the arbitral tribunal later determines that, in the circumstances then prevailing, the measure should not have been granted. The arbitral tribunal may award such costs and damages at any point during the proceedings.
(9) A request for interim measures addressed by any party to a judicial authority shall not be deemed incompatible with the agreement to arbitrate, or as a waiver of that agreement.

Article 27

(1) Each party shall have the burden of proving the facts relied on to support its claim or defence.
(2) Witnesses, including expert witnesses, who are presented by the parties to testify to the arbitral tribunal on any issue of fact or expertise may be any individual, notwithstanding that the individual is a party to the arbitration or in any way related to a party. Unless otherwise directed by the arbitral tribunal, statements by witnesses, including expert witnesses, may be presented in writing and signed by them.
(3) At any time during the arbitral proceedings the arbitral tribunal may require the parties to produce documents, exhibits or other evidence within such a period of time as the arbitral tribunal shall determine.
(4) The arbitral tribunal shall determine the admissibility, relevance, materiality and weight of the evidence offered.

Article 28

(1) In the event of an oral hearing, the arbitral tribunal shall give the parties adequate advance notice of the date, time and place thereof.
(2) Witnesses, including expert witnesses, may be heard under the conditions and examined in the manner set by the arbitral tribunal.
(3) Hearings shall be held in camera unless the parties agree otherwise. The arbitral tribunal may require the retirement of any witness or witnesses, including expert witnesses, during the testimony of such other witnesses, except that a witness, including an expert witness, who is a party to the arbitration shall not, in principle, be asked to retire.
(4) The arbitral tribunal may direct that witnesses, including expert witnesses, be examined through means of telecommunication that do not require their physical presence at the hearing (such as videoconference).

Article 29

(1) After consultation with the parties, the arbitral tribunal may appoint one or more independent experts to report to it, in writing, on specific issues to be determined by the arbitral tribunal. A copy of the expert's terms of reference, established by the arbitral tribunal, shall be communicated to the parties.
(2) The expert shall, in principle before accepting appointment, submit to the arbitral tribunal and to the parties a description of his or her qualifications and a statement of his or her impartiality and independence. Within the time ordered by the arbitral tribunal, the parties shall inform the arbitral tribunal whether they have any objections as to the expert's qualifications, impartiality or independence. The arbitral tribunal shall decide promptly whether to accept any such objections. After an expert's appointment, a party may object to the expert's qualifications, impartiality or independence only if the objection is for reasons of which the party becomes aware after the appointment has been made. The arbitral tribunal shall decide promptly what, if any, action to take.
(3) The parties shall give the expert any relevant information or produce for his or her inspection any relevant documents or goods that he or she may require of them. Any dispute between a party and such expert as to the relevance of the required information or production shall be referred to the arbitral tribunal for decision.
(4) Upon receipt of the expert's report, the arbitral tribunal shall communicate a copy of the report to the parties, which shall be given the opportunity to express, in writing, their opinion on the report. A party shall be entitled to examine any document on which the expert has relied in his or her report.
(5) At the request of any party, the expert, after delivery of the report, may be heard at a hearing where the parties shall have the opportunity to be present and to interrogate the expert. At this hearing, any party may present expert witnesses in order to testify on the points at issue. The provisions of article 28 shall be applicable to such proceedings.

Article 30

(1) If, within the period of time fixed by these Rules or the arbitral tribunal, without showing sufficient cause:
    (a) The claimant has failed to communicate its statement of claim, the arbitral tribunal shall issue an order for the termination of the arbitral proceedings, unless there are remaining matters that may need to be decided and the arbitral tribunal considers it appropriate to do so;
    (b) The respondent has failed to communicate its response to the notice of arbitration or its statement of defence, the arbitral tribunal shall order that the proceedings continue, without treating such failure in itself as an admission of the claimant's allegations; the provisions of this subparagraph also apply to a claimant's failure to submit a defence to a counterclaim or to a claim for the purpose of a set-off.

(2) If a party, duly notified under these Rules, fails to appear at a hearing, without showing sufficient cause for such failure, the arbitral tribunal may proceed with the arbitration.
(3) If a party, duly invited by the arbitral tribunal to produce documents, exhibits or other evidence, fails to do so within the established period of time, without showing sufficient cause for such failure, the arbitral tribunal may make the award on the evidence before it.

Article 31

(1) The arbitral tribunal may inquire of the parties if they have any further proof to offer or witnesses to be heard or submissions to make and, if there are none, it may declare the hearings closed.
(2) The arbitral tribunal may, if it considers it necessary owing to exceptional circumstances, decide, on its own initiative or upon application of a party, to reopen the hearings at any time before the award is made.

Article 32

A failure by any party to object promptly to any non-compliance with these Rules or with any requirement of the arbitration agreement shall be deemed to be a waiver of the right of such party to make such an objection, unless such party can show that, under the circumstances, its failure to object was justified.

SECTION IV. THE AWARD

Article 33

(1) When there is more than one arbitrator, any award or other decision of the arbitral tribunal shall be made by a majority of the arbitrators.
(2) In the case of questions of procedure, when there is no majority or when the arbitral tribunal so authorizes, the presiding arbitrator may decide alone, subject to revision, if any, by the arbitral tribunal.

Article 34

(1) The arbitral tribunal may make separate awards on different issues at different times.
(2) All awards shall be made in writing and shall be final and binding on the parties. The parties shall carry out all awards without delay.
(3) The arbitral tribunal shall state the reasons upon which the award is based, unless the parties have agreed that no reasons are to be given.
(4) An award shall be signed by the arbitrators and it shall contain the date on which the award was made and indicate the place of arbitration. Where there is more than one arbitrator and any of them fails to sign, the award shall state the reason for the absence of the signature.

(5) An award may be made public with the consent of all parties or where and to the extent disclosure is required of a party by legal duty, to protect or pursue a legal right or in relation to legal proceedings before a court or other competent authority.
(6) Copies of the award signed by the arbitrators shall be communicated to the parties by the arbitral tribunal.

Article 35

(1) The arbitral tribunal shall apply the rules of law designated by the parties as applicable to the substance of the dispute. Failing such designation by the parties, the arbitral tribunal shall apply the law which it determines to be appropriate.
(2) The arbitral tribunal shall decide as amiable compositeur or ex aequo et bono only if the parties have expressly authorized the arbitral tribunal to do so.
(3) In all cases, the arbitral tribunal shall decide in accordance with the terms of the contract, if any, and shall take into account any usage of trade applicable to the transaction.

Article 36

(1) If, before the award is made, the parties agree on a settlement of the dispute, the arbitral tribunal shall either issue an order for the termination of the arbitral proceedings or, if requested by the parties and accepted by the arbitral tribunal, record the settlement in the form of an arbitral award on agreed terms. The arbitral tribunal is not obliged to give reasons for such an award.
(2) If, before the award is made, the continuation of the arbitral proceedings becomes unnecessary or impossible for any reason not mentioned in paragraph 1, the arbitral tribunal shall inform the parties of its intention to issue an order for the termination of the proceedings. The arbitral tribunal shall have the power to issue such an order unless there are remaining matters that may need to be decided and the arbitral tribunal considers it appropriate to do so.
(3) Copies of the order for termination of the arbitral proceedings or of the arbitral award on agreed terms, signed by the arbitrators, shall be communicated by the arbitral tribunal to the parties. Where an arbitral award on agreed terms is made, the provisions of article 34, paragraphs 2, 4 and 5, shall apply.

Article 37

(1) Within 30 days after the receipt of the award, a party, with notice to the other parties, may request that the arbitral tribunal give an interpretation of the award.
(2) The interpretation shall be given in writing within 45 days after the receipt of the request. The interpretation shall form part of the award and the provisions of article 34, paragraphs 2 to 6, shall apply.

Article 38

(1) Within 30 days after the receipt of the award, a party, with notice to the other parties, may request the arbitral tribunal to correct in the award any error in computation, any clerical or typographical error, or any error or omission of a similar nature. If the arbitral tribunal considers that the request is justified, it shall make the correction within 45 days of receipt of the request.
(2) The arbitral tribunal may within 30 days after the communication of the award make such corrections on its own initiative.
(3) Such corrections shall be in writing and shall form part of the award. The provisions of article 34, paragraphs 2 to 6, shall apply.

Article 39

(1) Within 30 days after the receipt of the termination order or the award, a party, with notice to the other parties, may request the arbitral tribunal to make an award or an additional award as to claims presented in the arbitral proceedings but not decided by the arbitral tribunal.
(2) If the arbitral tribunal considers the request for an award or additional award to be justified, it shall render or complete its award within 60 days after the receipt of the request. The arbitral tribunal may extend, if necessary, the period of time within which it shall make the award.
(3) When such an award or additional award is made, the provisions of article 34, paragraphs 2 to 6, shall apply.

Article 40

(1) The arbitral tribunal shall fix the costs of arbitration in the final award and, if it deems appropriate, in another decision.
(2) The term "costs" includes only:
   (a) The fees of the arbitral tribunal to be stated separately as to each arbitrator and to be fixed by the tribunal itself in accordance with article 41;
   (b) The reasonable travel and other expenses incurred by the arbitrators;
   (c) The reasonable costs of expert advice and of other assistance required by the arbitral tribunal;
   (d) The reasonable travel and other expenses of witnesses to the extent such expenses are approved by the arbitral tribunal;
   (e) The legal and other costs incurred by the parties in relation to the arbitration to the extent that the arbitral tribunal determines that the amount of such costs is reasonable;
   (f) Any fees and expenses of the appointing authority as well as the fees and expenses of the Secretary-General of the PCA.
(3) In relation to interpretation, correction or completion of any award under articles 37 to 39, the arbitral tribunal may charge the costs referred to in paragraphs 2 (b) to (f), but no additional fees.

Article 41

(1) The fees and expenses of the arbitrators shall be reasonable in amount, taking into account the amount in dispute, the complexity of the subject matter, the time spent by the arbitrators and any other relevant circumstances of the case.

(2) If there is an appointing authority and it applies or has stated that it will apply a schedule or particular method for determining the fees for arbitrators in international cases, the arbitral tribunal in fixing its fees shall take that schedule or method into account to the extent that it considers appropriate in the circumstances of the case.

(3) Promptly after its constitution, the arbitral tribunal shall inform the parties as to how it proposes to determine its fees and expenses, including any rates it intends to apply. Within 15 days of receiving that proposal, any party may refer the proposal to the appointing authority for review. If, within 45 days of receipt of such a referral, the appointing authority finds that the proposal of the arbitral tribunal is inconsistent with paragraph 1, it shall make any necessary adjustments thereto, which shall be binding upon the arbitral tribunal.

(4) (a) When informing the parties of the arbitrators' fees and expenses that have been fixed pursuant to article 40, paragraphs 2 (a) and (b), the arbitral tribunal shall also explain the manner in which the corresponding amounts have been calculated;

(b) Within 15 days of receiving the arbitral tribunal's determination of fees and expenses, any party may refer for review such determination to the appointing authority. If no appointing authority has been agreed upon or designated, or if the appointing authority fails to act within the time specified in these Rules, then the review shall be made by the Secretary-General of the PCA;

(c) If the appointing authority or the Secretary-General of the PCA finds that the arbitral tribunal's determination is inconsistent with the arbitral tribunal's proposal (and any adjustment thereto)under paragraph 3 or is otherwise manifestly excessive, it shall, within 45 days of receiving such a referral, make any adjustments to the arbitral tribunal's determination that are necessary to satisfy the criteria in paragraph 1. Any such adjustments shall be binding upon the arbitral tribunal;

(d) Any such adjustments shall either be included by the arbitral tribunal in its award or, if the award has already been issued, be implemented in a correction to the award, to which the procedure of article 38, paragraph 3, shall apply.

(5) Throughout the procedure under paragraphs 3 and 4, the arbitral tribunal shall proceed with the arbitration, in accordance with article 17, paragraph 1.

(6) A referral under paragraph 4 shall not affect any determination in the award other than the arbitral tribunal's fees and expenses; nor shall it delay the recognition and enforcement of all parts of the award other than those relating to the determination of the arbitral tribunal's fees and expenses.

Article 42

(1) The costs of the arbitration shall in principle be borne by the unsuccessful party or parties. However, the arbitral tribunal may apportion each of such costs between the parties if it determines that apportionment is reasonable, taking into account the circumstances of the case.
(2) The arbitral tribunal shall in the final award or, if it deems appropriate, in any other award, determine any amount that a party may have to pay to another party as a result of the decision on allocation of costs.

Article 43

(1) The arbitral tribunal, on its establishment, may request the parties to deposit an equal amount as an advance for the costs referred to in article 40, paragraphs 2 (a) to (c).
(2) During the course of the arbitral proceedings the arbitral tribunal may request supplementary deposits from the parties.
(3) If an appointing authority has been agreed upon or designated, and when a party so requests and the appointing authority consents to perform the function, the arbitral tribunal shall fix the amounts of any deposits or supplementary deposits only after consultation with the appointing authority, which may make any comments to the arbitral tribunal that it deems appropriate concerning the amount of such deposits and supplementary deposits.
(4) If the required deposits are not paid in full within 30 days after the receipt of the request, the arbitral tribunal shall so inform the parties in order that one or more of them may make the required payment. If such payment is not made, the arbitral tribunal may order the suspension or termination of the arbitral proceedings.
(5) After a termination order or final award has been made, the arbitral tribunal shall render an accounting to the parties of the deposits received and return any unexpended balance to the parties.

ANNEX

Model arbitration clause for contracts

Any dispute, controversy or claim arising out of or relating to this contract, or the breach, termination or invalidity thereof, shall be settled by arbitration in accordance with the UNCITRAL Arbitration Rules.

Note. Parties should consider adding:

(a) The appointing authority shall be ... [name of institution or person];
(b) The number of arbitrators shall be .... [one or three];
(c) The place of arbitration shall be ... [town and country];
(d) The language to be used in the arbitral proceedings shall be ... .

Possible waiver statement

Note. If the parties wish to exclude recourse against the arbitral award that may be available under the applicable law, they may consider adding a provision to that effect as suggested below, considering, however, that the effectiveness and conditions of such an exclusion depend on the applicable law.

Waiver

The parties hereby waive their right to any form of recourse against an award to any court or other competent authority, insofar as such waiver can validly be made under the applicable law.

Model statements of independence pursuant to article 11 of the Rules

No circumstances to disclose

I am impartial and independent of each of the parties and intend to remain so. To the best of my knowledge, there are no circumstances, past or present, likely to give rise to justifiable doubts as to my impartiality or independence. I shall promptly notify the parties and the other arbitrators of any such circumstances that may subsequently come to my attention during this arbitration.

Circumstances to disclose

I am impartial and independent of each of the parties and intend to remain so. Attached is a statement made pursuant to article 11 of the UNCITRAL Arbitration Rules of (a) my past and present professional, business and other relationships with the parties and (b) any other relevant circumstances. [Include statement.] I confirm that those circumstances do not affect my independence and impartiality. I shall promptly notify the parties and the other arbitrators of any such further relationships or circumstances that may subsequently come to my attention during this arbitration.

Note. Any party may consider requesting from the arbitrator the following addition to the statement of independence:

> I confirm, on the basis of the information presently available to me, that I can devote the time necessary to conduct this arbitration diligently, efficiently and in accordance with the time limits in the Rules.

Appendix F

International Arbitral Institutions

LEADING INTERNATIONAL ARBITRAL INSTITUTIONS

International Chamber of Commerce ("ICC")

> 33–43, avenue du Président Wilson
> FR- 75116 Paris
> France
> Telephone: + 33 (0) 1 49 53 28 28
> Fax: + 33 (0) 1 86 26 67 44
> Website: http://www.iccwbo.org

Singapore International Arbitration Centre ("SIAC")

> 28 Maxwell Road
> #03–01, Maxwell Chambers Suites
> Singapore 069120
> Telephone: + 65 6713 9777
> Fax: + 65 6713 9778
> Website: http://www.siac.org.sg

American Arbitration Association ("AAA")/International Centre for Dispute Resolution ("ICDR")

> 120 Broadway, 21st Floor
> New York, NY 10271
> USA
> Telephone: + 1 (212) 716 5800 / + 1 (212) 484 4181
> Fax: + 1 (212) 484 4178
> Website: http://www.adr.org, https://www.icdr.org/

London Court of International Arbitration ("LCIA")

> 1 Paternoster Lane
> London, EC4M 7BQ

United Kingdom
Telephone: +44 (0)20 7936 6200
Fax: +44 (0)20 7936 6211
Website: http://www.lcia.org

International Centre for Settlement of Investment Disputes ("ICSID")

1818 High Street NW
MSN C3-300
Washington, D.C. 20433
USA
Telephone: +1 (202) 458 1534
Fax: +1 (202) 522 2615
Website: http://www.worldbank.org/icsid

Permanent Court of Arbitration ("PCA")

Peace Palace
Carnegieplein 2
2517 KJ The Hague
The Netherlands
Telephone: +31 70 302 4165
Fax: +31 70 302 4167
Website: http://www.pca-cpa.org

REGIONAL, SPECIALIZED, AND OTHER INTERNATIONAL ARBITRAL INSTITUTIONS

Asian International Arbitration Centre ("AIAC"), formerly the Kuala Lumpur Regional Centre for Arbitration ("KLRCA")

Bangunan Sulaiman
Jalan Sultan Hishamuddin
50000 Kuala Lumpur
Malaysia
Telephone: +603 2271 1000
Fax: +603 2271 1010
Website: https://www.aiac.world

Australian Centre for International Commercial Arbitration ("ACICA")

Level 16, 1 Castlereagh Street
Sydney NSW 2000
Australia
Telephone: +61 (0)2 9223 1099
Fax: +61 (0)2 9223 7053
Website: http://www.acica.org.au

Cairo Regional Centre for International Commercial Arbitration ("CRCICA")

1, Al-Saleh Ayoub Street
Zamalek, Cairo 11211
Egypt
Telephone: +202 2735 1333/1335/1337
Fax: +202 2735 1336
Website: http://www.crcica.org.eg

Centre for Effective Dispute Resolution ("CEDR")

100 St. Paul's Churchyard
London, EC4M 8BU
United Kingdom
Telephone: +44 (0)20 7536 6000
Fax: +44 (0)20 7536 6001
Website: http://www.cedr.com

Chartered Institute of Arbitrators ("CIArb")

International Arbitration Centre
12 Bloomsbury Square
London, WC1A 2LP
United Kingdom
Telephone: +44 (0)20 7421 7444
Fax: +44 (0)20 7404 4023
Website: http://www.ciarb.org

China International Economic and Trade Arbitration Commission ("CIETAC")

6/F, CCOIC Building, No. 2
Huapichang Hutong
Xicheng District
Beijing, 100035
China
Telephone: +86 10 6464 6688
Fax: +86 10 8221 7766
Website: http://www.cietac.org

Dubai International Arbitration Centre ("DIAC")

Dubai Chambers Building Level 14
Baniyas Road, Deira
Dubai, United Arab Emirates
Telephone: +971 4 364 5400
Website: https://www.diac.com/en/home/

German Institution of Arbitration ("DIS")

DIS Main Secretariat
Marienforster Str. 52
53177 Bonn
Germany
Telephone: +49 (0) 228 391 815 200
Fax: +49 (0) 228 391 815 222
Website: http://www.disarb.org/en/

Hong Kong International Arbitration Centre ("HKIAC")

38th Floor, Two Exchange Square
8 Connaught Place, Central
Hong Kong, S.A.R.
China
Telephone: +852 2525 2381
Fax: +852 2524 2171
Website: http://www.hkiac.org

Indian Council of Arbitration ("ICA")

Room 112, Federation House
Tansen Marg
New Delhi 110001, India
Telephone: +91 011 23719102
Website: http://www.icaindia.co.in/

Inter-American Commercial Arbitration Commission ("IACAC")

OAS Administration Building
17th Street and Constitution Ave., N.W.
Washington, D.C. 20006-4499
USA
Telephone: +1 (202) 370 5000
Fax: +1 (202) 458 3967
Website: http://www.sice.oas.org/dispute/comarb/iacac/iacac1e.asp

International Institute for Conflict Prevention & Resolution ("CPR")

30 East 33rd Street, 6th Floor
New York, N.Y. 10016
USA
Telephone: +1 (212) 949 6490
Fax: +1 (212) 949 8859
Website: http://www.cpradr.org

JAMS International

18881 Von Karman Ave., Suite 350
Irvine, CA 92612
USA
Telephone: +1 949 224 1810
Fax: +1 949 224 1818
Website: https://www.jamsadr.com/global/

Japan Commercial Arbitration Association ("JCAA")

3rd Floor, Hirose Building
3–17, Kanda Nishiki-cho, Chiyoda-ku
Tokyo 101-0054
Japan
Telephone: +81 (0)3 (5280) 5161
Fax: +81 (0)3 (5280) 5160
Website: http://www.jcaa.or.jp/en/

Korean Commercial Arbitration Board ("KCAB")

Samseong-dong, Trade Tower
43rd Floor, 511, Yeongdong-daero
Gangnam-gu, Seoul 06164
Republic of Korea
Tel: +82-2-551-2000
Fax: +82-2-551-2020
Website: http://www.kcab.or.kr

Netherlands Arbitration Institute ("NAI")

Weena 505 P.O. Box 21075
3013 AL Rotterdam
The Netherlands
Telephone: +31 10 281 6969
Fax: +31 10 281 6968
Website: http://www.nai-nl.org

Russian Arbitration Association ("RAA")

Lesnaya Plaza, office 405404
Dukhovskoy per 17 bld 12
115191125047, Moscow
Russia
Telephone: +7 495 201 29 59
Website: https://arbitration.ru/en

Russian Federation International Commercial Arbitration Court at the Chamber of Commerce and Industry ("ICAC")

Ulitsa Iliyinka 6
Moscow 109012
Russian Federation
Telephone: +7 (495) 620 0007
Fax: +7 (495) 620 0153
Website: http://mkas.tpprf.ru/en/

Stockholm Chamber of Commerce Arbitration Institute ("SCC")

The Arbitration Institute of the Stockholm Chamber of Commerce
P.O. Box 16050
SE-103 21 Stockholm
Sweden
Telephone: +46 (0)8 555 100 50
Fax: +46 (0)8 566 316 50
Website: http://www.sccinstitute.com

Swiss Arbitration Centre

Boulevard du Théâtre 4
1204 Geneva
Switzerland
Telephone: +41 22 819 91 57
Website: https://www.swissarbitration.org

Vienna International Arbitral Centre ("VIAC")

Wiedner Hauptstrasse 63
1045 Vienna
Austria
Telephone: +43 (0)5 90900 4398
Fax: +43 (0)5 90900 216
Website: http://www.viac.eu/en/

World Intellectual Property Organization ("WIPO")

34 Chemin des Colombettes
1211 Geneva 20
Switzerland
Telephone: +41 22 338 9111
Fax: +41 22 733 5428
Website: http://www.wipo.int

Appendix G

Select Bibliography on International Arbitration and Forum Selection Agreements

MAJOR WORKS ON INTERNATIONAL DISPUTE RESOLUTION

Bell, Andrew S., *Forum Shopping and Venue in Transnational Litigation* (Oxford University Press 2003)

Binder, Peter, *International Commercial Arbitration and Mediation in UNCITRAL Model Law Jurisdictions* (4th ed., Sweet & Maxwell 2019)

Blackaby, Nigel et al. (eds.), *Redfern and Hunter on International Arbitration* (6th ed., Oxford University Press 2015)

Born, Gary B., *International Commercial Arbitration* (3d ed., Kluwer 2021)

Born, Gary B., *International Arbitration: Law and Practice* (3d ed., Kluwer 2021)

Born, Gary B., *International Arbitration: Cases and Materials* (3d ed., Wolters Kluwer 2021)

Carter, James H. and Fellas, John, *International Commercial Arbitration in New York* (2d ed., Oxford University Press 2016)

Daly, Brooks et al., *A Guide to the PCA Arbitration Rules* (Oxford University Press 2014)

Derains, Yves and Schwartz, Eric A., *Guide to the ICC Rules of Arbitration* (2d ed., Kluwer 2005)

Friedland, Paul D., *Arbitration Clauses for International Contracts* (2d ed., JurisNet 2007)

Gaillard, Emmanuel and Di Pietro, Domenico, *Enforcement of Arbitration Agreements and International Arbitral Awards: The New York Convention in Practice* (Cameron May 2008)

Greenberg, Simon et al., *International Commercial Arbitration: An Asia-Pacific Perspective* (Cambridge University Press 2011)

Hanessian, Grant and Newman, Lawrence W., *International Arbitration Checklists* (3d ed., JurisNet 2016)

Joseph, David, *Jurisdiction and Arbitration Agreements and Their Enforcement* (3d ed., Sweet & Maxwell 2015)

Kronke, Herbert et al. (eds.), *Recognition and Enforcement of Foreign Arbitral Awards: A Global Commentary on the New York Convention* (Kluwer 2010)

Lew, Julian D.M. et al., *Comparative International Commercial Arbitration* (Kluwer 2003)

Mangan, Mark et al., *A Guide to the SIAC Arbitration Rules* (2d ed., Oxford University Press 2018)

McIlwrath, Michael and Savage, John, *International Arbitration and Mediation: A Practical Guide* (Kluwer 2010)

Moses, Margaret L., *The Principles and Practice of International Commercial Arbitration* (3d ed., Cambridge University Press 2017)

Moser, Michael J. and Bao, Chiann, *A Guide to the HKIAC Arbitration Rules* (Oxford University Press 2017)

Paulsson, Jan et al. (eds.), *The Freshfields Guide to Arbitration Clauses in International Contracts* (3d ed., Kluwer 2010)

Scherer, Maxi et al. (eds.), *International Arbitration and the COVID-19 Revolution* (Kluwer 2020)

Scherer, Maxi et al., *Arbitrating under the 2014 LCIA Rules: A User's Guide* (Kluwer 2015)

Schreuer, Christoph H. et al., *The ICSID Convention: A Commentary* (2d ed., Cambridge University Press 2009)

Schwarz, Franz T. et al., *A Guide to the ICDR International Arbitration Rules* (2d ed., Oxford University Press 2019)

Sutton, David St et al., *Russell on Arbitration* (25th ed., Sweet & Maxwell 2021)

Turner, Peter and Mohtashami, Reza, *A Guide to the LCIA Arbitration Rules* (Oxford University Press 2009)

van der Bend, Bommel et al. (eds.), *A Guide to the NAI Arbitration Rules: Including a Commentary on Dutch Arbitration Law* (Kluwer 2009)

Verbist, Herman et al., *ICC Arbitration in Practice* (2d ed., Kluwer 2015)

Wade, Shai et al., *A Commentary on the LCIA Arbitration Rules 2014* (Sweet & Maxwell 2015)

Webster, Thomas H., *Handbook of Investment Arbitration: Commentary, Precedents and Models for ICSID Arbitration* (Sweet & Maxwell 2012)

Webster, Thomas H., *Handbook of UNCITRAL Arbitration: Commentary, Precedents and Models for UNCITRAL Based Arbitration Rules* (3d ed., Sweet & Maxwell 2019)

Weigand, Frank-Bernd and Baumann, Antje (eds.), *Practitioner's Handbook on International Commercial Arbitration* (3d ed., Oxford University Press 2019)

Wolff, Reinmar (ed.), *New York Convention on the Recognition and Enforcement of Foreign Arbitral Awards: A Commentary* (2d ed., Hart 2019)

WORKS ON INTERNATIONAL DISPUTE RESOLUTION IN SPECIFIC JURISDICTIONS

Akinci, Ziya, *Arbitration Law of Turkey: Practice and Procedure* (Juris 2011)

Al-Mulla, Habib et al., *Comparison of Gulf International Arbitration Rules* (Juris 2010)
Al-Mulla, Habib et al., *Comparison of MENA International Arbitration Rules* (Juris 2011)
Berger, Bernhard and Kellerhals, Franz, *International and Domestic Arbitration in Switzerland* (3d ed., Hart 2015)
Böckstiegel, Karl-Heinz et al. (eds.), *Arbitration in Germany: The Model Law in Practice* (2d ed., Kluwer 2015)
Casey, Brian, *Arbitration Law of Canada: Practice and Procedure* (3d ed., Juris 2017)
Clay, Thomas, *Le Nouveau Droit Français de l'Arbitrage* (Lextenso 2011)
Delvolvé, Jean-Louis et al., *French Arbitration Law and Practice* (2d ed., Kluwer 2009)
El-Ahdab, Abdul Hamid and El-Ahdab, Jalal, *Arbitration with the Arab Countries* (3d ed., Kluwer 2011)
Heuman, Lars, *Arbitration Law of Sweden: Practice and Procedure* (Juris 2003)
Hobér, Kaj, *International Commercial Arbitration in Sweden* (Oxford University Press 2011)
Joseph, David and Foxton, David, *Singapore International Arbitration: Law & Practice* (2d ed., LexisNexis 2018)
Kidane, Won, *China-Africa Dispute Settlement: The Law, Economics and Culture of Arbitration* (Kluwer 2011)
Kim, Kap-You (Kevin) and Bang, John P. (eds.), *Arbitration Law of Korea: Practice and Procedure* (Juris 2012)
Kleinheisterkamp, Jan, *International Commercial Arbitration in Latin America* (Oceana Publications 2006)
Leung, Raymond H.M., *China Arbitration Handbook* (Sweet & Maxwell Asia 2011)
Ma, Justice Geoffrey and Brock, Denis (eds.), *Arbitration in Hong Kong: A Practical Guide* (4th ed., Sweet & Maxwell Asia 2017)
Menon, Sundaresh et al. (eds.), *Arbitration in Singapore: A Practical Guide* (2d ed., Sweet & Maxwell Asia 2018)
Moser, Michael J. and Choong, John (eds.), *Asia Arbitration Handbook* (Oxford University Press 2011)
Mourra, Mary H. and Carbonneau, Thomas E. (eds.), *Latin American Investment Treaty Arbitration: The Controversies and Conflicts* (Kluwer 2008)
Muniz, Joaquim T de Paiva and Basilio, Ana Tereza Palhares, *Arbitration Law of Brazil: Practice and Procedure* (2d ed., Juris 2015)
Nottage, Luke and Garnett, Richard (eds.), *International Arbitration in Australia* (Federation Press 2010)
Nottage, Luke and Bath, Vivienne (eds.), *Foreign Investment and Dispute Resolution Law and Practice in Asia* (Routledge 2011)
Ramsden, Peter A., *Law of Arbitration: South African & International Arbitration* (2d ed., Juta Law 2018)
Riegler, Stefan et al., *Arbitration Law of Austria: Practice and Procedure* (Juris 2007)

Schwarz, Franz T. and Konrad, Christian W., *The Vienna Rules: A Commentary on International Arbitration in Austria* (Kluwer 2009)
Tao, Jingzhou, *Arbitration Law and Practice in China* (3d ed., Kluwer 2012)
Vienna International Arbitration Centre, *Handbook Vienna Arbitration Rules: A Practitioner's Guide* (2014)
Williams, David A R QC and Kawharu, Amokura, *Williams & Kawharu on Arbitration* (2d ed., LexisNexis 2017)

ONLINE RESOURCES ON DRAFTING DISPUTE RESOLUTION CLAUSES

AAA Clause Builder

https://www.clausebuilder.org

Bilateral Investment Treaties 1959–1999 (UNCTAD)

http://www.unctad.org/en/docs/poiteiiad2.en.pdf

IBA Guidelines for Drafting International Arbitration Clauses

https://www.ibanet.org/MediaHandler?id=D94438EB-2ED5-4CEA-9722-7A0C928 1F2F2

ICDR Guide to Drafting International Dispute Resolution Clauses

https://www.icdr.org/clauses

ICSID Model Clauses

http://icsidfiles.worldbank.org/icsid/icsid/staticfiles/model-clauses-en/main-eng.htm

International Arbitration Clauses (Ashurst)

https://www.ashurst.com/en/insights/quickguide-international-arbitration-clauses/

International Commercial Arbitration: Resources in Print and Electronic Format (by Lyonette Louis-Jacques)

http://www.lib.uchicago.edu/~llou/intlarb.html

International Investment Agreements Navigator (UNCTAD)

http://investmentpolicyhub.unctad.org/IIA

JAMS International Clause Workbook

https://www.jamsadr.com/files/Uploads/Documents/JAMS-Rules/JAMS-ADR-Clauses.pdf

Permanent Court of Arbitration Model Clauses

https://pca-cpa.org/model-clauses-and-submission-agreements

WIPO Clause Builder

https://amc.wipo.int/clause-generator/

Appendix H

Model Submission Agreement

THIS AGREEMENT is made this ___ day of _________ between [A Corporation] and [B Corporation].

There presently exists a dispute between the parties arising out of and in connection with a contract between them dated _________ ("Dispute"). A brief description of the Dispute is set out in Schedule 1 to this Agreement.

The parties hereto agree to arbitrate, and hereby submit for final determination by arbitration the Dispute and the parties' respective claims. The seat of the arbitration shall be [_________].

The arbitration shall be conducted by three arbitrators, appointed as provided in this Agreement. [A Corporation] hereby designates [_________] of [_________] as one of the arbitrators and [B Corporation] hereby designates [_________] of [_________] as one of the arbitrators. The two arbitrators so designated shall, within a period of [30] days from the date of this Agreement, jointly designate in writing the third arbitrator. If the two named arbitrators do not jointly designate in writing the third arbitrator within a period of [30] days of the date of this Agreement, then, on the application of either party to this Agreement, the third arbitrator shall be designated by [insert appointing authority].

If a vacancy arises on the arbitral tribunal because any arbitrator dies, resigns, refuses to act, or becomes incapable of performing his or her duties, the vacancy shall be filled by the method by which that arbitrator was originally appointed. If that method fails, the appointment(s) shall be made by [insert appointing authority].

The arbitral tribunal may make its awards by a majority. In the event that no majority is possible, the presiding arbitrator may make the decision(s) as if acting as a sole arbitrator. After their designation, the arbitrators shall proceed forthwith to arbitrate and determine the Dispute and claims set out above. In so doing, the arbitrators shall act fairly and impartially as between the parties, giving each party a reasonable opportunity of presenting its case and replying to that of the other party. The arbitrators shall adopt procedures suitable to the circumstances of the Dispute, avoiding unnecessary delay or expense.

The arbitrators shall determine the Dispute and claims set out above in accordance with the laws of _________. The arbitrators shall have the power to decide all procedural and evidentiary matters, subject to the right of the parties to agree any matter, including:

(a) when and where any part of the proceedings is to be held;
(b) the language or languages to be used in the proceedings and whether translations of any relevant documents are to be supplied;
(c) whether, and if so, what form of written submissions are to be made, when these should be submitted, and the extent to which such statements can be amended;
(d) the extent to which documents or categories of documents should be subject to discovery between the parties;
(e) the extent to which interrogatories should be put to and answered by the respective parties, and when and in what form this should be done;
(f) whether to apply strict rules of evidence (or any other rules) as to the admissibility, relevance, or weight of any material (oral, written or other) and the time, manner and form in which such material should be exchanged and presented;
(g) whether and to what extent the tribunal should itself take the initiative in ascertaining the facts and the law;
(h) whether and to what extent there should be oral or written evidence or submissions.

The arbitrators [shall] [shall not] have the power to award a party all or part of its legal costs.

The arbitrators shall fix and state in their award their reasonable fees and expenses in connection with the arbitration, and each party agrees to pay one-half of the same. If the arbitrators so direct, the prevailing party shall pay the full amount of such fees and expenses, and one-half of the same may be included in the award in his favor against the other party.

The award of the arbitrators shall be final and binding upon the parties, who agree that each will faithfully abide by and perform any award rendered by the arbitrators, and that a judgment may be entered in any court of competent jurisdiction upon the award.

The parties intend that the award of the arbitrators shall conclusively determine the Dispute between them and hereby exclude any right which the parties might otherwise have under applicable law to challenge any award of the arbitrators in any court of competent jurisdiction.

Signed this ___ day of _________ 20__:

________________ for and on behalf of A Corporation

________________ for and on behalf of B Corporation.

Appendix I

Model Institutional Arbitration Clauses

ABU DHABI INTERNATIONAL ARBITRATION CENTRE

Any disputes, controversies, or claims of any nature (contractual or non-contractual), arising out of or having a connection with this contract, including, inter alia, the execution, interpretation or termination of the contract, ("Disputes"), shall be referred to and finally resolved by arbitration in accordance with the Rules of Arbitration of the Abu Dhabi International Arbitration Centre ("Rules").

The number of arbitrators shall be [one or three].

The seat of arbitration shall be ____________ [Abu Dhabi Global Market (ADGM), or other City/Country].

The language of the arbitration proceedings shall be ____________.

The law governing Disputes shall be the substantive law of ____________ [Jurisdiction].

AMERICAN ARBITRATION ASSOCIATION ("AAA")

Any controversy or claim arising out of or relating to this contract, or the breach thereof, shall be settled by arbitration administered by the American Arbitration Association in accordance with its Commercial [or other] Arbitration Rules, and judgment on the award rendered by the arbitrator(s) may be entered in any court having jurisdiction thereof.

ASIAN INTERNATIONAL ARBITRATION CENTRE ("AIAC")

Any dispute, controversy or claim arising out of or relating to this contract, or the breach, termination or invalidity thereof shall be settled by arbitration in accordance with the AIAC Arbitration Rules.

Recommended additions:

- The seat of arbitration shall be [...].
- The language to be used in the arbitral proceedings shall be [...].
- This contract shall be governed by the substantive law of [...].

- Before referring the dispute to arbitration, the parties shall seek an amicable settlement of that dispute by mediation in accordance with the AIAC Meditation Rules as in force on the date of the commencement of mediation.

AUSTRALIAN CENTRE FOR INTERNATIONAL COMMERCIAL ARBITRATION ("ACICA")

Any dispute, controversy or claim arising out of, relating to or in connection with this contract, including any question regarding its existence, validity or termination, shall be resolved by arbitration in accordance with the ACICA Arbitration Rules. The seat of arbitration shall be [Sydney/Melbourne/Perth/Brisbane/Adelaide], Australia [or choose another city]. The language of the arbitration shall be English [or choose another language]. The number of arbitrators shall be one [or three, or delete this sentence and rely on Article 11 of the ACICA Arbitration Rules].

BAHRAIN CHAMBER FOR DISPUTE RESOLUTION ("BCDR")

Any dispute arising out of or in connection with this contract, including any question regarding its existence, validity or termination, shall be finally settled by arbitration in accordance with the Rules of Arbitration of the Bahrain Chamber for Dispute Resolution. The arbitral tribunal shall consist of [specify one or three] arbitrator[s]. The place of arbitration shall be [specify town and country]. The language of the arbitration shall be [specify language].

CAIRO REGIONAL CENTRE FOR INTERNATIONAL COMMERCIAL ARBITRATION ("CRCICA")

Any dispute, controversy or claim arising out of or relating to this contract, including, but not limited to, its interpretation, execution, the termination or invalidity thereof, shall be settled by arbitration in accordance with the Arbitration Rules of the Cairo Regional Centre for International Commercial Arbitration.

Note: Parties should consider adding:

The number of arbitrators shall be ...
The place of arbitration shall be ... (city and country); and
The language to be used in the arbitral proceedings shall be...

Note: Parties may consider adding:

- The time limit within which the arbitral tribunal shall make its final award shall be...
- The governing law of the arbitration agreement; and
- The governing law of the contract [is/shall be] the substantive law of (country or state). Any dispute, controversy or claim arising out of or relating to this contract, its interpretation, execution, the termination or invalidity thereof, shall be settled by arbitration in accordance with the Rules for Arbitration of the Cairo Regional Centre for International Commercial Arbitration.

CHINESE INTERNATIONAL ECONOMIC AND TRADE ARBITRATION COMMISSION ("CIETAC")

Any dispute arising from or in connection with this Contract shall be submitted to China International Economic and Trade Arbitration Commission (CIETAC) for arbitration which shall be conducted in accordance with the CIETAC's arbitration rules in effect at the time of applying for arbitration. The arbitral award is final and binding upon both parties.

Or:

Any dispute arising from or in connection with this Contract shall be submitted to China International Economic and Trade Arbitration Commission (CIETAC)___________Sub-Commission (Arbitration Center) for arbitration which shall be conducted in accordance with the CIETAC's arbitration rules in effect at the time of applying for arbitration. The arbitral award is final and binding upon both parties.

Parties are also strongly advised to consider the below additions given CIETAC's default position on the language of arbitration and arbitrator selection:

- The language to be used in the arbitral proceedings shall be [...].
- No arbitrator shall be of the nationality of the place of incorporation or principal place of business of any of the parties [or any shareholders holding more than [5%] of such party's shares].
- When appointing an arbitrator, parties shall not be limited to arbitrators approved by the CIETAC Arbitrator Qualification Review Committee or any other list of arbitrators approved by CIETAC or any committees thereof.

DUBAI INTERNATIONAL ARBITRATION CENTRE ("DIAC")

Any dispute arising out of or in connection with this contract, including any question regarding its existence, validity or termination, shall be referred to and finally resolved by arbitration under the Arbitration Rules of the Dubai International Arbitration Centre, which Rules are deemed to be incorporated by reference into this clause.

The number of arbitrators shall be [one/three].

The seat of arbitration shall be [City and/or Country*].

The language to be used in the arbitration shall be [language].

The governing law of the contract shall be the substantive law of [State or Country].

GERMAN INSTITUTION OF ARBITRATION ("DIS")

All disputes arising out of or in connection with this contract or its validity shall be finally settled in accordance with the Arbitration Rules of the German Arbitration Institute (DIS) without recourse to the ordinary courts of law.

The arbitral tribunal shall be comprised of [please enter "a sole arbitrator" or "three members"].

The seat of the arbitration is [please enter city and country].

The language of the arbitration shall be [please enter language of the arbitration].

The rules of law applicable to the merits shall be [please enter law or rules of law].

HONG KONG INTERNATIONAL ARBITRATION CENTRE ("HKIAC")

Administered by the HKIAC:

Any dispute, controversy, difference or claim arising out of or relating to this contract, including the existence, validity, interpretation, performance, breach or termination thereof or any dispute regarding non-contractual obligations arising out of or relating to it shall be referred to and finally resolved by arbitration administered by the Hong Kong International Arbitration Centre (HKIAC) under the HKIAC Administered Arbitration Rules in force when the Notice of Arbitration is submitted.

- The law of this arbitration clause shall be [... (Hong Kong law)].
- The seat of arbitration shall be [... (Hong Kong)].
- The number of arbitrators shall be [... (one or three)].
- The arbitration proceedings shall be conducted in [... (insert language)].

Under UNCITRAL Rules:

Any dispute, controversy, difference or claim arising out of or relating to this contract, including the existence, validity, interpretation, performance, breach or termination thereof or any dispute regarding non-contractual obligations arising out of or relating to it shall be referred to and finally resolved by arbitration administered by the Hong Kong International Arbitration Centre (HKIAC) under the UNCITRAL Arbitration Rules in force when the Notice of Arbitration is submitted, as modified by the HKIAC Procedures for the Administration of Arbitration under the UNCITRAL Arbitration Rules.

- The law of this arbitration clause shall be [... (Hong Kong law)].
- The place of arbitration shall be [... (Hong Kong)].
- The number of arbitrators shall be [... (one or three)].
- The arbitration proceedings shall be conducted in [... (insert language)].

INTERNATIONAL CENTRE FOR DISPUTE RESOLUTION ("ICDR")

Any controversy or claim arising out of or relating to this contract, or the breach thereof, shall be determined by arbitration administered by the International Centre for Dispute Resolution in accordance with its International Arbitration Rules.

INTERNATIONAL CENTRE FOR SETTLEMENT OF INVESTMENT DISPUTES ("ICSID")

The [Government]/[name of constituent subdivision or agency] of name of Contracting State (hereinafter the "Host State") and name of investor (hereinafter the

"Investor") hereby consent to submit to the International Centre for Settlement of Investment Disputes (hereinafter the "Centre") any dispute arising out of or relating to this agreement for settlement by [conciliation]/[arbitration]/[conciliation followed, if the dispute remains unresolved within time limit of the communication of the report of the Conciliation Commission to the parties, by arbitration] pursuant to the Convention on the Settlement of Investment Disputes between States and Nationals of Other States (hereinafter the "Convention").

ICSID Additional Facility:

The Government of [name of host State] (hereinafter the "Host State") and [name of investor] (hereinafter the "Investor"), a national of [name of home State] (hereinafter the "Home State"), hereby consent to submit to the International Centre for Settlement of Investment Disputes (hereinafter the "Centre") any dispute arising out of or relating to this agreement for settlement by arbitration pursuant to:

(a) the Convention on the Settlement of Investment Disputes between States and Nationals of Other States (hereinafter the "Convention") if the Host State and the Home State have both become parties to the Convention at the time when any proceeding hereunder is instituted; or
(b) the Arbitration (Additional Facility) Rules of the Centre if the jurisdictional requirements ratione personae of Article 25 of the Convention remain unfulfilled at the time specified in (a) above.

INTERNATIONAL CHAMBER OF COMMERCE ("ICC")

Arbitration:

All disputes arising out of or in connection with the present contract shall be finally settled under the Rules of Arbitration of the International Chamber of Commerce by one or more arbitrators appointed in accordance with the said Rules.

Arbitration without emergency arbitrator:

All disputes arising out of or in connection with the present contract shall be finally settled under the Rules of Arbitration of the International Chamber of Commerce by one or more arbitrators appointed in accordance with the said Rules. The Emergency Arbitrator Provisions shall not apply.

ISTANBUL ARBITRATION CENTRE ("ISTAC")

Any dispute, controversy, difference or claim arising out of or relating to this contract, including the existence, validity, interpretation, performance, breach or termination thereof or any dispute regarding non-contractual obligations arising out of or relating to it shall be referred to and finally resolved by arbitration administered by the Istanbul Arbitration Centre (ISTAC) under the ISTAC Arbitration and Mediation Rules in force when the Notice of Arbitration is submitted.

- The law of this arbitration clause shall be [...].
- The seat of arbitration shall be [...].
- The number of arbitrators shall be [... (one or three)].
- The arbitration proceedings shall be conducted in [...].

JAMS INTERNATIONAL

Any dispute, controversy or claim arising out of or relating to this contract, including the formation, interpretation, breach or termination thereof, including whether the claims asserted are arbitrable, will be referred to and finally determined by arbitration in accordance with the JAMS International Arbitration Rules. The Tribunal will consist of [three arbitrators/one arbitrator]. The place of arbitration will be [location]. The language to be used in the arbitral proceedings will be [language]. Judgment upon the award rendered by the arbitrator(s) may be entered by any court having jurisdiction thereof.

JAPAN COMMERCIAL ARBITRATION ASSOCIATION ("JCAA")

All disputes, controversies or differences arising out of or in connection with this contract shall be finally settled by arbitration in accordance with the Commercial Arbitration Rules of The Japan Commercial Arbitration Association. The place of the arbitration shall be [city name], [country name].

KOREAN COMMERCIAL ARBITRATION BOARD ("KCAB")

Any disputes out of or in connection with this contract shall be finally settled by arbitration in accordance with the International Arbitration Rules of the Korean Commercial Arbitration Board.

- The number of arbitrators shall be [one/three].
- The seat, or legal place, of arbitral proceedings shall be [Seoul/Republic of Korea].
- The language to be used in the arbitral proceedings shall be [language].

LONDON COURT OF INTERNATIONAL ARBITRATION ("LCIA")

Any dispute arising out of or in connection with this contract, including any question regarding its existence, validity or termination, shall be referred to and finally resolved by arbitration under the LCIA Rules, which Rules are deemed to be incorporated by reference into this clause.

- The number of arbitrators shall be [one/three].
- The seat, or legal place, of arbitration shall be [City and/or Country].
- The language to be used in the arbitral proceedings shall be [...].
- The governing law of the contract shall be the substantive law of [...].

MUMBAI CENTRE FOR INTERNATIONAL ARBITRATION ("MCIA")

Any dispute, controversy, difference or claim arising out of or relating to this contract, including the existence, validity, interpretation, performance, breach or termination thereof or any dispute regarding non-contractual obligations arising out of or relating to it shall be referred to and finally resolved by arbitration administered by the Mumbai Centre for International Arbitration ("MCIA") under the MCIA Rules in force when the Notice of Arbitration is submitted.

- The law of this arbitration clause shall be [...].
- The seat of arbitration shall be [...].
- The number of arbitrators shall be [... (one or three)].
- The arbitration proceedings shall be conducted in [...].

NETHERLANDS ARBITRATION INSTITUTE ("NAI")

All disputes arising in connection with the present agreement, or further agreements resulting therefrom, shall be settled in accordance with the Arbitration Rules of the Netherlands Arbitration Institute.

Additionally, various matters may be provided for:

- The arbitral tribunal shall be composed of one arbitrator/three arbitrators.
- The arbitral tribunal shall be appointed according to the list procedure.
- The place of arbitration shall be [... (city)].
- The proceedings shall be conducted in the [... (language)].
- The arbitral tribunal shall decide as *amiable compositeur.*
- Consolidation of the arbitral proceedings with other arbitral proceedings, as provided for in Article 1046 of the Dutch Code of Civil Procedure and Article 39 of the Arbitration Rules of the Netherlands Arbitration Institute, is excluded.

PERMANENT COURT OF ARBITRATION ("PCA")

Administered by the PCA:

Any dispute, controversy or claim arising out of or relating to this contract, or the breach, termination or invalidity thereof, shall be settled by arbitration in accordance with the PCA Arbitration Rules 2012.

Under the UNCITRAL Rules:

Any dispute, controversy, or claim arising out of or relating to this contract, or the breach, termination or invalidity thereof, shall be settled by arbitration in accordance with the UNCITRAL Arbitration Rules in effect on the date of this contract.

The appointing authority shall be the Secretary-General of the Permanent Court of Arbitration.

Note: parties might wish to consider adding:

- The number of arbitrators shall be [... (one or three)].
- The place of arbitration shall be [... (The Hague) (or other location)].
- The language(s) to be used in the arbitral proceedings shall be [... (insert choice)].
- [For cases involving a State, a State-controlled entity or an intergovernmental organization] The case shall be administered by the International Bureau of the Permanent Court of Arbitration.

SINGAPORE INTERNATIONAL ARBITRATION CENTRE ("SIAC")

Any dispute arising out of or in connection with this contract, including any question regarding its existence, validity or termination, shall be referred to and finally resolved by arbitration administered by the Singapore International Arbitration Centre ("SIAC") in accordance with the Arbitration Rules of the Singapore International Arbitration Centre ("SIAC Rules") for the time being in force, which Rules are deemed to be incorporated by reference in this clause.

- The seat of the arbitration shall be [Singapore].
- Tribunal shall consist of [...] arbitrator(s).
- The language of the arbitration shall be [...].

STOCKHOLM CHAMBER OF COMMERCE ARBITRATION INSTITUTE ("SCC")

Any dispute, controversy or claim arising out of or in connection with this contract, or the breach, termination or invalidity thereof, shall be finally settled by arbitration in accordance with the Arbitration Rules of the Stockholm Chamber of Commerce Arbitration Institute.

Recommended additions:

- The arbitral tribunal shall be composed of three arbitrators/a sole arbitrator.
- The seat of arbitration shall be [...].
- The language to be used in the arbitral proceedings shall be [...].
- This contract shall be governed by the substantive law of [...].

SWISS CHAMBERS' ARBITRATION INSTITUTION ("SCAI")

Any dispute, controversy or claim arising out of, or in relation to, this contract, including the validity, invalidity, breach, or termination thereof, shall be resolved by arbitration in accordance with the Swiss Rules of International Arbitration of the Swiss Chambers' Arbitration Institution in force on the date on which the Notice of Arbitration is submitted in accordance with these Rules.

- The number of arbitrators shall be [... ("one," "three," "one or three")].
- The seat of the arbitration shall be in [... (name of city in Switzerland, unless the parties agree on a city in another country)].

- The arbitral proceedings shall be conducted in [... (insert desired language)].

UNCITRAL ARBITRATION RULES

Any dispute, controversy or claim arising out of or relating to this contract, or the breach, termination or invalidity thereof, shall be settled by arbitration in accordance with the UNCITRAL Arbitration Rules.

Note: parties may wish to consider adding:

- The appointing authority shall be [... (name of institution or person)].
- The number of arbitrators shall be [... (one or three)].
- The place of arbitration shall be [... (town and country)].
- The language(s) to be used in the arbitral proceedings shall be [...].

VANCOUVER INTERNATIONAL ARBITRATION CENTRE ("VanIAC")

All disputes arising out of or in connection with this agreement, or in respect of any legal relationship associated therewith or derived therefrom, shall be referred to and finally resolved by arbitration administered by the Vancouver International Arbitration Centre (VanIAC) pursuant to its applicable Rules.

The place of arbitration shall be Vancouver, British Columbia, Canada.

Options

The parties agree that either (any) party shall have a right of appeal pursuant to the VanIAC Rules with the grounds of appeal to be:

- on a question of law with leave of the Appeal Tribunal. Or
- on a question of law. Or
- on a question of law or a question of mixed fact and law. Or
- on a question of law, a question of mixed fact and law or a question of fact, in which case the appeal shall be only on the record.

Further Options

- Except for the appeal process under the VanIAC Rules, the parties agree that they will not appeal any arbitration decision, or decision of an Appeal Tribunal, to any court. Or:
- The parties agree that they will not appeal any arbitration decision to any court.

VIENNA INTERNATIONAL ARBITRAL CENTRE ("VIAC")

All disputes or claims arising out of or in connection with this contract including disputes relating to its validity, breach, termination or nullity shall be finally settled under the Rules of Arbitration of the International Arbitral Centre of the Austrian

Federal Economic Chamber in Vienna (Vienna Rules) by one or three arbitrators appointed in accordance with the said Rules.

Optional supplementary agreements on:

- the number of arbitrators (one or three) (Article 17 Vienna Rules);
- the language(s) to be used in the arbitral proceedings (Article 26 Vienna Rules);
- the substantive law applicable to the contractual relationship, the substantive law applicable to the arbitration agreement (Article 27 Vienna Rules), and the rules applicable to the proceedings (Article 28 Vienna Rules);
- the applicability of the provisions on expedited proceedings (Article 45 Vienna Rules);
- the scope of the arbitrators' confidentiality (Article 16 paragraph 2 Vienna Rules) and its extension regarding parties, representatives and experts.

Furthermore, the parties agree to jointly consider, after due initiation of the arbitration, to conduct proceedings in accordance with the Mediation Rules of the Vienna International Arbitral Centre (VIAC) of the Austrian Federal Economic Chamber (Vienna Mediation Rules). Settlements that are generated in such proceedings shall be referred to the arbitral tribunal appointed in the arbitration. The arbitral tribunal may render an award on agreed terms reflecting the content of the settlement (Article 37 paragraph 1 Vienna Rules).

In case of participation of Russian parties, the following addition to the model clause is advisable:

All disputes or claims arising out of or in connection with this contract, including disputes relating to its validity, breach, termination or nullity, shall be submitted to the Vienna International Arbitral Centre (VIAC) of the Austrian Federal Economic Chamber and shall be finally settled under the Rules of Arbitration (Vienna Rules) of VIAC by one or three arbitrators appointed in accordance with the said Rules.

WORLD INTELLECTUAL PROPERTY ORGANIZATION ("WIPO")

Any dispute, controversy or claim arising under, out of or relating to this contract and any subsequent amendments of this contract, including, without limitation, its formation, validity, binding effect, interpretation, performance, breach or termination, as well as non-contractual claims, shall be referred to and finally determined by arbitration in accordance with the WIPO Arbitration Rules. The arbitral tribunal shall consist of [a sole arbitrator] [three arbitrators]. The place of arbitration shall be [specify place]. The language to be used in the arbitral proceedings shall be [specify language]. The dispute, controversy or claim shall be decided in accordance with the law of [specify jurisdiction].

Appendix J

Representative International Arbitration and Forum Selection Clauses

The draft clauses in this Appendix are intended as the basis for more detailed analysis and drafting in particular cases. The validity and usefulness of particular clauses depend on the circumstances of individual cases, the applicable national law and other factors. Before using particular clauses, careful analysis and expert advice must be sought.

Drafting Forum Selection Clauses (Chapter 2) (p. 21)

Exclusive forum selection clauses (p. 27)

To provide exclusive jurisdiction to the specified courts:

> The parties agree that any dispute relating to this Agreement shall be resolved exclusively by the courts of _________, and no others.

Alternatively:

> The courts of _________ shall have exclusive jurisdiction over all disputes relating to this Agreement.

Or:

> All disputes relating to this Agreement shall be resolved exclusively by the courts of _________, and no others. [Each of the parties irrevocably submits to the jurisdiction of the courts of _________ for the purpose of resolving such disputes.]

Or:

> In relation to any legal action or proceedings arising out of or in connection with this Agreement ("Proceedings"), each of the parties irrevocably submits to the exclusive jurisdiction of the ________ courts with regard to such Proceedings and waives any objections to Proceedings on the grounds of venue or on the grounds that proceedings have been brought in an inappropriate forum.

Non-exclusive forum selection clauses (p. 27)

To provide non-exclusive jurisdiction to the specified courts:

> The parties submit to the non-exclusive jurisdiction of the courts of ________ for any disputes relating to this Agreement.

Or:

> The parties irrevocably submit to the non-exclusive jurisdiction of the courts of ________ for any disputes relating to this Agreement.

Or:

> The courts of ________ shall have non-exclusive jurisdiction to decide actions relating to this Agreement, without prejudice to the right of either party to commence such actions in any other court of competent jurisdiction.

Or:

> All disputes relating to this Agreement may be submitted by either party to the non-exclusive jurisdiction of the courts of ________. [The parties irrevocably submit to the non-exclusive jurisdiction of the courts of ________ for the purpose of resolving such disputes.] Nothing contained herein shall affect the rights of either party to submit any such dispute to any other courts of competent jurisdiction.

Or:

> In relation to any legal action or proceedings arising out of or in connection with this Agreement ("Proceedings"), each of the parties irrevocably submits to the non-exclusive jurisdiction of the courts of ________ save that this submission shall not affect the right of any party to take Proceedings in any other court or courts having jurisdiction, to the extent permitted by law.

Scope of Forum Selection Clauses (p. 31)

To provide a broad scope to the jurisdiction of the specified courts:

All disputes, claims, controversies, and disagreements relating to or arising out of this Agreement, or the subject matter of this Agreement, shall be subject to the exclusive [or non-exclusive] jurisdiction of the courts of ________, and no others.

To provide a broad scope to the jurisdiction of specified courts using a common law perspective:

All disputes relating to this Agreement shall be subject to the exclusive [or non-exclusive] jurisdiction of the courts of ________.

To exclude certain categories of disputes from its coverage:

All disputes relating to this Agreement, with the exception of claims arising under Article III [or: claims for payment under Article IV], shall be resolved exclusively in the courts of ________.

Asymmetrical Forum Selection Clauses (p. 34)

To permit one party to pursue a claim in an alternate jurisdiction:

The parties agree that all disputes relating to this Agreement shall be resolved exclusively in the courts of ________, provided however that [Party A] shall be also free to pursue claims in any court of competent jurisdiction, including, without limitation, the courts of ________ and ________.

Or:

The parties agree that all disputes relating to this Agreement shall be resolved exclusively in the courts of ________, unless [Party A] chooses to bring action in ________.

Or:

This Agreement shall be governed by and construed in accordance with English Law and the parties irrevocably agree for the exclusive benefit of the Lenders that the courts of England are to have jurisdiction to settle any disputes which may arise out of or in connection with this Agreement and that accordingly any suit, action, or proceeding arising out of or in connection with this Agreement (in this Article [X] referred to as "Proceedings") may be brought in such courts and the Company hereby irrevocably submits to the jurisdiction of such courts.

Nothing contained in this Article [X] shall limit the right of the Lender to take Proceedings against the Company in any other court of competent jurisdiction, nor shall the taking of proceedings in one or more jurisdictions preclude the taking of Proceedings in any other jurisdiction, whether concurrently or not.

To permit one party to elect to arbitrate (rather than litigate) future disputes:

The parties irrevocably submit to the non-exclusive jurisdiction of the courts of ________ for resolution of any disputes, claims or controversies relating to this Agreement. Notwithstanding the foregoing sentence, and at the sole option of [Party A], any disputes, claims or controversies relating to this Agreement shall be finally resolved by arbitration. ... If a court action has been initiated by [Party B] prior to or at the time that [Party A] elects to submit the dispute(s) to arbitration, then [Party B] shall forthwith take all necessary steps to discontinue and dismiss such court action.

To ensure that an asymmetrical clause complies with the requirement of clarity of the Brussels I Regulation (Article 17 of EC Regulation 44/2001 and Article 19 of EU Regulation 1215/2012):

All disputes relating to this Agreement shall be submitted to the courts of ________. This provision is for the sole benefit of ________, which shall retain the option of submitting any such disputes to any other courts of competent jurisdiction.

To specify that the defendant's domicile is contractual forum:

Any suit relating to this Agreement brought by Buyer shall be brought in ________ [or: the place where Seller's principal place of business is located]; any suit relating to this Agreement brought by Seller shall be brought in ________ [or: the place where Buyer's principal place of business is located].

Consent to Service of Process (p. 37)

To specify an agent within the contractual forum for service of process:

________ irrevocably designates, appoints, and empowers ________, with offices on the date hereof at ________, as its agent with respect to any action or proceeding in ________ to receive, on its behalf, and in respect of its property, service of any and all legal process, summons, notices, and documents which may be served in any such action or proceeding and agrees that the failure of the agent to notify _________ of any such service of process will not impair or affect the validity of service. _________ further irrevocably consents to the service of process out of any of the courts listed in Article [X] by the mailing of copies by registered or certified mail, postage prepaid, to _________ at its address set forth in Article [X], such service to become effective 30 days after such mailing. If for any reason _________ shall cease to be available to act as agent, _________ agrees to designate a new agent in _________ on the same terms and for the same purposes.

To specify an agent within the contractual forum for service of process: under English law, is:

_________ hereby irrevocably appoints _________ of _________ as his agent for the service of process in England in connection with this Agreement. Service of process on _________ at the above address shall be deemed, for all purposes, to be due and effective service, and service shall be deemed completed whether or not forwarded to or received by _________.

Waiver of Sovereign Immunity (p. 38)

To provide a standard waiver of sovereign immunity:

The parties agree that the matters that are subject to this choice of court agreement are commercial transactions and agree not to claim and to waive any immunity from suit, execution, pre-judgment, or post-judgment attachment, or other legal process in any jurisdiction in connection with any litigation between the parties pursuant to this choice of court agreement or otherwise.

To provide a waiver of sovereign immunity in accordance with U.S. law:

The Borrower is subject to civil and commercial law with respect to its obligations under this Agreement. The execution, delivery, and performance by the Borrower of this Agreement constitute private and commercial acts rather than public or governmental acts. Neither the Borrower, nor any of its Properties or revenues, is entitled to or will claim any right of immunity in any jurisdiction from suit, jurisdiction, judgment, attachment (whether before or after judgment), set-off, or execution of a judgment or from any other legal process or remedy relating to the obligations of the Borrower under this Agreement.

To provide a waiver of state immunity under English law:

> To the extent that the Borrower may in any jurisdiction claim for itself or its assets immunity from suit, execution, attachment (whether in aid of execution, before judgment or otherwise), or other legal process and to the extent that in any such jurisdiction there may be attributed to itself or its assets any such immunity (whether or not claimed), the Borrower hereby irrevocably agrees not to claim and hereby irrevocably waives such immunity to the full extent permitted by the laws of such jurisdiction.

Waiver of Forum Non Conveniens (p. 39)

To provide waiver of forum non conveniens defense:

> The Parties irrevocably waive any objection to venue in those Courts and any objection based on the doctrine of *forum non conveniens* or similar grounds that those Courts are inconvenient for determination of a dispute.

Waiver of Jury Trial (p. 39)

To provide waiver of jury trial:

> [Borrower] expressly waives any right to a trial by jury with respect to disputes relating to this Agreement, and agrees not to seek or claim any such right.

Or:

> Each party to this Agreement waives its prospective right to a jury trial of any claim or cause of action arising out of this Agreement, or any dealings between any of the parties hereto relating to the subject matter of this Agreement. The scope of this waiver is intended to be all-encompassing of any and all disputes that may be filed in any court and that relate to the subject matter of this Agreement or the loan documents, including, without limitation, contract claims, tort claims, and all other common law and statutory claims. This waiver is irrevocable, meaning that it may not be modified either orally or in writing, and this waiver shall apply to any subsequent amendments, supplements or modifications to this Agreement, or to any other document or agreement relating to the transactions. The parties acknowledge that they have consulted with legal counsel regarding this provision and that they have freely and voluntarily entered into it.

Application of Forum Selection Clauses to Actions Seeking Provisional or Interim Relief (p. 41)

To exclude provisional or interim relief from a forum selection clause:

> Nothing in this Agreement shall prevent either party from applying to a court that would otherwise have jurisdiction for provisional or interim measures, including, but not limited to, any claim for preliminary injunctive relief.

To allow licensors relief outside the contractual forum when their licensee makes unlicensed use of their property:

> All disputes relating to this Agreement shall be resolved exclusively in the courts of ________, provided that claims alleging unlicensed or otherwise unauthorized use of the [Trademarks] may be asserted in any court of competent jurisdiction.

Or:

> All disputes relating to this Agreement (with the exception of claims arising under Article [X]) shall be resolved exclusively in the courts of ________.

To specify the party's domicile, combined with an equally simple choice-of-law clause:

> All disputes relating to this Agreement shall be subject to the exclusive jurisdiction of the courts of ________, and shall be decided in accordance with the laws of ________.

Forum Selection Clauses in Routine Transactions (p. 42)

> All disputes relating to this Agreement shall be subject to the exclusive jurisdiction of the courts of ________, and shall be decided in accordance with the laws of ________.

Selecting International Courts (p. 42)

To submit to the exclusive jurisdiction of the SICC:

> Each party irrevocably submits to the exclusive jurisdiction of the Singapore International Commercial Court all disputes arising out of or in connection with the present contract, including any question relating to its existence, validity or termination.

To submit to the exclusive jurisdiction of the DIFC:

> Any dispute arising out of or in connection with this contract, including any question regarding its existence, validity or termination, shall be subject to the exclusive jurisdiction of the Courts of the Dubai International Financial Centre.

Drafting International Arbitration Agreements (Chapter 3) (p. 45)

Scope of Arbitration Agreement (p. 47)

To extend the scope of the arbitration agreement:

> All disputes, claims, controversies, and disagreements relating to or arising out of this Agreement, or the subject matter of this Agreement, shall be finally resolved by arbitration. ...

Or:

> All disputes, claims, controversies, and disagreements relating to or arising out of this Agreement (including the formation, existence, validity, enforceability, performance, or termination of this Agreement), or the subject matter of this Agreement, shall be finally resolved by arbitration. ...

Concise example of a broad arbitration clause:

> All disputes relating to this Agreement shall be finally resolved by arbitration.

To exclude certain matters from the scope of the arbitration agreement:

> With the exception of those claims which are specifically excluded (pursuant to Article [X](2) below) from arbitration under this Article [X](1), all disputes, claims, controversies, and disagreements relating to or arising out of this Agreement shall be finally resolved by arbitration. ...

Or:

> Claims under the following Articles of this Agreement are specifically excluded from arbitration hereunder: [Articles V, VII, and ...].

Injunctive Relief for Intellectual Property Rights (p. 51)

To increase flexibility to seek injunctive relief in case of a violation of intellectual property rights:

> Any violation of Article [X] hereof [relating to trademarks, patents, trade secrets, copyrights] would cause irreparable injury to [Licensor]. [Licensor] may, in addition to any other rights under this Agreement and notwithstanding the arbitration agreement contained in this Article [Y], seek specific performance of Article [X] and any other available provisional relief in any court of competent jurisdiction against any violation of such Article [X].

To provide for injunctive relief in case of intellectual property rights in a graduated manner:

> Prior to the appointment of the arbitrator(s), either party may seek provisional or interim measures from any court of competent jurisdiction. After the appointment of the arbitrator(s), the arbitrator(s) shall have exclusive power to consider and grant requests for provisional or interim measures.

Validity of Intellectual Property Rights (p. 52)

To exclude validity and ownership of intellectual property, from the scope of the arbitration agreement:

> All disputes arising out of or relating to this Agreement, except "Licensed Mark Disputes" (as defined below), shall be finally resolved by arbitration in accordance with [identify institutional rules]. "Licensed Mark Disputes" shall constitute all disputes relating to the Licensor's ownership of, the validity of, or the registration of any Licensed Mark.

To provide a forum for issues such as the validity or ownership of intellectual property after they have been excluded from the scope of the arbitration agreement:

> All Licensed Mark Disputes shall be subject to the [exclusive] [non-exclusive] jurisdiction of ________.

Exclusion of Payment Obligations (p. 46)

To exclude payment obligations from the scope of the arbitration agreement:

> With the exception of Buyer's payment obligations under Article [X] hereof, all claims, controversies, disputes, and disagreements arising under or relating to this Agreement shall be finally resolved by arbitration in accordance with ...

Forum selection clause to be used with a clause that excludes payment obligations from the scope of the arbitration agreement:

> All disputes [arising under] [in connection with] the Buyer's payment obligations under Article [X] hereof shall be subject to the [exclusive] [non-exclusive] jurisdiction of the courts of ________.

Ad Hoc Arbitration (p. 76-78, 106-109)

UNCITRAL ad hoc arbitration clause:

> Any dispute, controversy, or claim arising out of or relating to this contract, or the breach, termination or invalidity thereof, shall be settled by arbitration in accordance with the UNCITRAL Arbitration Rules as at present in force.
>
> *Note. Parties should consider adding:*
>
> (a) The appointing authority shall be [name of institution or person].
> (b) The number of arbitrators shall be [one or three].
> (c) The place of arbitration shall be [town and country].
> (d) The language to be used in the arbitral proceedings shall be ________.

Ad hoc arbitration clause:

> All disputes, claims, controversies, and disagreements relating to or arising out of this Agreement, or the subject matter of this Agreement, shall be finally resolved by arbitration. The seat of the arbitration shall be ________. The language of the arbitration shall be ________.
>
> The arbitration shall be commenced by a request for arbitration delivered by the claimant to the respondent. The request for arbitration shall set out the parties to the arbitration, the agreement to arbitrate, the applicable law, the general nature of the claim(s), and the relief requested, and shall attach a copy of this Agreement. Within [30] days of receipt of the request for arbitration, the respondent shall deliver to the claimant an answer together with any counterclaim(s), setting out the nature of the counterclaim(s) and the relief requested.
>
> The number of arbitrators shall be three. The arbitrators shall be appointed as follows: (a) the claimant shall appoint an arbitrator in the request for arbitration, and the respondent shall appoint an arbitrator in the answer, and the two arbitrators so appointed shall, within [30] days of delivery of the answer,

appoint a third arbitrator who shall be the presiding arbitrator; (b) if either party fails to appoint an arbitrator within [the foregoing time limits], such arbitrator shall, at the written request of that other party, be appointed by [insert appointing authority]; (c) if the two arbitrators appointed by the parties fail to agree upon the presiding arbitrator within [30] days of the appointment of the second arbitrator, the third arbitrator shall be appointed at the written request of either party by [insert appointing authority]; (d) any challenge to an arbitrator for lack of independence or impartiality, or any other ground, shall be decided by [insert appointing authority]; and (e) if a vacancy arises on the arbitral tribunal, the vacancy shall be filled by the method by which that arbitrator was originally appointed. The presiding arbitrator shall not be of the same nationality as either of the two arbitrators or of the parties. The procedure to be followed during any arbitration under this Article [X] shall be agreed to by the parties or, failing such agreement, by the arbitral tribunal. Default by any party shall not prevent the arbitrators from proceeding to render an award.

The arbitral tribunal may make its decisions by a majority. In the event that no majority is possible, the presiding arbitrator may make the decision(s) as if acting as a sole arbitrator. If an arbitrator appointed by a party fails or refuses to participate, the two other arbitrators may proceed with the arbitration and render an award if they determine that the failure or refusal to participate was unjustified.

Any award(s) made by the arbitral tribunal under this Article [X] shall be final and binding on the parties, and each party waives to the fullest extent permitted by law any right it may otherwise have under the laws of any jurisdiction to any form of appeal, annulment, action to set-aside or vacate, collateral attack, or any other challenge to such award(s).

A representative ad hoc arbitration agreement provides:

All disputes, claims, controversies, and disagreements relating to or arising out of this Agreement (including the formation, existence, validity, enforceability, performance, or termination of this Agreement) or the subject matter of this Agreement shall be finally resolved by arbitration [in accordance with the UNCITRAL Arbitration Rules].

The number of arbitrators shall be [one] [three]. The appointing authority shall be ________.

The arbitral tribunal shall be composed of three arbitrators. Each party shall appoint one arbitrator. The two arbitrators so appointed shall appoint the presiding arbitrator. If either party fails to appoint an arbitrator within [30] days of receiving written notice of the appointment of an arbitrator by the other party, such arbitrator shall be appointed by ________. If the two arbitrators to be appointed by the parties fail to agree upon a third arbitrator within [30] days of the appointment of the second arbitrator, the third arbitrator shall be appointed by ________.

The seat of the arbitration shall be ________.

The language of the arbitration shall be ________.

This Agreement will be governed by, and all disputes relating to or arising in connection with this Agreement [or the subject matter of this Agreement] shall be resolved in accordance with, the laws of ________.

An alternative ad hoc agreement, from the IBA Guidelines for Drafting International Arbitration Clauses:

All disputes arising out of or in connection with this agreement, including any question regarding its existence, validity or termination, shall be finally resolved by arbitration.

The place of arbitration shall be [city, country].

The language of the arbitration shall be [...].

The arbitration shall be commenced by a request for arbitration by the claimant, delivered to the respondent. The request for arbitration shall set out the nature of the claim(s) and the relief requested.

The arbitral tribunal shall consist of three arbitrators, one selected by the claimant in the request for arbitration, the second selected by the respondent within [30] days of receipt of the request for arbitration, and the third, who shall act as presiding arbitrator, selected by the two parties within [30] days of the selection of the second arbitrator. If any arbitrators are not selected within these time periods, [the designated appointing authority] shall, upon the request of any party, make the selection(s).

If a vacancy arises, the vacancy shall be filled by the method by which that arbitrator was originally appointed, provided, however, that if a vacancy arises during or after the hearing on the merits, the remaining two arbitrators may proceed with the arbitration and render an award.

The arbitrators shall be independent and impartial. Any challenge of an arbitrator shall be decided by [the designated appointing authority].

The procedure to be followed during the arbitration shall be agreed by the parties or, failing such agreement, determined by the arbitral tribunal after consultation with the parties.

The arbitral tribunal shall have the power to rule on its own jurisdiction, including any objections with respect to the existence, validity or effectiveness of the arbitration agreement. The arbitral tribunal may make such ruling in a preliminary decision on jurisdiction or in an award on the merits, as it considers appropriate in the circumstances.

Default by any party shall not prevent the arbitral tribunal from proceeding to render an award.

The arbitral tribunal may make its decisions by a majority. In the event that no majority is possible, the presiding arbitrator may make the decision(s) as if acting as a sole arbitrator.

If the arbitrator appointed by a party fails or refuses to participate, the two other arbitrators may proceed with the arbitration and render an award if they determine that the failure or refusal to participate was unjustified.

Any award of the arbitral tribunal shall be final and binding on the parties. The parties undertake to carry out any award without delay and shall be deemed to have waived their right to any form of recourse insofar as such waiver can validly be made. Enforcement of any award may be sought in any court of competent jurisdiction.

Drafting Provisions Specifying An Arbitral Seat (p. 91-92)

To specify the seat of arbitration:

The seat of the arbitration shall be [city/nation].

Or:

The place of the arbitration shall be [city/nation].

Alternatively:

The seat of the arbitration shall be [city/nation]. The arbitrators may hold hearings or meetings in any other locations for convenience.

To provide for seat of arbitration based on the identity of the applicant:

The seat of the arbitration shall be [identify Party B's principal place of business (e.g., Singapore)], if the arbitration is commenced by [Party A], and the place of arbitration shall be [identify Party A's principal place of business (e.g., Rome, Italy)] if the arbitration is commenced by [Party B].

Or:

> Unless otherwise agreed in writing by the parties, the seat of the arbitration shall be either (a) in the case of claims initiated by Licensor, in the city with a population of 500,000 or more which is located nearest Licensee's main office, or (b) in the case of claims initiated by Licensee, in ________.

Name of Arbitrator (p. 93)

To name the arbitrator:

> The [arbitrator] [sole arbitrator] shall be [Ms. Natascha Born] ...

Number of Arbitrators (p. 93-94)

To provide for the number of arbitrators:

> Any dispute, claim, or controversy relating to, arising out of, or in connection with this agreement shall be finally resolved under the [Rules of Arbitration of the International Chamber of Commerce] by [three arbitrators] appointed in accordance with the said Rules.

Or:

> Any dispute, claim, or controversy relating to, arising out of, or in connection with this agreement shall be finally resolved under the [Arbitration Rules of the Singapore International Arbitration Centre] by [a sole arbitrator] appointed in accordance with the said Rules.

Methods of Selecting Arbitrators (p. 95-98)

UNCITRAL Rules model clause providing for an appointing authority:

> The appointing authority shall be [name of institution or person].

To deal with cases in which the parties did not agree on an appointing authority:

> If any arbitrator is not selected within the foregoing time limits, the [appropriate court (virtually always in arbitral seat)] will appoint such arbitrator(s).

To allow party-nominated arbitrators to choose presiding arbitrator:

> The arbitral tribunal shall be composed of three arbitrators. Each party shall appoint one arbitrator. The two arbitrators so appointed shall appoint the presiding arbitrator. If either party fails to appoint an arbitrator within [30] days of receiving written notice of the appointment of an arbitrator by the other party, such arbitrator shall be appointed by ________. If the two arbitrators to be appointed by the parties fail to agree upon a third arbitrator within [30] days of the appointment of the second arbitrator, the third arbitrator shall be appointed by ________.

Alternatively:

> The number of arbitrators shall be three. One arbitrator shall be [nominated] [selected] by the claimant in its [request for arbitration]. The second arbitrator shall be [nominated] [selected] by the respondent within [30] days of its receipt of the [request for arbitration]. The third arbitrator, who shall be the presiding arbitrator, shall be jointly [nominated] [selected] by the [two other arbitrators] [parties] within [30] days of the [nomination] [selection] [appointment] of the second arbitrator. If any arbitrator is not [nominated] [selected] within these time periods, the [appointing authority] shall appoint such arbitrators.

To provide for parties' selection of presiding arbitrator:

> Within [30] days after the commencement of the arbitration, each party shall [appoint] [select] an arbitrator. The parties shall then [appoint] [select] the presiding arbitrator within [20] days after selection of the party-[appointed] [selected] arbitrators. If any arbitrators are not selected within these time periods, the [International Centre for Dispute Resolution] shall, at the written request of any party, complete the appointments that have not been made.

To provide for simultaneous selection of arbitrators by the parties:

> The number of arbitrators shall be three. Each party shall [nominate/select] one co-arbitrator. On the [30th] day following receipt by the respondent(s) of the request for arbitration, the parties shall simultaneously exchange their respective [nomination/selections] of co-arbitrators. Within [30] days after [nomination/selection] of the two co-arbitrators, the co-arbitrators shall [nominate/select] a third arbitrator, who shall be the presiding arbitrator. If any arbitrator is not [nominated/selected] within these time periods, the [(add appointing authority)] shall appoint such arbitrator(s).

Qualifications and Nationality of Arbitrators (p. 98-100)

To require the arbitrator(s) to have certain technical expertise:

> [Each arbitrator] [The presiding arbitrator] shall be an [electrical engineer] knowledgeable in ________.

To require the arbitrator(s) to be fluent in a particular language:

> [Each arbitrator] [The presiding arbitrator] shall be fluent in written and spoken [English and German].

To require the arbitrator(s) to have specific qualifications:

> [Each arbitrator] [The presiding arbitrator] shall be legally qualified and experienced in [oil and gas contracts] [intellectual property] [construction projects].

Or:

> Each arbitrator shall be [a Certified Public Accountant] [an electrical engineer].

To prevent that any arbitrator be of the same nationality as one of the parties:

> No arbitrator shall be of the nationality of the place of incorporation or principal place of business of any of the parties [or any shareholders holding more than [5%] of such party's shares].

To exclude arbitrators of certain nationalities:

> The presiding [or sole] arbitrator shall not be a national of ________.

To provide a contractual definition of "nationality":

> In ascertaining an arbitrator's or proposed arbitrator's nationality for purposes of this Article [X], any national of a Member State of the European Union shall be deemed to have the nationalities of both the European Union and each of its Member States.

Independence and Impartiality of Arbitrators (p. 100-101)

To provide for impartiality and independence of the arbitrators:

> Each of the arbitrators shall be and remain impartial and independent of the parties.

To require a formal commitment to impartiality and independence by the arbitrators:

> Prior to commencement of the arbitral proceedings, each of the arbitrators shall provide an oath or undertaking of impartiality.

To incorporate the IBA Guidelines on Conflicts of Interest in International Arbitration:

> The parties agree to comply with the IBA Guidelines on Conflicts of Interest in Arbitration in matters concerning prospective arbitrator appointments and disclosure of relationships between parties, party representatives and arbitrators.

Language of the Arbitration (p. 102)

To provide for the language of the arbitral proceedings:

> The language of the arbitration shall be ________.

Or:

> The arbitration proceedings shall be conducted in the ________ language. All written submissions shall be made in the ________ language. All evidence, including all witness statements, shall be submitted in the ________ language, or with a translation into the ________ language. Oral testimony shall be in the ________ language or shall be simultaneously translated into the ________ language by a translator. Each party shall bear its own translation costs.

Law Applicable to Arbitration Agreement and to Arbitral Proceedings (p. 103-104)

To specify the law governing the arbitration agreement:

> This Article [X] shall be governed by the laws of ________.

To specify the procedural law of the arbitration:

> The arbitration agreement and the arbitral proceedings shall be governed by the laws of ________.

Provisions Allocating Legal Costs (p. 109-112)

To provide for award of legal fees and costs to the prevailing party:

> The prevailing party shall be entitled to recover its [reasonable] costs, including administrative fees and expenses, arbitrators' fees and expenses, and fees and expenses of legal representation, incurred in the arbitration proceedings.

Or:

> The arbitral tribunal shall award to the prevailing party, if any, all of its costs and fees. "Costs and fees" means all reasonable pre-award expenses of the arbitration, including the arbitrators' fees, administrative fees, travel expenses, out-of-pocket expenses such as copying and telephone, court costs, witness fees, and costs of legal representation in the arbitration.

To provide for award of fees and costs of all related arbitration and judicial proceedings to the prevailing party:

> The prevailing party may recover its reasonable fees for legal representation and related costs in any arbitration under this Article [X] and in any action to enforce this Article [X] or any award made under this Article [X] in any judicial or arbitration proceeding.

To ensure that time costs incurred by in-house counsel, experts and management are recoverable:

> ... including all costs of in-house or internal lawyers, legal staff, experts, or management in connection with these arbitral proceedings.

To obligate parties to pay for their own costs and expenses:

> Notwithstanding any provision to the contrary in the [ICC Arbitration Rules], each party shall bear its own costs and expenses, including fees for legal representation.

Or:

The fees and expenses of the arbitrators shall be borne in equal shares by the parties. Each party shall bear the fees and expenses of its legal representation in the arbitration. The arbitral tribunal shall not reallocate the fees and expenses of either the arbitrators or the parties' legal representation.

Or:

Each party shall bear its own costs and expenses (including costs and expenses of legal representation in the arbitration) and an equal share of the arbitrators' fees and expenses and all administrative fees and expenses of the arbitration.

To give arbitrators the discretion to allocate all costs related to the arbitral proceedings and legal representation:

The arbitrators shall have the power to make an award allocating the costs of the arbitration between the parties, including administrative fees and expenses, arbitrators' fees and expenses, and the fees and expenses of legal representation.

To give arbitrators the discretion to award all costs and expenses except legal representation costs:

The arbitral tribunal may include in any award an allocation of the costs and expenses of the arbitration, but it shall not have the authority to allocate or award costs of legal representation in the arbitration.

ICSID-recommended clause relating to the tribunal and the administrative services of the arbitral institution:

In any arbitration proceeding conducted pursuant to this agreement, the fees and expenses of the members of the Arbitral Tribunal as well as the charges for the use of the facilities of the Centre shall be [borne equally by the parties hereto]/[divided between the parties hereto as follows: ...].

Award of Interest (p. 112)

To require award of interest against the breaching party, with a rate deemed by the tribunal, and set out the time period of accrual:

Any monetary award shall include interest from the date of any breach or violation of this agreement. The arbitrator(s) shall fix the appropriate rate of interest from the date of the breach or other violation to the date when the award is paid in full.

To require award of interest against the breaching party with instructions on accrual period and interest rate:

> The arbitral tribunal shall include in any award of monetary damages interest from the date of loss or default until the date of payment of the award in full, at the prime commercial lending rate published by the [name of bank] at its principal office in [city, country] for [90-day commercial loans to substantial borrowers] averaged over the period from the date of the loss or default until the date of the award.

To require award of interest, compounded, if appropriate, against the breaching party and set out the accrual period:

> The arbitral tribunal shall include in any award of monetary damages interest (including, if appropriate, compound interest) from the date of loss or default until the date of payment of the award.

To permit award of interest against the breaching party, giving the tribunal full discretion to decide the rate:

> The arbitral tribunal may order that simple or compound interest shall be paid by any party on any monetary amounts awarded at such rates as the arbitral tribunal determines to be appropriate without being bound by legal rates of interest applicable in any national courts.

Payment of Award (pp. 113)

To specify currency for arbitral award:

> Any award shall be made payable in [Euros] [U.S. Dollars].

To require that award be expressed in freely-convertible currency:

> An award may be expressed in [any currency] [any freely-convertible currency].

To require award of pre-award interest against the breaching party:

> Any monetary award in an arbitration initiated under this Article [X] shall include pre-award interest [(including compound interest [compounded [daily] [monthly] [annually])] at the rate of ___% from the time of the act or acts giving rise to the award.

To require payment of full award without any deductions:

> Any award of monetary relief shall be promptly paid, without any set-off, allowance for tax, or other deduction.

Disclosure or Discovery (pp. 113-116)

To prescribe procedures for disclosure and discovery:

> The parties shall be entitled to engage in reasonable discovery, including requests for the production of relevant documents. [Depositions may be ordered by the arbitrator upon a showing of need.]

Or:

> The parties shall be entitled to engage in discovery as provided for by the [U.S. Federal Rules of Civil Procedure] [other procedural rules, with or without modification].

To require detailed disclosure requests and give the Tribunal discretion to order disclosure after party requests are made:

> At the request of a party, the Tribunal shall have the discretion to order the disclosure of specified documents by the parties. Such a request shall identify the document(s) with a reasonable degree of specificity and establish the relevance of the document(s) to the arbitration.

To give the tribunal discretion in ordering disclosure after reasonable requests by the parties or the tribunal itself:

> The arbitral tribunal shall have the authority to order the parties to produce such [documents] [categories of documents] as are reasonably requested by another party or by the arbitral tribunal.

To give the tribunal discretion in ordering disclosure upon showing by a party of justifiable need:

> The arbitral tribunal shall have the authority to order production of documents relevant and material to the issues in dispute, upon the showing by either party of a justifiable need for such document(s).

To give the tribunal discretion in ordering oral depositions while limiting the number of deposition requests:

> The arbitral tribunal shall have the authority to order the examination by deposition of any witness [or officer or director of any party]. No party shall request more than ___ depositions.

To prescribe procedures and deadlines for disclosure and discovery:

> After the arbitrators are selected, the parties shall confer jointly with the arbitral tribunal at the earliest convenient date (not to exceed [30] days after selection of the last arbitrator) to determine the discovery that shall take place. Each party shall have the right to take no more than ___ depositions of potential witnesses, and each shall have the right to serve no more than ___ sets of interrogatories, none of which shall include more than ___ interrogatories. Additional discovery shall be in the discretion of the arbitral tribunal. All discovery shall be completed within ___ months after the selection of the last arbitrator, unless this period of time is extended by the arbitral tribunal for good cause.

To exclude disclosure or discovery:

> The parties shall not be entitled to discovery, and the arbitrators shall have no power to order discovery or disclosure of documents, oral testimony, or other materials.

IBA Rules on the Taking of Evidence in International Arbitration (pp. 116-118)

To incorporate the IBA Rules on the Taking of Evidence:

> The IBA Rules of Evidence shall apply together with the _________ Rules governing any submission to arbitration incorporated in this contract. Where they are inconsistent with the before said _________ Rules, these IBA Rules of Evidence shall prevail but solely as regards the presentation and reception of evidence.

To incorporate only some aspects of the IBA Rules on the Taking of Evidence:

> Direct testimony of fact or expert witnesses shall be submitted in any arbitration pursuant to this Article [X] through written witness statements made in accordance with the procedures set forth in the IBA Rules on the Taking of Evidence in International Arbitration, as such procedures may be varied by the arbitral tribunal.

To prescribe the manner of evidence-taking:

> Direct testimony of fact or expert witnesses shall be submitted in any arbitration pursuant to this Article [X] through written witness statements made in accordance with the procedures directed by the arbitral tribunal. Any party submitting a written witness statement shall make the witness providing any such statement available for cross-examination as directed by the arbitral tribunal. If cross-examination is requested by another party and the witness is not made available, the written witness statement will be excluded from evidence except for good cause shown.

To incorporate the Prague Rules on the Efficient Conduct of Proceedings in International Arbitration:

> The Prague Rules on the Efficient Conduct of Proceedings in International Arbitration shall apply to any arbitration conducted under this Article [X].

To prescribe optional procedures on the manner of gathering and submitting witness statements:

> Either party may submit direct testimony through written witness statements (in accordance with procedures directed by the arbitral tribunal). Any party submitting a written witness statement shall make the witness providing any such statement available for cross-examination as directed by the arbitral tribunal. If cross-examination is requested by another party and the witness is not made available, the written witness statement shall be excluded from evidence except for good cause shown.

To provide expert guidelines and give the tribunal the authority to appoint experts:

> The arbitral tribunal shall have the authority, [after consulting the parties], to appoint experts to advise it with respect to any issue in the arbitration. If the arbitral tribunal appoints an expert, such expert shall render a report in writing, and the parties shall have the right to examine such expert at a hearing before the arbitral tribunal.

Pre-Arbitration Notice and/or Consultation (pp. 118-119)

To require pre-arbitration notice and consultations and establish their time deadlines:

> All disputes relating to this Agreement shall be referred to management representatives of the parties for resolution. If such representatives are unable to resolve any dispute(s) referred to them within [30] days of referral, either party may submit

such dispute(s) to arbitration in accordance with the provisions of Article [X] hereof.

To require good-faith negotiations to settle and, if negotiation fails, establish notice deadlines for arbitration:

The parties shall endeavor in good faith to resolve any dispute, claim, controversy, or disagreement relating to or arising out of this Agreement, or the subject matter of this Agreement ("Dispute"), by negotiation. Any Dispute which remains unresolved [45] days after either party gives written notice of the existence of such Dispute, shall be finally resolved by arbitration.

To require negotiation between specified party representatives:

The parties shall use their best efforts to resolve all disputes relating to this Agreement by amicable negotiations. If either party gives notice to the other party that a dispute has arisen, and the parties are unable within thirty (30) days of such notice to resolve the dispute, then it shall be referred to [the Vice-President for Sales] of Seller and [the Vice-President for Quality Control] of Buyer. If these officers are unable within thirty (30) days to resolve the dispute, then it shall be referred to the [Chief Executive Officers] of Seller and Buyer. If the Chief Executive Officers of Seller and Buyer are unable within thirty (30) days to resolve the dispute, then either party may submit the dispute to arbitration in accordance with the provisions of Article [X] hereof.

To permit arbitration only after negotiation attempts:

The parties shall attempt to settle any dispute relating to this Agreement amicably. Nothing in this Article shall preclude either party from commencing arbitration in accordance with the provisions of Article [X] hereof [at any time] [within ___ days after written notice that efforts to amicably settle any dispute have commenced].

Multi-Tiered Dispute Resolution Clauses (pp. 120-123)

To require mediation under the AAA Rules before arbitration:

If a dispute arises from or relates to this contract or the breach thereof, and if the dispute cannot be settled through direct discussions, the parties agree to endeavor first to settle the dispute by mediation administered by the American Arbitration Association under its Commercial Mediation Procedures before resorting to arbitration. Any unresolved controversy or claim arising from or relating to this contract or breach thereof shall be settled by arbitration administered by the American Arbitration Association in accordance with its Commercial Arbitration

Rules, and judgment on the award rendered by the arbitrator may be entered in any court having jurisdiction thereof. If all parties to the dispute agree, a mediator involved in the parties' mediation may be asked to serve as the arbitrator.

To require mediation under the CEDR Rules before arbitration:

If any dispute arises in connection with this agreement, the parties agree to enter into mediation in good faith to settle such a dispute and will do so in accordance with the CEDR Model Mediation Procedure. Unless otherwise agreed between the parties within 14 [working] days of notice of the dispute, the mediator will be nominated by CEDR. To initiate the mediation a party must give notice in writing ("ADR notice") to the other party[ies] to the dispute, referring the dispute to mediation. A copy of the referral should be sent to CEDR. Unless otherwise agreed, the mediation will start not later than [28] days after the date of the ADR notice. No party may commence any court proceedings/arbitration in relation to any dispute arising out of this agreement until it has attempted to settle the dispute by mediation and either the mediation has terminated or the other party has failed to participate in the mediation, provided that the right to issue proceedings is not prejudiced by a delay.

To require negotiation or, in the alternative, mediation in accordance with the CPR Mediation Rules before arbitration commences:

Negotiation Between Executives (A): The parties shall attempt to resolve any dispute arising out of or relating to this [Agreement] [Contract] promptly by negotiation between executives who have authority to settle the controversy and who are at a higher level of management than the persons with direct responsibility for administration of this contract. To initiate a negotiation, a party shall give the other party written notice of any dispute not resolved in the normal course of business. Within [30] days after delivery of the notice, the executives of both parties shall meet at a mutually acceptable time and place, and thereafter as often as they reasonably deem necessary, to attempt to resolve the dispute. All negotiations pursuant to this clause are confidential and shall be treated as compromise and settlement negotiations for purposes of applicable rules of evidence.

Mediation (B): If the dispute has not been resolved by negotiation as provided herein within [45] days after delivery of the initial notice of negotiation, [or if the parties failed to meet within [20] days,] the parties shall endeavor to settle the dispute by mediation under the International Institute for Conflict Prevention & Resolution ("CPR") Mediation Procedure [currently in effect OR in effect on the date of this Agreement], [provided, however, that if one party fails to participate in the negotiation as provided herein, the other party can initiate mediation prior to the expiration of the [45] days.] Unless otherwise agreed, the parties will select a mediator from the CPR Panels of Distinguished Neutrals.

Arbitration (C): Any dispute arising out of or relating to this [Agreement] [Contract], including the breach, termination or validity thereof, which has not been resolved by mediation as provided herein [within [45] days after initiation of the mediation procedure] [within [30] days after appointment of a mediator], shall be finally resolved by arbitration in accordance with the International Institute for Conflict Prevention and Resolution ("CPR") Rules for Administered Arbitration [currently in effect OR in effect on the date of this Agreement], by [a sole arbitrator] [three independent and impartial arbitrators, of whom each party shall designate one] [three arbitrators to be appointed in accordance with the "screened" appointment procedure provided in Rule 5(4)] [three independent and impartial arbitrators, none of whom shall be appointed by either party]; [provided, however, that if one party fails to participate in either the negotiation or mediation as agreed herein, the other party can commence arbitration prior to the expiration of the time periods set forth above.] Judgment upon the award rendered by the arbitrator(s) may be entered by any court having jurisdiction thereof. The place of the arbitration shall be [city, country]. The language of the arbitration shall be [language].

To require mediation in accordance with the ICDR Rules before arbitration commences:

Any controversy or claim arising out of or related to this contract, or a breach thereof, shall be resolved by arbitration administered by the International Centre for Dispute Resolution in accordance with its International Arbitration Rules. Once the demand for arbitration is initiated, the parties agree to attempt to settle any controversy or claim arising out of or relating to this contract or a breach thereof by mediation administered by the International Centre for Dispute Resolution under its International Mediation Rules. Mediation will proceed concurrently with arbitration and shall not be a condition precedent to any stage of the arbitration process.

To require mediation in accordance with the ICC Mediation Rules before arbitration commences:

In the event of any dispute arising out of or in connection with the present contract, the parties shall first refer the dispute to proceedings under the ICC Mediation Rules. If the dispute has not been settled pursuant to the said Rules within [45] days following the filing of a Request for Mediation or within such other period as the

> parties may agree in writing, such dispute shall thereafter be finally settled under the Rules of Arbitration of the International Chamber of Commerce by one or more arbitrators appointed in accordance with the said Rules of Arbitration.

Fast-Track Arbitration and Contractual Time Limits (pp. 123-124)

To provide fast-track procedures for arbitration:

> The arbitral tribunal shall make a final award within ___ months from the date of [the respondent's receipt of the claimant's notice of arbitration] [appointment of the [sole] [presiding] arbitrator].

Or:

> The arbitrators shall conclude the arbitration no later than ___ days from the date that the claimant's statement of claim is received by the arbitrators. Unless the parties otherwise agree, a single hearing (lasting no more than ___ days) shall be conducted commencing no later than ___ days from the date that the claimant's statement of claim is received by the arbitrators. If the arbitrators determine that the interests of justice so require, they may extend the dates for the hearing and/or for conclusion of the arbitration by up to a total of ___ days.

To provide fast-track procedures for arbitration unless the tribunal sees a need for an extension:

> The final award in any arbitration under this Article [X] shall be made by the arbitral tribunal within [180] days from the appointment of the [sole arbitrator] [presiding arbitrator], unless the arbitral tribunal concludes that the interest of justice requires that such limit be extended [by an additional period not to exceed [45] days].

To provide fast-track procedures for arbitration unless the parties have agreed in writing for an extension:

> The parties mutually desire and intend that, barring exceptional and unforeseen circumstances, the final award of any arbitration under this Article [X] shall be made ___ days from the appointment of the [sole arbitrator] [presiding arbitrator]. The parties may extend this time limit by written agreement. The arbitral tribunal may extend this time limit in its discretion if it considers that the interest of justice so requires. The arbitral tribunal shall use its best efforts to issue the final award within such time period. The arbitral tribunal's failure to make a final award within

> this time limit shall not be a basis for refusing to comply with or for challenging or resisting enforcement of any such award.

Expedited Procedures (p. 124)

To exclude the possibility of expedited procedures under the SIAC Rules:

> Unless otherwise agreed, no arbitration conducted pursuant to this Article [X] shall be subject to expedited procedures under [Rule 14 of the SIAC Arbitration Rules] or otherwise.

To exclude the possibility of appointment of a sole arbitrator even if an arbitration is expedited:

> The number of arbitrators shall be three, including in any arbitration conducted pursuant to the Expedited Procedures under [Rule 14 of the SIAC Arbitration Rules].

Amiable Compositeur or Ex Aequo et Bono (pp. 124-125)

To confer the arbitral tribunal with the power to decide a dispute ex aequo et bono:

> The Arbitral Tribunal shall have the power to decide a dispute *ex aequo et bono*.

Entry-of-Judgment Clause (p. 125)

To ensure the enforceability of the arbitral awards in U.S. courts:

> Judgment upon any award made by the arbitrator(s) may be entered in any state or federal court having jurisdiction thereof.

Multi-Contract, Non-Signatories, and Multi-Party Contracts (pp. 125-129)

Clause addressing issues of consolidation:

> Each Party agrees that it may be joined as an additional Party to an arbitration involving other Parties under this Agreement. If more than one arbitration is begun under this Agreement and any Party contends that two or more arbitrations are substantially related and that the issues should be heard in one proceeding, the

> arbitral tribunal appointed in the first-filed of such proceedings shall have the power to determine whether, in the interests of justice and efficiency, the proceedings should be consolidated before that arbitral tribunal.

Or:

> Any Party may, either separately or together with any other Party, initiate arbitration pursuant to this Article [X] by sending a request for arbitration to all other Parties. In any arbitration pursuant to this Article [X], any Party may submit claims, counterclaims, or cross-claims against any other Party, regardless whether such Party was named as a respondent in a request for arbitration, counterclaim, or cross-claim, provided that (A) each such new claim, counterclaim, or cross-claim is substantially related to the dispute, claim, controversy or disagreement in a previously submitted request for arbitration, counterclaim or cross-claim, and (B) such new claims, counterclaims, or cross-claims are submitted by written notice to all other Parties within [30] days from the receipt by such Party of the relevant request for arbitration, counterclaim, or cross-claim.

Or:

> Any Party against whom claims, counterclaims, or cross-claims are submitted may submit counterclaims or cross-claims against any Party, provided that (A) each such new counterclaim or cross-claim is substantially related to the dispute, claim, controversy, or disagreement in a previously submitted request for arbitration, counterclaim, or cross-claim, and (B) such new counterclaim or cross-claim is submitted by written notice to the other Parties within [30] days from the receipt by such Party of the relevant notice of arbitration, counterclaim, or cross-claim.
>
> Any joined or intervening Party shall be bound by any award rendered by the arbitral tribunal even if such Party chooses not to participate in the arbitral proceedings.

To provide for the enforceability of the arbitration agreement against successors and assigns:

> This agreement to arbitrate shall be binding upon the parties and their successors, assigns, and affiliates.

To limit the transferability of an arbitration agreement:

> This agreement to arbitrate is binding only upon the signatories hereto and not, unless otherwise agreed in writing by the signatories hereto, their successors, assigns, or affiliates.

Or:

The arbitration agreement contained in this Article [X] binds only the signatories to this Agreement.

To provide for consolidation:

If more than one arbitration is begun under this Agreement, the [second Agreement], and/or the [third Agreement] and any party contends that two or more arbitrations are substantially related and that the issues should be heard in one proceeding, the arbitral tribunal appointed in the first-filed of such proceedings shall have the power to determine whether, in the interests of justice and efficiency, the proceedings should be consolidated before that arbitral tribunal.

Or:

An arbitral tribunal constituted pursuant to this Article [X] may consolidate an arbitration hereunder with an arbitration (or arbitrations) under Article [XX] of [insert related agreement(s)], provided that the arbitrations involve common questions of law or fact. If two or more arbitral tribunals constituted under this Article [X] or under Article [XX] of [insert related agreement(s)] issue decisions providing for consolidation of different arbitrations, the order issued first shall prevail.

Or:

The parties shall agree to join any dispute resolution proceeding under this Agreement with any other dispute resolution pending in respect of any other Project Contract relating to substantially the same matter.

The AAA's model clause for consolidation of construction dispute provides:

The owner, the contractor, and all subcontractors, specialty contractors, material suppliers, engineers, designers, architects, construction lenders, bonding companies, and other parties concerned with the construction of the structure are bound, each to each other, by this arbitration clause, provided that they have signed this contract or a contract that incorporates this contract by reference or signed any other agreement to be bound by this arbitration clause. Each such party agrees that it may be joined as an additional party to an arbitration involving other parties under any such agreement. If more than one arbitration is begun under any such agreement and any party contends that two or more arbitrations are substantially related and that the issues should be heard in one proceeding, the arbitrator(s)

> selected in the first-filed of such proceedings shall determine whether, in the interests of justice and efficiency, the proceedings should be consolidated before that (those) arbitrator(s).

Exclusion of Judicial Review (pp. 130-131)

To exclude judicial review:

> The arbitrators' award will be final and binding. The parties expressly exclude any and all rights to appeal, set aside or otherwise challenge any award by the arbitrators, insofar as such exclusion can validly be made.

Or:

> Any award(s) made by the arbitral tribunal under this Article [X] shall be final and binding on the parties, and each party waives to the fullest extent permitted by law any right it may otherwise have under the laws of any jurisdiction to any form of appeal, annulment, action to set aside or vacate, collateral attack, or any other form of recourse against or challenge to such award(s).

UNCITRAL Rules' model provision for the waiver of rights to seek annulment:

> The parties hereby waive their right to any form of recourse against an award to any court or other competent authority, insofar as such waiver can validly be made under the applicable law.

To exclude judicial review under English law:

> The parties expressly agree that leave to appeal under section 69 of the English Arbitration Act 1996 shall not be sought with respect to any question of law arising during the course of the arbitration or with respect to any award made.

Heightened Judicial Scrutiny (pp. 131-132)

To allow parties to appeal award in the jurisdiction in which it was made with heightened judicial scrutiny:

> The arbitrators' award shall be final and binding, but any party hereto shall have the right to seek judicial review of such award in the courts of the place where the award is made in accordance with the standards of appellate review applicable to decisions of courts of first instance in that place.

The AAA's model provision for opting in to the AAA Optional Appellate Arbitration Rules provides:

> Notwithstanding any language to the contrary in the contract documents, the parties hereby agree: that the Underlying Award may be appealed pursuant to the AAA's Optional Appellate Arbitration Rules ("Appellate Rules"); that the Underlying Award rendered by the arbitrator(s) shall, at a minimum, be a reasoned award; and that the Underlying Award shall not be considered final until after the time for filing the notice of appeal pursuant to the Appellate Rules has expired. Appeals must be initiated within thirty (30) days of receipt of an Underlying Award, as defined by Rule A-3 of the Appellate Rules, by filing a Notice of Appeal with any AAA office. Following the appeal process, the decision rendered by the appeal tribunal may be entered in any court having jurisdiction thereof.

"Documents Only" Arbitration (pp. 132-133)

To agree to a "documents only" arbitration:

> The arbitration shall be conducted on a documents only basis and no party shall have the right to a hearing.

To allow the arbitral tribunal to have discretion as to whether a hearing should be conducted:

> Neither party shall have the right to request or require a hearing before the arbitral tribunal. The arbitral tribunal shall have the power to decide, in its discretion, whether or not to conduct a hearing.

To apply the "documents only" arbitration rules of the European Court of Arbitration:

> Any dispute arising from the relationships between the parties to this Agreement shall be subject to determination by a sole arbitrator selected and appointed by the European Court of Arbitration being part of the European Centre of Arbitration having its seat in Strasbourg in accordance with the Documents Only Arbitration Rules of the Court in force at the time the application for arbitration is filed.

Remote Hearings and Testimony (pp. 133-134)

To grant the arbitral tribunal power to examine witnesses and conduct hearings remotely:

> The Arbitral Tribunal shall have the power to either hear witness evidence by [telephone or] videoconference or conduct hearings by [telephone or]

> videoconference. No party shall have the right to either in-person examination of any witness or an in-person hearing in the physical presence of the arbitral tribunal.

To allow the arbitral tribunal to have discretion as to whether hearings should be in person, remote, or a combination thereof:

> The Arbitral Tribunal shall have the power to establish the conduct of a hearing, including whether it may take place physically or remotely (including by video or telephone conference) or a combination thereof.

Alternatively:

> At a request of a Party or on its own motion, the Arbitral Tribunal, after having heard the Parties, may decide to conduct a hearing either physically or remotely (including by video or telephone conference) or a combination thereof.

To require the arbitral tribunal to consider conducting remote hearings:

> The Arbitral Tribunal should consider conducting hearings remotely where possible and unless there are good reasons why a physical hearing is necessary, taking into account all circumstances of the case.

To require the arbitral tribunal to conduct in-person hearings:

> Any examination of witnesses or hearing shall be in person in the physical presence of the arbitral tribunal, unless otherwise agreed by the parties.

Provisional Measures (pp. 134-135)

To allow the arbitral tribunal to grant provisional measures:

> Any provisional, interim, or conservatory measures which would be available from a court of law shall be available from the arbitral tribunal.

Or:

> Without prejudice to the parties' right to seek provisional measures from any court of competent jurisdiction, the arbitral tribunal shall have the power to grant provisional, interim, or conservatory measures, including, but not limited to, provisional injunctive relief. The parties undertake to comply forthwith with any such provisional, interim, or conservatory measures ordered by the arbitral

tribunal and agree that such measures may, to the extent not precluded by applicable law, be enforceable as a final award in any court of competent jurisdiction.

To limit provisional measures that can be granted by the arbitral tribunal:

Without prejudice to the parties' right to seek provisional measures from any court of competent jurisdiction, the arbitral tribunal shall have the power to grant provisional, interim, or conservatory measures, but only in order to maintain the status quo until either a final award is made by the arbitral tribunal or the dispute is otherwise resolved.

An alternative and more expansive clause provides:

Each party hereby acknowledges that it would not have an adequate remedy at law for money damages in the event that this Agreement was not performed in accordance with its terms and therefore agrees that each party shall be entitled to specific performance and/or interim relief. The parties hereby acknowledge and agree that they may apply to the arbitral tribunal [or to any court of competent jurisdiction] for conservatory or interim measures.

To reserve the parties' rights to seek provisional remedies from national courts:

Nothing in this provision shall prevent any party from seeking conservatory or interim measures, including, but not limited to, temporary retaining orders or preliminary injunctions or their equivalent, from any court of competent jurisdiction before the arbitral tribunal is constituted or, thereafter, upon the order of the arbitral tribunal.

A more expansive provision is as follows:

Nothing in this Article [X] shall prevent any party from seeking provisional, interim, or conservatory measures from any court of competent jurisdiction at any time. Any such request by a party to a court for provisional, interim, or conservatory measures shall not be deemed incompatible with the agreement to arbitrate in this Article [X] or a waiver of the right to arbitrate.

ICSID-recommended clause providing for court-ordered provisional measures:

Without prejudice to the power of the Arbitral Tribunal to recommend provisional measures, either party hereto may request any judicial or other authority to order any provisional or conservatory measure, including attachment, prior to the institution of the arbitration proceeding, or during the proceeding, for the preservation of its rights and interests.

To exclude the right to seek provisional measures from either the courts or the arbitral tribunal:

Notwithstanding any other provision of this Article [X] or the [applicable institutional rules], [the arbitral tribunal shall not have the power to order any provisional, interim, or conservatory measures] [and] [the parties irrevocably undertake and agree not to seek any provisional, interim, or conservatory measures from any court or judicial authority].

Emergency Arbitrators (pp. 136-137)

To exclude the ICC emergency arbitrator procedures:

All disputes arising out of or in connection with the present contract shall be finally settled under the Rules of Arbitration of the International Chamber of Commerce by one or more arbitrators appointed in accordance with the said Rules. The Emergency Arbitrator Provisions shall not apply.

Limitations on Arbitrators' Remedial Authority (pp. 137-138)

To forbid the arbitral tribunal from awarding consequential damages:

The arbitrator(s) shall not award consequential damages in any arbitration initiated under this section.

To forbid the arbitral tribunal from awarding punitive damages:

The arbitrator(s) will have no authority to award punitive or other damages not measured by the prevailing party's actual damages, except as may be required by statute.

To limit the arbitral tribunal from awarding monetary damages:

Any award in an arbitration initiated under this clause shall be limited to monetary damages and shall include no injunction or direction to any party other than the direction to pay a monetary amount.

High-Low and Baseball Arbitrations (pp. 138-139)

To limit the remedial powers of the arbitrators (a high-low clause):

> Any award of the arbitration in favor of [X], but against [Y], shall be at least [specify amount] but shall not exceed [specify amount]. [X] expressly waives any claim in excess of [specify amount] and agrees that its recovery shall not exceed that amount. Any award of damages shall be in satisfaction of all claims by [X] against [Y].

Baseball arbitration clause (where the arbitral tribunal is not aware of the baseball clause):

> In the event the arbitral tribunal denies the claim or awards an amount less than the minimum amount of [specify], then this minimum amount shall be paid to claimant. Should the arbitral tribunal's award exceed the maximum amount of [specify], then only this maximum amount shall be paid to the claimant. It is further understood between the parties that if the arbitral tribunal awards an amount between the minimum and the maximum stipulated range, then the exact awarded amount will be paid to the claimant. The parties further agree that this agreement is private between them and will not be disclosed to the arbitral tribunal.

Baseball arbitration clause (where the arbitral tribunal is aware of the baseball clause):

> Each party shall submit to the arbitrator and exchange with each other in advance of their hearing their last best offers. The arbitrator shall be limited to awarding only one or the other of the figures submitted by the parties.

Or:

> The parties agree that the arbitration to be employed by the arbitral tribunal shall be "baseball" arbitration. On a date specified by the arbitrators, each party shall submit to the arbitrators and to each other its proposed valuation of all the claims before the arbitrators, as an aggregate amount. The parties shall include any specifics or breakdown of the amounts included within their respective figures, as they may desire. The arbitrators shall be limited to awarding only one or the other of the two proposed aggregate figures, being the amount closest to the arbitrators' own valuation of the aggregate of all submitted claims.

Expert Determination (pp. 139-142)

To provide for expert determination instead of arbitration in highly technical matters:

> If the parties are unable to agree on [identify issue(s)], either party may request that the matter be referred for decision to [identify individual or company to serve as expert] OR [the expert selected by the [ICC Centre for Expertise] (the "Expert")]. The Expert shall attempt to agree with the parties upon the procedure and timetable to be followed in the expert determination. If and to the extent that any such matter cannot be agreed upon, the Expert may in its sole discretion adopt such procedures and timetables as it shall consider appropriate and these shall be binding on the parties.

WIPO Model Clause:

> Any dispute or difference between the parties arising under [describe matter referred to expert determination] shall be referred to expert determination in accordance with the WIPO Expert Determination Rules. The determination made by the expert shall [not] be binding upon the parties. The language to be used in the expert determination shall be [specify language].

To provide for expert determination for use in a corporate acquisition:

> If the Vendors and the Purchasers are unable to agree on [the Completion Accounts and calculation of Net Current Assets as at the Completion Date] by [date], the matter in dispute shall be referred, at the request of either the Vendors or the Purchasers, for decision to an Independent Chartered Accountant (the "Independent Accountant") who shall be appointed by agreement between the Vendors and the Purchasers, or, if they have not agreed within 14 days of the [first date above or date of request to refer by one of the parties], by the President for the time being of the Institute of Chartered Accountants in England and Wales ("the President") on the application of either party. If an Independent Accountant has been appointed but is unable to complete the reference, another independent accountant shall be appointed by the parties, or if they have not agreed on the appointment within 14 days of the request to do so by one of the parties, by the President.

To provide for the binding effect of expert determination unless expedited arbitration under the WIPO Rules is requested:

> The determination made by the expert shall be binding upon the parties, unless within [30] days of the communication of the determination to the parties, the matter referred to expert determination is, upon the filing of a Request for Arbitration by either party, referred to arbitration in accordance with the WIPO [Expedited] Arbitration Rules. [The arbitral tribunal shall consist of [a sole

arbitrator] [three arbitrators]]. The place of arbitration shall be [specify place]. The language to be used in the arbitral proceedings shall be [specify language]. The dispute or difference referred to arbitration shall be decided in accordance with the law of [specify jurisdiction].

(* The WIPO Expedited Arbitration Rules provide that the arbitral tribunal shall consist of a sole arbitrator.)

To provide for mediation followed, in the absence of a settlement, by expert determination:

Any dispute or difference between the parties arising under out of or relating to [describe scope of the matter referred to expert determination] under this contract and any subsequent amendments of this contract to mediation in accordance with the [WIPO Mediation Rules]. The place of mediation shall be [specify place]. The language to be used in the mediation shall be [specify language].

If, and to the extent that, any such dispute or difference has not been settled pursuant to the mediation within [60] [90] days of the commencement of the mediation, it shall, upon the filing of a Request for Expert Determination by either party, be referred to expert determination in accordance with the WIPO Expert Determination Rules. Alternatively, if, before the expiration of the said period of [60] [90] days, either party fails to participate or to continue to participate in the mediation, the dispute or difference shall, upon the filing of a Request for Expert Determination by the other party, be referred to expert determination in accordance with the WIPO Expert Determination Rules. The determination made by the expert shall [not] be binding upon the parties. The language to be used in the expert determination shall be [specify language].

To provide for expert determination and costs:

Each party shall bear all costs (internal and external) that it incurs in the course of the expert determination unless the expert determines otherwise. If any party does not pay its share of the expert's fees and costs, the other part(y)/(ies) may advance such share of the expert's fees and costs on the defaulting party's behalf, and the expert determination shall proceed. The part(y)/(ies) which pay the defaulting party's share of the expert's fees and costs shall have the right to request that the expert or an arbitral tribunal constituted under Article [X] of this Agreement direct the defaulting party to reimburse such fees and costs.

To provide for a case where the parties have not complied with the expert determination:

> The expert determination shall be final and binding, and each party undertakes to comply forthwith with such expert determination. If a party does not comply fully with an expert determination, the other party may refer this failure to arbitration under Article [X] of this Agreement [or, at its sole option, seek to enforce its rights under such expert determination in any court of competent jurisdiction].

Technical Expertise (p. 142)

ICC model clause for optional use of administered expert proceedings:

> The parties may at any time, without prejudice to any other proceedings, agree to submit any dispute arising out of or in connection with [clause X of the present contract] to administered expert proceedings in accordance with the Rules for the Administration of Expert Proceedings of the International Chamber of Commerce.

ICC model clause for mandatory use of administered expert proceedings:

> In the event of any dispute arising out of or in connection with [clause X of the present contract], the parties agree to submit the dispute to administered expert proceedings in accordance with the Rules for the Administration of Expert Proceedings of the International Chamber of Commerce. [The parties agree that the findings of the expert shall be contractually binding upon them.]

CEDR model agreement for submitting dispute for expert determination:

> 1. **Appointment of Expert** CEDR will appoint an Expert to resolve the Dispute and has exclusive rights to do so under this Procedure. The Parties agree that the Expert will resolve the Dispute by Expert Determination. The Expert will act as an expert and not as an arbitrator or legal adviser.
> 2. **Purpose of Expert Determination** Unless the Parties subsequently agree otherwise, this Expert Determination leads to a decision ("the Decision") being issued by the Expert via CEDR. The Decision will be final and binding on the Parties ...
> 11. **Implementation of the Decision** The Parties agree to implement the Decision within [e.g.—seven] days of the Decision being published to them.

> **12. Challenge to the Decision** The Parties agree that the decision of the Expert is final and binding and that the dispute cannot be referred to a subsequent tribunal ...

Confidentiality of Arbitral Proceedings (pp. 142-144)

To provide for confidentiality of the arbitral proceedings:

> The parties to any arbitration under this Article [X] shall keep the arbitration confidential and shall not disclose to any person, other than those necessary to the proceedings, the existence of the arbitration, any information submitted during the arbitration, any documents submitted in connection with it, any oral submissions or testimony, transcripts, or any award unless disclosure is required by law or is necessary for permissible court proceedings, such as proceedings to recognize or enforce an award.

Or:

> The parties agree to keep confidential all awards in any arbitration conducted under this Article [X], together with all materials submitted or exchanged in any such arbitration (including all documents and other materials produced by another party in such arbitration), except insofar as such documents are already in the public domain or to the extent that disclosure may be required by legal duty, to protect or pursue a legal right, or to recognize, enforce, or challenge an award in legal proceedings before a court or other judicial authority.

To provide for more detailed confidentiality of the arbitral proceedings:

> The arbitrators, any party, any witness, and any other participant in the arbitration shall not disclose, transmit, or disseminate (a) anything said or done in the arbitration, (b) any documents disclosed or provided during or in connection with the arbitration, (c) any information disclosed during or in connection with the arbitration, and (d) the existence or result of the arbitration, including, without limitation, the arbitration award and any explanations or reasons for the award.

ICDR model confidentiality clause:

> Except as may be required by law, neither a party nor its representatives may disclose the existence, content, or results of any arbitration hereunder without the prior written consent of (all/both) parties.

To provide that arbitral proceedings will not be confidential:

> Neither party shall be under any confidentiality obligations with respect to any arbitration pursuant to this Article [X], and either party shall be free to publicly disclose any award made in any such arbitration and any materials submitted or exchanged in any such arbitration (including all documents and other materials produced by another party in such arbitration).

Or:

> Any award made by the arbitrators pursuant to this Article [X] may be disclosed by either party (including to non-parties to this Agreement or to any arbitration conducted pursuant to this Article [X]).

Asymmetrical Arbitration Clauses (pp. 144-145)

To allow one party and not the other to initiate arbitral proceedings:

> All disputes, claims, controversies, and disagreements relating to or arising out of this Agreement, or the subject matter of this Agreement, shall be finally resolved by arbitration in accordance with [institutional arbitration rules]. Notwithstanding the foregoing, [Party A] shall be free at its sole option to seek judicial or non-judicial relief to enforce [specified provisions imposing monetary obligations or specified agreements]. [Party A]'s request for judicial or non-judicial relief pursuant to the foregoing sentence shall not constitute a waiver of its right to arbitrate under this Article [X] or to enforce the arbitration agreement contained in this Article [X]. If an arbitration has been initiated by [Party B] prior to or at the time that [Party A] elects to pursue judicial or non-judicial remedies, then [Party B] shall forthwith take all necessary steps to discontinue and dismiss such arbitration and shall in no event proceed with such arbitral proceedings.

Or:

> The courts of England shall have jurisdiction to settle any disputes which may arise out of or in connection with this Agreement but [Party A] shall have the option of bringing any dispute hereunder to arbitration. ... Any dispute arising from the provisions of this Agreement or its performance which cannot be resolved by mutual agreement which [Party A] determines to resolve by arbitration shall be referred to arbitration. ...

Preliminary Decision of Dispositive Issues (pp. 145-146)

To allow the arbitrators to make preliminary decisions on dispositive issues:

> The arbitral tribunal shall have the authority to decide at any stage of the arbitration any issue claimed by a party to be dispositive of any claim or counterclaim, in whole or part, in accordance with such procedures as the arbitral tribunal prescribes. The arbitral tribunal shall have the authority to make a partial, final, or other award with respect to any such issue.

Decisions Regarding Time Bars and Similar Defenses (pp. 146-147)

To allow the arbitrators to decide on the timeliness of claims:

> The arbitral tribunal shall have the authority to decide any defense that any claim or counterclaim is not timely by reason of contractual limitations period, statute of limitations, prescriptive periods, laches, or any similar defense.

To provide for the courts to decide any question of timeliness:

> Any decision of whether a claim or counterclaim is timely under this Agreement or applicable law shall be determined by a court of competent jurisdiction, and not by the arbitral tribunal. The parties irrevocably consent to the exclusive jurisdiction of _________ for the decision of any such issue of timeliness.

Or:

> Notwithstanding [the arbitration agreement], determination of whether a dispute is timely under this Agreement or the applicable law shall be determined by a court of competent jurisdiction, and not by the arbitral tribunal.

Or:

> If a claim sought to be arbitrated would be barred by limitation of time had the claim sought to be arbitrated been asserted in a court under the law applicable to the arbitration, a party may apply to a court of competent jurisdiction—and not to the arbitral tribunal—to stay arbitration or to vacate any award as untimely.

To provide for the arbitrators or the courts to decide any question of timeliness:

> If, at the time that a demand for arbitration was made or a notice of intention to arbitrate was served, the claim sought to be arbitrated would have been barred by limitation of time or other time bar had it been asserted in a court under the law applicable to the arbitration, a party may assert the limitation as a bar to the

arbitration on an application to a court of competent jurisdiction. The failure to make such an application in court shall not preclude a party from subsequently asserting it before an arbitral tribunal.

Jurisdictional Decisions (pp. 147-148)

To give the arbitral tribunal the authority to rule on its own jurisdiction:

The arbitral tribunal shall have the authority to rule upon its own jurisdiction, including any objection to the formation, existence, validity, or effectiveness of the arbitration agreement in this Article [X]. The arbitral tribunal's decision on any such jurisdictional matter shall be final and binding and the parties agree not to apply to any national court or other judicial authority to annul or deny recognition to any such decision.

To give a specific court the authority to rule on the jurisdiction of an arbitral tribunal:

Any objection to the jurisdiction of the arbitral tribunal shall be submitted exclusively to the courts of ________ [ordinarily the courts of the arbitral seat].

To give a specific court the authority to rule on actions to enforce or challenge its agreement to arbitrate:

Without prejudice to the arbitral tribunal's authority to consider challenges to its jurisdiction, the courts of ________ [ordinarily the courts of the arbitral seat] shall have exclusive jurisdiction over any judicial action to enforce or challenge the agreement to arbitrate contained in this Article [X], and each of the parties irrevocably submits to the exclusive jurisdiction of such courts for such purpose. [Notwithstanding the preceding sentence, any party may apply to any court or other judicial authority seeking recognition or enforcement of any award(s) made by the arbitral tribunal under this Article [X]].

Submission Agreement (p. 148)

To agree to submit an existing dispute to arbitration:

This agreement is between [Party A] and [Party B] as of [date]. A dispute has arisen between the parties concerning ________ (the "Dispute"). The parties agree to submit such Dispute, and all claims, controversies, disputes, or differences in connection with such Dispute, for final resolution by arbitration in accordance with this Agreement. The seat of the arbitration shall be ________. The language of the arbitration shall be ________.

> There shall be three arbitrators. [Party A] hereby designates ________ as one of the arbitrators. [Party B] hereby designates ________ as the second of the arbitrators. The two arbitrators so designated shall, within [30] days of the effective date of this agreement, jointly designate in writing a third arbitrator, who shall be the presiding arbitrator. If the two arbitrators fail jointly to designate in writing the presiding arbitrator within such period, then, on the application of either party, the presiding arbitrator shall be selected within [30] days by [appointing authority].
>
> The procedures to be applied in the arbitration shall be agreed upon by the parties or, failing such agreement, shall be directed by the arbitral tribunal. Default by any party shall not prevent the arbitrators from proceeding to render an award.

Class Action Arbitration Waivers (p. 149)

To waive the right to bring class action claims in arbitration:

> All claims shall be arbitrated on an individual basis and no party shall have any right or authority to assert or pursue any claims subject to this agreement to arbitrate as a class action of any sort.

Or:

> All claims arising out of or relating to this Agreement, or the subject matter of this Agreement ("Claims") must be brought in the name of an individual person or entity and must proceed on an individual (non-class, non-representative) basis. The arbitrator shall not be authorized to, and shall not, award relief for or against anyone who is not a party to this Agreement and to an individual arbitration. If any party requires arbitration of any Claim, no party nor any other person may pursue any such Claims in arbitration as a class action, private attorney general action, or other representative action [nor may such Claim be pursued on behalf of any party in any court]. Claims, including any assigned Claims, of two or more persons or entities may not be joined or consolidated in the same arbitration.

Investment Arbitration (pp. 151-155)

To explicitly stipulate that the transaction is an "investment":

> It is hereby stipulated that the transaction to which this agreement relates is an investment.

To stipulate the nationality of the investor:

> It is hereby stipulated by the parties that the Investor is a national of [name of another Contracting State].

To stipulate the nationality of the local subsidiary's parent company:

> It is hereby agreed that, although the Investor is a national of the Host State, it is controlled by nationals of [name(s) of other Contracting State(s)] and shall be treated as a national of [that]/[those] State[s] for the purposes of the Convention.

To stipulate that the host state entity has consented to ICSID jurisdiction:

> The [name of constituent subdivision or agency] is [a constituent subdivision]/[an agency] of the Host State, which has been designated to the Centre by the Government of that State in accordance with Article 25(1) of the Convention. In accordance with Article 25(3) of the Convention, the Host State [hereby gives its approval to this consent agreement (if this government is also a party to the agreement)] [has given its approval to this consent agreement in [citation of instrument in which approval is expressed]]/[has notified the Centre that no approval of [this type of consent agreement]/[of consent agreements by the [name of constituent subdivision or agency] is required]].

To stipulate that acts of the state entity are attributable to the host state:

> The parties agree that, for the purposes of Article 25(1) of the ICSID Convention, the acts of [State entity] are attributable to [the State] within the meaning of the ILC Articles on State Responsibility.

To provide for preservation of other remedies:

> The consent to the jurisdiction of the Centre recorded in [citation of basic clause] above shall not preclude either party hereto from resorting to the following alternative remedy: [identification of other type of proceeding]. While such other proceeding is pending, no arbitration proceeding pursuant to the Convention shall be instituted.

To require exhaustion of local remedies:

> Before either party hereto institutes an arbitration proceeding under the Convention with respect to a particular dispute, that party must have taken all steps necessary to exhaust the [following] [administrative] [and] [judicial] remedies available under the laws of the Host State with respect to that dispute [list of required remedies], unless the other party hereto waives that requirement in writing.

ICSID-recommended clause for waiver of sovereign immunity:

> The Host State hereby waives any right of sovereign immunity as to it and its property in respect of the enforcement and execution of any award rendered by an Arbitral Tribunal constituted pursuant to this agreement.

PCA-recommended clause for waiver of sovereign immunity:

> This agreement to arbitrate constitutes a waiver of any right to sovereign immunity from execution to which a party might otherwise be entitled with respect to the enforcement of any award rendered by an arbitral tribunal constituted pursuant to this agreement.

Drafting Choice-of-Law Clauses (Chapter 8) (pp. 179-190)

Scope of Choice-of-Law Clauses (p. 179)

To select the law governing the agreement:

> This agreement shall be interpreted in accordance with, and governed by, the laws of ________.

Or:

> This agreement shall be construed in accordance with the laws of ________.

To provide a choice-of-law clause that mirrors the scope of the original arbitration agreement:

> This Agreement will be governed by, and all disputes relating to or arising in connection with this Agreement [or the subject matter of this Agreement] shall be resolved in accordance with, the laws of ________.

Renvoi Versus "Whole Law" (p. 180-181)

To provide that the substantive laws of a country rather than its conflict of law rules will apply to the proceedings:

> This Agreement will be governed by, and all disputes relating to or arising in connection with this Agreement shall be resolved in accordance with, the laws of ________ (to the exclusion of its conflict of laws rules).

Choice-of-Law Clauses in Investment Contracts (pp. 181-185)

To select both national and international law to investment disputes:

> For purposes of this Contract, the laws of ________ existing and in force on the Effective Date of this Contract and generally accepted principles of international law shall govern this Contract.

ICSID model provision for investment agreements:

> Any Arbitral Tribunal constituted pursuant to this agreement shall apply [specification of system of law] [subject to the following modifications: ________].

To select general principles of international law:

> This contract, and all disputes arising out of a relating to this contract, shall be governed by general principles of law, to the exclusion of any rules of national law.

Tiered choice-of-law clause referring to both national law and general principles of law:

> This concession shall be governed by and interpreted in accordance with the principles of [Libya] common to the principles of international law, and in the absence of such common principles then by and in accordance with the general principles of law as may have been applied by international tribunals.

UNIDROIT Principles of International Commercial Contracts (p. 185)

To provide that the contract be governed by the UNIDROIT Principles of International Commercial Contracts:

> This contract shall be governed by the UNIDROIT Principles (2016) [except as to Articles _____], supplemented when necessary by the law of [jurisdiction X].

"Concurrent" Choice-of-Law Clause (p. 186)

To provide for a "concurrent" choice-of-law clause (in state contracts):

> The laws of [State] will apply, insofar as they are consistent with international law.

Stabilization Clauses (for Investment Contracts) (pp. 186-188)

To seek protection against future changes in applicable law ("stabilization clause"):

> No new laws, regulations, modifications or interpretation which could be conflicting or incompatible with the provisions of this Agreement shall be applicable.

An example of an economic equilibrium clause provides:

> In the event that any provisions contained in the laws, rules or regulations of the Government are inconsistent with the terms and conditions of this Agreement, the Government shall take such action as is necessary to relieve the Company from any loss, liability or jeopardy as a result of such inconsistency and shall also take such action as may be necessary to maintain the economic equilibrium existing between the Parties on the Effective Date of this Agreement.

Or:

> The Government guarantees to the Contractor, for the entire duration of this Agreement, that it will maintain the stability of the fiscal and economic conditions of this Agreement, as they result from this Agreement and as they result from the Laws in force on the Effective Date. The Contractor has entered into this Agreement on the basis of the legal, fiscal and economic framework prevailing at the Effective Date. If there are any changes with respect to any provisions of any Law which may detrimentally and unfairly affect the Contractor's economic position during the Stability Period, this Agreement shall be amended as may be necessary to restore the Contractor to the economic position it would have enjoyed during the Stability Period but for such changes.

Energy Charter Secretariat "Model Host Government Agreement for Cross-Border Pipelines" hybrid freezing and economic equilibrium clause:

> If any Change of Law has the effect of impairing, conflicting or interfering with the implementation of the Project, or limiting, abridging or adversely affecting the value of the Project or any of the rights, indemnifications or protections granted or arising under this Agreement or any Project Agreement, or of imposing (directly or indirectly) any Costs on any Project Investor, the Project Investor shall, within [one year] of the date when it could with reasonable diligence have become aware of the effect of the Change of Law upon the project as aforesaid, give notice thereof in writing to the Host Government. During the [90 days] following the Host Government's receipt of this notice, the Project Investor and the Host Government shall endeavour to resolve the matter through amicable negotiations. Failing such a resolution, the Host Government shall, by the end of this [90-day] period, do one of the following:

(a) take all actions available to it to reverse the effect of that Change of Law upon the Project, the value of the Project or the relevant rights, indemnifications or protections. The foregoing obligation shall include the obligation to take all appropriate measures to resolve promptly by whatever means may be necessary, including by way of exemption, legislation, decree and/or other authoritative acts, any conflict or anomaly between this Agreement and any Project Agreement and [insert name of State] law; or

(b) compensate the Project Investor for the Costs incurred by that Project Investor as a result of the Change of Law. Such compensation shall, if the relevant Project Investor so requires, be paid in Convertible Currency and shall, at the option of the Host Government, take the form of:
   - reimbursement by the Host Government of the Costs incurred by the Project Investor as a result of the Change of Law, promptly as and when such Costs are incurred;
   - reimbursement by the Host Government of the Costs incurred by the Project Investor as a result of the Change of Law, in the form of equal annual payments to the Project Investor during the remaining expected life of the Project ...;

provided however that the obligation to take one of the actions referred to above shall not apply in relation to a Change of Law if the Host Government establishes that that Change of Law reflects a change in standards generally applicable in relation to standards of environmental protection, safety, employment, training, social impact or security in the [petroleum] [gas] industry internationally.

Exclusion of CISG (p. 188)

To opt out of the CISG:

The parties agree that this Agreement, and any disputes, claims, controversies, or disagreements relating to or arising under this Agreement, shall not be subject to the 1980 United Nations Convention on Contracts for the International Sale of Goods ("CISG") and that the provisions of the CISG Convention are hereby excluded. This Agreement, and any disputes, claims, controversies, or disagreements relating to or arising under this Agreement, shall be governed by the law of ________ (without regard to its conflict of laws rules and without regard to the CISG).

Index

D

E

N

P

Q

R

S

www.ingramcontent.com/pod-product-compliance
Ingram Content Group UK Ltd.
Pitfield, Milton Keynes, MK11 3LW, UK
UKHW020133290926
15471UKWH00003B/450

9 789403 532998